From Twitter to Tahrir Square

From Twitter to Tahrir Square
Ethics in Social and New Media Communication

Volume 2

Bala A. Musa and Jim Willis, Editors

 PRAEGER

AN IMPRINT OF ABC-CLIO, LLC
Santa Barbara, California • Denver, Colorado • Oxford, England

Library of Congress Cataloging-in-Publication Data

From Twitter to Tahrir Square : ethics in social and new media communication /
Bala A. Musa and Jim Willis, editors.
      volumes ; cm
   Includes index.
   ISBN 978-1-4408-2841-6 (hardback) — ISBN 978-1-4408-2842-3 (ebook)
1. Social media—Moral and ethical aspects.   2. Online social networks—
Moral and ethical aspects.   I. Musa, Bala A., editor of compilation.   II. Willis, Jim,
1946 March 19– editor of compilation.
   HM741.F76   2014
   302.30285—dc23   2014000304

ISBN: 978-1-4408-2841-6
EISBN: 978-1-4408-2842-3

18 17 16 15 14   1 2 3 4 5

This book is also available on the World Wide Web as an eBook.
Visit www.abc-clio.com for details.

Praeger
An Imprint of ABC-CLIO, LLC

ABC-CLIO, LLC
130 Cremona Drive, P.O. Box 1911
Santa Barbara, California 93116-1911

This book is printed on acid-free paper ∞

Manufactured in the United States of America

Contents

Appreciation

A project like this takes a lot of support to accomplish. To this end, the editors wish to acknowledge, with sincere gratitude, the support and assistance of many people who helped to make this project possible. Special gratitude go to Jim Willis's spouse, Anne Kindred Willis; and to Bala Musa's spouse, Maureen Ifeyinwa Musa, for their support, insights, and patience, that we have each relied on in the course of our careers, and during this project, in particular.

Thank you to our colleagues across the country and across the globe, who contributed their research, scholarship, and professional expertise to this project, thereby providing the rich array of perspectives and insights contained in these two volumes.

Appreciation goes to our students and colleagues at Azusa Pacific University. We appreciate the opportunity to exchange ideas, even in their formative stages, and to receive input from you. The collegial atmosphere you create makes it possible to collaborate on projects like these. Thank you to the administration at Azusa Pacific University, whose support for the Annual David C. Bicker Communication Ethics Conference laid the seed for this project. Special gratitude to Mrs. Debbie Cram, administrative coordinator, Department of Communication Studies, Azusa Pacific University, for her administrative skills and tireless assistance.

We are greatly indebted to the editorial support team at ABC-CLIO for their support, cooperation, gracefulness, and expertise in guiding this project. Special thanks to Ms. Beth Ptalis, Acquisitions Editor; Ms. Rebecca Matheson, Editorial Assistant; Vanessa Naranjo, Marketing Assistant; Barbara Patterson, Books Department; Gregg Carter, Enduring Questions Series Editor; and others on their team.

We thank God for all His blessings; and thank you to all who have helped in various ways in the course of this project.

Bala A. Musa and Jim Willis
(Editors and Contributors)

Introduction to Volume 2

This volume of the anthology looks at the micro- and mid-range-level issues of new media use, effects, and ethics. Much of the analysis here focuses on how individuals and groups interact with social and new media. Social media permeate every aspect of today's society, from the personal to the professional, from the private to the public. The contributors in this volume, drawn from various backgrounds and diverse research and scholarly interests, bring their insightful scholarly, intellectual, cultural, and professional perspectives to bear on changes occurring in society in light of emerging new media technology. While Volume 1 focuses more on the macro and larger trends, this volume focuses on how social media are woven into personal and group lives. It examines the ethical issues relating to social media use and consumption, changes in popular culture, self-concept and identity, and information use and abuse by communicators and audience members. It examines ethical challenges posed by new and social media adoption and application. These include navigating lifestyle and value changes in the new mediascape, as well as balancing the tensions of "musts," "oughts," and "wants."

Every new technological epoch opens new possibilities and also poses new dilemmas. The dawn of the digital age is no different. Excitement of new media adoption, from Facebook to Instagram, and from Twitter to Wikis, has provided instant connectivity, instant information, and instant self-disclosure at the stroke of the computer or mobile device key. The opening section of this volume analyzes how the individuals and groups encounter the larger popular culture and entertainment culture. Pauline Cheong, Joe Hight, and Cindy Phu show how popular culture consumption in the new media age has become a very personal experience. Society has moved from mass production and dissemination to personal branding, and individually tailored marketing and consumption. Likewise, Tim

Posada, at Claremont Graduate University; and Joseph Bentz argue that digital media are changing the art of storytelling and the relationship between "stories lived" and :stories told."[1] Both digital storytelling in the form of fan trailers and the novel, as a medium, are adapting to the changing habits of the audience. If, even in storytelling, content reflects the medium and vice versa, what responsibility do source and receiver have in the narrative dance between storyteller, the story, and the participatory audience?

If the television era was the age of "Amusing Ourselves to Death,"[2] the new media age can be seen as one of "addicting ourselves to death," when it comes to entertainment. Video game consoles as well as games with friends, Facebook games, and others games that can be played on digital devices have created a generation addicted to nonstop, mind-numbing, addictive entertainment. In Chapter 6, Pavica Sheldon examines the motive for playing video games. Sheldon questions whether video games offer more than just distractions.

Using the storied life of Evangelist Aimee Semple McPherson, Musa returns to an earlier argument that media can enhance credibility, empathy, and effect of secular and sacred messages alike.[3] Musa draws a line from McPherson's dramatizing of the gospel and use of radio, the modern mass medium of her time, to today's adoption of social media as evangelistic tools. The chapter shows the mutual interface between medium and message necessary to reach a changing audience. It examines the ethical boundaries of this negotiation between medium and message in the search for relevance.

In Part II Jim Willis looks at young peoples' sense of self and individual identities in the virtual world. He analyzes how young people (re)define themselves on take-on different personas in the virtual world. They are able to present themselves as they seem themselves or want to be seen. In the same way, Franklin Nii Amankwah Yartey writes on race and identity in Second Life, demonstrating that people are able to create a perfect and preferred image of themselves in the virtual world. The ethical question this raises is whether the self is objectified or the real self could be despised if it fails to live up the ideal virtual self.

Kris D. Boyle at the University of Texas at Austin also studies how people present themselves in social media. The chapter examines the psychology behind self-promotion in online media. Social media by nature is a space where people can selectively put images of themselves for the rest of the world to see. Oftentimes, people may show their bad-hair days, but most of the time, in Myspace, Instagram, Facebook, YouTube, and other social media, others post their achievements or present the most favorable view of the themselves. The question one would ask is whether social media are enabling people's self-absorption and narcissism. In asking the question, "Is Jar Jar Racist?" Tim Posada shows how digital depictions of movie characters perpetuate racial stereotypes. Using the example of Jar Jar Binks in *Star Wars: Episode I—The Phantom Menace* (1999), he argues that films like these act as "reminders that as new media transforms the cinematic landscape, the dangers of Hollywood's greatest sin—the misrepresentation of non-whites—lingers behind each pixel."

Other chapters in this part, by Sue Aspley, Bala Musa, Brooke Van Dam, and Jim Willis take up the issue of privacy in the new media environment. Using her legal background, Aspley discusses both the legal and ethical privacy paradox posed by social media use. The chapter identifies the tension points of privacy invasion that could arise from ignorance of the law or ethical misjudgment on the part of social media users. Van Dam points out that social media privacy policies are fraught with ethical concerns as they are very ambiguous and allow businesses, news media, and other institutions to bend on change the rules at will. Jim Willis looks at the evolving standards of online piracy, privacy, and surveillance, showing how various stakeholders wrestle with finding appropriate boundaries. Willis also calls into question the ethical practices of marketers who invade customers' information privacy as they gather massive personal data on existing and potential customers. In the same vein, Musa suggests that consumers, the courts, and corporations all have responsibilities to held set reasonable expectations and standards of social media privacy. According to Musa, the government, as well as private organizations, must put public interest first in setting media privacy guidelines. Likewise the public must not only be vigilant but also be social responsible and savvy when disclosing personal information on social media sites.

Part III addresses ethics in social and new media in relation to information access, use, and abuse, in educational, social, and religious settings. Contributor Anne Willis, using her extensive experience in teaching English as a second language to international students, highlights the "uses and abuses of the Internet by international students in American universities." While there are many positive uses such as researching, taking entrance exams, staying connected with friends and family, there are also abuses such as cheating, plagiarism, and so forth. Etim Anim and his colleague, Stanley Ngoa, at Wits University come to similar conclusion in their survey of Nigerian students' use of the Internet. Both chapters recommend ways of curbing students' misuse of the Internet. These include stricter monitoring and lessening the pressure of competition to gain admission or outdo other students.

Arguing that social media, in themselves, are a neutral, not deterministic tool, Linda Chiang, at Azusa Pacific University, demonstrates the potential for positive and negative use of social media in the classroom. According to Chiang, social media can be used to support or hurt student learning. Effective and ethical use of social media as a tool for learning requires intentionality and commitment on the part of both instructors and learners.

Writing on "rumors in social media," Agnes Lando shows how social media provide a fertile atmosphere for the spread of rumors, whether true or false, and the effects of such rumors in individuals and society at large. The chapter cites specific rumors about Kenyan government officials, politicians, and stars. Using the case of the Kenya–Nigeria "tweef," it even shows how rumors on social media have the potential to affect relations between groups and nations.

Using a combination of critical communication theory and liberation theory, coauthors David Olali, Gbenga Dasylva, and Saliu Imaledo underscore the potential for social media to serve tools of evangelization, gospel outreach on one hand, and tools for abuse of power and domination of the laity by the clergy. The chapter analyzes the use of social media among leading independent churches in Nigeria.

Given the ubiquitous, pervasive, and amorphous nature of social media's role in today's society, Bala Musa and Ibrahim M. Ahmadu call for renewed commitment to media literacy, with special attention to new and social and new media literacy among young people. In their view, young people, as digital natives, are prone to adopt and use the medium first and think about its effects later. The chapter identifies the benefits of new media literacy and the dangers of new media illiteracy. It proposes policy strategies for advancing prosocial entertainment and new media literacy, with a view to promoting responsible social media behavior among digital natives and the society as a whole.

Notes

1. W. Barnnett Pearce and Kimberly A. Pearce, "Transcendent Storytelling: Abilities for Systematic Practitioners and Their Clients," *Human Systems: The Journal of Systematic Consultation & Management* 9 (1998): 178–79; cited in Em Griffin, *A First Look at Communication Theory*, 8th ed. (New York: McGraw-Hill, 2012), 73.

2. Neil Postman, *Amusing Ourselves to Death: Public Discourse in the Age of Show Business* (New York: Penguin Books, 2005).

3. Bala Musa and Ibrahim M. Ahmadu, "New Media, Wikifaith and Church Brandversation: A Media Ecology Perspective," in *Digital Religion, Social Media and Culture: Perspectives, Practices, and Futures,* ed. Pauline Hope Cheong, Peter Fischer-Nielsen, Stafan Gelfgren, and Charles Ess (New York: Peter Lang, 2012), 63–80.

PART I

Popular Culture

CHAPTER ONE

Considering Ethical Tensions in Transmedia Culture

Pauline Hope Cheong

Introduction

In February 2010, Dr Gloria Gadsden, a sociology professor was suspended from her duties and was put on leave by her university. Her offense? She posted some remarks about her teaching frustrations on her Facebook account, some remarks which were interpreted as threats. In January, she wrote, "Does anyone know where to find a very discreet hitman? Yes, it's been that kind of day." Another post said, "had a good day today, DIDN'T want to kill even one student :-). Now Friday was a different story." In her defense, she said that she was sharing her comments only to 32 members of her family and friends. She had not added students to her account and had no students among her Facebook friends. So she was unsure how her messages wound up at the provost's office.[1]

You will recognize that her case is not unique. Several other cases involving social media have caused significant challenges in educational institutions, including incidents where students have been punished and even suspended after posting derogatory remarks about their pedagogical authorities online. More recently, the compound phrase cyber-bullying attracted renewed media attention after a series of suicides by students who have been taunted and teased online, including one highly profiled case on a college freshman who jumped to his death following the circulation of a video about his gay relationship on YouTube by his peers.[2]

I submit that these recent confrontations point to how new and social media are facilitating changes in the educational landscape, including changes in informational boundaries between the so-called private and the public spheres in a dynamic communication environment. This is perhaps in part why universities have for years been relying on individuals' internal virtue ethics, by reminding students that they ought to keep their Facebook and Myspace pages free of inappropriate material but recently, several colleges have begun to erect social media policies to govern how faculty and other employees use communication technologies. These regulations, no doubt well intentioned, usually offer a list of guidelines or best practices. Yet, while considering any official policy or disciplinary action, we must attend to the larger informational and social landscape, including competing discourses, tensions, and contradictions inherent in the new cultural logics of social media.

Thus, the dialectical approach is key to what I want to discuss today as we think about our communication and the conference theme of information ethics in an increasingly mediated world. This chapter is organized into two parts. First, for the benefit of scholars unfamiliar with the dialectical approach, I open with a short summary of dialectics, and mediated dialectics as I have framed it to understand new media and culture. Second, I offer several observations about the emerging cultural developments and dynamics underpinning concepts like ambience and transmediation. I propose that these new cultural logics converge and diverge on several aspects of our established beliefs and norms regarding access and privacy. I draw upon the broader field of communication and Internet studies, as well as my own personal experience of conducting research in the area of social media, religion, and culture. As the study of ethics per se is not my research specialty, I am not here to preach or prescribe particular solutions. Instead, I will reflect on my research experiences to highlight emergent social tensions in order to further our understanding of the ethical challenges that new and social media practices might pose. These tensions bring both hope and ethical tribulations worthy of our collective attention and hopefully provide fodder for future debate.

Mediated Tensions

Borrowing from Mikhail Bakhtin's work on dialogue that emerges from the interplay of different, often competing discourses, communication scholars have applied the dialectical perspective in a variety of investigative contexts like in face-to-face interpersonal and family relationships and in organizational settings.[3] In investigating cultural communication phenomena, Judith Martin and Martin Nakayama offered the dialectic perspective as a way to move beyond traditional paradigmatic scholarship by emphasizing the relational, rather than individual aspects of interaction and holding two contradictory ideas simultaneously.[4] As noted by many contemporary scholars, a dialectical approach underscores the dynamic character of culture, as well as our knowledge about cultures and communication and cultural others.[5]

I employ the notion of mediated dialectics or tensions in my scholarship in light of the affordances of the Internet, which may facilitate multiple seemingly opposing relations, including liberating and dominating, empowering and fragmenting, universalizing but non-totalizing relationships. Notably, former International Communication Association President Ronald Rice recently commented that given the "social and technological interdependencies of new media," which "forces us to collaborate with people and systems not rewarded or designed to do so with us," "tensions among interdependence, collaboration and dysfunctional sociotechnical interactions" are developing, embedded, and pervasive, which should prod us toward further research in mediated dialectics.[6] Furthermore, to avoid essentializing others in mediated intercultural encounters, attention to mediated dialectics experienced by online users help highlight differences experienced within groups and individuals as these tensions shift—driven by many different forces, including media convergence and globalization. It is worth noting that Jacques Ellul, priest, sociologist, and author of *The Technological Society*, argued for dialectical thinking in the face of his experiences in the then technological innovations of the 20th century which has significant import for our times.[7] In his words,

> Dialectic, then is not just a way of reasoning by question and answer. It is an intellectual way of grasping reality, which embraces the positive and the negative, white and black. . . . It includes contradictory things that do not exclude one another but co-exist. Hence a system of vigorous thought ought to take account of both the yes and the no without ruling out either, without choosing between, since every choice excludes on part of reality.[8]

Accordingly, consideration of mediated dialectics broadens the conventional notion of Internet use in terms of time or activities online, to include the management of conflicting tensions, uneven gains, multiple opportunities, and challenges that people face in their contemporary social media experiences. My dialogically grounded approach to media thus departs from mainstream and popular communiqués which tend to either stress the hype about the revolutionary advantages of new media or the moral panic and dystopia that new media bring. In other words, in recognizing that mediated communication is inherently dynamic, I recognize that virtue and vice may coexist in mediated platforms, which are sites of power and inequality of discourses in struggle.

Approaching Ambience

When we utter or hear the term ambient, we tap into the enveloping presence of new media communication in our daily lives. Ambience as a condition of our contemporary existence helps us to make sense of our wired connectivity, or what Sonia Livingstone terms as the "mediation of everyday life."[9] According to several other theorists like Stig Harvard, Internet use has mediatized our daily existence to such a pervasive and deep extent that major alterations are at work in how we relate to one another and how key institutions including governments, schools, and churches work.[10]

By ambient, I refer to the ubiquity of mediated communication. My experiences inform me that mediated processes and outcomes are increasingly interwoven into our cultural surround that they are increasingly taken for granted and opaque, at least largely in parts of the wired world's consciousness. In increasingly wired contexts, online communication is associated with computer hardware but now also with a range of cell phones and Web-enabled electronic devices like Kindle and the iPad. Social media are commonly referred to as "Web 2.0," but I see signs that signal a need to start stretching our social and ethical comprehension toward "Web 3.0."

In popular conception, social media represent a paradigm shift from Web 1.0, which is an e-mail era with read-only content, static HTML Web sites, directories, to Web 2.0, with read–write user-generated content like YouTube, Facebook, Flickr, and Digg. Ambience is evoked particularly in the third wave of Web 3.0, which entails the portable personal Web. We are said to be moving to the semantic Web, or as the International Telecommunications Union report puts it, "the Internet of things," whereby the meaning of information and services on the Web is defined, making it possible for people as well as machines to understand and appropriate Web content. For example, lifestreaming applications are enabling technologies which import RSS feeds from various sites and services. Ambient lifestreaming helps gather the messages you have already produced elsewhere on various social media platforms online and consolidates them, bringing them all together into a single ongoing stream for other people and apps.

Several statistics and studies aptly illustrate how many of us are situated within a Web 2.0 paradigm, and moving toward Web 3.0. For instance, a report by the Pew Internet and American life Project shows a slight dip in blogging activities among those under 30, while wireless connectivity continues to rise. Fourth-fifths of young adults between the ages of 18 and 29 are wireless Internet users, and while many of them are getting to the Web using their laptops, they're also using netbooks, cell phones, game consoles, and e-readers. Nearly three quarters of online teens and young adults and 40 percent of adults over 30 use social networking sites.[11] Facebook reports that it has more than 400 million active users. Therefore, if we reimagine Facebook as a country it would be one of the largest countries in the world. About one-fifth of online American adults said that they used a microblogging service to send messages or tweets.[12]

Thus, it seems that each of us unknowingly or knowingly operate a personal communication system, where we use multiple media to connect to people and information on a regular basis. As Ralph Schroeder at the Oxford Internet Institute puts it, we are faced with the "inexorable advance of multimodal connectedness."[13] And as if "multi"-modal is not superlative enough, many students in my class on new media and culture this semester, report in their weekly essays that they are super or very multimodal. The result is that for many, being always connected through multiple media becomes the new normal. Hence, in light of the ambient quality of mediated communication, what are the ethical tensions and considerations associated with new media use?

Back to the case of Professor Gloria Gadsden. Multimodal connectivity enables one to engage in life logging, to log content and share your life stories with others on a frequent basis. On the other hand, it also makes it easy for others to publicly access, view, and follow your latest news and online publishing habits. Integrated multimodal connectivity might mean for us, as it did for sociology professor Gloria Gadsden, that she is proverbially on the record, all the time. Until recently, Gadsden said, she thought that by limiting her cyber friendships she could maintain the boundary or firewall between her personal life and her role as a professor. It is reported that she said, "I actually did see that page as something that was not a part of ESU [her university of employment], not a part of my professional life." She said, "I don't invite students into that part of my life."[14]

But this Facebook incident points out how our postings, even offhand musings may not be considered private in the age of Web 3.0 social networking. Professor Gadsden believes an update to Facebook's software automatically altered her settings, removing the privacy barriers she had erected. This brings up the dialectics associated with Web 2.0 and the semantic Web 3.0.

For many, new and social media bring on the many benefits associated with increased access. In dominant discourse, online authorship and creative participation is highly encouraged. Many social networks allow the putatively free and efficient exchange of textual, visual, and video information by Internet users, who are now framed as agentic participants known by the portmanteaus "pro-sumers" or "produ-sers." But what is less known and publicized are the high costs of these allegedly seamless and free connections between people and technological implements.[15] For instance, in the case of Facebook, the social networking grew dramatically promising privacy and control at the center of what it offered: the default setting is that your information is private, visible only to people whom you, approve as friends. But just months ago in the winter, several changes were unfurled in a significant, perhaps ethically heartburning way.

In December 2009, Facebook launched a set of communication rules which was viewed by many to be an infraction to user control. In the past, it could be said that the friends we chose represent the limit of the privacy we want but now the default setting to many layers of information has been changed to public. And as always, most people click through the list of updates and accept automatic settings which may go well against what they really want or understand. In addition, Facebook users are no longer allowed to restrict access to their profile photos and the list of pages they have subscribed to updates from. In other words, certain profile details, such as your name, profile picture, gender, current city, networks, friends list, and all the pages you subscribe to are now publicly available information on Facebook. This means everyone on the Web can see it; it is also searchable by other people and can be (and in many cases has been) accessed and permanently archived by external applications like the Google search engine and other Web crawlers. In April 2010, the Facebook site started giving third-party applications more access to user data, where "Instant Personalization" lets sites share Facebook user data to create recommendation engines in a system where users were automatically enrolled.[16] Is it good bye Web 2.0 privacy and security, and hello the open Web 3.0? Facebook CEO Mark Zuckerberg seemed to think so, when he commented that a privacy change for social media is necessary. In his words, "A lot of companies would be trapped by the conventions and their legacies of what they've built, doing a privacy change—doing a privacy change for 350 million users is not the kind of thing that a lot of companies would do. But we viewed that as a really important thing, to always keep a beginner's mind and what would we do if we were starting the company now and we decided that these would be the social norms now and we just went for it."[17]

Given the Web's dynamic connectivity, this change has wide-reaching implications on the visibility of the data on social networks which are still being debated. And while I do not want to paint a dystopian future, given some of the benefits that might come with the semantic Web including a more telepathic and tailored information search environment which means convenience and profitability to some, there is evidence that for people like Professor Gadsden, ambient connectivity is an unwelcome entry into a Web 3.0 reality.

Indeed, power matters and creates inequalities in terms of user experiences and control. Asymmetry in mediated tensions or dialectics means that many capabilities of social media are dictated by those in macro or corporate formations that are differently served depending on the dictates of the major players, with significant implications for those positioned away from powerful interests.[18] For example, some Facebook users have reported that they were not given adequate warning of the default privacy changes. As a result, many could not defriend people on their list which reveal their religious, sexual, or political orientation, and other sensitive information about themselves. Their frustrations have been voiced on many blogs, and Web sites, and many have threatened to terminate their Facebook account in protest (since this change affects all their past posted information and tagged photos, highly lucrative data which in all probability have already been cached by organizations like search engine companies). For instance, in his now famous or infamous open letter to Facebook CEO Mark Zuckerberg, Craig Kanalley wrote,

> Because here's the thing, Mark. Behind all those numbers, and behind the dollar signs that may be in the back of your mind, there are people. Real people. Human beings. With lives. And friends. And family. And employers. And they're all connected on Facebook. And if the wrong piece of information gets to the wrong person, or if a private detail gets to a marketing company, or if criminals or stalkers find info they need to attack people, you will ruin people's lives. Literally—ruin people's lives. . . . Don't forget that any changes you make have a significant impact on everybody in the network. And if data isn't private by default, and if you go more and more in the public direction, people will withhold what they share.[19]

He goes on to say,

> I'm not going to waste time revamping my entire Facebook presence, go back to old pictures and delete, untag, and get rid of my all private info on

there. I'm not going to waste time deleting old wall posts or posts I've made elsewhere. I'm not going to waste time trying to understand new privacy settings or learning the "new way" of using Facebook.[20]

Craig Kanalley's comments describe how one now needs to painstakingly remove data, clean up digital traces, restore one's privacy settings one at a time in order to try and reclaim back previous levels of protection. His frustrations stem from the paradox that users' ability to post frequently on social media gives them the feel of uninhibited, oral expression yet the cultural logic of ambient connectivity preserves these comments as published material and spreads them beyond the intended or imagined audience. Reconsidering the case of Professor Gadsen, it seemed that she never imagined that her comments on an assumed private Web site were publicly shared by her so-called friends in common, nor interpreted as threats by her dean. Indeed, it was reported that five comments followed her post which had a smiley face emoticon, suggesting that those to whom she was linked understood the joke. One said she was "ROFL," shorthand for "rolling on the floor laughing."

Thus, it is hard not to witness the dialectical irony, of how the ease of online connectivity can also become a disease when it becomes so easy and quick for information and disinformation to spread. Updates as fragments can be misinterpreted to negative effect. Furthermore, as some of us will attest, we simply click through the choices offered to us in new programs issued by software companies without fully investigating the default settings which can change, and quickly alter communication rules. Hence, it is of significant concern when users perceive that their expectations of trust and privacy are violated, and also when users do not realize, cannot understand, or are automatically enrolled into new programs unaware of the changing conditions of online information exchanges and the context in which information spreads. This brings us to consider my second point on a related cultural logic, that of transmediation.

Transmedia and Digital Memes

By transmediation, I refer to the flow of media content across multiple media platforms. According to Henry Jenkins, the convergence of old and new media represents "a cultural shift as consumers are encouraged to seek out new information and make connections among dispersed media content."[21] Unlike traditional top-down dissemination of information, transmediation is related to the nonlinear circulation and multidirectional remediation and reappropriation of media content.[22] This can result in the creation of remixes,[23] mash-ups, and memes—the latter are compelling ideas, catchphrases, or stories which cultural dissemination generates virus-like imitations and reproductions. In the realm of entertainment where transmediation is highly valued for branding, viral marketing allow fans to participate in the production and sharing of new meanings supplementary and additional to what is developed in the original main script. This allows fans to recreate their identities online, engage on a deeper level to build stronger emotional connections to media products.

But beyond entertainment, transmediation can work in other areas of social participation, bringing about both positive and negative social and ethical implications. In religious communication for example, my research on faith memes examines how religion-related tweets may function as memes to accelerate the speed and intensity of gospel message spread.[24] To literally spread the word about Christianity online, multiple faith memes have been developed.[25] For example, one of the first and more popular memes is entitled "Twitter of Faith." In the Twitter of Faith challenge, one is to write a statement of faith in 140 words and pass it forward,

> What do you believe? You have 140 characters—give us your statement of faith in 140 characters. #TOF.

This meme was first created on November 22, 2008, when Minister Adam Cleveland was tasked with composing his essay statement of faith for his ordination and was challenged to condense his beliefs into a tweet of 140 characters. Subsequently, Minister Cleveland urged his Twitter friends and followers to respond by composing their own TOF and add the hash tag #TOF to permit identification and categorization of this tweet. The twitter brand icon was also appropriated to form the accompanying "Twitter of Faith" graphic meme.

Within days, multiple # TOF tweets were sent in response through the creation of this viral game. Many were declarations of faith and summaries of theological truths into punchy, memorable phrases:

> sirmikelittle: #TOF "Life is art. Get to know the Artist."
>
> mattkelley468: #TOF Jesus Christ is the invasion of the infinite into the finite, allowing we who are finite to experience the fullness of God's being.
>
> david_a_zimmerm: One God in three persons created creation and actively pursues its redemption. Redeemed people love God and one another and life itself.#TOF
>
> MattEB: #TOF Saved by faith in Christ. Jesus died for my sins. Jesus lives.

ktday: #tof God was, is, and shall be with us always, and loves us ridiculously.
We are called to love one another likewise.

Various other tweets were condensations inspired from verses from the
Bible, as in the following cases, from the New Testament book of First
Corinthians and the Old Testament book of Micah respectively:

Josielle: #TOF And now these three remain: faith, hope and love. But the greatest of these is love.

fritzg: Do justice, love mercy and walk humbly with God. #TOF

To further spread the meme, besides composing and sharing their own
#TOF, twitterers were also asked to retweet and transmediate this message
on multiple Web 2.0 platforms.

Please post about this on your blog (with a link back to this post here), feel
free to use the above image as well, and Twitter about it or put it on your
Facebook. . . .—it could be interpreted as a cool social experiment in sharing your faith with the Twitter world.

These faith memes purposefully instigate conversation about spiritual
beliefs. Like mutating chain letters, the (re)circulation of faith tweets may
be conceived of as media viral codes, with the ability to influence a society's agenda, with real effects. They can help, for example, to build an
imagined community among microbloggers, bloggers, and other online
users.[26] Although it is arguable how effective religious messages reduced
to tweets of 140 characters are, faith memeing provides a thread to connect like-minded seekers and online evangelists to manipulate and spiritually shape the twitter verse.

Yet, as you might suspect, this thought contagion may present perverse
effects. Critics of religious tweeting have pointed out the limitations of
"byte-sized theology" which dilutes truths in the gospel message. Religious
leaders have also debated the difficulty in balancing twitter chatter with
the need for quiet reflection that spirituality entails.[27] Moreover, transmediation can contribute to Internet radicalization of a more malevolent
kind, where we see communication between extremist networked believers who create compelling memes to spread radical views or instigate
militant interpretations of faith. In light of ambience and transmediation,
microblogging may accelerate extremist "cyber-herding" or what Cass
Sunstein calls an "echo chamber effect" among fundamentalist ideologues,
which may lead to cultural polarization, public disorder, and violence.[28]

In this way, we see how transmediation can facilitate swift changes in the multimodal communication ecology. Creative possibilities of the social Web are facilitating different kinds of representations and constructions of truth. Indeed, new and social media can facilitate what has been called "hive" or "collective intelligence," whereby civic collaboration in information seeking and the constructions of Wikis, become the legitimate standard for truth. In higher education, for example, we have long debated the functional utility and limitations of Wikipedia as a source of information and knowledge. Yet in today's ambient and transmedia culture, the wiki mentality may extend into our everyday lives, raising newer forms of ethical concerns for privacy and security.

To illustrate the ethical tensions involved in transmediation and collective intelligence practices, I bring up one final example with regard to a research study I recently conducted with a doctoral student on the "human flesh search in China."[29]

Human flesh search, a literal translation from its Chinese name *ren rou sou suo,* was rated one of China's top 10 catchphrases in 2008. Human flesh search involves mediated processes whereby online participants mobilize to track down demographic and geographical information of deviant individuals, often with the shared intention to expose, shame, and punish them to reinstate legal justice or public morality. In China, the first widely publicized cyber manhunt was sparked off in 2006 by the circulation of online videos showing a woman killing a kitten to death with her high heels. Enraged netizens posted the woman's photograph online and urged people to track her down. This virtual collaboration brought to light the woman's name and details about her workplace, eventually leading to her giving an online apology for the cruelty after being dismissed from her job.

Recently, human flesh search has become an increasingly popular public recourse to identify and punish corrupt public officials. Our research paper, for example, examined two prominent cases of human flesh searches which involved the identification of corrupt high-ranking officials in Shanghai and Shenzhen and the mass circulation of their private data online through blogs, forums, and social networking sites as video mash-ups of political parodies, which led to amplified attention on their abuse of power, criminal investigation, and ultimately their removal from public office.

Here again, we witness the dialectical ethical implications of new media since transmediation processes helped diminish corruption as netizens collaboratively constructed private details of social deviants to bring them to public attention. Yet privacy risks of this sort of cyber manhunt are high, especially considering the ethical implications of the exposure of individual public records overtime, like in the case of publishing personal details of criminal offenders in open access databases.[30]

Particularly, deeply entrenched online narratives of social deviants may rule out their second chances in life. As Amitai Etzioni and Radhika Bhat recently wrote in *The American Scholar* in an article entitled, "Second Chances, Social Forgiveness and the Internet," the Internet may erode "an important American value" of "social forgiveness" rooted in the Judeo-Christian belief in redemption and the nation's immigration history of providing people a fresh start in life. In their words, the internet "casts a shadow of people's past far and fast; like a curse they cannot undo, their records now follow them wherever they go."[31] They point out that we must protect people not only from crime but also from our own propensity to evil in response to the crimes of others. Therefore, rather than open databases, we should think of restricting access by sealing a record on a database after a certain amount of time, limiting access to certain databanks to those who are trained to understand the limitations of these databanks, and make media companies who control Internet databases accountable for the information they provide. Hence, it would be interesting to discuss how communities regulate legal, technological, and social means to extend or alter civic memory, long after perpetrators are persecuted for their misconduct.

Conclusion

I have discussed two emergent cultural logics underlying Web 2.0 and Web 3.0. The dialectical approach sensitizes us to various ethical tensions in an ambient and transmedia culture. Mediated dialectics compel us to broaden our ethical focus, to accept the dynamic complexities in social media communication, and perhaps to think about extending social forgiveness to those tainted by prior error or falsehoods online. To some extent, this might help resist operational closures even while we grapple with new social norms, and while universities struggle to codify and enforce official new media policies. In Professor Gloria Gadsden's case, for example, this brings up other issues that perhaps could have been considered before her suspension, including the context of her post and how it spread online, the recent changes to Facebook's policy which remain opaque to many social media users, and other socio-technological entanglements in the semantic Web 3.0, where interminable flows of information are exchanged, stored, and archived today, much in ambience.

Notes

1. Jack Stripling, "Not So Private Professors," 2010. http://www.insidehighered.com/news/2010/03/02/Facebook.

2. Bonnie Rochman, "Cyberbullying? Homophobia? Tyler Clementi's Death Highlights Online Lawlessness," 2010. http://healthland.time.com/2010/10/01/cyberbullying-homophobia-tyler-clementis-death-highlights-online-lawlessness/.

3. Mikhail Bakhtin, "Discourse in the Novel," in *The Dialogic Imagination: Four Essays by M. M. Bakhtin,* ed. M. Holquist, trans. C. Emerson and M. Holquist (Austin: University of Texas Press, 1982), 259–422. (Original work published 1975). See also Leslie Baxter, *Voicing Relationships: A Dialogic Perspective* (Thousand Oaks, CA: Sage, 2011); Jensen Chung, "The Chi/Qi/Ki of Organizational Communication: The Process of Generating Energy Flow with Dialectics," *China Media Research* 4, no. 3 (2008): 92–100.

4. Judith Martin and Thomas Nakayama, "Thinking Dialectically about Culture and Communication." *Communication Theory* 9 (1999): 1–25.

5. Pauline Cheong, Judith Martin, and Leah Macfadyen, "Mediated Intercultural Communication Matters: Understanding New Media, Dialectics and Social Change," in *New Media and Intercultural Communication: Identity, Community and Politics*, ed. Pauline Cheong, Judith Martin, and Leah Macfadyen, 1–20 (New York: Peter Lang, 2012).

6. Ronald Rice, "Sociological and Technological Interdependencies of New Media." *Journal of Computer-Mediated Communication* 14 (2009): 714–19.

7. Jacques Ellul, *The Technological Society*, trans. John Wilkinson (New York: Random House, 1964).

8. Jacques Ellul, *What I Believe,* trans. G.W. Bromiley (London: Marshall Morgan & Scott Publications, 1989), 31.

9. Sonia Livingstone, "On the *Mediation* of Everything: ICA Presidential Address 2008," *Journal of Communication* 59, no. 1 (2009): 1–18.

10. Stig Hjarvard, "The Mediatization of Society," *Nordicom Review* 29, no. 2 (2008): 105–34.

11. Amanda Lenhart, Kristen Purcell, Aaron Smith, and Kathryn Zickuhr, "Social Media and Young Adults," 2010. http://www.pewinternet.org/Reports/2010/Social-Media-and-Young-Adults.aspx.

12. Susannah Fox, Kathryn Zickuhr, and Aaron Smith, "Twitter and Status Updating." Pew Internet & American Life Project Web. 2009. http://www.pewinternet.org/~/media//Files/Reports/2009/PIP_Twitter_Fall_2009_web.pdf.

13. Ralph Schroeder, "Mobile Phones and the Inexorable Advance of Multimodal Connectedness," *New Media and Society* 12, no. 1 (2010): 75–90.

14. Stripling, "Not So Private Professors."

15. Jose Van Dijck, "Users Like You? Theorizing Agency in User-Generated Content." *Media, Culture and Society* 31, no. 1 (2009): 41–58.

16. Dan Fletcher, "Friends without Borders." *Time*, May 31, 2010, 32–38.

17. http://www.ustream.tv/recorded/3848950.

18. David Beer, "Social Network(ing) Sites . . . Revisiting the Story So Far: A Response to danah boyd and Nicole Ellison." *Journal of Computer-Mediated Communication* 13 (2008): 516–29.

19. http://www.huffingtonpost.com/craig-kanalley/Facebook-privacy-concerns_b_418031.html.

20. Ibid.

21. Henry Jenkins, *Convergence Culture: Where Old and New Media Collide* (New York: New York University Press, 2006), 3.

22. Jay Bolter and Richard Grusin, *Remediation: Understanding New Media* (Cambridge, MA: MIT, 2003).

23. Lawrence Lessig, *Remix: Making Art and Commerce Thrive in the Hybrid Economy* (New York: Penguin Group, 2008).

24. Pauline Cheong, "Faith Tweets: Ambient Religious Communication and Microblogging Rituals," *M/C Journal: A Journal of Media and Culture* 13, no. 2 (2010), http://journal.media-culture.org.au/index.php/mcjournal/article/viewArticle/223.

25. Pauline Cheong, "Twitter of Faith: Understanding Social Media Networking and Microblogging Rituals as Religious Practices," in *Digital Religion, Social Media and Culture: Perspectives, Practices, Futures*, ed. Pauline Cheong, Peter Fischer-Nielsen, Stephen Gelfgren, and Charles Ess (New York: Peter Lang, 2012), 191–206.

26. James Sanderson and Pauline Cheong, "Tweeting Prayers and Communicating Grief over Michael Jackson Online," *Bulletin of Science, Technology, & Society* 30, no. 5 (2010): 328–40.

27. Pauline Cheong, "Christianity-Lite: In 140 Characters or Fewer," *Religion Dispatches*, December 4, 2009, http://www.religiondispatches.org/archive/mediaculture/1346/christianity-lite%2C_in_140_characters_or_fewer.

28. Cass Sunstein, *Going to Extremes: How Like Minds Unite and Divide* (New York: Oxford University Press, 2009).

29. Pauline Cheong and Jie Gong, "Cyber Vigilantism, Transmedia Collective Intelligence, and Civic Participation," *Chinese Journal of Communication* 3, no. 4 (2010): 471–87.

30. Anne Cheung, "China Internet Going Wild: Cyber-Hunting versus Privacy Protection," *Computer Law and Security Review* 25, no. 3 (2009): 275–79.

31. Amitai Etzioni and Radhika Bhat, "Second Chances, Social Forgiveness and the Internet," 2009, 1. http://www.theamericanscholar.org/.

CHAPTER TWO

The ME BRANDS of Social Media

Joe Hight

The age of social media has created new ways for public officials, celebrities, and even journalists to build audiences through what I call "ME BRANDs."

You only have to look at the 2012 Grammy Awards to understand why ME BRANDs are important. Adele, Lady Gaga, Chris Brown, Nicki Minaj, and LL Cool J all have different brands based on their choice of music and how they present themselves in public and act in private. They all have ME BRANDs that are entirely different and are evolving based on what they do in public and what is revealed in their private lives.

A ME BRAND is your own brand of personalization and how you relate to a community. Whether you have 100 or 5,000 friends or followers on Facebook, Twitter, or another social medium, you have to consider the importance of your brand.

For those considering a media career, a ME BRAND becomes more important to success today because of the choices that audiences are given, from social media to multimedia and megascreen televisions with hundreds of cable offerings to YouTube and on-demand video.

The ME BRAND must understand that platforms are changing in which people collect information, read stories, or see content. They are changing in how they communicate. Good or bad, the changes are fundamental and will continue to evolve for many years.

Those who still doubt the emergence of social media should consider the story[1] from Lanet Umoja, a village about 100 miles west of Nairobi in Kenya. According to The Associated Press (AP), administrative chief Francis Kariuki didn't call the local police when thugs were robbing a teacher's home at 4 A.M. one day in 2012. He tweeted it. Within minutes, AP reported, villagers converged on the house and chased the thieves from the scene.

Kariuki said he no longer writes letters or print posters, but uses Twitter to send messages about missing children and farm animals. One tweet even prompted a thief to return a stolen cow, leaving it abandoned but tied to a pole.

Kariuki has created his own ME BRAND through how he relates to his audience of 28,000 residents of the area. He does all this, AP reports, with only 300 followers.

Journalists should consider the same as they relate to their audiences. They must report or edit on many more different platforms than when journalists pounded out their stories on typewriters or offered reports through fuzzy black-and-white images on a small screen. The vast number of changes in the media industry and the fact there are fewer journalists have made it even more challenging.

Then there's social media, which create different ways for how we gather in our society and how we report on it. Sites like Facebook and Twitter provide news on a wide-ranging and personal level. Others like Pinterest provide for those with more visual interests. Instead of public gatherings, people can gather in even more informal ways on social media and even help each other through the usage of it.

Such power is why today's journalists must not only know how to report the news, write it, and tell stories in different ways and platforms, but they must also understand how the power of ME BRANDS can influence and spread the message of what they are writing about, photographing, or videotaping. Those who do are advancing rapidly in their careers.

Jay Rosen, a professor at New York University, one of the founders of what was known as public journalism and a frequent user of Twitter, wrote about 27-year-old Tracy Samantha Schmidt, who in four years at *The Chicago Tribune* became brand manager and lead trainer at 435 Digital, a Tribune subsidiary.[2]

"Journalism is going to need a lot more like her if it's going to secure itself as a business. But I think they're out there: talented young journalists who can help with the revenue puzzle, and who want to help solve it because they want journalism to survive."

This doesn't mean all journalists will have to become revenue producers, but it does mean they will have to become the solution, the ones who adapt in this age and become valuable to a media organization, or, in some cases, to their own audiences. Singers such as Adele are successful because they have loyal audiences. Journalists must do the same by developing their own audiences and/or understanding their needs, not only to help their media companies but also to help themselves.

Kristina Ackermann wrote in a story for Editor & Publisher[3] that content will still be king in 2020 as it always has been. But in 2020 "content . . . is more than words on paper (or screen). Content is the end-user's entire experience: from delivery and first read to sharing an article with a cousin in another state. The experience of content is why alumni of the old school wax nostalgic about sitting in a favorite chair to read the paper with a hot cup of coffee on a Sunday morning. Producing content is as much about building trust and inspiring engagement as it is about reporting, writing, and editing," she wrote.

"2020 will bring the opportunity to distribute your content farther than ever before on a range of available platforms. Your content must be distributed to every platform available—online, smartphones, tablets, mobile Web, social media, email, and new mediums we haven't heard of yet."

She referred the new age as the one of hyperpersonalization, in which readers will pull information and content from sources they want. Social media have and will change the way people view content. They are now tuning in to links provided by their followers, content recommended by friends, or visuals that a follower has pinned. It's content that's personalized to their tastes and needs, rather than force-fed to them. If you use social media, you know what this means.

The ME BRAND must learn to provide content through multiple platforms and then know how to use social media effectively. Journalists need to know not only the audience that is served by their media company, but the audience that they serve as well.

However, despite the increasing number of platforms and choices, the foundations of journalism remain the same and ultimately will determine a journalist's ME BRAND credibility.

David Espo, a correspondent with AP, tells the story[4] of White House reporters for United Press International (UPI) and AP who were covering the President John F. Kennedy's visit to Dallas on November 22, 1963. Both shared a car in the presidential motorcade with only one phone available for the both of them. When Kennedy was shot, the UPI reporter was the first to get to the phone with this bulletin: "THREE SHOTS WERE FIRED AT PRESIDENT KENNEDY'S MOTORCADE IN DOWNTOWN DALLAS."

"Note what Merriman Smith didn't write that day," Espo said. "Nothing about whether anyone had been hit, or injured, or killed." Just the simplest sentence based on what he heard and on the chaos in the president's car that he witnessed at close range.

"Imagine the pressure on Smith that day to say more than he did, and in fact, to say more than he knew. I'm going to guess that then, as now, the questions flooding everyone's mind were: Had the president in fact been shot, and if so, how seriously?"

"So the need to be first has been around for a long time, and the need to be ethical about your reporting, too."

Pulitzer Prize winner Albert Merriman Smith understood the need for credibility in 1963, as much as journalists should understand the need for it today. That credibility will help journalists rise above the pressure that is put on them to place facts over fiction that may drive increased readership or audience, but creates damaging long-term effects. It helps them rise above the tabloid newspapers, Web sites, and television shows that strive to be more sensationalistic and intrusive on innocent victims trust into a public tragedy.

A case involving a tabloid newspaper that should concern all journalists is the News of the World scandal. Allegations ranged from the hacking of a missing 13-year-old girl's phone messages as well as phones of parents of murdered children and relatives of dead soldiers to bribery of law enforcement to use of private investigators who were convicted criminals.

Most journalists might simply shrug when hearing the allegations. The excuses may vary: *It was just one of those sensationalistic, now-defunct British tabloids. It wasn't even in our country. It had no ethical standards like we do.*

However, the allegations affect journalists worldwide for two primary reasons:

- *Public perception:* To the public, the News of the World was part of the media. A poll for ITV News at Ten in Great Britain showed 80 percent of respondents no longer trust the media because of the scandal.[5] That compares to a 2010 Gallup poll that showed 57 percent of respondents in the United States "have little or no trust in the mass media to report the news fully, accurately and fairly."[6]
- *Questioning of our ethical practices:* Did the News of the World cross boundaries that traditional journalists would never cross?

"Every journalist, not only those working for the tabloids, is called upon to take risks in the pursuit of truth—usually within agreed-upon limits. And it is true that, to a remarkable degree, even the most egregious news outlets adhere to those limits," Ryan Linkof, a lecturer in history at the University of Southern California whose doctoral dissertation was on the origins of tabloid photojournalism in Britain, wrote in an op-ed piece for *The New York Times*.[7] "The tabloids may be sneakier and more persistent than more respected news sources, but this is a matter of degree, not kind." The "matter of degree" has been blurring for years, as noted by the growing number of instances worldwide in which traditional media may have crossed the lines.

One example came after the Oklahoma City bombing in which a local television station hired a private investigator to look into an Iraqi refugee as the possible "John Doe 2." The restaurant worker claimed later that he was subjected to "unbelievable harassment" from the station and was beaten and spat upon because of the reports.[8] He was never arrested or charged.

Rupert Murdoch, whose media empire included News of the World, even noted during a parliamentarian hearing in London: "I think all news organizations have used private detectives and do so in their investigations from time to time, I don't think illegally."[9]

Other instances have occurred, too, in which journalists have dressed up in uniforms or used their celebrity to gain access to areas in which other media have been barred by authorities. Some are even ludicrous, such as the journalist who dressed up in a brown dress and carried apple crisp in an effort to cross police lines in her coverage of the massacre of Amish schoolgirls in Nickels Mine, Pennsylvania.[10]

Even if the lack of access was questionable, the deceptions to cross boundaries can be found in the coverage of almost any disaster or massacre worldwide and erode public perception even further.

"So long as sensation and intrusion continue to sell newspapers, journalists will remain under pressure to produce material to meet demand," researchers Eileen Berrington and Ann Jemphrey wrote in "Pressures on the Press: Reflections on reporting tragedy," a 2003 study that explored journalists covering the massacre at Dunblane Primary School, Scotland, in 1996. "They were driven by commercial imperatives to produce copy, a pressure that at times overrode ethical considerations and sensitivity."

As Linkof asserts, tabloids may have a place in this world, especially as long as people buy them or, most importantly, advertise in them. However, the tabloid newspapers and television shows are also putting more pressure on legitimate media to become sensationalistic even beyond the coverage of a mass tragedy or questionable acts of public officials. It now includes everyday coverage of murder victims and missing children that tends to inflict more harm on grieving relatives.

So while journalists can deny that they don't have any ties to what transpired at News of the World, the links are inevitable and should cause them to consider what boundaries we will cross to get a story.

Journalists can enhance their ME BRAND credibility through accuracy, fairness, and sensitivity to victims. The Oklahoman's Standards Team has this as part of the News and Information Center Ethics Code's mission statement: "Our ventures into multimedia should not lessen our need for ethical standards in the gathering of news and information for those products and platforms."

Margaret Holt, senior editor for *The Chicago Tribune*, said journalists must understand the "language of engagement" and how people crave community and connection to others. Today's social media provides that community and connections more than ever before. However, Holt stresses that accuracy must be the foundation that provides meaning to those communities.

"We must pursue more facts to allow for a deeper, richer truth. We as journalists have to engage in the world . . . and seek more voices to truly tell the truth," she said.

"And that is what ethical journalists must do—every day—the changing world of media."

Journalists should also understand the increasing number of ways to verify and fact-check their content, writes Craig Silverman, author of the "Regret the Error" blog for the Poynter Institute for Media Studies. He called the emerging area the "New Verification."[11]

"Never before in the history of journalism—or society—have more people and organizations been engaged in fact checking and verification. Never has it been so easy to expose an error, check a fact, crowdsource and bring technology to bear in service of verification," he wrote for *The Nieman Reports*.

"Not surprisingly, the price for inaccuracy has never been higher."

This should not, however, dissuade anyone already pursuing or considering a career in journalism.

Kristen Daum, a reporter for *The Lansing State Journal*, expresses the perfect attitude for journalists of the future: "Keep an open mind, learn all the tools you can, offer fresh ideas and be enthusiastic for the adventure ahead!" She expressed this in a tweet.[12]

Journalists are on an adventure ride of the future. Those with ME BRANDs will have to learn, adapt quickly to changes, but those with talent, hard work, and credibility will be the ones who ultimately will succeed, as they have in the past.

They will still pride themselves on the art of storytelling through multiple platforms. They will still think that ethics are vital, so much that they will take great pride when someone tweets that getting a retweet from them means much more than getting one from others with less credibility.

Numbers matter to those in the media, but the quality of the content and audiences should matter most. The same goes for journalists who care more about people than numbers in their stories.

Two-time Pulitzer Prize winner Anthony Shadid, who died while seeking to cover the civil war in Syria, believed that when he said: "The best stories are those about people. The best journalism comes when you care about what you're writing about."[13]

Whether journalists have aspirations to be war correspondents like Anthony Shadid or work in their own communities, their ME BRAND must be passionate, care about people, and understand that credibility is vital for the future.

As Thomas Jefferson wrote, "The only security of all is in a free press. The force of public opinion cannot be resisted when permitted freely to be expressed. The agitation it produces must be submitted to. It is necessary, to keep the waters pure."[14]

Journalists' ME BRAND audiences continue to depend on them "to keep the waters pure."[15]

Notes

1. Dan Berrett, "ESU Professor Suspended for Comments Made on Facebook Page," *Pocono Record,* February 26, 2010, http://www.poconorecord.com/apps/pbcs.dll/article?AID=/20100226/NEWS/2260344.

2. Jay Rosen, "From the Expense Column to the Revenue Stream: Q & A with Tracy Samantha Schmidt," *Press Think,* http://pressthink.org/2012/01/from-the-expense-column-to-the-revenue-stream-q-a-with-tracy-samantha-schmidt/.

3. Editor & Publisher, "2020 Vision: Newspaper Content, Evolved," February 2012, http://www.editorandpublisher.com/Features/Article/2020-Vision--Newspaper-Content--Evolved.

4. University of Central Oklahoma Media Ethics Conference 2011.

5. Press Gazette, Journalism Today, and other sources, July 2011.

6. "Distrust in U.S. Media Edges Up to Record High," Gallup.com, September 2010.

7. "Why We Need Tabloids," *The New York Times,* July 19, 2011.

8. Ed Godfrey, "Lawsuit Says TV Station Falsely Labeled City Man," *The Oklahoman,* August 25, 1995. http://newsok.com/lawsuit-says-tv-station-falsely-labeled-city-man/article/2512240.

9. CBSNews.com, July 19, 2011.

10. "Local Tragedy, National Spotlight," dartcenter.org, December 26, 2006.

11. "Truth in the Age of Social Media." *Nieman Reports,* Summer 2012.

12. Twitter statement after request from Joe Hight.

13. Anthony Shadid, in speech to The Oklahoman's News and Information Center, February 2012.

14. Thomas Jefferson to Lafayette, 1823.

15. Part of this chapter appeared originally in Joe Hight's column "Hacking Scandal Returns: Should Journos Care?" which appeared September 6, 2011, on the Dart Center for Journalism & Trauma's Web site at dartcenter.org.

CHAPTER THREE

Lighten Up: A Rhetorical Performance Critique of Gap's Online Khaki Campaign

Cindy N. Phu

Introduction

The Spring 2007 Gap Campaign was "Gap's New 'Khakis With Attitude' Lighten Up Wardrobes" that featured Kyra Sedgwick, Kate Mara, Chris O'Donnell, Wentworth Miller, Daniel Dae Kim, Dermot Mulroney, and Chris Brown. This campaign primarily focused on bringing back the khaki image to both males and females during the spring season. They utilized famous individuals to perform advertisements on television commercials, billboards, magazine ads, Web site homepage, and in-store images to promote their new clothing line. According to the Gap's Press Release:

> The look for women is all about wide-leg pants, which makes Gap's boyfriend trouser a must-have item. Made of lightweight cotton and featuring clean lines with a wide cut leg, the boyfriend trouser offers women an updated twist on a classic favorite. . . . Men will love the casual attitude of this season's khakis including everything from relaxed khaki pants and cargo shorts to weekend jackets and military shirts.[1]

This research study is essential because Gap is one of the largest specialty retailers with more than 3,100 stores and with fiscal revenues in 2006 of $15.9 billion.[2] There is not enough research on the critical rhetorical implications of advertising campaigns, especially with this new campaign that was released Spring 2007.

To better understand the social implications of this National Apparel Marketing Campaign, it is important to draw theories from a performance lens because the issues from this perspective can easily be overlooked. In analyzing the detrimental effects of the Gap's Spring 2007 Khaki Campaign, this will allow us to better understand the influences of the Euro-centric standards of beauty. Therefore, I argue that there are rhetorical underlying messages behind Gap's Spring 2007 Khaki Campaign that can be analyzed through a performance perspective of the construction of ethnicity and gender. In addition, Melvin Carlson explains that "the term 'performance' has become extremely popular in recent years in a wide range of activities in the arts, in literature, and in the social science,"[3] which justifies the need to explore all avenues of performance within our society, especially in marketing and advertising. To promote awareness of the social implications of the effects of this campaign, I will first investigate the 2007 Spring Khaki Marketing Campaign by examining the Gap's online marketing via its homepage. Secondly, I will explore several performance theories and then apply the theories toward the perpetuation of the Euro-centric standards of beauty in the Gap campaign.

Gap's 2007 Spring Khaki Marketing Campaign

The first Gap store was opened in 1969 on Ocean Avenue in San Francisco, California. Ever since that summer, Gap has become one of the world's largest specialty retailers. In 2007, Gap began a new Spring Khaki Marketing Campaign, "'Khakis with Attitude' Lighten up Wardrobes." According to Gap's Press Release, the campaign images were "shot by acclaimed photographer Mikael Jansson, Gap's spring print campaign features Gap's new "khakis with attitude" in a series of laid-back images. The ads are shot against a faded khaki backdrop capturing the light, relaxed mood of the season. Each person in the campaign is photographed wearing an item from Gap's new khaki collection for spring."[4] The "khakis with attitude" print campaign, was developed by "Gap's creative agency Laird + Partners" and ran in March issues of publications such as *Vogue, Vanity Fair, Elle, Allure, Glamour, Lucky*, and *GQ*. The campaign also includes outdoor elements such as billboards and bus shelters in select markets. This was a highly marketed campaign to address the need for the casual look of the spring season. The words "Lighten Up" accompanied all of the campaign images throughout their marketing advertisements.

In examining specifically the Gap's homepage during March 2007, there are two sides to the Web site. First, on the left side, there is an image of the famous individual, Kyra Sedgwick, which takes up the entire side of the Web site which demonstrates the image as one of the main focus of the campaign. Kyra Sedgwick was presented on the homepage wearing Gap's "boyfriend trousers" with her hands in the pockets and a white shirt against a light khaki background. She was standing to the side giving a backward glance toward the audience with the words "Lighten Up" also on the left side. The words "Lighten Up" was in white text framed inside a darker khaki clothing tag hanging from the top.

Aside from Kyra Sedgwick, on the right side of the homepage, there were six other snapshot images of individuals promoting the khaki look for Gap. However, above the images of the performers of the ad, there is text that states "Khakis with attitude" in white with brown-khaki outline of the text. The next line of text states "Lighten up your look with a little khaki: pants, shirts, dresses, jackets, and more" in the same brown-khaki color. Beneath both the text is a textbox that is of the same brown-khaki color that states "Shop khaki looks for men, women, petites, tall" with hyperlinks attached to each one of the categories to allow the audience to shop under those specific categories. The lower half of the right side of the homepage presents six images framed as snapshot photos with a white frame around each image. The images overlap each other to form a collage of the collection of photographs. The women in the snapshots were all sitting or standing in provocative poses in khaki attire. In the overall homepage of the Gap's Web site, including Kyra Sedgwick, there were five images of women and only two of men. The two men have on a pair of khaki pants with an inside shirt and a khaki jacket. In addition, they both are in standing poses with their hands in their pants' pockets. The women depicted in the campaign are wearing: khaki pencil skirt, khaki drawstring dress, cropped khaki cardigans, khaki tank tops and spaghetti straps, khaki pants, khaki capris, khaki oversized jackets, and other khaki clothing. Furthermore, all of the images seem to have an overlaying khaki tone tint with a washed-out look while all of the faces of the performers have a lightened tone.

Performance Theories

Performance

Carlson believes that performance is a demonstration of a conventional skill, restored behavior, and acting performance. The author states that "performing" and "performance" are arts that "require the physical presence of trained or skilled human beings whose demonstration of their skills is the performance."[5] Essentially, performance requires the demonstration of the physical presence of the individual that have been educated or experienced. When referencing the terms "trained or skilled," it is not directly in reference to only staged theater but also the everyday life. Keeping this in mind, Carlson also claims that the notion of restored behavior is also "the recognition that our lives are structured according to repeated and socially sanctioned mode of behavior raises the possibility that all human activities could potentially be considered as 'performance.'"[6] Ultimately, this means that life is a performance, and each of the scenes in our lives are acts within the performance. Whether it is a play on stage or the engagement of teaching a class, each event or moment is constituted as a performance based on the conscious attitude of the individual. In addition, Carlson believes that the self-consciousness toward attitude choices provides a quality of performance. The ability to choose self-presentation, rhetoric, emotions, attitudes, and so forth, is similar to having to choose costumes and characters for an on-stage performance. Essentially, the Gap campaign can be categorized as a performance because it is considered as an act used to capitalize the clothing industry. Also, the Gap Campaign's performers are famous individuals who wear Gap clothing to promote the product, but the Campaign in itself is also a performance.

Similarly, Jon McKenzie discusses the challenges with performances of artists and activists. McKenzie argues that "indeed, within Performance Studies, performance has taken on a particular political significance; with increasing consistency, performance has become defined as a 'liminal' process, a reflective transgression of social structures."[7] This means that through the use of performance, we are able to use it as resistance and contrast to the social system that currently prevails. Another issue is that "beyond these relatively specialized discourses, technological performance is perhaps most familiar to consumers through the use of 'performance' to market brands and products."[8] This elucidates that performance can be used through the technological discourse by performing products and brands through use of commercials or advertisements. The Gap Campaign of Khaki Apparel is an example of a brand that is performed by famous individuals to promote use of their product.

Lastly, Judith Hamera believes that individuals' presentation and actions in "the everyday life" is a performance within itself.[9] Furthermore, the author claims that "aesthetics is inherently social,"[10] which means that the interlinking of production and consumption of works of art "binding them together in material and highly situated interpretive communities"[11] provides a foundation for exchange in conversations in multiple areas of our lives. Acknowledging that aesthetics is a social element for conversation demonstrates the existence of the performance of inanimate objects.

This provides the foundation to justify that the Gap Campaign is a performance of an aesthetic social element within the context of the everyday life because the Gap Campaign can be accessed or viewed on a regular basis. The Gap Campaign has integrated itself into the everyday lives by performing on television, magazine ads, billboards, social media, and even bus stops.

Furthermore, the media and social media contribute to the social construction of the performance of reality by influencing how viewers experience a sense of attachment through the advertising campaigns. Elza Ibroscheva et al. explain that "the social experiences we accumulate, directly or through various channels of mediation, cultivate a sense of belonging to a certain group to which we develop individual and social attachment and by which we learn to define social reality."[12] With this in mind, Gap has used their Web site as a means of social media to expand their advertising campaign. With the growing importance of online and social media marketing, there has been a stronger need for social personalization. According to *Business News* of August 2, 2013, their research revealed that two thirds of social network users have claimed to only follow people or brands that they are genuinely interested in. With the Gap campaign using well-known actors and actresses wearing their casual attire, it creates relatability with the viewer because the viewer will be able to purchase the same clothing. If the viewers feel a social personalization or connection to people in the advertisement, then it will increase the effectiveness of the social media campaign.

Performance of Ethnicity

After understanding the fundamental elements of performance, it is crucial to this chapter to also comprehend the significance of ethnicity in our society and the roles it plays in social media marketing. Feminist theorist bell hooks explains the media play a significant role in perpetuating "white supremacy."[13]

Furthermore, hooks explains that marginalization is "to be part of the whole but outside the main body,"[14] and those that are oppressed have "the absence of choices."[15] The author argues that the current system of "white supremacist capitalist patriarchy" endorses domination and subjugation to share the principle of having a "superior and inferior."[16] With this ideology in mind, I believe that Dwight Conquergood would argue that despite the injustice placed upon those on the boundaries and borderlands, these individuals and groups are still able to transcend themselves by establishing their own identities.[17]

Furthermore, Conquergood explains that "marginal cultures that obliged them figuratively and literally to live on the boundary did not prevent them from still seeing identity and culture, self and other, as discrete, singular, integral, and stable concepts."[18] In essence, Conquergood argues that marginalized cultures are still able to discover their identity and culture despite the fact that cultures and individuals are marginalized literally or figuratively. Examples are communities such as China Town, Little Tokyo, Korean Town, Little Saigon, and many others where minorities choose to live on the borders rather than in the center. Their establishment of such communities allows them to identify with marginalized individuals in order to create a representation of their culture. Yet, with the accessibility of social media, the assumption is that social media lend itself to niche marketing and product positioning, which should lead to less stereotyping. Unfortunately, this is still not the case. As with the Gap campaign, the same images are presented in the traditional marketing as it is with the social media marketing. The major difference is that with the traditional case, the image placements are based on the selective target audiences. However, with social media, in attempts to reach the entire audience, Gap's Web site includes all of their images from their campaign. With this all-encompassing approach, the patriarchal system is still apparent in their selection of their front page Web site featuring Kyra Sedgwick, who happens to be a white female versus the other images from their campaign.

Conquergood contends that "The major epistemological consequence of displacing the idea of solid centers and unified wholes with borderlands and zones contest is a rethinking of identity and culture as constructed and relational, instead of ontologically given and essential."[19] The notion that we can redefine or choose the position of marginalization impacts our views of identity and culture. Conquergood further notes that "Cities throughout the United States have become sites of extraordinary diversity as refugees and immigrants, increasingly from the hemisphere of the South and the East, pour into inner-city neighborhoods."[20] There is not a need to go to "Third World" countries to witness marginalization because refugees and immigrants from all over the world have found their homes within the inner-city neighborhoods of the United States. Additionally, social media marketing has done the same. It has found its way through the inner-city neighborhoods, all around the world, and simply, into the homes of anyone with Internet access.

Performance of Gender Constructions

Elin Diamond analyzed Judith Butler's book, *Gender Trouble,* where she contends that "gender is just an act, but that gender is materially 'performative': it 'is real only to the extent that it is performed,"[21] and that "gender, then is both a doing—a performance that puts a conventional gender attributes into possibly disruptive play—and a thing done—a pre-existing category."[22] By understanding Judith Butler's concept that gender is an act or a performance, it will allow our society to be able to reconstruct the socialized gender norms through the use of performance to be more accepting toward homosexuals and transgender individuals. Butler provides hope to our society because by establishing gender as an act or materially performative means that there is room for reconstruction and to re-establish the concept of gender.

hooks explains that people have internalized racism and sexism and so would not recognize domination and oppression because they have already accepted the subordinated genders roles.[23] In addition, "It is the woman's overall acceptance of the value system of the culture that leads her to passively absorb sexism and willingly assume a pre-determined sex role."[24] This means that even though women are marginalized, it is their acceptance of the position that allows the patriarchal system to continue to oppress the female gender. This is especially true in the interactive and participatory nature of social media; images of gender performance perpetuate the gender norms in marketing campaigns that can go completely unnoticed. It is not only this acceptance of oppression but also the lack of awareness to the potential impacts that social media marketing has on the viewer. When individuals do not question the degrading sexualized images of the bodies presented in social media, it becomes an example of the continued allowance of the patriarchal system to objectify the female body for the purpose of consumerism.

Application Analysis

With Gap's 2007 Spring Khaki Marketing Campaign, there are underlying social implications that are detrimental to our society. In uncovering the implications, I will investigate the Gap Campaign through an analysis of performance of ethnicity and the performance of gender constructions in order to discover the underlying rhetorical message that perpetuates the discrimination of ethnicity and stereotypical gender roles.

Performing Ethnicity

On the Gap's 2007 Spring Khaki "Lighten Up" homepage, there are several elements that require analysis: (1) The performance of only "white" people on the homepage, (2) The words "Lighten Up" used in the campaign, and (3) The overall color tonality of the images. Because there are only "white" people modeling for Gap's Homepage, hooks would claim that Gap is a corporation that is selling whiteness as a means to fame. Furthermore, hooks claims that, "capitalist investors in the cosmetics and fashion industry feared that feminism would destroy their business. They put their money behind mass-media campaigns which trivialized women's liberation by portraying images which suggested feminists were big, hypermasculine, and just plain old ugly."[25] The performance of only "white" people on the homepage represents the ideal standard of beauty and fashion to the public. The underlying message is that the images represent what is acceptable and deemed as fashionable in our society. Furthermore, hooks contends that "even though most black communities were and remain segregated, mass media bring white supremacy into our lives, constantly reminding us of our marginalized status."[26] Essentially, this means that despite the fact that "white supremacy" is not obvious in our society, it still exist in the world of the mass media where most of the main characters in television shows, commercials, and advertisements are primarily white. Even though there may be some portrayal of other token ethnicities, those characters are usually minor characters that support the white main characters. This is also the case with the Gap's 2007 Spring Khaki "Lighten Up" marketing campaign because there are token minority characters that also modeled for Gap's khaki clothing. However, their images were not displayed on Gap's homepage but on Gap's shopping bags. This clearly demonstrates a representation that reinforces the hooks' "white supremacy" because the marginalized minority images are on shopping bags that are often used once and torn away. Yet, in contrast, the images on the Internet homepage can be viewed internationally and is the representation Gap's Spring Khaki Campaign with "white" models.

In understanding underlying message of Gap's Spring Khaki Campaign utilizing only white representations on their homepage, it is also equally significant to note the connotation of the words "Lighten Up" displayed on the Web site. By definition, the term "Lighten Up" can have two meanings. The first definition could be "to relax," which the Gap Campaign wants their khaki clothing to perform a relax ambiance. However, the second definition could also mean "moving from a darker tone to a lighter tone." These two words, "Lighten Up," are critical because by the second definition, it is reinforcing a Eurocentric standard of beauty and acceptance in our society. As observed on the Web site, it is imperative to note that the entire Web site showed only white models to advertise Gap's Khaki Apparel, which demonstrates that the meaning of "Lighten Up" on the homepage is a direct message linked to "white" models represented. hooks would argue that there is a Euro-centric standard of beauty to promote a need to become more "white." Even on the right side of the homepage, the words "Lighten up your look with a little khaki" reinforces the notion that one's look needs to be lighten up in order to have the same feel represented in the images.

To further implement the notion of "Lighten Up," the entire homepage has an overall tonality layer of a lighter tone because of the lighting choices as well as the background. This can be noted by observing the skin color of the individual models on the Web site. They all have an unnatural shade of "white" that almost appears "pasty" or "pale." Specially, for the close-up snapshot of the female model in the middle of the top row, her skin is so colorless that she almost appears to be in poor health. This overlay of color tone can also be noted on their shopping bags because the African American model and Asian model also have an off-set pasty look to their skin tones. Allowing the African American and Asian model to have the same ashen look as the "white" models reveals what hooks explains as the internalization of racism because the depiction of both minority groups are not true to their skin tones. *The Hamilton Spectator* (Ontario, Canada) of August 21, 2006 explains that skin-whitening cream is not only geared toward women and men of color but also to "white women" that are not white enough because of aging spots or skin damage. Moreover, the article also noted that in Yaba Blay's thesis, "Yellow Fever: Skin Bleaching and the Aesthetico-cultural Gendered Politics of Skin Color in Ghana," Blay stated that, "It appears that in the context of global white supremacy, skin bleaching represents an attempt to gain access to the social status and mobility often reserved not only for whites, but for lighter-skinned persons of African descent."[27] Understanding that lighter skin color matters in regard to social status (or Gap homepage status), as a society, we need to acknowledge the internalization of "global white supremacy" in order to create social change.

Performance of Gender Construction

Aside from the performance of ethnicity, the Gap Campaign also demonstrates promise in regard to the performance of gender construction by use of their clothing as a performative element of gender roles. In the two snapshots of the male models, they are both wearing a pair of pants, a shirt, and a jacket. Their outfit fits the gender role stereotype of men's clothing. However, the female's clothing provides room for a rhetorical analysis. The snapshot images of the four females performing female stereotypical gender constructions by having them wearing skirts and dresses, but also wearing oversized jackets.

Kyra Sedgwick is the only female on the homepage wearing khaki pants. One would argue that Kyra Sedgwick is breaking out of the gender construction because she is not wearing clothing that represents the typical female role. Furthermore, McKenzie explains that "marginal, on the edge, in the interstices of institutions and at their limits, liminal performances are capable of temporarily staging and subverting their normative functions."[28] This means that through performance, one can break free from social constructions by allowing the audience to see a world without the restraints of gender roles. Kyra Sedgwick's pants could have been one form of transcendence above the socially constructed gender roles because pants were socially constructed for males, yet the underlying message within Kyra Sedgwick's pants is in its name.

Her pants are referred to as the "boyfriend's trousers," which means that the pants are not hers but are made to look like her boyfriend's trousers. In addition, "boyfriend's trousers" also demonstrate that she does not own a pair of trousers but had to borrow her boyfriend's trousers. Just the name of the pants, "boyfriend trousers," reframes the notion of gender construction because females traditionally did not wear pants. This presents the notion that even females' pants are dominated by the patriarchal system because she cannot even have her own pair of trousers without the interference of socially constructed gender roles.

Even in our contemporary society, where it is socially acceptable for women to wear pants, this campaign reinforces the notion that women's pants are not comfortable by design due to the social expectations on female beauty. The objectification of women and the "boyfriend's trousers" are twofold. First, there are sexual connotations to her wearing his pants, which is an inference to their sexual relationship. Secondly, this can be interpreted as she "wears the pants," meaning she holds the power that is typically seen as belonging to the men in the relationship. Both of these interpretations allow for Gap to reach multiple female audiences. Jean Kilbourne further explains that "advertisers are aware of their role and do not hesitate to take advantage of the insecurities and anxieties of young people, usually in the guise of offering solutions. A pair of designer jeans or sneakers convey status."[29]

Kilbourne reveals that the relationship between women and really tight jeans or pant is not new in advertising. An example of an ad for jeans stated, "You can learn more about anatomy after school," which Kilbourne contends "manages to trivialize sex, relationships, and education all in one sentence."[30] These traditional marketing strategies have worked in the past, and still are apparent in our social and new media marketing. The main difference is that those are now more accessible than ever.

Furthermore, Butler explains that "acts and gestures, articulated and enacted desires create the illusion of an interior and organizing gender core, an illusion discursively maintained for the purposes of the regulation of sexuality within the obligatory frame of reproductive heterosexuality."[31] Essentially, this means that there are performances created to reinforce gender constructions by use of acts and gestures to create and socialize the ideology of the hetero-normative patriarchal system. It is important to acknowledge the perpetuation of gender stereotype types within the world around us and also through the mass communication. Even within the Gap Stores, there are television screens that show the Gap's Khaki Campaign Commercial with a female dancing and singing, "Anything you can do, I can do better. Anything you can wear, I can wear too!" This message demonstrates the possibility of the female dancer breaking out of the socially gender constructions, however, the name "Boyfriend's Trousers" frames the female gender's place in society. In addition, the use of the term "Boyfriend's" in "Boyfriend's Trousers" are targeted toward females, which also promote a hetero-normative notion that marginalizes homosexuals and transgender individuals.

Conclusion

In endorsing awareness of the social repercussion of the possible ramifications of Gap's 2007 Spring Khaki Marketing Campaign, I examined Gap's homepage, explored several performance theories, and then applied the theories toward the perpetuation of the Euro-centric standards of fashion and beauty. Furthermore, I argued that the Gap 2007 Spring Khaki Marketing Campaign perpetuated the internalization of racism and reinforced the stereotypical social constructions of gender roles through their social media marketing strategies. At first glance, the campaign may simply be seen as a way of advertising Gap's khaki apparel. However, viewing it through a performance perspective revealed the continued marginalization of those who do not meet the Euro-centric beauty and fashion standards.

In comprehending the detrimental consequences of advertising campaigns such as Gap's 2007 Spring "New 'Khakis With Attitude' Lighten Up Wardrobes" that featured Kyra Sedgwick, Kate Mara, Chris O'Donnell, Wentworth Miller, Daniel Dae Kim, Dermot Mulroney, and Chris Brown, it is crucial to acknowledge and not accept the socialized performance of ethnicity and gender constructions. Although we have all been socialized with images of discrimination, there is still hope because hooks states that "Until all Americans demand that mass media no longer serve as the biggest propaganda machine for white supremacy, the socialization of everyone to subliminally absorb white supremacist attitudes and values will continue."[32] hooks continues to fight the battle against the unconscious socialization of the white supremacy through use of mass media; the author argues that it is up to everyone to take agency to enact social change within the community. In alleviating the social constructions of stereotypes and discrimination, whether through traditional or social media marketing, there still is optimism for a utopian society within capitalism and consumerism. Therefore, whether it is through voice, action, or performance, it is critical for individuals to take personal advocacy in order to remedy attitudes and values that discriminate against ethnicity, gender, and sexuality in any marketing medium.

Notes

1. Gap Inc., "About Gap," 2007, http://www.gapin.com/public/About/about .shtml.

2. Ibid.

3. Marvin Carlson, "Introduction: What Is Performance?" in *Performance: A Critical Introduction* (New York: Routledge, 1996), 1–7.

4. Gap Inc., "About Gap."

5. Marvin Carlson, *Performance*, 3.

6. Ibid.

7. Jon McKenzie, *Perform or Else: From Discipline to Performance* (New York: Routledge, 2002), 8.

8. Ibid., 10.

9. Judith Hamera, "Performance, Performativity, and Cultural Poeisis in the Practice of Everyday Life." In *SAGE Handbook of Performance Studies*, ed. Judith Hamera and D. Soyini Madison (Thousand Oaks, CA: SAGE, 2006)), 46–64.

10. Ibid., 46–47.

11. Ibid.

12. Elza Ibroscheva, "Do Media Matter." *Journal of Intercultural Communication* 14 (2008): 1404–634.

13. bell hooks, *Killing Rage: Ending Racism* (New York: Henry Holt Ltd., 1996), 108–18.

14. bell hooks, *Feminist Theory: From Margin to Center* (Cambridge, MA: South End Press, 1984), xvi.

15. Ibid., 5.

16. Sonja K. Foss, Karen, A. Foss, and Robert Trapp, *Contemporary Perspectives on Rhetoric* (Prospect Heights, IL: Waveland Press, Inc., 2002), 270–71.

17. Dwight Conquergood, "Rethinking Ethnography." In *SAGE Handbook of Performance Studies*, ed. Judith Hamera and D. Soyini Madison (Thousand Oaks, CA: Sage, 2006), 351–65.

18. Ibid., 358.

19. Ibid., 359.

20. Ibid., 361.

21. Elin Diamond, ed., *Performance and Cultural Politics* (New York: Routledge, 1996) 1–7.

22. Ibid., 4–5.

23. bell hooks, *Feminist Theory: From Margin to Center* (Cambridge, MA: South End Press, 1984), 87.

24. Ibid.

25. bell hooks, *Feminism Is for Everybody: Passionate Politics* (Cambridge, MA: South End Press, 2000), 32.

26. bell hooks, *Killing Rage: Ending Racism* (Harmondsworth, UK: Penguin, 1996), 110.

27. Evelyn Myrie, Skin-Bleaching Products Promote "Whiteness as Rightness." *The Hamilton Spectator,* August 21, 2006, p. A15,. http://pqasb.pqarchiver.com/hamiltonspectator/doc/270260113.html?FMT=ABS&FMTS=ABS:FT&type=current&date=Aug+21%2C+2006&author=Myrie%2C+Evelyn&pub=The+Spectator&edition=&startpage=&desc=Skin-bleaching+products+promote+%27whiteness+as+rightness%27; Yaba Amgborale Blay, Yellow Fever: Skin Bleaching and the Politics of Skin Color in Ghana. *ProQuest Dissertations and Theses database.* (2007), https://www.academia.edu/492351/Yellow_fever_Skin_bleaching_and_the_politics_of_skin_color_in_Ghana.

28. Jon McKenzie, *Perform or Else: From Discipline to Performance* (New York: Routledge, 2002), 8.

29. Jean Kilbourne, "The More You Subtract, The More You Add Cutting Girls Down to Size." Deadly Persuasion, 1999, http://www.aef.com/industry/news/data/hot_issues/1361.

30. Ibid.

31. Judith Butler, "Gender Trouble, Feminist Theory, and Psychoanalytic Discourse." In *Feminism/Postmodernism*, ed. Linda J. Nicholson (New York: Routledge, 1990), 337.

32. hooks, *Killing Rage,* 116.

CHAPTER FOUR

Fan Trailers as Digital Storytelling

Tim Posada

Introduction

On July 10, 2009, *Variety* announced that Ryan Reynolds would play the DC Comics superhero Green Lantern in a live-action film adaptation of the galactic police officer who wields a ring with the power of imagination. But on May 22 earlier that year, a trailer for *Green Lantern* appeared on YouTube, garnering more than 500,000 hits in its first week, along with hundreds of positive comments by site users. Many respondents were in awe of the trailer for its *authenticity*, although it was in fact a fan-made trailer created by Jaron Pitts, featuring 33 film and television clips, with actor Nathan Fillion (of *Dr. Horrible's Sing-Along Blog* and *Castle*) as Hal Jordan or Green Lantern. Fan trailers are a largely under-researched genre of online storytelling, but their presence continues to grow as more amateur filmmakers participate in this digital act of *copying and creating*. Their existence—created without financial compensation as a form of homage—implies a more personal relationship with popular media texts, thus I propose that when placed alongside the online medium Digital Storytelling (DST), fan trailers are similarly an individualized narrative experience that function like a first-person narrative, creating the "I" voice just as DST does. Through reappropriated film and television clips and the creator's implied film adaptation, the *Green Lantern* trailer and other similar fan trailers reflect their creators' consumer filmography, revealing just how personal fictional material can be to a fan. Taking a cue from Green Lantern's power set, then, the agency of the fan requires a post-copyright approach and a theoretical model as academically imaginative as fan fiction.

Variance and Convergence

Digital Storytelling seems a simple enough concept to understand. For Ruth Sylvester and Wendy-lou Greenidge, it serves as "an example of a multimedia text that encompasses both traditional and new literacies and has the potential for stimulating struggling writers,"[1] taking on a truly open form. *Digital story* can refer to anything from a Web series like *The Guild* and ESPN podcasts to motion comic books and the Old Spice Channel on YouTube; Digital Storytelling (capitalized), however, is something quite different, even if the name implies a broader use. Knut Lundby characterizes DST in six key ways, several of which align with fan-made trailers: "small-scale stories"; "bottom-up" and "self-made" media that gives voice to underrepresented people; storytelling that occurs on a "macro" level; a medium that questions the "norm" of narrative conventions; first-person stories that reveal something "authentic" about the maker's identity; and storytelling that uses digital technology.[2] Adding to this, multiple media organizations host DST workshops to teach communities how to use new media, thus the medium consists of "local narratives" based on "personal memory."[3] While DST's definition remains influx, these six (negotiable) characteristics are a helpful beginning.

The amateur creators who make both fan trailers and Digital Stories utilize the video and audio equipment available to them, often outside the realm of professional production—or through professionally lead workshops, in the case of DST. Running less than 10 minutes long, both fan trailers and DST create small-scale narratives with a specific focus. Outside mainstream budgeting and conventional style, these mediums only find an audience online, echoing Henry Jenkins's claim that the Internet is the "Do It Yourself" refrigerator that allows for greater representation of minority groups.[4] For DST and fan trailers, the primary limitation is access to technology. But unlike DST, fan trailers stem from a position of socioeconomic privilege. Due to the workshop structure, DST requires no prior technical knowledge to properly participate in the medium due to its open form, while fan trailers are only as effective as their creators' ability to watch films or television series and reimagine their audial and visual function—an activity unavailable to those without access to a television or the disposable income necessary to attend movie theaters, let alone a computer, editing software, and an Internet subscription. The first challenge to this comparison is knowledge—a cultural knowledge gained through pop culture consumption that results in a familiarity with trailer conventions and televisual clips to properly conduct a *snatch-and-grab*. We find here that participation, for the fan, is both financial and cultural, or as

John Fiske says, "Cultural capital thus works hand in hand with economic capital to produce social privilege and distinction."[5] Thus, even though DST and fan trailers are amateur productions, fan trailers require greater financial independence and, most likely, self-motivation. DST does not.

Media-based organizations often use DST as an educational tool to help students and sample groups merge "old and new literacies,"[6] but Jaron Pitts is not a student in the midst of formal education or a member of a community sought out by, say, the BBC for a DST project; his video projects are hobbies conducted between his job as a worship leader at a church and home life as a husband and father.[7] This does not mean Pitts and others who (assumedly) share his leisure association with the medium do not function outside the *bottom-up* structure of DST; anyone outside the production system remains in a marginalized position, though DST is often more associated with less socioeconomically privileged groups or older individuals unfamiliar with new media. The key issue, again, is knowledge: DST seeks to educate, while fan trailers are largely created by those with preexisting knowledge as a part of digital community.

Even though DST appears to emphasize the process more than the final product, Rebecca Thumin's research found that DST participants associated quality productions with access to equipment; with increasing media literacy, agency was determined by how participants defined quality.[8] Considering this DST concern, the *Green Lantern* trailer is fascinating for its emphasis on quality. While many clips remain recognizable, added digital effects, audio and video transitions, and narrative cohesion create an effective illusion of authenticity—something as convincing as other popular fakes, like *The Shining* recut as a comedy and *Sleepless in Seattle* as a serial stocker flick. Even YouTube user WormyT's *Thundercats* fake trailer—a video Pitts names as one inspiration—is far easier to debunk: disjointed voice dubbing and less convincing digital effects. Pitts's trailer is a rare example of the fake that nearly surpasses its namesake. In the YouTube comments section, Pitts expresses concern for the flaws that do exist. One user notes that the ring, the root of Green Lantern's power, switches between the character's right and left hand. To this, Pitts admitted he should have mirrored the scenes to make the ring consistently appear on the right hand, though he was glad someone caught the error. Finding flaws means someone is paying attention; part of the game is finding the Easter eggs. Responding to another user, Pitts also expressed dissatisfaction with the audio clip of the Green Lantern Corps' oath. He admitted to the limited availability of audio clips, regretting that he did not simply recite the oath himself. The concern for authenticity here comes not from a first-person story but through complete suspension of disbelief, highlighting visible and audible seams that cause the illusion's haze to lift. But rather than fix the audio—perhaps because he enjoys editing too much[9]—Jaron Pitts stays the course of *fan-trailerdom*, accepting the challenge to tell an original story with the voices of others. The "I" comes afterward, participating in the forum and explaining his choices as a new media auteur. Through auteur theory of mid-1950s and 1960s, the film director became the most important author of a film, more than producers, screenwriters, and performers.[10] The films of directors like Jean-Luc Godard and Alfred Hitchcock (especially noted for his cameos, further invoking a personal narrative) became extensions of their personality and creativity. Likewise, the fan trailer creator becomes an auteur, revealing personal characteristics and creative choices.

For Lundby, the motivation behind DST is personal, while fan trailers create an "increasing interactivity between the trailer and the audience" taking "the trailer beyond the studio's control."[11] DST uses new media to enhance the personal lives of its users, while fan trailers create a dialogue between creators, users or participants, and production companies. The end goal for each medium appears very different. This variation alone is enough to place fan trailers beyond the grasp of DST, but the "I" in fan trailers is much more subtle, appearing through the cultural capital earned by using multiple recognizable film clips and providing a personal statement on what a potential adaptation could or should look like.

The Self in Fiction

The most substantial support for my argument comes not from an academic work, but from the film *High Fidelity* (2000). To the confusion of his friend, vinyl shop owner Rob (played by John Cusack) reorganizes his record collection in an unrecognizable pattern. When asked what it is, Rob simply says, "Autobiographical." He has to remember when he purchased an album in order to find it on his shelves. For Rob, music defines moments in his life. He constantly creates "Top 5" song lists to reflect his changing state of mind. Music is not escapism but a tool—a language—that helps him navigate life's challenges. Similarly, Glynda A. and Mira-Lisa Hull address how DST participants re-authored themselves through songs, dance, and image.[12] In one example, a woman from Nepal utilized a music genre "to illustrate how the narratives that people learn to tell and retell about themselves have particular structures, allow particular roles, and promote certain values."[13] Similarly, Jenkins compares participatory culture to "American folks songs of the nineteenth century" where ideology is questioned "sometimes inside and sometimes outside the cultural logic of commercial entertainment."[14] The use of music in forming identity provides a significant bridge to understanding the fan trailer's autobiographical attribute. Popular texts become the harmonies and melodies of American folk music that reflect their creators, turning Pitts's fan trailer into a digital folk song that sings an epic tale about a superhero vanquishing evil throughout the galaxy. Just as a musician's influence can be heard in a guitar solo or vocal tone, Pitts's viewing habits and technical influences are put on display. He views popular science fiction, fantasy, action, and superhero films and television shows. He was also most likely moved (as I was) by the song "Freedom Fighters" by Two Steps from Hell that set the emotional tone of the *Star Trek* (2009) trailer and decided to replicate that mood in his fan trailer. Furthermore, choosing Nathan Fillion to play Green Lantern demonstrates a familiarity with the actor's work, especially his performance as a space cowboy in the cult series *Firefly*. As his statements in the user comments prove, Pitts has a personal investment in the Green Lantern character. Through the trailer's visuals, he argues that Fillion would be the best actor to play the intergalactic law enforcer. However, while the trailer does reveal several films Pitts has viewed, his personal feelings about them are known only to him. He possibly disliked the critically ill-received *Fantastic 4: Rise of the Silver Surfer* (2007), but saw within its frames potential footage for something far more engaging. What remains true for all clips is their function as mediatized fodder. In folk music, the story changes the more the songs are sung, and fan trailers follow in that tradition.

In "Out of the Closet and into the Universe: Queers and *Star Trek*," Jenkins researches a group of gay and lesbian *Star Trek: The Next Generation* fans, the Boston Area Gaylaxians, who organized and petitioned the show's executive producers, requesting they include gay and lesbian characters.[15] In a show with the tagline, "To boldly go where no one has gone before,"[16] the Gaylaxians demanded the show live up to its intergalactic creed. As bell hooks addresses in much of her research, representation, sex, race, and class are pivotal components in how we relate to characters—how we suspend disbelief and become sutured into the story, not simply joining the protagonists but partly becoming them.[17] Likewise, Pitts's trailer serves a personal purpose, reflecting the role of the character (and Fillion's other performances) in his life. While many user comments addressed Pitts's technical skill, some discussion revolved around the upcoming film's casting and the earlier announcement that Martin Campbell would direct it. In response, Pitts expanded on his motivation for making the trailer: "I hope this trailer has pushed the bar a little higher so they HAVE to do it right instead of just throwing a piece of garbage out there knowing it will make money because it's called Green Lantern. I have faith that Martin Campbell is up to the challenge."[18] By creating a trailer for a film he cannot bring to fruition, Pitts provides a personal account of the character, and in so doing, allows the character to take on a more significant role in his life, much like a toy. In *When Toys Come Alive*, Lois R. Kuznets argues that toys are stories that "come alive" outside the parameters of a book (or any other passive narrative structure): "When the unconscious objects that are toys become self-consciously alive, they blur the lines between self and other, subject and object, and require the reader to note those blurred dividing lines, imaginatively if not analytically."[19] When someone, like a fan, spends enough time watching *Star Trek*, discussing canonical details, and collecting show paraphernalia, does that fictional universe not become an aspect of one's personality—something worth using, mentioning, or highlighting in a first-person narrative?

Fan trailers do not tell specific stories about family life as most DST does, instead revealing a privileged participant whose identity can be seen through consumer-based products. Fan trailers can be a form of daydreaming and wish fulfillment that allow creators to imagine themselves as filmmakers actively involved in forging the narrative path of beloved characters. But just as the movements of an action figure are limited, so too are there limits to what can be done with someone else's ideas. However, this fact does not stop Jaron Pitts, or others like him, from trying to make all the pieces fit.

User and Producer

As of the summer 2013, Pitts's trailer on YouTube has been viewed more than 7 million times and includes more than 18,000 comments—mostly praise. With clips from films like *The Lord of the Rings* films, *Star Trek* (2009), *The Matrix Revolutions* (2003), and *Planet of the Apes* (2001), the *Green Lantern* trailer features both familiar and obscure media texts. While fan fiction has largely gone unpunished for copyright infringement, some corporations became uncomfortable with its growing popularity more than 15 years ago, attempting to cease all unofficial use of certain properties.[20] Now, fake trailers appear to exist outside copyright concern, though ownership of the fan-made work holds greater authority in fan communities. In the user comments for the *Green Lantern* trailer, some users expressed concern when another YouTube user claimed credit for creating it. Using copyrighted material remains an invalid concern, dismissed by users and Pitts in the comments section. Everyone knows where the source material came from, but they may not know of Pitts and other creators. Furthermore, Pitts informed other users in the comments section that he nearly fell prey to YouTube's "guilty until proven innocent policy on copyright disputes"[21]—a policy that restricts reproducing copyrighted material, sometimes without concern for educational or fair use laws, echoing Jenkins's earlier assessment of the fan psyche: "fans also reject the studio's assumption that intellectual property is a 'limited good,' to be tightly controlled lest it dilute its value. Instead, they embrace an understanding of intellectual property as 'shareware,' something that accrues value as it moves across different contexts, gets retold in various ways, attracts multiple audiences, and opens itself up to a proliferation of alternative meanings."[22]

He goes on to say, "Fan works can no longer be understood as simply derivative of mainstream materials but must be understood as themselves open to appropriation and reworking by the media industries."[23] An interesting case occurred when artist Shepard Fairey was sued by the Associated Press (AP) for using their copyrighted photo of President Barack Obama to create the popular "Change" and "Hope" paintings of the president during the 2008 presidential campaign. Fairey countersued the AP for infringing his rights under fair use law. In an unexpected resolution, both sides decided to agree to disagree: both would share the rights to the previous Obama images, Fairey would not use anymore AP photos without licensing permission, and the AP would provide Fairey with images for another series of pieces.[24] We are seeing more examples of private creators and mass producers working together. The fan community provides multiple examples with similar conclusions, like *Star Wars* fan videos now featured at pop culture convention screenings. As media convergence expands, the relationship between amateur creator and production company is changing. The battle has become more a ballet, with both sides attempting to feel out the movements of the other.

Along with the changing relationship between mass culture and marginal groups, the fan trailer questions the trailer's *proper* function. McLuhan's famous claim, "the medium is the message,"[25] states that content does not matter as much as how it is used. For example, a televangelist can broadcast a regular church sermon every Sunday and not effectively relay a message without properly analyzing the differences between a live service, with a pastor feeding off the congregation's mood, and a television screen, where the experience is completely passive. Kathleen Williams states that a recut trailer "challenges the tools of promotion" by making the trailer an end in and of itself.[26] The form, just as much as the content, of the fan trailer develops a cultural space "that would not exist without the world wide web," as Nick Couldry says of DST.[27] The trailer is no longer a direct marketing tool but an original story that can take any shape its creator chooses. In an almost poetic move, fan trailers call attention to the cyclic nature of trailers and the predictability of popular film and television; multiple clips can only be combined through the standardization of mass production.

Fan trailers change both the trailer's longtime function and reimagine the path to authenticity—a path bathed in the recontextualized material of others. But can fan trailers be authentic—especially with the word "fake" in the medium's title? Yet DST is far from innocent in this arena. Like varying broadcast forms, borrowing media texts is a common practice. In "My Life in Toronto" from the Center for Digital Storytelling, Amber Sabah uses the image of a fish in the sea to describe her relocation to another city. A fish cutout moves across an image of other fish and then across images of Toronto landmarks. Sabah employs a symbolic visual in her story—the little fish in the big sea—telling an authentic story with more than just personal photos or on-the-nose footage of her life outside the sea she once knew so well. In "Me and the Sailor Moon," a participant created cartoon characters to tell her personal story.[28] Finally, another author used music to create a narrative, constructing "authority through his appropriation and recontextualization of images linked to words and music."[29] These examples show that DST does not have to take place in live-action settings, using only personal photos (as found through the BBC's DST project), but can reappropriate unrelated media texts for personal use.

Copyrighted material actually sneaks into DST, without proper reference, just like fan trailers. For example, the fish image in Sabah's Digital Story is not her own, but an image titled "School of Tropical Fish," taken by photographer Steve Allen (and most of the Toronto images are most likely copyrighted as well). Through both borrowed images and music, we find examples of copyrighted material used to reach autobiographical goals. This tactic is employed by news outlets as well: news radio uses film audio for political and cultural story packages and newspapers run film images with stories. A rather humorous example of this occurred when *The New York Times* covered Google's decision to ban Cougar— older women seeking younger men—profiles from its advertising system. Accompanying the story was not a Cougar profile image from a Web site but a film still from *The Graduate* (1967), depicting a young Dustin Hoffman and Anne Bancroft, playing Mrs. Robinson, perhaps the first Cougar in popular culture. The caption read: "MRS. ROBINSON, ARE YOU . . . Anne Bancroft played the original cougar in 'The Graduate.' Dustin Hoffman was the cub."[30]

Nicholas Mirzoeff believes photography can no longer be trusted with the advent of photo editing.[31] Like an almost unreal photograph featured in *National Geographic*, we must trust that images in Digital Stories are authentic. Fan trailers, however, cannot be authentic in the same way as DST, perhaps making them a more trustworthy medium. In the end, authenticity must be the result of agency. When something is given worth, it becomes important (true), but that might not be something the academy is ready to do with fan trailers.

Determining Agency

An ethical response to fan trailers does not stem from the expected place (fair use) since production companies are distancing themselves from such lawsuits, instead seeing the trend as an opportunity for greater exposure. Furthermore, the victory of the fan trailer has also begun to trickle into other new media spheres as well. The U.S. Copyright Office ruled that "jailbreaking," also known as hacking, iPhones and other Apple products is lawful, to the dismay of progressive tech-giant Apple. Once the product leaves the production company's hands, the owner has complete control. Could audio and video footage be used in a similar way? Replication poses significant problems (your copy belongs to you, not those who did not purchase it), but a fan trailer is not easily defined as replication for profit, nor are film or television files being copied in whole. For Roberta Pearson, the fan is not infringing on copyright laws but perhaps doing major studios a service: "Unlike the music industry, which has a first-order commodity relationship with its consumers, selling a product directly to them, advertising-supported television has a second-order commodity relationship with its consumers, indirectly selling the sponsors' products rather than directly selling the text itself."[32] Furthermore, popular texts cannot exist without the public's continuing financial support. So, again, who owns these texts, the producers or the customers who purchase them? In a time when real estate tycoon Donald Trump tried to copyright the phrase, "You're fired"—two words used by many employers in American culture—the waters of ownership are not likely to settle anytime soon. Still, this very arguable point is less important than the real issue at work here: an old bourgeois mentality that prevents scholarly eyes from gazing upon something like the fan trailer with any sense of real agency. Much of the research available on fan fiction focuses on the fascinating legal issues that surround user-created contend based on popular franchises; as Jenkins discusses in much of his work, fan scholars still spend too much time defending the merits of the entire field. In the field of visual culture,

W.J.T. Mitchell critiques *purists* who desire a return to the divide between image and text: to combine the two enters the lowbrow realm of advertising or, even (the bourgeoisie forbid), a comic book. These purists are less concerned with aesthetic value, but seek a return to *high art* and old class hierarchies, along with it.[33] From this point of view, spending time on fake trailers is as wasteful as engaging Superman (or, perhaps, Green Lantern) on a scholarly level, even if those popular icons reach more than 7 million people online—something high art can rarely boast. As hooks points out, *The Color Purple* may be a racially naive film, but it has generated more discussion about race than any theoretical work.[34] The broad study of fan communities is an important first step in engaging what varying groups spend their time consuming, even if it *appears* trivial.[35]

For Pearson, fandom ignited the digital revolution, pioneering technology and utilizing online space through the creation of unofficial Web communities dedicated to popular media texts like *Star Wars*, *Star Trek*, and *Twin Peaks*. Pitts did not attend a formal workshop, but spent two months learning how to use Adobe After Effects to create the appropriate visuals for his trailer, continuing a long history of fans motivating themselves. What began in the margins of emerging technological became something else entirely. On December 25, 2006, *Time* magazine declared "You" the "Person of the Year," with a reflective cover that allowed any reader to see herself as the new face of the digital age: participants and content generators of user-run sites like YouTube, Wikipedia, and Facebook. A digital narrative has been developing for years, and it would be insufficient to ignore the personal investment of contributors, retorting with base criticism (*if only they cared this much about something that matters*). While responses to fan fair vary, established organizations are noticing. Even *The Hollywood Reporter* covered the creation of a *Captain America* fan trailer, where footage from the 2011 summer film was recut to a comical soundtrack with two songs from the irreverent, puppet film *Team America*, created by the makers of *South Park*.[36] But YouTube remains a sore subject for authentic dialogue. CNN and YouTube presented a virtual discourse where users generated questions for political candidates, including questions by some very informal (if not flat out goofy) users, though their content was sincere. Perhaps understandably, former Massachusetts Governor Mitt Romney mocked the debate, claiming presidential forums should be taken more seriously.[37] However, the user-run public sector can be a dangerous sphere for candidates who are used to controlling the flow of information. On the other side, a digital space where everyone has a voice can also successfully silence the significance of all messages as well. It will be some time before the climate is truly ready to examine these Web sites without doubt of their importance, though Jean Burgess and Joshua Green extensive qualitative study on YouTube culture paves the way.[38]

When examining the agentive function of fan trailers, Stuart Hall's work exposes a paradox. He breaks media readers into three groups (with some crossover):

1. Passive reader: taking in all mediatized messages without resistance.
2. Negotiated reader: agreeing with some messages and resisting others.
3. Oppositional reader: completely resistant to media messages, seeing the ideology subtext of every broadcast.[39]

As fan studies grew, Fiske and Jenkins pioneered the concept of the active reader, which acknowledged the holes in Hall's three categories. The active reader reveals certain levels of resistance and passivity; active can be passive, negotiated, or oppositional. As Martin Barker and Kate Brooks say, active involvement does not necessarily mean resistance,[40] thus the fan trailer creator, as an active participant, straddles a popular and marginal position. Pearson puts it this way: "Fandom, then, is a peculiar mix of cultural determinations. On the one hand it is an intensification of popular culture which is formed outside and often against official culture, on the other it expropriates and rewords certain values and characteristics of that official culture to which it is opposed."[41] At its most pessimistic, promoting an active reader or participant leads to what Slavoj Žižek refers to as "double deception."[42] In this case, we are being duped into finding something akin to the *truth*, but become even more lost in the trappings of ideology. *Ironic racism* in sitcoms reflects double deception by acknowledging racism's presence whilst freeing us to laugh nonetheless. I propose that the fan trailer creator practices *assimilated resistance*, as it allows the creator to safely resist one mainstream text in support of another.

Conclusion

Returning once more to DST, it can be summed up as "local narratives" based on "personal memory."[43] Personal memory is a simple enough concept, but what constitutes personal memory is not always limited to lived experience. Any given dream can include a combination of lived and imaginary interactions between friends and what was on television last night. In waking life, personal memory also faces a similar blurring of fiction and nonfiction—a blurring fan trailers, and fan fiction in general, expose. But these local narratives are not set in physical places or recognizable neighborhoods; the familiar spaces are the films or television series them-selves—recognizable landmarks in the City of YouTube. The mayor of the Green Lantern district is Nathan Fillion, beloved space cowboy and pro-tector of the YouTube galaxy. In making his fan trailer, Jaron Pitts develops strong cultural capital that allows him to "surf the publicity" of a popular character, as Jenkins would say, through the use of fan fiction.[44]

Jean Burgess uses the term *vernacular creativity* when referring to new media that demands a different language and aesthetic follow media into the digital age.[45] As new media, fan trailers require a similarly unique cri-teria to analyze their worth, and I have proposed that comparing them to DST provides the appropriate framework:

1. Amateur filmmakers create pieces for enjoyment, not profit.
2. Participants develop new media skills that emphasize content and form.
3. First-person stories use any media texts, fiction or nonfiction.
4. The community is created through content.
5. Production companies and creators share a paradoxical relationship.
6. The Internet provides the only venue for an audience.

After my extensive search for commonality, I now conclude that fan trailers are in fact not a form of DST, when compared to examples pro-vided by Lundby, Couldry, and others. But this does not mean that my experiment has been a failure, for briefly considering this possibility better defines the purpose of each medium and supports the idea that popular texts can directly influence the "I" in both documentary and fic-tional forms. Furthermore, acknowledging the differences between each does not prove null this rhetorical debate but provides a needed coun-terpoint to the current definition of DST, exposing formal ambiguities and its audaciously broad name. More so, the same arguments used to promote DST's function in educational settings segue into the fan trailer's potential educational role as well. At the very least, creating fan trailers encourages participants to actively engage with popular media texts and reappropriate them for personal use, in the process forming resistance to dominant ideologies by taking the text's final say away from the produc-tion company and placing it in the digitized hands of the amateur creator. Furthermore, the practice of creating fan trailers encourages individuals to become aware of how a popular medium rhetorically persuades; previ-ously passive spectators can now see studio manipulation with new eyes.

The *authenticity* of DST raises questions about the fan's commitment to films, television shows, music, and other media texts, revealing consid-erations like social privilege and hegemony in the formation of fan taste that warrant further study. Yet in the end, I remain drawn to fan trailers because they challenge my knowledge of film, recontexualize film clips (sometimes for the better), provide me with opportunities to see something unoriginal in an original way, and speak to my enjoyment of film trailers. Like the toy, fan trailers (when made with greater precision) allow films to be seen anew; Lego pieces meant for something more engaging than the mediocre films from whence they came. After all, the directions on the back of the box are meant for kids, not adults.

Notes

1. Ruth Sylvester and Wendy-lou Greenidge, "Digital Storytelling: Extending the Potential for Struggling Writers," *The Reading Teacher* 63, no. 4 (2009): 286.

2. Knut Lundby, "Introduction: Digital Storytelling, Mediatized Stories," *Digital Storytelling, Mediatized Stories: Self-Representations in New Media*, ed. Knut Lundby (New York: Peter Lang Publishing, Inc., 2008), 1–8.

3. Helen Klaebe, Marcus Foth, Jean Burgess, and Mark Bilandzic, "Digital Storytelling and History Lines: Community Engagement in a Master-Planned Development," *Proceedings 13th International Conference on Virtual Systems and Multimedia (VSMM'07)* (Brisbane, Australia: Springer, 2007), http://eprints.qut .edu.au/archive/00008985/01/8985.pdf, 12.

4. Henry Jenkins, "Quentin Tarantino's Star Wars?: Digital Cinema, Media Convergence, and Participatory Culture," *Rethinking Media Change: The Aesthetics of Transition*, ed. David Thorburn and Henry Jenkins (Boston: The MIT Press, 2004), 287.

5. John Fiske, "The Cultural Economy of Fandom," *The Adoring Audience: Fan Culture and Popular Media*, ed. Lisa A. Lewis (New York: Routledge, 1992), 31.

6. Sylvester and Greenidge, "Digital Storytelling," 284.

7. Lance Berry, "*Popdose* Interview: The Man behind Green Lantern's (Fan-Made) Power Ring," *Popdose*, May 28, 2009, http://popdose.com/popdose-interview-the-man-behind-green-lanterns-fan-made-power-ring.

8. Nancy Thumim, "'It's Good for Them to Know My Story': Cultural Mediation as Tension," *Digital Storytelling, Mediatized Stories: Self-Representations in New Media*, ed. Knut Lundby (New York: Peter Lang Publishing, Inc., 2008), 98.

9. Berry, "*Popdose* Interview."

10. David Bordwell and Kristin Thompson, *Film Art: An Introduction*, 8th ed. (New York: McGraw Hill, 2008), 461.

11. Kathleen Williams, "Never Coming to a Theatre Near You: Recut Film Trailers," *M/C Journal* 12, no. 2 (2010), http://www.journal.media-culture.org.au/ index.php/mcjournal/article/viewArticle/139.

12. Glynda A. Hull and Mira-Lisa Katz, "Crafting an Agentive Self: Case Studies of Digital Storytelling," *Research in the Teaching of English* 41, no. 1 (2006): 46–48.

13. Ibid., 46.

14. Jenkins, "Quentin Tarantino's Star Wars," 288.

15. Henry Jenkins, *Fans, Bloggers, and Gamers: Exploring Participatory Culture* (New York: New York University Press, 2006), 90–91.

16. *Start Trek: The Next Generation* was particularly known for elevating the role of female characters, even changing the 1966 series' tagline from "no man" to a gender-inclusive "no one."

17. See "The Oppositional Gaze" in bell hooks, *Reel to Real: Race, Sex, and Class at the Movies* (New York: Routledge, 1996).

18. From the comments (July 2009) of Jaron Pitts, *Green Lantern Trailer*, video file, 2:39 minutes, May 22, 2009, http://www.youtube.com/watch?v =_hTiRnqnvDs.

19. Lois R. Kuznets, *When Toys Come Alive: Narratives of Animation, Metamorphosis, and Development* (New Haven: Yale University Press, 1994), 5.

20. Rebecca Tushnet, "Legal Fictions: Copyright, Fan Fiction, and a New Common Law," *Loyola of Los Angeles Entertainment Law Journal* 17, no. 3 (1997): 653.

21. From the comments (October 2009) of Pitts, *Green Lantern Trailer*.

22. Jenkins, "Quentin Tarantino's Star Wars," 289.

23. Ibid., 305.

24. Julie Gerstein, "Shepard Fairey–AP Obama Lawsuit Settled [Updated]," *New York*, last date modified January 11, 2011, http://nymag.com/daily/ intel/2011/01/shepherd_faireys_obama_lawsuit.html. It is worth noting that since this decision, the case became more problematic when Fairey admitted to destroying evidence.

25. Marshall McLuhan, *Understanding Media: The Extensions of Man* (New York: McGraw-Hill Book Company, 1964), 7.

26. Williams, "Never Coming to a Theatre Near You."

27. Nick Couldry, "Mediatization or Mediation? Alternative Understandings of the Emergent Space of Digital Storytelling," *New Media & Society* 10, no. 3 (2008): 374.

28. Hull and Katz, "Crafting an Agentive Self," 64.

29. Ibid., 68.

30. Sarah Kershaw, "Google Tells Sites for 'Cougars' to Go Prowl Elsewhere," *The New York Times*, May 15, 2010, http://www.nytimes.com/2010/05/16/fashion/ 16cougar.html.

31. Nicholas Mirzoeff, *An Introduction to Visual Culture* (New York: Routledge, 1999), 86–87.

32. Roberta Pearson, "Fandom in the Digital Era," *Popular Communication* 8 (2010): 85.

33. W. J. T. Mitchell, *Picture Theory: Essays on Verbal and Visual Representation* (Chicago: University of Chicago Press, 1995), 93.

34. hooks, *Reel to Real,* 229.

35. I still remain baffled at the popularity of the film *Transformers: Revenge of the Fallen*, especially for its incredibly offensive depictions of minorities, like the

blackface robots called the Twins. Still, it made $836,303,693 at the box office, warranting a deeper examination, and the *people-are-stupid* response should not be sufficient for the academy.

36. Borys Kit, "'Team America'/Alan Jackson Music Mash-Up for Funny 'Captain America' Trailer," *The Hollywood Reporter*, March 28, 2011, http://www.hollywood reporter.com/heat-vision/team-americaalan-jackson-music-mash-171993.

37. Henry Jenkins, *Convergence Culture: Where Old and New Media Collide*, 2nd ed. (New York: New York University Press, 2008), 272.

38. Jean Burgess and Joshua Green, *YouTube: Online Video and Participatory Culture* (Malden: Polity Press, 2009).

39. Stuart Hall, "Encoding/Decoding," *The Cultural Studies Reader*, 2nd ed., ed. Simon During (New York: Routledge, 2007), 507–17.

40. Martin Barker and Kate Brooks, *Knowing Audiences: Judge Dredd, Its Friends, Fans, and Foes* (Luton, UK: University of Luton Press, 1998), 96.

41. Pearson, "Fandom in the Digital Era," 34.

42. Slavoj Žižek, *Looking Awry: An Introduction to Jacques Lacan through Popular Culture* (Cambridge, MA: The MIT Press, 1991), 73.

43. Klaebe, Foth, Burgess, and Bilandzic, "Digital Storytelling," 12.

44. Jenkins, "Quentin Tarantino's Star Wars," 295.

45. Burgess, Jean, "Hearing Ordinary Voices: Cultural Studies, Vernacular Creativity and Digital Storytelling," *Journal of Media & Cultural Studies* 20, no. 2 (2006): 205–6.

CHAPTER FIVE

Will the Novel Remain Relevant in the Twitter Generation?

Joseph Bentz

If the novel didn't already exist, would anyone bother to invent it today? Think of what a traditional novel is: a huge chunk of pages containing tens of thousands of words. That's it. No videos. No photos. No graphics. Just hundreds of pages of unbroken text.

That might sound fine to readers who fell in love with the novel long before things such as YouTube videos or text messages were invented. But for newer generations of readers who will now become saturated with these online forms of information *before* ever reading a novel, how attractive will those long books be?

As our culture's tastes change, as our brains change, as our attention spans shrink, as information floods over us 24 hours a day in Tweets, Facebook posts, video games, Web sites, journals, magazines, blogs, vlogs, e-mails, memes, films, television shows, commercials, and many other sources of information, will the novel continue to be relevant, or will it be tossed aside as hopelessly old-fashioned?

Here are some of the challenges the novel faces today.

Reading Is an Unnatural Act

In her book, *Proust and the Squid: The Story and Science of the Reading Brain*, cognitive neuroscientist and reading specialist Maryanne Wolf writes, "In the evolution of our brain's capacity to learn, the act of reading is not natural, with consequences both marvelous and tragic for many people, particularly children."[1] She explains, "We were never born to read. Human beings invented reading only a few thousand years ago. And with this invention, we rearranged the very organization of our brain, which in turn expanded the ways we were able to think, which altered the intellectual evolution of our species."[2] Reading changes us not only intellectually, but also physiologically, as our brain creates new neuron pathways to allow the complex set of skills we call "reading" to take place. The only reason we can learn to read is because of the plasticity or "open architecture" of the brain, which allows for these neuronal changes. But many things within the brain have to happen just right for these pathways to be created correctly.

In her book, Wolf gives a glimpse of just how difficult it is to read a book, or even a few paragraphs. She gives a 233-word excerpt from one of Proust's works and asks the reader to read it. Then she briefly describes what the reader has just done. Here is her description:

> In response to this request, you engaged an array of mental or cognitive processes: attention; memory; and visual, auditory, and linguistic processes. Promptly, your brain's attentional and executive systems began to plan how to read Proust speedily and still understand it. Next, your visual system raced into action, swooping quickly across the page, forwarding its gleanings about letter shapes, word forms, and common phrases to linguistic systems waiting for the information. These systems rapidly connected subtly differentiated visual symbols with essential information about the sounds contained in words. Without a single moment of conscious awareness, you applied highly automatic rules about the sounds of letters in the English writing system, and used a great many linguistic processes to do so. . . . As you applied all these rules to the print before you, you activated a battery of relevant language and comprehension processes with a rapidity that still astounds researchers.[3]

That sounds complicated enough, but within those processes she mentions are further complexities. For example, cognitive scientists say that as we determine the meaning of each word, we activate every possible association we have for that word before settling on the correct meaning. When we read the word bug, we call up not only the idea of an insect, but also other meanings such as a recording device, a Volkswagen, and a computer glitch.[4]

So reading is doable, but it is *hard*. It's harder than we can even consciously be aware that it is. Many people are going to avoid it without really knowing why. While Maryanne Wolf approaches this difficulty of reading from a scientific viewpoint, Alan Jacobs, in his book *The Plea-sures of Reading in an Age of Distraction*, describes the difficulty from a different perspective. He quotes from a Martin Amis novel in which a character named John Self attempts to read George Orwell's novel, *Animal Farm*, because a woman he is interested in won't have anything to do with him unless he reads it. Self dutifully tries to read it but is barraged with every imaginable distraction. Even when he does settle into the reading, he finds it tough slogging. He describes the experience this way:

> Reading takes a long time, though, don't you find? It take such a long time to get from, say, page twenty-one to page thirty. I mean, first you've got page twenty-three, then page twenty-five, then page twenty-*seven*, then page twenty-nine, not to mention the even numbers. Then page thirty. Then you've got page thirty-*one* and page thirty-*three*—there's no end to it. Luckily *Animal Farm* isn't that long a novel. But novels . . . they're all long, aren't they. I mean, they're all so *long*. After a while I thought of ringing down and having Felix bring me up some beers. I resisted the temptation, but that took a long time too. Then I rang down and had Felix bring me up some beers. I went on reading.[5]

Most of us can relate to that description, and we've heard it from our students or from our children or others who find book-reading difficult. For many of us, those difficulties, or at least our perception of them, diminish over time as we read more and enjoy it more. But many are not willing to push through those complex, difficult processes. Even if they are, another problem arises.

We May Be Too Distracted to Read Novels

Why are we so distracted? Because our brains are changing in ways that make it easier to take in short segments of information as delivered by the Internet, but harder to focus on longer works such as novels.

An entire body of literature has emerged over the past few years about how distracted we are. In terms of the novel, the disturbing aspect of this is that these reports of distraction are not just about people who normally wouldn't be interested in the novel anyway, but they are from people whose livelihood often depends on books. For example, David Ulin, who makes his living as the book review editor of *The Los Angeles Times*, began a 2009 article with these words: "Sometime late last year—I don't remem-ber when, exactly, I noticed I was having trouble sitting down to read. That's a problem if you do what I do, but it's an even bigger problem if you're the kind of person I am."[6] What kind of person is he? The kind who always has stacks of books around him, and who has stuffed reading into every corner of his life. He says that the problem now "isn't a failure of desire so much as one of will. Or not will, exactly, but focus: the ability to still my mind long enough to inhabit someone else's world, and to let that someone else inhabit mine." Why does he have trouble doing that now? He explains, "These days . . . after spending hours reading e-mails and fielding phone calls in the office, tracking stories across countless websites, I find it difficult to quiet down. I pick up a book and read a paragraph; then my mind wanders and I check my e-mail, drift onto the Internet, pace the house before returning to the page."[7]

A more famous analysis of our age of distraction is Nicholas Carr's disturbing book, *The Shallows: What the Internet Is Doing to Our Brains.* Carr writes that the Internet seems to be chipping away at his "capacity for concentration and contemplation. Whether I'm online or not, my mind now expects to take in information the way the Net distributes it: in a swiftly moving stream of particles. Once I was a scuba diver in the sea of words. Now I zip along the surface like a guy on a Jet ski."[8] He quotes a former magazine editor who confesses that he has stopped reading books altogether: "I was a lit major in college, and used to be [a] voracious book reader. . . . What happened?" He speculates on the answer: "What if I do all my reading on the web not so much because the way I read has changed, i.e. I'm just seeking convenience, but because the way I THINK has changed?"[9]

Carr quotes a prominent academic who says, " 'I can't read *War and Peace* anymore.' . . .'I've lost the ability to do that. Even a blog post of more than three or four paragraphs is too much to absorb. I skim it.' "[10]

What is the reason for all this distraction, and what is the answer to it? Some, like David Ulin, lament the loss of concentration on long books and are trying to get it back. Some, like Carr, argue that our habits *and* our brains are changing because of the new ways of taking in information, so reading books will continue to become more and more challenging not only for established readers of books, but especially for people who never cared for them that much in the first place. Carr writes, "For some people, the very idea of reading a book has come to seem old-fashioned, maybe even a little silly—like sewing your own shirts or butchering your own meat."[11]

What if people do decide to set aside these old-fashioned, long novels that seem so hard for our brains to absorb? Are there any acceptable substitutes for that pleasurable, meaningful literary experience that we get from novels? That question leads to a third challenge for literature:

Other, Newer Media Forms Can Meet Many of the Needs That Used to Drive People to Novels

Among the newer media forms that are replacing literature for some readers is one that faces perhaps the strongest resistance from many parents, teachers, and literature lovers generally: video games. Many critics of video games think of them as little more than random and repetitive violence on the screen. But just as a whole body of literature has emerged about how distracted we are, so also has a whole set of books emerged by scholars extolling the value of video games—their educational value, their social value, and even their literary value.

The argument here is not that video games and other new media forms are *equal* to literature simply because they mimic so many aspects of it. Rather, because these new forms meet so many of the needs that used to drive people to literature, many people who otherwise might have become readers of literature will instead choose these newer forms that are easier to digest (they don't require the difficult act of reading for the most part) and that are satisfying enough, or as many practitioners and players would attest, even more satisfying than novels.

What needs does literature meet? What is its purpose? There is no simple answer to that, but consider the claims that literature professors and textbooks make about their subject. For example, a college-level literature anthology called *Retellings* states "literature provides us with entry into others' worlds. It allows us to interact, at least in our imaginations, with people of different times, cultures, socioeconomic groups, genders and ethnic backgrounds other than our own."[12]

When literary authors and thinkers write about the purpose of literature, that idea of "connectedness"—the reader connecting to one another and to ideas and to the mind of the author and to worlds beyond themselves—often emerges as the most important rationale for literature. Contemporary American novelist David Foster Wallace said, "I guess a big part of serious fiction's purpose is to give the reader, who like all of us is sort of marooned in her own skull . . . imaginative access to other selves."[13] Jonathan Franzen, author of *The Corrections* and *Freedom*, wrote, "Readers and writers are united in their need for solitude . . . in their reach inward, via print, for a way out of loneliness."[14] Susan Sontag said, "A great writer of fiction both creates a new, unique, individual world . . . and responds to a world, the world the writer shares with other people but that is unknown or mis-known by still more people, confined in their worlds.[15]

Literature, then, connects readers to other selves, other worlds, other minds, but what about video games? Aren't video games little more than people blowing up zombies?

According to video game scholars, the games have far more value than the stereotypes about them would indicate. In his book, *What Video Games Have to Teach Us about Learning and Literacy*, Arizona State University Literary Studies professor James Paul Gee shows how video games help people connect in many of the ways people associate with literature. One of the reasons people love and value literature is that it allows them to vicariously live the experience of someone else. You experience what it's like to be Huckleberry Finn or Jake Barnes or Lily Bart. Through novels, readers can be anyone, from any century, any race, any gender.

Video games also allow that connection to the lives of fictitious characters and other places and times. In fact, the games allow players not only to vicariously *experience* these characters but also to help *create* them. In many video games, people create their own avatars and then live the experiences of those people. In this sense, players become not only the equivalent of *readers*, but they also perform some of the functions of an *author*, creating characters. In one game he mentions, *EverQuest*, "character creation breaks down into 14 professions (bard, cleric, druid, enchanter, magician, monk, necromancer, paladin, ranger, rogue, shadowknight, shaman, warrior, or wizard) and 12 'races,' composed of three human cultures, three cultures of elves, and six others."[16] Beyond that, players may choose other characteristics such as gender, religion, race, and personal attributes, such as stamina, dexterity, and charisma.

Many people now play video games online, with other players all over the world. So at the same time that they are connecting to their characters, they are also connecting to other real people. Like the characters who can be either good or bad or a mixture of the two, players, who use screen names that are different from their own real names and different from the names of their characters, may behave rudely to other players, cause disruptions, and they may also get to know new people, have fun together, and connect as friends. As Gee points out, players may meet people online that they would never encounter anywhere else in their lives. He says, "At the same time, as our society becomes ever more segregated by race and class—as people spend more and more time with people like themselves in terms of values and lifestyle—games like *World of WarCraft* become new 'public spheres.' They are worlds where people come into contact with a now global public. People of all ages, countries, and value systems meet within these worlds."[17] In terms of connecting to characters and other people, then, video games offer a rich experience.

People go to novels not only to connect with characters but also to plunge into a rich, sumptuously imagined world that an author has created.

We want to spend time floating down Mark Twain's Mississippi River or inhabit Faulkner's Yoknapatawpha County or walk the streets of Dickens's grimy London or jet around John le Carré's exotic cities of Europe. Can video games compete with that? An article about the creation of the video game, "Star Wars: The Old Republic," shows to what elaborate lengths its creators went to develop a detailed, fully realized world for its players to inhabit: "More than 800 people on four continents have spent six years and nearly $200 million creating it. The story runs 1,600 hours, with hundreds of additional hours still being written. Nearly 1,000 actors have recorded dialogue for 4,000 characters in three languages. The narrative is so huge that writers created a 1,000-page 'bible' to keep the details straight."[18]

Jonathan Gottschall, author of *The Storytelling Animal: How Stories Make Us Human*, loves novels, but he sees video games, specifically a particular type of game called a massively multiplayer online role-playing game, or (MMORPG) (pronounced "Mor-Peg") as an important part of our story-telling future, not to mention the *present*. Gottschall explains that these experiences, which are often based on novels and other popular stories, "invite us to become characters in classic hero stories. As one player put it, playing a MMORPG is like living 'inside a novel as it is being written.' Another said, 'I'm living inside a medieval saga. I'm one of the characters in the novel, and, at the same time, I'm one of the authors.'"[19] How popular are these games? Twelve million people play *World of Warcraft* online. Overall, in the United States alone, 183 million people are active players of video games, meaning that they play them regularly, on average 13 hours a week.[20]

Besides video games and other new media forms, the ongoing relevance of the novel faces one further threat.

What Is a "Novel" Anyway? The Proliferation of New Categories "Flattens Out" Experience and Makes the Genre Less Distinct and Harder to Define

Increasingly, people experience information not in terms of distinct categories but rather in terms of a steady, flowing stream that moves across our various computer, tablet, and cell phone screens. We move seamlessly from news article to Facebook post to YouTube video to e-mail to blog to short story to novel to film to tweets. People not only have *more* forms of information than ever before, but they also make fewer distinctions about the genres of what they're reading or viewing. Is a reality television show fiction or nonfiction? Is a blog post journalism? Or is it memoir? Or fiction? Or a blending of all those?

In his book *Reality Hunger: A Manifesto*, David Shields calls genre a "minimum-security prison." He says, "Just as out-and-out fiction no longer compels my attention, neither does straight-ahead memoir." He writes,

> I want the contingency of life, the unpredictability, the unknowability, the mysteriousness, and these are best captured when the work can bend at will to what it needs: fiction, fantasy, memoir, meditation, confession, reportage. Why do I so strenuously resist generic boundaries? Because when I'm constrained within a form, my mind shuts down, goes on a sit-down strike, saying, This is boring, so I refuse to try very hard. I find it very nearly impossible to read a contemporary novel that presents itself unself-consciously as a novel, since it's not clear to me how such a book could convey what it feels like to be alive right now.[21]

Many other readers are abandoning the novel. A 2007 study by the National Endowment for the Arts, called *To Read or Not to Read*, found that Americans were spending less time reading now than 10 or 20 years earlier, and their reading comprehension skills had eroded over that period.[22] The study also reported these disturbing findings:

- "Nearly half of all Americans ages 18 to 24 read no books for pleasure."
- "The percentage of 18- to 44-year-olds who read a book fell 7 points from 1992 to 2002."
- "Less than one-third of 13-year-olds are daily readers."
- "The percentage of 17-year-olds who read nothing at all for pleasure has doubled over a 20-year period."[23]
- "15- to 24-year-olds spend only 7–10 minutes per day on voluntary reading, about 60% less time than the average American."[24]

That was in 2007. In 2008, the NEA released a report called *Reading on the Rise* that was more optimistic and that showed an increase in reading among young people after 2002. So the statistics about reading trends are not conclusive, but the trends are more negative than positive.

In spite of all the challenges to literature's relevance, there are still plenty of reasons for optimism among those who value the novel:

1. Online technology and new media forms, which in some ways may replace the novel, also offer new ways for novel readers to connect with one another and with authors.

   Goodreads, the social media site devoted to books, has 16 million users. Many readers also now have direct contact with authors and each other through Twitter and Facebook author pages. Online book clubs are thriving, Authors reach out through YouTube video talks and book trailers, e-mail, Amazon pages, and in many other ways.

2. People keep reinventing the novel in ways that may connect with new readers.

In 2013, *The New York Times* reported that filmmaker Steven Soderbergh had written and had begun to release a hard-boiled suspense novella called *Glue* on Twitter. He was releasing the novella, along with some photographs, one 140-word tweet at a time, and as of May 1 seven chapters of the book had appeared in that forum.[25]

In his novel *Extremely Loud and Incredibly Close*, and in other books, contemporary American novelist Jonathan Safran Foer tries all kinds of experiments in his novels—with typography, with photographs, with color. In his novel *Tree of Codes*, Foer took someone else's book, Bruno Schulz's *The Street of Crocodiles*, and literally sliced out lines and pages in order to create his own story.

Other novelists are experimenting with e-books that contain video clips, music clips, maps, and other extra-literary material. Some readers are still content with 700-page novels that are nothing but words, but these new novels may bring in readers who won't settle for that.

3. Nothing has managed to defeat literature yet.

In an article titled, "Is There Any Reason to Read?" Alberto Manguel argues that something about literature must be very powerful "if every dictator, every totalitarian government, every threatened official tries to do away with it, by burning books, by banning books, by censoring books, by taxing books, by paying mere lip-service to the cause of literacy, by insinuating that reading is an elitist activity."[26]

If none of those political and dictatorial forces could destroy the novel, in spite of strenuous efforts to do so, then perhaps none of the current challenges will manage to obliterate it either.

4. The irresistible power of words will keep the novel alive.

Those who love literature know the incomparable joy of losing oneself in a novel. The power of this experience goes beyond characters, it goes beyond the world the novelist describes, it goes beyond the plot of the story itself. The words, the rhythms of the sentences, the precision of the dialogue, the narrative voice all work together to create an experience that is not reducible—and not capable of being imitated or replaced—by any other form. Films and video games may be able to copy some elements of a novel, and they may be able to do some aspects even better. But the *language* is something they can't match.

Reading blends the words and ideas of the novelist with the thoughts and ideas of the reader unlike any other media or art form. A novel is not the same for any two readers. When reading a novel, we don't simply *respond* to what is given to us, the way we do with a film or a video game. Instead, we take the words, interpret them, mix them up with our own thoughts and images and ideas, and form the story in our brain. We are co-creators to a greater degree than even with the most interactive video game, and yet at the same time we are more deeply influenced—and more deeply enmeshed—in the writer's own vision. There is simply nothing else like it.

In his book on the pleasures of reading, Alan Jacobs quotes from Dickens's *David Copperfield*, when David is living with the gloomy and unpleasant Murdstone family, and books are his only refuge. David has his own little collection of novels his father had left him, and no one else in the family bothers them. In his little room upstairs, David reads *Humphrey Clinker, Tom Jones,* the *Vicar of Wakefield,* and other books. "This was my only and my constant comfort," David says. "When I think of it, the picture always rises in my mind, of a summer evening, the boys at play in the churchyard, and I sitting on my bed, *reading as if for life.*"[27]

Because of the many challenges the novel faces, the genre has already lost and probably will continue to lose millions of potential readers to other forms, but because enough people in the world still understand this phrase "reading as if for life," the novel still has a bright future for millions more.

Notes

1. Maryanne Wolf, *Proust and the Squid: The Story and Science of the Reading Brain* (New York: Harper, 2007), x.

2. Ibid., 10.

3. Ibid., 8.

4. Ibid.

5. Martin Amis, quoted in Alan Jacobs, *The Pleasures of Reading in an Age of Distraction* (Oxford: Oxford University Press, 2011), 77.

6. David L. Ulin, "Finding Your Focus," *Los Angeles Times,* August 9, 2009, E10.

7. Ibid.

8. Nicholas Carr, *The Shallows: What the Internet Is Doing to Our Brains* (New York: Norton, 2011), 6–7.

9. Ibid., 7.

10. Ibid.

11. Ibid., 8.

12. M. B. Clarke and A. G. Clarke, eds., *Retellings: A Thematic Literature Anthology* (New York: McGraw-Hill, 2004), xv.

13. David Foster Wallace, quoted in Zadie Smith, "Brief Interviews with Hideous Men," in *Changing My Mind: Occasional Essays* (New York: Penguin Press, 2009), 255.

14. Jonathan Franzen, "Why Bother?" in *How to Be Alone: Essays* (New York: Farrar, Straus and Giroux, 2002), 88.

15. Susan Sontag, "Essay: The Truth of Fiction Evokes Our Common Humanity," *Los Angeles Times*, June 1, 2012, http://www.latimes.com/news/obituaries/la-122804sontag_archives,0,3146156,print.story.

16. James Paul Gee, *What Video Games Have to Teach Us about Learning and Literacy* (New York: Palgrave, Macmillan, 2007), 181.

17. Ibid., 182.

18. Ben Fritz and Alex Pham, "Will Star Wars Game Reshape the Online Universe?," *Los Angeles Times,* January 20, 2012, A1.

19. Jonathan Gottschall, *The Storytelling Animal: How Stories Make Us Human* (New York: Houghton Mifflin Harcourt, 2012), 192–93.

20. Jane McGonigal, *Reality Is Broken: Why Games Make Us Better and How They Can Change the World* (New York: Penguin, 2011), 3.

21. David Shields, *Reality Hunger: A Manifesto* (New York: Alfred A. Knopf, 2010), 70–71.

22. National Endowment for the Arts, *To Read or Not to Read: A Question of National Consequence* (Washington, DC: NEA, 2007), 5.

23. Ibid.

24. Ibid., 7.

25. A. O. Scott, "A Novella Emerges Tweet by Tweet," *The New York Times*, May 1, 2013, http://www.nytimes.com/2013/05/02/books/soderbergh-explores-a-new-medium.html?ref=books&_r=0&pagewanted=print.

26. Alberto Manguel, "Is There Any Reason to Read?," *Salon*, June 8, 2012, http://www.salon.com/2012/06/08/is_there_any_reason_to_read/.

27. Charles Dickens, quoted in Jacobs, *The Pleasures of Reading in an Age of Distraction*, 32 (emphasis mine).

CHAPTER SIX

Distraction or Sensation Seeking: Understanding Motivations for Playing Facebook Games

Pavica Sheldon

Facebook is not a new medium, but a social medium, and even more than that—it is a virtual country. With over 1 billion users in 2013, the site has more than triple the population of the United States and more than the entire European continent. A number of studies[1] conducted in the past six years showed that the main motives for Facebook use are relationship maintenance and entertainment. However, another important reason for using Facebook is game playing. Every day tens of millions of people log on to Facebook to play games like *Farmville*, *Candy Crush Saga*, and *Texas HoldEm Poker*. Most popular games on Facebook are owned by Zynga, a San Francisco company. In times of economic recession, game businesses flourish as games are a kind of cheap home entertainment.[2] Only 10 years ago, players would have had to buy software for monthly accounts to play a game online. Thanks to Facebook, many games are free today.

Despite online games' constant evolvement, there has been relatively little research studying the positive aspects of game playing. So far, studies have been mostly focused on adolescent players and negative effects, such as addiction[3] and aggressive behavior.[4] In order to make profits, computer game developers need to have customers going back to their sites repeatedly. Therefore, understanding what factors influence the continued intention to play online games is an important issue that both academics and creators of online games want to know. According to uses and gratifications theory (U&G), individual differences influence motivations for engaging with different media.[5] The purpose of this study is to examine what the main reasons for playing Facebook games are, and how certain factors drive people to play them.

Despite evidence linking sensation seeking to Internet and violent media exposure, no study has explored the degree to which high-sensation-seeking individuals would enjoy playing Facebook games. Similarly, studies did not document the relationship between locus of control and motivations for playing Facebook games. Previous research showed that externals enjoyed online games more and played online games more frequently than internals.[6] Will the same occur with Facebook games? Life satisfaction is another construct often ignored when studying motivations for media consumption. Do individuals who are happy with their lives depend on Facebook games less than those who are not satisfied with their lives? Who plays Facebook games more often: women or men, older or younger individuals?

Theoretical Background

The assumption of U&G theory is that people are active in choosing and using media based on their needs.[7] For example, some people may use Facebook to meet their need for meeting new people, while others may use it to play games. According to the theory, audiences differ in the gratifications that they seek from the mass media. While those gratifications are not equally important for all types of media, the main ones include: diversion (escape from problems; emotional release), personal relationship (social utility of information in conversation; substitute of the media for companionship), personal identity (value reinforcement; self-understanding), and surveillance.[8] For example, most people watch television or use Facebook when nothing important is happening—to relax and escape from daily problems. They also use it in the company of friends (television) or to talk to their long-distance friends (Facebook). By choosing the channel and the content they like, they are reinforcing their personal values and their identity.

U&G theory has been applied to various new media related to communication technology, including video game playing.[9] However, different studies have suggested different gratifications for playing video and online games, including challenge,[10] entertainment,[11] and escapism.[12] Recently, a new concept called flow state has emerged to explain why users continue playing online games. Flow state explains how individuals become absorbed in the activity of playing, while losing self-consciousness.[13] Other studies[14] emphasized the difference between traditional media and new media: "Unlike more passive media such as film and television, computer games proceed only through the player's motivation to continue, and this continuation requires a user's focused attention and action" (p. 1340).

Early U&G studies used television U&G as a model for understanding video game playing.[15] Two decades later, Sherry and Lucas first developed a comprehensive U&G scale for video game playing.[16] This scale has been utilized in this study. Based on focus groups and interviews, they categorized six main reasons why people play video games: (1) competition, (2) challenge, (3) social interaction, (4) diversion, (5) fantasy, and (6) arousal. Competition was motivated by the desire to be the best player of the game. Challenge was measured as pushing oneself to beat the game or to get to the next highest level. Social interaction referred to playing with friends as a way of socializing. Diversion included playing games to pass time or to stop boredom. The fantasy motive included doing things you might not be able to do in real life, such as driving race cars or flying. Arousal was measured as playing games because it is exciting. No studies, however, have explored motivations for playing Facebook games. Thus, the following research question was asked:

RQ1: What are the most important motivations for playing Facebook games?

U&G theory suggest that factors such as one's social and psychological circumstances, motives, and expectations influence media use and effects.[17] However, "no single factor is theorized to drive media use; it is the interaction among needs, individual differences, and social context that predicts use."[18] This study investigates how four psychological constructs—sensation seeking, locus of control, life satisfaction, and sex and age—are related to motives for playing Facebook games and the time spent playing them.

Sensation Seeking

Sensation seeking is a psychological personality trait used to document individuals' need for novelty, complexity, and intensity.[19] High sensation seekers attempt to fulfill their need for stimulation by utilizing a variety of mediated and non-mediated sources.[20] According to the activation model of information exposure, activation levels vary from individual to individual. When the level of activation drops below the level that is comfortable, the person will engage in behavior designed to increase activation. The activation model further proposes that individuals with higher needs would be more likely to be in a state of *stimulus hunger* or *arousal-seeking* than individuals with lower needs. Individuals with a low need would be in an *arousal-avoidance* mode.[21] Sensation seeking is the arousal-seeking mode. Sensation seekers, therefore, enjoy thrill-seeking activities, such as bungee jumping, parachuting, fast and risky driving, and gambling.[22] They are also drawn to the Internet because of its potential to be dynamic, mentally arousing, and fast-paced.[23] Despite evidence linking sensation seeking to Internet and violent media exposure, no study has explored the degree to which high-sensation-seeker individuals would enjoy playing Facebook games. Therefore, the following question is asked:

RQ2: How is sensation seeking related to playing Facebook games?

Since research has shown that high sensation seekers are attracted to the Internet, it is hypothesized that they will also play Facebook games more often:

H1: Sensation seeking will be positively related to the frequency of playing Facebook games.

Another construct that might relate to playing Facebook games is locus of control.

Locus of Control

Locus of control is a personality construct that measures individuals' perceptions of how much control they have over their own lives.[24] Individuals who believe that they can control their own destiny tend to possess an internal locus of control while individuals who believe outer forces such as luck or fate determine their destiny possess an external locus of control.[25] External locus of control is the perception that one's life is controlled by chance or powerful others, but not by oneself.[26] On the other hand, people with an internal locus of control believe that they are the masters of their destiny.[27]

In the context of online game playing, a study of young male South Koreans[28] showed that externals enjoyed online games more and played online games more frequently than internals. This is consistent with previous studies[29] that found that internals tend to believe that they are responsible for the outcomes they experience and believe that they can control, cut, or stop playing online games whenever they want. Therefore, this study hypothesizes that internals would spend less time playing Facebook games when compared to externals.

H2: External locus of control will positively relate to time spent playing Facebook games.

Since there is no research on locus of control and motivations for playing Facebook or video games, the following research question is asked:

RQ3: What is the relationship between locus of control and motivations for playing Facebook games?

Life Satisfaction

Life-position elements, such as physical health, mobility, life satisfaction, interpersonal interaction, social activity, and economic security, are more informative than just demographics in explaining interpersonal needs and motives.[30] For example, research[31] showed that individuals who are more satisfied with their lives have multiple communication alternatives and are less dependent on one communication channel. Is it then possible that individuals who are happy with their lives would depend on Facebook games less than those who are not satisfied with their lives? Because there is no research on life satisfaction and online gaming, we asked a research question:

RQ4: Is there a relationship between playing Facebook games and life satisfaction?

Sex and Age

Past research[32] confirmed different intentions and consequences for playing online games between adolescents and adult online game players. Males and adolescents spent much more time on online games than females and adults.[33] Males were found to be faster in figuring out game strategies, and were more enthusiastic about playing online games than females.[34] Research[35] has consistently showed that boys play games more often than girls and for longer consecutive periods of time. The reasons cited included the emphasis of most games on competition and violence,[36] navigation through a route or maze, and targeting directed motor skills that males are better at.[37] In a Lucas and Sherry study,[38] females were less likely to be video game players, played for fewer hours, and did not seek out game-play situations for social interaction as much as male players did. Based on the previous findings, we hypothesized that:

H3: Women will spend less time playing Facebook games than men will.

H4: Women will be less motivated by competition than men will.

While young adults have consistently been the most likely to use social networking sites, Internet users in other age groups have seen faster rates

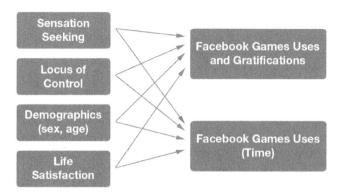

Figure 6.1 Facebook Games Uses and Gratifications Model

of growth in recent years. Social networking site use among Internet users 50–64 years old more than doubled between 2006 and 2013—from 24 percent to 52 percent.[39] Researchers[40] found that players of massively multiplayer online (MMO) games over 50 were more likely to be women. Their primary motivation for online game play was social connectedness to family. Moreover, those over 50 were more likely to note self-growth or learning motivations than those under 50. Because of the changing trends in the usage of social networking sites between older and younger adults, we asked a research question:

RQ5: Is there a difference in frequency and motivations for playing Facebook games between younger and older adults?

The model in Figure 6.1 represents the relationships tested in this study.

Method

Participants

Participants included 408 adults—of which 267 (65.4%) were women and 141 (34.6%) were men, ranging in age from 18 to 68 (mean age 29 years). Surveys were first distributed to college students at a medium-size research university. Older adults were then recruited by students who were asked to take home two questionnaires and have them filled out by any adult older than 40. By surveying older participants, we attempted to get a more representative sample. Studies have employed individuals' social networks in order to access "hard to reach" and "sensitive" populations.[41] In our case, not every Facebook user will play Facebook games.

Measurement

Facebook Games U&G

Participants were asked how often (4 = *very often;* 1 = *never*) they played Facebook games for the following reasons: challenge, arousal, diversion, competition, social interaction, and fantasy. The items from Lucas and Sherry scale[42] were adapted so that they fit Facebook game playing ("Facebook games allow me to pretend I am someone/somewhere else," and "I find that playing Facebook games raises my level of adrenaline"). Factor analyses extracted factors related to gratifications of playing Facebook games. The factor analysis used a principal component solution and varimax rotation and specified the retention of factors with eigenvalues greater than 1.0. This resulted in five factors that accounted for 73.6 percent of the variance (Table 6.1). Of six categories that were tested in the study, results showed that participants could not relate to social interaction motives for playing Facebook games. This makes sense considering that Facebook games are solitary (a person plays them from their own computer), unlike video games that can be played with a group of persons gathered in the same room. Excluded items measuring social interactions were "My friends and I use Facebook games as a reason to get together," and "Often, a group of friends and I will spend time playing Facebook games." In addition, the item measuring competition ("I get upset when I lose to my friends") loaded on three different factors and was excluded from the analysis.

Sensation Seeking

A brief sensation-seeking scale (BSSS)[43] was used to assess sensation seeking among Facebook users. The BSSS scale contains four components—thrill and adventure seeking, experience seeking, disinhibition, and boredom susceptibility. Participants responded to eight questions (two for each dimension) using a 5-point Likert-type scale (5 = *strongly agree;* 1 = *strongly disagree*). Items included "I would like to explore strange places," and "I prefer friends who are exciting and unpredictable." The eight questions were aggregated and averaged to form an indicator. A higher score implied that the respondents were more willing to engage in risky behaviors. The mean score of all of the items for the BSSS was 3.24, *SD* = .83, Cronbach's alpha = .82.

Locus of Control

Eight items on the locus of control were chosen from Levenson's locus of control scale.[44] Three items measured the internal locus of control

Table 6.1 Motives for Facebook game playing: primary factor analysis

	Loading	Eigenvalue	Variance	α
Factor 1: Fantasy				
I play Facebook games because they let me do things I can't do in real life.	.87			
Facebook games allow me to pretend I am someone/somewhere else.	.88			
I like to do something that I could not normally do in real life through a Facebook game.	.85	7.43	37.1	.94
I enjoy the excitement of assuming an alter ego in a game.	.87			
Factor 2: Competition				
I like to play to prove to my friends that I am the best.	.76			
When I lose to someone, I immediately want to play again in an attempt to beat him or her.	.75	2.88	14.4	.78
It is important to me to be the fastest and most skilled person playing the game.	.68			
Factor 3: Challenge				
I feel proud when I master an aspect of a game.	.74			
I find it rewarding to get to the next level.	.84	1.72	8.6	.80
I play until I complete a level or win a game.	.56			
I enjoy finding new and creative ways to work through Facebook games.	.61			
Factor 4: Arousal				
I find that playing Facebook games raises my level of adrenaline.	.66			
Facebook games keep me on the edge of my seat.	.72	1.38	6.9	.82
I play Facebook games because they excite me.	.46			
Factor 5: Diversion				
I play Facebook games when I do not have other things to do.	.90	1.13	5.6	.87
I play Facebook games instead of other things I should be doing.	.85			

(e.g., "My life is determined by my own actions"), while the others measured the external locus of control (e.g., "When I get what I want, it is usually because I am lucky."). All of the items were measured on a 5-point Likert scale (1 = *strongly disagree;* 5 = *strongly agree*). The items were summed into a scale, such that the larger the value of each scale, the greater the internal or external locus of control. For the internal locus of control, $M = 3.93, SD = .73$, Cronbach's alpha = .64. For the external locus of control, $M = 2.24, SD = .69$, Cronbach's alpha = .78.

Life Satisfaction

The A. Rubin and R. Rubin life position scale[45] was used to measure life satisfaction. Respondents reported their agreement with three statements (1 = *strongly disagree;* 5 = *strongly agree*): "I find a great deal of happiness in my life," "I have been very successful in achieving my aims or goals in life," and "I am very content and satisfied with my life." A higher score indicated that the respondents were more satisfied with their current life, $M = 3.86, SD = .80$, Cronbach's alpha = .84.

Facebook Use

Participants were asked if they have a Facebook account, how many hours per day they spend on Facebook, how often they play Facebook games and, if they play, how long their sessions are. They also indicated which Facebook games they played most often.

Results

Of the total number of participants who had a Facebook account ($N = 363$), about 20 percent ($n = 73$) answered that they played Facebook games. Most participants said that they played "sometimes" ($n = 55$), nine said they played them "often," and nine said they played them "very often." When asked how many times per week they played them, 75 percent of game players said that they do it once to three times per week. When asked about the length of an average game session, 80 percent of players said that they are less than an hour. No player said that they played for more than 2.5 hours consecutively.

On average, Facebook game players spent 2 hours on Facebook per day and had 346 Facebook friends. This number is significantly lower than the number of friends that non-gamers had (440 friends). Non-gamers also spent less time on Facebook (1.4 hours per day). The most popular Facebook game was *Words with Friends* (12 out of 73 players), followed by

Bejeweled Blitz (4 out of 73 players), and *Family Feud* (4 out of 73 players). Other mentioned games included *Castleville, Mafia Wars, Scrabble,* and *Cityville.*

RQ1. Motivations for Playing Facebook Games

The first research question asked about the most important motivation for playing Facebook games. Results showed that the main motivation was challenge (*M* = 2.36; *SD* = .75; 4-point scale). Facebook gamers in this study are motivated by achieving that next level. The second most important motivation was diversion or playing games to pass time or to stop boredom (*M* = 1.70; *SD* = .72). Third place is fantasy, or doing things you cannot do in real life (*M* = 1.65; *SD* = .79). The last two motivations were arousal or playing for excitement (*M* = 1.62; *SD* = .66), and competition or a desire to be the best player of the game (*M* = 1.58; *SD* = .65). Competition was the least mentioned reason for playing Facebook games (Table 6.2).

Table 6.2   Measures of central tendencies for gaming motives

	M[a]	SD
Factor 1: Fantasy		
I play Facebook games because they let me do things I can't do in real life	1.56	.84
Facebook games allow me to pretend I am someone/ somewhere else.	1.65	.94
I like to do something that I could not normally do in real life through a Facebook game.	1.77	.86
I enjoy the excitement of assuming an alter ego in a game.	1.56	.83
Factor 2: Competition		
I like to play to prove to my friends that I am the best.	1.59	.86
When I lose to someone, I immediately want to play again in an attempt to beat him/her.	1.73	.81
It is important to me to be the fastest and most skilled person playing the game.	1.50	.66
Factor 3: Challenge		
I feel proud when I master an aspect of a game.	2.50	.93
I find it rewarding to get to the next level.	2.62	.96
I play until I complete a level or win a game.	2.17	.90
I enjoy finding new and creative ways to work through Facebook games.	2.20	.96

Factor 4: Arousal

I find that playing Facebook games raises my level of adrenaline.	1.52	.75
Facebook games keep me on the edge of my seat.	1.47	.66
I play Facebook games because they excite me.	1.89	.93

Factor 5: Diversion

I play Facebook games when I do not have other things to do.	1.71	.72
I play Facebook games instead of other things I should be doing.	1.67	.79

[a]Means for a 4-point scale (very often = 4; often = 3; rarely = 2; never = 1).

RQ2 and H1. Sensation Seeking and Facebook Game Playing

The second research question asked about the relationship between sensation seeking and motivations for playing Facebook games. Pearson product–moment correlations were computed. Results showed no significant relationship between sensation seeking and motivations for playing Facebook games ($p > .5$).

The first hypothesis predicted that sensation seeking would be positively related to the frequency of playing Facebook games. Pearson product-moment correlation results showed no support for this hypothesis, $r(363) = -.04$, $p = .25$.

RQ3 and H2. Locus of Control and Facebook Game Playing

The second hypothesis predicted that the external locus of control would be positively related to time spent playing Facebook games. This hypothesis was supported. The external locus of control was positively and significantly related to the frequency of playing Facebook games, $r(363) = .10$, $p = .029$. In other words, individuals who are trying to escape the real world are more prone to playing Facebook games.

The third research question asked what the relationship between locus of control and motivations for playing Facebook games is. Results showed two significant relationships. First, the internal locus of control was positively correlated with a competition motivation for playing Facebook games, $r(71) = .28$, $p = .009$. Individuals who believe that they can control the world around them play competitive games more often. Second, external locus of control was negatively associated with both the challenge motivation, $r(71) = -.20$, $p = .048$. Individuals who believe that others control them are less likely to play challenging Facebook games.

RQ4. Life Satisfaction and Facebook Game Playing

The fourth research question asked about the relationship between life satisfaction and frequency for playing Facebook games, and life satisfaction and motivations for playing Facebook games. Of those who played Facebook games, the more satisfied individuals played them less often, $r(71) = -.40$, $p = .001$. The amount of time was a significant predictor of life satisfaction, explaining 16 percent of variance in the dependent variable, $B = -.16$, $SE = .04$, $\beta = -.40$, $t(68) = -3.58$, $p = .001$, $R^2 = .16$. When looking at the life satisfaction of all Facebook users (gamers and non-gamers), results also showed a significant and negative relationship between life satisfaction and the time spend playing Facebook games, $r(363) = -.10$, $p = .05$.

Life satisfaction was, however, positively related with competition motives, $r(71) = .30$, $p = .011$, and challenge, $r(71) = .25$, $p = .034$. Individuals who were satisfied with their current lives play competitive, challenging, and stimulating games with their friends. Additional results showed that they also scored higher on the internal locus of control, $r(73) = .47$, $p = .001$.

H3 and H4. Sex and Facebook Game Playing

The third hypothesis predicted that women would spend less time playing Facebook games than men will. This hypothesis was not supported. There was no significant difference in the amount of time spent playing Facebook games. The fourth hypothesis predicted that women would be less motivated by competition than men. There were no significant sex differences in the competition motivation for playing Facebook games. However, sex differences emerged in other motives for playing Facebook games. Men were significantly more motivated to play for diversion, $M_m = 2.09$, $SD_m = .80$, than women, $M_f = 1.52$, $SD_f = .61$, $t(69) = 3.320$, $p = .002$.

RQ5. Age and Facebook Game Playing

The fifth research question asked about the difference in motivations and frequency of playing Facebook games by younger and older adults. Pearson product–moment correlations were first computed between age and different gratifications. Results showed that younger people played for competition, $r(71) = -.20$, $p = .047$, and arousal, $r(71) = -.26$, $p = .016$, more often than older adults. However, there was no relationship between age and the amount of time spent playing Facebook games, $r(71) = .17$, $p = .077$.

Discussion

Video game playing is linked to many positive benefits, including acquisition of computer literacy,[46] as well as improvement of cognitive and attention skills.[47] However, there has been almost no research studying why people play Facebook games, and who the people playing them are. U&G theory argues that individuals are motivated to acquire certain gratifications from their media use. They use media to fulfill certain needs. Facebook games are one of the most popular and cheap options for home entertainment for millions of Americans. Are the individuals who play Facebook games bored or need an excitement in their lives?

First, the present study asked what the main motivations for playing Facebook games are. Research on motivations for playing online or video games showed contradictory findings. Previous studies[48] found that the main motive for playing online games is challenge. According to Wu et al., the most important gratification is entertainment.[49] In a study of South Korean online game players,[50] escapism was the most important motive. In this study, the main motivations for playing Facebook games are challenge and diversion (or playing when nothing else is going on) (RQ1). In order to understand this finding, it is important to look at the content of Facebook games that participants in this study played. The most often played Facebook game—*Words with Friends*—is a multiplayer game with two opponents. It resembles the traditional word game *Scrabble*. The game challenges players to create the highest-scoring word while playing against the opponent. It also allows users to exchange messages with each other through a chat feature. The biggest difference from Scrabble might be the fact that users can leave the game at any time and return later, thus allowing them to play at their own convenience or when nothing else is going on (diversion). The game is challenging so it is not surprising that the challenge was the main motive for playing this Facebook game.

U&G theory[51] also emphasizes that we need to study individual differences that might influence motivations for engaging with different media. The present study focuses on the sensation-seeking trait, locus of control construct, and life satisfaction—to understand how they are related to motives for playing Facebook games. The first hypothesis predicting that sensation seekers would be attracted more often to game playing on Facebook was not supported. A possible reason might be the fact that Facebook games are not violent. In fact, past research[52] found that high-sensation-seeking adolescents are drawn more to *violent* video games. *Words with Friends* and *Candy Crush* are fun and challenging games, but they do not contain aggression.

Previous studies[53] also indicate that high sensation seekers always look for "novel, complex, and intense sensations and experiences," and it is therefore possible that they try to play games even though they have other tasks to do because games provide them with the stimulus that they are searching for. However, sensation seeking was not related to any motivations for playing Facebook games (RQ2).

The findings of this study extend our knowledge about external locus of control construct. A high external locus of control was positively associated with the amount of time spent playing Facebook games (H2). It is likely that internals believe that they are responsible for the outcomes that they experience and therefore are able to control, cut, or stop playing Facebook games whenever they want. Externals cannot control themselves when it comes to how much time they spend playing those games. In addition, this study indicates that they tend to avoid risky and conflicting games and play those that are less challenging (RQ3). This finding makes sense considering that externals do not like competition and challenge in their real life. Their trait attributes do not change in the virtual world. Externals are more prone to depression and anxiety, while internals can wait longer to obtain gratification.[54]

A. Rubin and R. Rubin[55] emphasized the importance of studying life-position elements, such as life satisfaction, that might influence how individuals use media, or even communicate to each other. They argued that life-position indicators are more informative than just demographics in explaining interpersonal needs and motives. However, no study has examined the relationship between life-position indicators and Facebook or even online game playing. Therefore, this study asked if there is a relationship between playing Facebook games and life satisfaction. Results show that people who are less satisfied with their lives play Facebook games more often. The question is, why? It is possible that those less satisfied with their lives perceive Facebook games as a way of escape or diversion from the real world. Games are fun and often seen as a substituted entertainment for more expensive options that might include hanging out with friends (e.g., movies). However, those individuals are not playing competitive games. This study's findings show that the more satisfied individuals are with their lives, the more often they will play competitive, challenging, and cooperative games with their friends (RQ4). This is related to the internal locus of control. Individuals with an internal locus of control play competitive games. In this study, they also score higher on life satisfaction than individuals with an external locus of control.

Past research[56] shows that men and younger adults play video and online games more often than women and older adults. This was not the case in the present study (H3 not supported). It is plausible to conclude that these unexpected findings are due to the Facebook game design. Two recent studies[57] also discredited the stereotype that gamers are white, heterosexual young men.

Interestingly, this study found no gender difference in the competition motive for playing Facebook games (H4 not supported). Although we traditionally expect that men are more competitive and play games in order to compete, this did not reflect in our sample. The explanation, again, might be in the design of Facebook games. They are challenging but not as competitive as traditional video games. However, this study shows that men were significantly more likely to play games for diversion when compared to women. Future studies should try to answer this finding.

When comparing the age of Facebook players, there was no difference in the amount of time spent playing Facebook games between older and younger users (RQ5). This is somewhat surprising considering the previous research on online gaming.[58] However, a possible explanation might be the increase in the Baby Boomer generation's presence on social networking sites. In 2013, more than 50 percent of Baby Boomers in America maintained a profile on the social Web. Boomers also like Facebook more than any other social media sites. Some speculate[59] that senior social media users have picked up Facebook as a new hobby. Moreover, games provide mental stimulation that also improves health. In addition, older individuals have more time to spend on Facebook. However, compared to younger people, older individuals play less often for competition or arousal. This might be due to their age and sensation seeking. Delwiche and Henderson's study[60] of MMO gamers also confirmed that older players spend more time playing games, and were less likely to cite social achievement and competition motivations.

Conclusion

From the U&G perspectives, this study suggests that we should study both motives for using a certain medium and its by-products (e.g., games), but also life-position and psychological characteristics that affect its use. This study found that those who spend more time playing Facebook games are less satisfied with their lives and score higher on external locus of control. Those who are more satisfied and those who score high on internal locus of control play Facebook games less often, but their motives are different. More satisfied individuals and those in control play to challenge an opponent, while less satisfied individuals and those with an external locus of control play to escape from the real world.

Another unexpected finding of this study is that women and men do not differ in the amount of time they spend playing Facebook games. Traditionally, men have always been drawn to video games more than women. It is evident that Facebook is changing this trend. Social networking sites attract women more than men. Similarly, age differences are disappearing. Facebook games attract both young and old.

Overall, these are important findings as they provide a better understanding of how one's personality and demographic characteristics influence Facebook gaming. Future research could expand on other life-position indicators (e.g., physical health, mobility, economic security) to better understand why somebody decides to grow virtual crops or crush the candies. This study, however, made a first and important step toward understanding U&G of playing Facebook games.

Limitations

This study was conducted both in 2012. In 2012, the most popular Facebook game was *Words with Friends*. According to insidesocialgames.com, in May 2013, the most popular Facebook game was *Candy Crush*, followed by *Farmville* and *Texas HoldEm Poker*. This, however, does not change the type of personality that is attracted to Facebook games. Another limitation was low means for some Facebook game use motivations. Future research should include a larger sample size.

Notes

1. Pavica Sheldon, "The Relationship between Unwillingness to Communicate and Students' Facebook Use," *Journal of Media Psychology* 20 (2008): 67–74.

2. "Are Revenue Gains in the Same Game Industry Coming at the Expense of Profits?," http://www.dfcint.com/wp/?p=236.

3. Mark D. Griffiths, "Video Games and Children's Behavior," in *Elusive Links: Television, Video Games, Cinema and Children's Behavior*, ed. Tony Charlton and Kenneth David (Gloucester, UK: GCED/Park Publishers, 1997), 66–93.

4. Lily S. Chen, "The Impact of Perceived Risk, Intangibility and Consumer Characteristics on Online Game Playing," *Computers in Human Behavior* 26 (2010): 1607–13.

5. Elihu Katz, Jay G. Blumler, and Michael Gurevitch, "Uses and Gratifications Research," *The Public Opinion Quarterly* 37 (1974): 509–23.

6. Dong-Mo Koo, "The Moderating Role of Locus of Control on the Links between Experiential Motives and Intention to Play Online Games," *Computers in Human Behavior* 25 (2009): 466–74.

7. Jen-Her Wu, Shu-Ching Wang, and Ho-Huang Tsai, "Falling in Love with Online Games: The Uses and Gratifications Perspective," *Computers in Human Behavior* 26 (2010): 1862–71.

8. Denis McQuail, Jay G. Blumler, and J. R. Brown, "The Television Audience: A Revised Perspective," in *Sociology of Mass Communication*, ed. David McQuail (Middlesex, UK: Penguin, 1972), 135–65.

9. Kristen Lucas and John L. Sherry, "Sex Differences in Video Game Play: A Communication-Based Explanation," *Communication Research* 31 (2004): 499–523.

10. Ibid.

11. Wu, Wang, and Tsai, "Falling in Love," 1862–71.

12. Koo, "The Moderating Role," 466–74.

13. Chin-Lung Hsu and His-Peng Lu, "Consumer Behavior in Online Game Communities: A Motivational Factor Perspective," *Computers in Human Behavior* 23 (2007): 1642–59.

14. Nicholas D. Bowman and Ron Tamborini, "Task Demand and Mood Repair: The Intervention Potential of Computer Games," *New Media & Society* 14 (2012): 1339–57.

15. Gary W. Selnow, "Playing Videogames: The Electronic Friend," *Journal of Communication* 34 (1984): 148–56.

16. John Sherry and Kristen Lucas, "Video Game Uses and Gratifications as Predictors of Use and Game Preference" (paper presented at the annual meeting of the International Communication Association, San Diego, California, 2003).

17. Katz, Blumler and Gurevitch, "Uses and Gratifications," 509–23.

18. Lucas and Sherry, "Sex Differences in Video Game Play," 503.

19. Jeffrey Arnett, "Sensation Seeking: A New Conceptualization and a New Scale," *Personality and Individual Differences* 16 (1994): 289–96; Marvin Zuckerman, *Sensation Seeking: Beyond the Optimal Level of Arousal* (Hillsdale, NJ: Lawrence Erlbaum Associates, 1979); Marvin Zuckerman, *Behavioral Expression and Biosocial Bases of Sensation Seeking* (New York: Cambridge University Press, 1994).

20. Kathryn Greene and Marina Krcmar, "Predicting Exposure to and Liking of Media Violence," *Communication Studies* 56 (2005): 71–93.

21. Lewis Donohew, Philip Palmgreen, and Jack Duncan, "An Activation Model of Information Exposure," *Communication Monographs* 47 (1980): 295–303.

22. Zuckerman, "Sensation Seeking"; Jonathan W. Roberti, "A Review of Behavioral and Biological Correlates of Sensation Seeking," *Journal of Research in Personality* 38 (2004): 256–79.

23. Jakob Jensen, Rebecca Ivic, and Kristen Imboden, "Seeds of Deviance: Sensation Seeking and Children's Media Use" (paper presented at the annual

meeting of the International Communication Association, Chicago, Illinois, May 20–26, 2009).

24. Julian B. Rotter, "Generalized Expectancies for Internal versus External Control of Reinforcement," *Psychological Monographs* 80 (1966): 9–28.

25. Colleen Ward and Antony Kennedy, "Locus of Control, Mode Disturbance, and Social Difficulty during Cross-Cultural Transitions," *International Journal of Intercultural Relations* 16 (1992): 175–94.

26. Rotter, "Generalized Expectancies," 9–28.

27. Philip J. Auter and Ray Lane Jr., "Locus of Control, Parasocial Interaction, and Usage of Radio or TV Ministry Programs," *Journal of Communication and Religion* 22 (1999): 93–120.

28. Koo, "The Moderating Role," 466–74.

29. Christophe Boone, Bert De Brabander, and Arjen van Witteloostuijn, "CEO Locus of Control and Small Firm Performance. An Integrative Frame Work and Empirical Test," *Journal of Management Studies* 33 (1996): 667–99.

30. Alan M. Rubin and Rebecca B. Rubin, "Contextual Age and Television Use," *Human Communication Research* 8 (1982): 228–44.

31. Rebecca B. Rubin and Alan M. Rubin, "Antecedents of Interpersonal Communication Motivation," *Communication Quarterly* 40 (1992): 305–17.

32. Mark D. Griffiths, Mark N. O. Davies, and Darren Chappell, "Online Computer Gaming: A Comparison of Adolescent and Adult Gamers," *Journal of Adolescence* 27 (2004): 87–96; Nick Yee, "Motivations for Play in Online Games," *CyberPsychology and Behavior* 9 (2006): 772–75.

33. Chen, "The Impact of Perceived Risk," 1607–13.

34. Ibid.

35. Lucas and Sherry, "Sex Differences in Video Game Play," 499–523; John Sherry, "Flow and Media Enjoyment," *Communication Theory* 14 (2004): 328–47, http://icagames.comm.msu.edu/flow.pdf.

36. Jeanne B. Funk and Debra D. Buchman, "Playing Violent Video and Computer Games and Adolescent Self-Concept," *Journal of Communication* 46 (1996): 19–32.

37. Doreen Kimura, *Sex and Cognition* (Cambridge, MA: MIT Press, 1999).

38. Lucas and Sherry, "Sex Differences in Video Game Play," 499–523.

39. "Pew Internet: Social Networking," Pew Research Center, http://pewinternet.org/Commentary/2012/March/Pew-Internet-Social-Networking-full-detail.aspx.

40. Aaron A. Delwiche and Jennifer Henderson, "The Players They Are A-changin': The Rise of Older MMO Gamers," *Journal of Broadcasting & Electronic Media* 57 (2013): 205–23.

41. Sherry M. Bergeron and Charlene Senn, "Body Image and Sociocultural Norms—A Comparison of Lesbian and Heterosexual Women," *Psychology of Women Quarterly* 22 (1998): 385–401; Sotirios Sarantakos, "Sex and Power in Same-Sex Couples," *Australian Journal of Social Issues* 33 (1998):17–36.

42. Lucas and Sherry, "Sex Differences in Video Game Play," 499–523.

43. Rick H. Hoyle et al., "Reliability and Validity of Scores on a Brief Measure of Sensation Seeking," *Personality and Individual Differences* 32 (2002): 401–14.

44. Hanna Levenson, "Activism and Powerful Others: Distinctions within the Concept of Internal-External Control," *Journal of Personality Assessment* 38 (1974): 377–83.

45. Rubin and Rubin, "Contextual Age," 228–44.

46. Patricia M. Greenfield et al., "Cognitive Socialization by Computer Games in Two Cultures: Inductive Discovery or Mastery or an Iconic Code?" *Journal of Applied Developmental Psychology* 15 (1994): 59–85.

47. C. Shawn Green and Daphne Bavelier, "Action Video Game Modifies Visual Selective Attention," *Nature* 423 (2003): 534–37.

48. John L. Sherry et al., "Video Game Uses and Gratifications as Predictors of Use and Game Preference," in *Playing Video Games: Motives, Responses, and Consequences,* ed. Peter Vorderer and Jennings Bryant (Mahwah, NJ: Lawrence Erlbaum Associates, 2006), 213–24; Lucas and Sherry, "Sex Differences in Video Game Play," 499–523.

49. Wu, Wang, and Tsai, "Falling in Love," 1862–71.

50. Koo, "The Moderating Role," 466–74.

51. Katz, Blumler, and Gurevitch, "Uses and Gratifications," 509–23.

52. Michael D. Slater, "Alienation, Aggression, and Sensation Seeking as Predictors of Adolescent Use of Violent Film, Computer and Website Content," *Journal of Communication* 53 (2003): 105–21.

53. Zuckermann, "Behavioral Expression," 27.

54. Philip C. Miller et al., "Marital Locus of Control and Marital Problem Solving," *Journal of Personality and Social Psychology* 51 (1986): 161–69.

55. Rubin and Rubin, "Contextual Age," 228–44.

56. Chen, "Online Game Playing," 1607–13; Lucas and Sherry, "Sex Differences in Video Game Play," 499–523; Sherry et al., "Video Game Uses," 213–24.

57. Delwiche and Henderson, "MMO Gamers," 205–23; Adrienne Shaw, "Do You Identify as a Gamer? Gender, Race, Sexuality, and Gamer Identity," *New Media & Society* 14 (2012): 28–43.

58. Chen, "Online Game Playing," 1607–13.

59. "Baby Boomers and Seniors Are Flocking to Facebook," http://mashable.com/2010/01/28/baby-boomers-social-media/.

60. Delwiche and Henderson, "MMO Gamers," 205–23.

CHAPTER SEVEN

Mediating Faith through Popular Culture: The Voice of Aimee Semple McPherson in the New Media Marketplace

Bala A. Musa

Introduction

Media ecologists would argue that the public communication environment is more saturated today than at any time in human history. The information rate has increased exponentially due to the proliferation of communication channels. The cacophony of voices in the media marketplace has made it increasingly difficult for any single message, intellectual, commercial, or religious, to stand out. The result is that today's public square has become the site for a clash of creeds, values, ideologies, beliefs, and systems.

In every civilization and cultural epoch, three institutions that have sought to capture the soul of the city and shape society have been the temple of worship (religious center), the city square or piazza (the site of commerce and culture), and the city hall (the seat of government). The temple, the marketplace, and the city hall, while all necessary for the good of society, seek different paths toward that good. The ascendance of any of these over the others moves the culture in a different direction.

This enduring struggle was also evident at the turn of the early 20th century in America. Society was undergoing a transition from rural to urban, agricultural to industrial, religious to secular, and homogeneous to diverse. The turn of that century set in motion trends in technological advancement, rising mega cities, an increase in education, the greater role of government, growth in commerce, an expanding entertainment and consumer culture, an increasing religious fervor alongside secularization, and a growing cultural diversity.

It was against this background that Aimee Semple McPherson (Sister Aimee, as she was known) emerged as an international evangelist, revivalist, pastor, media ministry pioneer, philanthropist, educator, and leader. This chapter looks at the communication strategy used by Sister Aimee in her evangelistic ministry and the influence it had on popular culture. It examines her effective and creative use of what were new communication media and approaches in her time to disseminate the gospel in a fast-changing media marketplace. It leaps forward to today's era to examine what bearing today's information revolution would have had on her work and vice versa.

The Cultural Environment

It is beyond the scope of this work to provide a detailed biography of Sister Aimee's life and ministry. Besides, much of that has been well researched and written about by others[1] The focus of this discourse is to examine the slice of her work and legacy that relates to gospel communication and their implications for Christian engagement with contemporary culture.

After years of itinerant tent and church revival ministry across the United States and overseas, Sister Aimee settled in Los Angeles in 1919. The time and place were providential and crucial to the impact of her ministry from there on. Los Angeles was arguably the fastest-growing city, the city with the most jobs, a city with an influx of people of diverse backgrounds, and, thanks to Hollywood, it was becoming a world entertainment and cultural capital. It was the budding city on the West Coast. Not only the country but also the world was moving there. Its economic boom created opportunities for social mobility. It was the strongest real estate market at that time. Its population was growing rapidly.

Prior to moving to Los Angeles, Aimee had been enchanted by the lively cultural and art scene in New York. Edith Blumhofer noted that, while in New York, Aimee and her soon-to-be second husband, Harold, were enchanted by the theater. The two "relished rubbing shoulders with theater people."[2] And Aimee was taken by the artistry and spectacle of the elaborate productions. "The bustle of the city, the lights of Broadway, the fashionable silk gowns so different from the practical attire of the farm women and missionaries she knew, the vivacity of the theatre crowds thrilled her."[3] She would later incorporate many design and production elements of Broadway and Hollywood theater and entertainment into her gospel communication.

The turning of the 20th century was also an era of increasing acceptance of women's role and leadership in public life. The decades preceding this era, including the 19th-century revivals, "brought women to the visible forefront of the churches and even, to some extent, to the forefront of public life in general."[4] Also, "changing social conditions and new theological emphases began to offer them [women] more opportunities for public ministry."[5] Blumhofer opines, "The technological and media revolution of the 1920s combined with new images of femininity to assist her [Aimee's] popularity."[6]

World War I, the Great Depression, and the rapid social and economic transitions caused people to want to find something to hold on to. Many were open to having God as a source of hope and stability. Most of the immigrants to the cities, including the city of Los Angeles, had come from rural areas of other countries where faith was an important part of their lives. They were drawn to the gospel, among other things, as a way for finding stability, comfort, and assurance in the quickly changing environment.

The newcomers to the city, removed from kith and kin, sought and found new community in various circles. Clubs, work, social causes, churches, political organizations, and so forth, offered them the sense of place and belonging. Different institutions offered identity, meaning, community, and sanctuary.

All sorts of preachers and doctrines fed that spiritual hunger and sought to capitalize on it. One minister lamented how,

> Lately the city's overrun with fakes, . . . Satan's own false prophets are converging upon Los Angeles by the dozens. Cultists in this town preach salvation through everything from weight lifting to orgies of the flesh. . . . We've got the temperance crowd, the brain-breathing cult, the evangelical atheists.[7]

There were divisions and competitions among Christian ministers. The church scene was described as one in which "some, respected preachers of the Gospel, would slit your throat if by so doing they could add your congregation to their own. It's money in their pockets, and that's the beginning and end of it."[8] Obviously, the church community in Los Angeles was in need of a strong unifying presence to fill the leadership void that had been created by conflict, rivalry, and personality clashes.[9]

Sister Aimee arrived just at the right time. She had not been part of the local conflicts or church politics. She was respected and admired by other ministers and was not seen as a threat to their ministries. She had a strong, yet warm, and charming personality that made her welcoming, not threatening to others. She immediately filled the existing leadership void. Not only was she respected in Christian circles, she raised the presence, profile, and visibility of the church in Los Angeles and, one could say, in American culture. In particular, she became one of the leading voices and the face of Pentecostal Christianity. According to Blumhofer,

> Despite the fact that the Apostolic Faith Mission on Azusa Street in Los Angeles loomed large in worldwide Pentecostal memory, Pentecostalism had never really become a cultural force in the city. Aimee's arrival changed that: within a few years, thanks largely to her efforts, Pentecostalism took its place among the city's enduring religious currents.[10]

The inherent desire to belong drives people in multiple directions. Some pursue external sensation and pleasure. Others pursue inward peace and spiritual development. Popular culture offers a range of avenues for people to realize these desires. These outlets include sports, leisure, entertainment, religion, social activism, business, and so forth. Sister Aimee's ministry, likewise, drew audiences who came for a variety of reasons. There were sensation seekers and observers who were drawn to the energy, drama, and excitement. Some came seeking to draw closer to God. Others came out of curiosity, drawn by the advertisement and stories of miracles.

The brotherhood and sisterhood of believers became new home for many. As the subtitle of one of her biographies reads, Aimee Semple McPherson was indeed "everybody's sister."[11] Angelus Temple, which she founded in Los Angeles, soon became a "house of prayer for all nations."[12] It had round-the-clock prayer tower and many services daily.

Perspectives on Christianity and Popular Culture

God created the world, but humans created culture. Scripture makes a distinction between the created world of humans and nature, and the world system that humans have constructed. The world system is considered by many believers to be in opposition to God's purpose and principles because of sin. The church has always had a nuanced and conflicted relationship with the world. Jesus' relationship to the culture was rather nuanced and ambivalent.[13] Christians are supposed to love all the people of the world, but at the same time, not love the world. The Bible teaches Christians to "not love the world or anything in the world."[14]

The era of Sister Aimee's ministry and its impact on the cultural scene coincided with the emergence of modern popular culture in North America. As a result, this chapter looks at her engagement with and impact on the popular culture of her time. As Thomas Bertonneau observes, "The notion of popular culture first emerged in the early modern period, coincident with intensified town- and city-life, the expansion of the market, and the diffusion of literacy."[15] Popular culture has come to connote that which belongs to the people or the masses. It refers to what is liked and shared by the majority of the people or the average person. When used in terms of art and entertainment, it is viewed as different from high and sophisticated art, or different from underground, alternative, or counter-cultural art.

The perception of popular culture, particularly among Christians, as summed by Dick Staub is that it consists of "diversionary entertainment," "mindless amusement," and "soullessness."[16] That it is "celebrity driven," "centered in money," "spread by marketing," and "sustained by technology." Critics as well as fans of popular culture agree that it is a significant force in socialization, teaching values, telling stories, and shaping identity. Some have argued that "popular culture *is* a religion."[17] This school believes "More theology is conveyed in, and probably from one hour of popular television, than from all the sermons that are delivered on any given weekend in America's synagogues, churches, and mosques."[18] "Hollywood," they argue,

> has created a great and very successful religion. Through its successful missionaries—the films produced in Hollywood—it has spread around the globe, gaining adherents faster than any other religion in the world.[19]

That said, the questions remains, how have Christians responded to the power and influence of secular culture? The history of Christianity shows a wide range of varying perspectives on the ideal relationship between the church and the surrounding culture. Different churches, preachers, and denominations have embraced different interpretations and approaches in their attempts to walk the fine balance between being in the world but not of the world, and loving the people of the world but not loving the world.

Richard Niebuhr's treatise on this subject remains the reference point for analyzing the various the diverse positions on Christianity and culture.

In his classic, *Christ and Culture,* he identifies the approaches as (1) Christ against Culture, (2) Christ of Culture, (3) Christ above Culture, (4) Christ and Culture in Paradox, and (5) Christ the Transformer of Culture.[20]

This model synthesizes many doctrinal perspectives and traditions that preceded Niebuhr's work and remain today. Other theologians and authors have built on and/or provided various critiques of that analysis by Charles Kraft, David Hasselgrave, Douglas Ottati, Paul Luis Metzer, and William Dyrness.[21] They examine how theologians, philosophers, preachers, and Christian workers like Tertullian, Thomas Aquinas, Karl Barth, Friedrich Schleiermacher, Martin Luther, John Calvin, Phoebe Palmer, Paul Tillich, Jonathan Edwards, Billy Sunday, Dorothy Day, Frances Day, and Aimee Semple McPherson have responded to this dilemma. Typically, Christians and ministers approach culture in ways consistent with the doctrines of their denominations or faith traditions.

Each view is founded on particular scriptures or interpretations of scripture. The broad outlines include the view that Christ's kingdom is in opposition to culture, and scripture is the sole authority for the believer, as represented by the Christ against Culture typology. Most holiness churches lean in this direction.

The Christ of Culture view sees Christ's dominion as embracing all realms, natural and spiritual, and temporal. Christians in this school see no contradiction between their faith and their culture.

The Christ above Culture view sees neither inherent contradiction nor compatibility between Christ and culture. Instead, the two are viewed as operating on different planes and serving differing purposes. The demands of God's kingdom provide spiritual guidance, while human laws guide human affairs.

The Christ and Culture in Paradox perspective is the view that the demands of God's Kingdom and of society balance and perfect each other. They are dialectical because they serve different goals, yet they are para-doxical, not oppositional.

Christ Transforming Culture is the view that culture is corrupted by sin and needs to be redeemed by Christ. Through conversion, there will be change of nature in the believer, a new culture and, eventually, a new heaven and earth.

A look at Christiandom shows the ascendance of different typologies in different settings and periods. The puritanical era, the temperance move-ment, the holiness movement, the social gospel era, the Jesus movement, the Pentecostal and Charismatic movement, faith and prosperity gospel, and the civil rights and pro-justice movements all highlighted different points on this continuum.[22]

Ethics, Gospel Communication, and Popular Culture

Sister Aimee's personal and spiritual journey from the Methodist Church in Ingersoll, Canada, through the Pentecostal experience, missionary work overseas, and Salvation Army work in New York, all were vital in shaping her perspective on the gospel and popular culture. Her approach to popular culture did not fit neatly into any of the typologies described earlier. Instead, it spanned the spectrum from the Wesleyan Methodist holiness view of Christ against Culture to the Social Gospel, the Christ of Culture, the approach of the Salvation Army, and everything in between. As an evangelist, she worked hard to win souls and to see them transformed by Christ. She took the gospel to the red-light district, took on the Ku Klux Klan, and was a thorn in the side of bootleggers as well as city officials. Yet she did not view popular culture as inherently evil or something to be avoided. In her effort to transform culture, she was counter-cultural as a minister. She preached comfortably in nightclubs just as she did in Angelus Temple. According to Blumhofer, "Sister did not merely insist on lifestyle changes, however, she offered alternatives, many of which were clearly influenced by secular popular culture."[23]

The fact that Aimee's style did not fit neatly into the cookie-cutter box ministry format alienated her from some fellow ministers. When she was opposed and turned away from the pulpit of a Pentecostal Holiness Church in Virginia because "she was not 'straight' on sanctification," she moved her meeting to the open-air.[24] Moving the meeting from inside the church to open air turned out to be a blessing in disguise as it attracted a crowd that would not have been possible to accommodate inside the church.

She often held meetings in civic auditoriums, theaters, and large public arenas. And her meetings were usually larger than any other meetings in such venues, thus making them notable and memorable cultural events whose impact reverberated across the city and nation. "Day after day, newspapers put her on the first page and described the crowds as the greatest ever assembled in the city."[25]

She was ecumenical, not sectarian. "Baptist, Methodist, and Episcopalian ministers shared the platform with Sister and other independent evangelicals and Pentecostals."[26] Aimee said she was not Baptist, Methodist, or Pentecostal, just Christian. And she saw that her gospel was based on the word of God not denominational doctrine. She did not build a wall between the kingdom of God and the kingdom of darkness. Instead, she believed in building a bridge that allowed sinners to cross over to the church. She didn't wait for sinners to come to church; she went to where the sinners were, often to minister to them and to invite them to her meetings.

In 1920, the Pentecostal Assembly of God, Winnipeg, Canada, invited her to conduct a revival meeting. She found that most people in Winnipeg did not attend church. Instead the city was "busy, worldly, pleasure-seeking, and wonderful."[27] Sister Aimee chose to go to the red-light district, pool rooms, and dance halls in order to encounter the people where they lived. Afterward, she went to the nightclub and announced that "she was an army recruiter, . . . recruiting for 'the army of the King of Kings, and the blood stained banner of the cross.'"[28] She visited, hugged, cried, and prayed with the women in the red-light district. By the time her meeting began, the hall was packed as many she had invited from the nightclubs showed up.

This was a promotion and advertising strategy she repeated in New York, Texas, and other areas. Often in such settings, she would have the nightclub band accompany her in singing a gospel song. She viewed popular culture, and communication media in particular, not to be deterministic in relation to culture and the gospel, and others conceive as neutral.[29] Sister Aimee saw that elements of popular culture can be equally effective tools in the hands of God and of Satan. She decried a situation where the devil's army had "the greatest bag of tricks," including "the automobile, the movies, novels of immorality, and decadence. Godless science texts, false prophets. Drinking, dancing, and debauchery among our youth . . . Atheism rampant. Jazz and jitterbug, bobbed hair and painted lips," while "the Gospel of salvation . . . the most stunning dramatic story ever told" is made to appear dull and boring.[30] In her view, "An orchestra isn't *sinful*— it's what we do with the orchestra that makes it a weapon in the devil's army—or the *Lord's!*"[31] She exhorted the church to "throw Christian musicians into the front lines of battle!" she opined.[32]

Sister believed in using the latest media and every medium possible to reach as many people as she could. Being conscious of the fact that the gospel message was competing for attention with other voices in entertainment and popular culture, she made every effort to present the basic gospel of salvation in as colorful and compelling a manner as possible. Early in her ministry, "she delivered that message with considerable skill, using charts and illustrations before she had the resources to invest in the illustrated sermons for which she later became famous."[33] Commenting on the innovative and creative communication approaches used by the evangelist, Tona Hangen observed that Aimee

> Seemed to possess an innate capacity for successful promotion, with no hesitation to use colorful and unorthodox techniques for reaching a broader audience. . . . Her illustrated sermons drew on popular culture

for subject matter and were executed with elaborate costumes rented from Hollywood studios and huge sets with special effects, thanks to the help of her vaudeville-trained stage manager, Thompson Eade.[34]

Sister Aimee was a strong believer in the power of the mass media and was an innovator when it came to adoption of new media technology. "Through Angelus Temple's various outreaches, she would exploit the ongoing revolution in communication for spreading the gospel."[35] Her magazine, *Bridal Call,* was an effective medium for sharing the gospel, announcing upcoming events, and raising support. An editorial note in the magazine said, "We want the *Bridal Call Four Square* to take its place, among the 'biggest sellers' on the news stands all over the country, as the messenger of God's word and gospel."[36]

She employed the whole gamut of media available in her time in the course of her ministry. In 1917 in St. Petersburg, Florida, she got a flat-bed truck, mounted a replica of her meeting tent and an organ on it, and joined an ongoing parade through town. The publicity it generated paid off. In 1920 in San Diego, she scattered leaflets over the city from an airplane. She entered floats in the Pasadena Rose Parade believing that it would help win souls for Christ. In her view, it was one way of "proving to the world that things of the Lord can be every bit as colorful and impressive as those of the devil."[37] The Angelus Temple float won first place prize in the January 1, 1925 parade.

The view that Christian music, art, performance, and media need not be mediocre or of lesser quality than secular productions also informed her productions . Hollywood was fast becoming the movie and entertainment capital of the world. Its impact on culture was undeniable. "Sister's presentations," it was said, "competed successfully against local theater productions. She got ideas for titles, props, staging, and music from the entertainment world around her."[38] She also acquired the best talents in the entertainment industry to work on her elaborate productions. Newspapers reported that "Angelus Temple offered the best show in town."[39] In the growing celebrity culture, Sister's fame and popularity was equal to, if not greater than, any Hollywood celebrity.

Aimee was a pioneer and a leading voice in the emerging new media marketplace. In 1923, she commissioned the first religious broadcast radio station in the United States, the KFSG (*Kall Four Square Gospel*). It was the third radio station licensed in Los Angeles and went on air on February 6, 1924. Those in attendance at the commissioning of the radio station featured many of the city's most important figures, including some from city hall, the Chamber of Commerce, the entertainment industry, and the religious community.

The radio station offered an extensive variety program comparable to commercial radio. Most other religious radio stations in her time could afford only few hours of limited programming while KFSG's programming provided an alternative to secular radio shows. Programs included music, live worship, the Crusaders Rally, the Sunshine Hour, the Bethesda Hour, and the Foursquare Junior. It carried weekly radio dramas like *Useless, the Studio Janitor, The Red Comet,* and *The Adventures of Jim Trask—Lone Evangelist,* among others. She recorded her sermons on discs for national and international broadcasting and distribution.

In her broadcast license renewal application to the Federal Radio Commission, Aimee said the station existed to provide "'educational advantages' to its listeners, with 'world famous speakers [to] bring messages of national, civic, social, educational, and religious interest.'"[40] Church of the Foursquare International was truly a multimedia endeavor evidenced by the range and versatility of Sister's share of voice and footprint on popular culture.

> She published several books of her sermons and stories from her life and in the early forties prepared a screenplay for a feature film about her life, in which she was to star, titled "Clay in the Potter's Hands." She prepared to use the new medium of television, too: shortly before her death in 1944, McPherson received a license to construct an experimental television broadcasting station.[41]

Although she did not have a television ministry, her radio and stage interviews of guests served as a model for modern television hosting and interviewing. Many evangelical and Pentecostal ministers after her were influenced by her visionary, enterprising, and creative use of media and an array of communication strategies in disseminating the gospel and engaging the culture.

It is worth mentioning that Sister Aimee was a pioneer of the emerging industry and art of promotions through modern public relations and advertising, both of which owe their existence and growth to the mass media. She effectively rebranded herself in a way that positioned her to relate comfortably to believers and people of all backgrounds. She was careful to avoid extremes of religious conservatism and liberalism. Hangen noted that Sister's "promotional machine was well oiled. In advance of her speaking engagements, she sent to host organizations stacks of material to use in media promotions."[42] Like a seasoned public relations professional, she courted the mass media, not antagonized them. Even during controversies and media obsession about her disappearance, she was willing to answer any questions journalists asked her. She advertised and promoted her campaigns intensively in the media.

What Would Sister Do?

There are important parallels between the early 20th century and the early 21st century in terms of the challenges and opportunities for gospel communication. Sister Aimee ministered at a time of significant change in the culture and in the church. The turn of the 20th century witnessed population growth, the rise of urban centers, increasing cultural diversity, and a technological revolution. Today's global metropolis provides access to a worldwide audience just as the new cities of the early 1900s enabled ministers, marketers, and the media to reach large segments of the populations. The new media revolution of the 21st century can be viewed as a throwback to the rapid technological changes of the 20th century, only on a larger scale and at a faster rate.

Sister Aimee ministered in the new media marketplace characterized by the proliferation of media outlets and the rise of new channels of mass communication. While some Christians suspected new media technology, radio in particular, as controlled by Satan, prince of the air, and therefore not of God, she saw it as a God-given tool to reach the world with the gospel. In the April 1924 edition of *Bridal Call,* she summoned her followers to "Picture for the moment, the mighty work which lies before that invisible spirit." To her, the radio was a

> Messenger of the gospel of God, speeding to the far lands, encircling the globe in one second! Harbinger of faith, and hope, and salvation traveling on the wings of the winds to one million listeners gathered in the Cathedral of God, which is the earth and all who dwell in it.[43]

As one who dealt with the media, she was not naïve to its potential for both good and evil. However, it was in her nature to see and harness its power for good to advance the kingdom of God. While she sought to convert the Hollywood types from their sinful and empty ways, she readily borrowed from Hollywood talents, themes, and technology she could use for gospel purposes.

How would Sister Aimee engage today's culture? In this age of social and new media, what would she do to promote the gospel? Just as there were many voices seeking to drown out the voice of God in her time, likewise today's media marketplace continues to experience an even greater cacophony of voices. To what extent is the voice of the church being heard in popular culture? If Sister Aimee were ministering today, what would she do to gain visibility in a seemingly chaotic communication environment where fewer and fewer people are paying reasonable attention to anything, not to mention the gospel?

One thing we can tell is that she would not be a spectator in the new media marketplace or be an inconsequential player in it. If through the eyes of radio broadcasting, she saw the whole earth as the "Cathedral of God," how would the world appear to her in the age of the Internet? Definitely she would relish the .com era. To use the words of John Reynolds and Roger Overton reflected in the subtitle of their book, Sister would be "blogging, vlogging, and podcasting for Christ."[44]

Sister chose to be a pacesetter. She defined the landscape of gospel communication rather than let others dictate it. Even as the new media landscape continues to emerge, Christians have to engage with it and define it rather than be defined by it. Many have suggested some of the ways the church can take its place and assert its voice in the YouTube, Facebook, Google church, and wikifaith era.[45]

Hangen notes that through the mass media, Sister Aimee "legitimized the Bible-based evangelical way of thinking" in mainstream culture, and at the same time, "introduced into this insular community aspects of the secular media."[46] In Hangen's view, Aimee "remains a fascinating example of the way religion functions as a form of popular culture entertainment in America and how faithful believers—religion's spokespeople—become transformed through their relationship with media into objects of intense interest ranging from ridicule to reverence."[47]

The church is seeking to find its identity in a changing culture. In a society where the religion of the new generation is popular culture, there is a need for new marketplace theology in how the church can engage today's pop culture. Craig Detweiler and Barry Taylor describe Jesus's method of communicating the gospel as countercultural within the religious tradition of His day. They noted that

> Jesus spent a lot of time in public places, engaging people, hearing their stories, and telling his. He developed his theological approach within the marketplace, telling stories that made God's kingdom relevant to the people he encountered. . . . Pop culture is our marketplace—the arena we visit daily to encounter issues of life and death, to discover what it means to be human, to hear the questions society asks, to meet God. The marketplace can (and must!) inform our theology.[48]

Throughout time, teachers, preachers, merchants, and cultural crusaders have used the latest available communication medium to disseminate their messages. Religion has played an essential pioneering role in the advancement of communication technology. Likewise new media technology has benefitted religion. The dawn of the digital age has been no different. Aimee Semple McPherson, who stood on the edge of the dawn of the electronic communication era, showed herself as an innovator when it came to adopting new media technology and techniques in communicating faith.

Conclusion

Today's entertainment-obsessed, technologically driven, consumer-oriented, highly pluralistic popular culture creates both an opportunity and a challenge to the gospel. The challenges we face today, and the world's attempt to drown out or marginalize the voice of the church, have always been challenges to saints through the centuries. Paul had to find a way to be heard in the Areopagus. Sister Aimee would not let the world's fair take center stage in the emerging popular culture marketplace. Instead, she "competed successfully with Hollywood in the show-business world of Southern California."[49]

New media technology opens new vistas of cultural exchange and engagement for all groups. Religious groups are still in the forefront of adopting and using cutting-edge communicating tools to propagate their causes. The question over time remains which strategies are regarded as religiously sound. Pioneers like Aimee Semple McPherson are always confronted with how to balance religious orthodoxy with contemporary tools and styles, and how to put the old wine of their faith into the new wineskins of communication media. This is always not without controversy. Yet the symbiotic relationship continues to thrive. Innovative approaches and styles always pose threats and opportunities. There will always be a mutual interface between religion and popular culture. As faith communities wrestle with the question of how to "be in the world but not of the world," it is enlightening to see how one person whose legacy has spanned two centuries navigated her new media landscape.

Notes

1. See Edith W. Blumhofer, *Aimee Semple McPherson: Everybody's Sister* (Grand Rapids, MI: William B. Eerdman's Publishing Co., 1993); Daniel Mark Epstein, *Sister Aimee: The Life of Aimee Semple McPherson* (San Diego: A Harvest Book, 1993); Robert Bahr, *Least of All Saints: The Story of Aimee Semple McPherson* (Englewood Cliffs, NJ: Prentice-Hall, Inc., 1979).

2. Blumhofer, *Aimee Semple McPherson: Everybody's Sister,* 99.

3. Ibid., 100.

4. Mark A. Noll, *A History of Christianity in the United States and Canada* (Grand Rapids, MI: William B. Eerdmans Publishing Co., 1992), 180.

5. Ibid., 181.

6. Blumhofer, *Aimee Semple McPherson: Everybody's Sister,* 231.

7. Bahr, *Least of All Saints,* 143.

8. Ibid., 145.

9. Blumhofer, *Aimee Semple McPherson: Everybody's Sister.*

10. Ibid., 141.

11. Ibid.

12. Mark 11:17, *The Holy Bible,* New King James Version (Nashville, TN: Thomas Nelson, 1992).

13. Steve Taylor, *The Out of Bounds Church?* (Grand Rapids: MI: Zondervan, 2005).

14. 1 John 2:15a, *The Holy Bible.*

15. Thomas F. Bertonneau, "A Counter-Curriculum for the Pop Culture Classroom," *Popular Culture and the Academy* 23 (2010): 421.

16. Dick Staub, *The Culturally Savvy Christian* (San Francisco: John Wiley & Sons, Inc., 2007).

17. Ibid., 17.

18. Ibid.

19. Ibid.

20. Richard Niebuhr, *Christ and Culture* (New York: Harper & Row, 1951).

21. See Charles H. Kraft and Marguerite G. Kraft, *Christianity in Culture: A Study in Dynamic Biblical Theologizing in Cross-Cultural Perspective* (Maryknoll, NY: Orbis Books, 2005); David J. Hesselgrave, *Communicating Christ Cross-Culturally,* 2nd ed. (Grand Rapids, MI: Zondervan Publishing House, 1991); William A. Dyrness, *Reformed Theology and Visual Culture: The Protestant Imagination from Calvin to Edwards* (Cambridge: Cambridge University Press, 2004); Douglas F. Ottati, *Reforming Protestantism: Christian Commitment in Today's World* (Louisville, KY: Westminster John Knox Press, 1995); Paul L. Metzer, *The Word of Christ and the World of Culture* (Grand Rapids, MI: William B. Eerdmans Pub. Co., 2003).

22. See Brett McCracken, *Hipster Christianity: When Church and Cool Collide* (Grand Rapids, MI: Baker Books, 2010); Shirley R. Steinberg and Joe L. Kincheloe, eds., *Chritotainment: Selling Jesus through Popular Culture* (Boulder, CO: Westview Press, 2009); Louise Nelstrop and Martyn Percy, eds., *Evaluating Fresh Expressions: Explorations in Emerging Church* (Norwich: Canterbury Press, 2008).

23. Blumhofer, *Aimee Semple McPherson: Everybody's Sister,* 226.

24. Ibid., 126.

25. Ibid., 226.

26. Ibid., 202.

27. Ibid., 149.

28. Ibid., 150.

29. See Geraldine E. Forsberg, "Media Ecology and Theology," *Journal of Communication and Religion* 32 (2009): 135–56; Clifford G. Christians, "Religious Perspectives on Communication Technology," *Journal of Media & Religion* 1, no. 1 (2002): 37–47; Jacques Ellul, *The Technological Society* (New York: Vintage Books, 1967).

30. Bahr, *Least of All Saints,* 146–47.

31. Ibid., 147.

32. Ibid.

33. Blumhofer, *Aimee Semple McPherson: Everybody's Sister,* 203.

34. Tona J. Hangen, *Redeeming the Dial: Radio, Religion, and Popular Culture in America* (Chapel Hill: The University of North Carolina Press, 2002), 62–63.

35. Blumhofer, *Aimee Semple McPherson: Everybody's Sister,* 237.

36. *Bridal Call,* April 1924, 14.

37. Bahr, *Least of All Saints,* 178.

38. Blumhofer, *Aimee Semple McPherson: Everybody's Sister,* 262.

39. Ibid.

40. Hangen, *Redeeming the Dial,* 73.

41. Ibid., 63.

42. Ibid.

43. *Bridal Call,* April 1924, 18.

44. John Mark Reynolds and Roger Overton, eds., *The New Media Frontier: Blogging, Vlogging, and Podcasting for Christ* (Wheaton, IL: Crossway Books, 2008).

45. See Gene E. Veith Jr and Christopher L. Stamper, *Christians in a .Com World: Getting Connected without Being Consumed* (Wheaton, IL: Crossway Books, 2000); Bala A. Musa and Ibrahim M. Ahmadu, "New Media, Wikifaith and Church Brandversation: A Media Ecology Perspective," in *Digital Religion, Social Media and Culture: Perspectives, Practices, and Futures,* ed. Pauline H. Cheong, Peter Fischer-Nielsen, Stefan Gelfgren, and Charles Ess (New York: Peter Lang, 2012), 63–80.

46. Hangen, *Redeeming the Dial,* 78.

47. Ibid.

48. Craig Detweiler and Barry Taylor, *A Matrix of Meanings: Finding God in Pop Culture* (Grand Rapids, MI: Baker Academic, 2003), 27.

49. Bob Lochte, *Christian Radio* (Jefferson, NC: McFarland & Co. Inc. Pub. 2005), 29.

PART II

Self, Identity, and Privacy

CHAPTER EIGHT

The Virtual World and Individual Identity among Young People

Jim Willis

Experts in intercultural communication remind us of the importance that *narratives* and *rituals* play in our lives and in orienting us to our own identities, history, and the norms and expectations of our society. Each society uses rituals and narratives for this purpose, and they combine to form powerful tools to teach us.

I'm thinking of the opening scenes of the Robert Redford film, *A River Runs through It,* where Norman MacLean describes beautifully how he and his brother learned at the feet of their father, a Presbyterian pastor who taught them the value of faith, fluid writing, and fly fishing, in equal measures. Fly fishing is one of many lessons that have been passed down from one generation to the next. In the process, values such as preparedness and patience are learned as well. But what happens to those life lessons as younger generations spend more and more time in the virtual world of the Web rather than the real world of their culture and traditions?

As Norman said in the film, based on the story of his own life:

> We were left to assume, as my younger brother Paul and I did, that all first-class fishermen on the Sea of Galilee were fly fishermen and that John was a *dry* fly fisherman.[1]

Learning the Values

Hours of painstaking practice, on a daily basis, reinforced their father's instructions on these three values which had long been central characteristics of this Montana family of the early 20th century. Norman and Paul learned the lessons well. When I see that film, I can't help but think of the times my own grandfather took me trout fishing, and of the times I took my own two sons to hunt for the big bass on Indiana lakes. Then I think about the much greater amount of time the three of us have spent apart, glued to our laptops, tablets, and smartphones.

Let's face it: you don't get much connection to the family or your own identity from the Internet. You may learn *about* them, but they don't become ingrained in your DNA as Norman's and Paul's lessons did.

Instead, our time spent in the virtual world of the Web provides us with narratives that are snippets or sound bites, constantly interrupted by hyperlinks to related stories to which we happily leap, distracting our attention from the main story or narrative that—frankly—was getting a little too long anyway for our short attention spans.

And instead of the rituals of the family dinner, learning writing or fly fishing from dad, we spend hour after hour vicariously living others' experiences, often with a stand-in avatar for us as we get lost in some online video game or doing armchair traveling around the world.

We already know we have become more splintered as families as everyone heads off to their own laptops to explore their virtual worlds which may not be representative of the corner of the world we inhabit at all. That being so, how do we expect to understand that culture as our parents and grandparents did?

It's not just family members going their own way, but also members of the same culture or society doing the same thing. The younger we start out exploring the world on the Web instead of the real world in front of us, the more time we spend away from the rituals and narratives that teach us about that culture. And, since we learn a lot about our own identity from our culture, we make it harder to discover that identity.

No Mall Directory

Is it surprising that we wake up one day to discover that, like the first-time shopper in a huge shopping mall, we have no idea where we are in relation to the places we want to be or how to get there? There is no mall directory, because there have been no narratives and few real-life rituals to point us to our destinations.

The other day I was watching a television commercial for one of those online services that helps you track your family tree. Something like Ancestry.com. There was this woman who was talking about her great-grandfather as if he were someone from an alien planet whom she knew absolutely nothing about until she paid this online service to discover his identity.

Then I realized, I don't even know who my *own* great-grandfather was. As a child raised on television, I can tell you the name of Tonto's horse, but not the name of my grandfather's dad or mom. Come to think of it, I know next to nothing about my own grandfather on my mother's side. Yes, he divorced my grandmother and wasn't part of the picture when I was growing up, but shouldn't I at least know his name or what he was all about? A telling sign about how we're losing our sense of our own culture? Wouldn't our grandparents chide us for side-stepping the importance of knowing our own family history?

Is our time spent in the virtual world, as opposed to the real one, exacerbating that disconnect from our own culture? At best, it doesn't help.

When I posted these comments in a blog I write called *A Virtual Unknown*,[2] I got a number of interesting responses and observations from readers about their own experiences in identity searching in a virtual world. Among those comments were the following,[3] all from readers were between the ages of 19 and 23 at the time:

- It's a really sad thing to think and reflect on how important technology and this "virtual world" we live in really is. It can consume our time, energy and relationships. I think we need to really be cautious and intentional not to let this day and age of technology take over our lives and our relationships. We learn and grow from being present with someone or with life's circumstances, and with technology as a barrier or distraction, we can't grow and mature in our own identity.
- The online world has helped to make each of us disconnected with reality. Many people will be able to tell us more about the backgrounds of their favorite celebrities before they could talk about their family history. It has become such a problem that people's goals aren't to go to college and make something for themselves anymore. Everyone wants to get famous on YouTube or from their blogs and be instantly immersed into fame and fortune.
- It is so true that today we are often more in touch with our media outlets than we may be with our family or history of our family. As a child I could think of numerous times my parents would discuss a family history story and instead of listening I would be glued to the television set.
- We have disconnected ourselves from reality and we have we have emigrated to the Internet. It is time that we start living our lives and stop caring of what the rest of the people are doing. Family values are disappearing in our society because everyone is doing anything to become popular online. People are posting their lives and secrets online, not knowing that anyone can assess them. As time goes by technology is becoming very important in our daily lives. We feel lost when we don't have our cellphones and computers.
- I have a 7-month-old son and the last thing I want is for him to fall into the trap of media, the Internet, the television, or video games. I want

him to know his culture and his identity and not identify himself with what he sees on a screen. It is scary that the reliance on media and technology is only going to increase and people are going to lose touch with their families and family history. Because of how much this very concept saddens my husband and I are leaving California for Montana to raise our son in (hopefully) an atmosphere that is not as consumed by technology.

- People are becoming more disconnected everyday, and sadly people will not be learning the values and traditions that others learned before the internet came about.

- I, too, have never wondered about any relatives that died before I was born. The time of children sitting around their grandparents listening to stories about the "good old days" is over, replaced by hand-held video games and TV. I'm ashamed that I haven't questioned my grandparents about their childhoods or their parents, because they are the people who shaped my grandparents, who then helped shape my parents, who then helped shape me. I wouldn't be who I am today, no one would, were it not for the indirect influence of their ancestors. It is so sad that people's legacies are dying out because kids are more interested in electronics and technology than spending quality time with family members, listening to stories about their pasts.

- I do actually know a good amount about my family history. However, I usually only hear it in bits and pieces at family gatherings. It is true that the times of sitting with our relatives and listening to them tell stories is in the past. The Internet and television can be so distracting. Although the internet can be helpful for some when trying to learn about their relatives, it is usually just a distraction to those of us who have the ability to sit and talk to ours.

- I think of my life as a child and how I spent it with my parents. My mom and I would bake things together, anything with chocolate really. With my dad and I would go down to the park with my baseball glove and I would insist that he throw endless pop-up balls because they were my favorite to catch. Now when I go home I see my 14-year-old sister glued to the TV, the Internet, her I-pod, or all three at the same time! I always try to get her to go to Caribou with me when I visit and play chess, which we always end up loving. I think now in a world of social media, it is up to the older siblings or parents to suggest fun outing with their children or younger siblings. They just need that extra push and once they are out the door I think most of them would admit they are having more fun then sitting in front of a screen.

- There was so much fun in spending family time together. However, after the video games and online games appeared when growing up, we started spending a lot of time on them and forgot about family time. The technology is too convenient for us to connect each other's, so it makes us become lazy and never spend time together again. The good thing for me is that Taiwanese culture pays respects to a dead person from our family. Therefore, we will have our family picture on our house wall and we go to their grave to clean it and bring the food for them every year. My culture helps me to remember my family and respect them. I am happy about it because I think it is really important to know our own family.

- As someone who is interested in the development of the youth of this next generation, this has been a constant circulating discussion. The warning signs are clear: 1. Today we constantly need a wifi connection. Hotspots are no longer enough for us. We need the assurance that our Facebook profiles, twitter accounts, gmails and other sites are available for us at any time. Addiction? 2. Today we constantly trade one conversation for another . . . we do it all the time when we text in the middle of a conversation or pick up a phone while talking to someone. How is it that we cannot focus on the person who is already investing their own time in this conversation. Addiction? 3. Today we constantly spend time with our friendly technology. How is it that we have come to a point where apps replace live entertainment? Where video games are put in place of actual recreational events? Addiction? And today's youths are beginning to experience the world of technology at much younger ages than ever before.

- The virtual world is where we spend most of our time now. It is sad to know that we do not spend enough time learning about ourselves and where we come from and what our story is. Yet, we know the creator of Facebook and who the latest YouTube stars are. I think that we all must have a balance in our lives between reality and how much time we spend in the virtual world. I was lucky enough to know my great grandparents and their stories. I learned where I came from and how strong we all are as a family and as people. I am lucky enough to have dinner every night with my family. We must remember and know where we come from and what our values are and only then can we grow.

- Unfortunately we spend our daily lives living in a virtual world. Although the Internet is a very useful thing, it has taken away much of that personal bonding time with other people. The cyber world makes our relationships with people different. It also takes away from us learning about ourselves and living our own lives. We identify ourselves by what we post on the Internet and also hide our real selves because of what we post. We do not take the time to be with people, but rather follow them online. Instead of going out and experiencing life, we look at people's pictures and posts about things they are doing or looking at places online wishing we could go there instead of making it happen. I see it as a lazy way of living.

These comments all came from college students, but the identity problem is just as difficult, if not more so, for younger teens as well. In their case, they have even less emotional maturity to discern between the real and the virtual than do their older counterparts.

Tough Growing Up

It's never been easy being a teenager, has it? We all have our own bittersweet memories of those years ourselves, and high on the list of challenges was this nagging question: Who am I? Educators and psychologists call the troubled years "adolescence." Singer Pat Boone once wrote a book simply calling them, "twixt twelve and twenty."[4] Teens and parents alike often just call them frustrating. One of the key reasons is that it's hard to identify who you really are, even as you are seeking out that identity for the first time, in a virtual world. Life is a roller coaster during the teenage years, and sometimes the social media don't help adolescents who are trying to figure out who they are.

After all, actuality and virtuality are not the same thing, and the latest studies show the average teen spends 31 hours per week online.[5] Adding in some additional time for cell phone texting, and you could say the average teen has a full-time job of living and interacting in a virtual world.

That's about 50 percent of an adolescent's waking week spent in a world where they and other teens can say pretty much anything they like on Facebook, Twitter, YouTube, and so forth, without having to worry about any immediate nonverbal reaction from the person they are saying it about. That can release all kinds of inhibitions and bypasses a lot of internal censors normally in place when an individual is interacting with others in a face-to-face setting.

Censors Off

My own years in teaching online college classes have proven that to be true. Students released from their perceptions of how other facial expressions in the room are evaluating them feel a lot freer to jump in and shoot from the lip. That can be great when it comes to student participation in a topical discussion, but it can also turn sour if students don't realize they shouldn't say, online, what they wouldn't say in face-to-face conversations. Words still hurt, whether they stare at you from the computer screen or come in aurally through your ears. Sadly, as all of us who ever wished to un-strike the send key know, talking before thinking is not always such a great thing.

Extreme Results

The recent cases of teen suicide resulting from embarrassing, personal, social media disclosures[6] made about them show the extreme tragic reaction that can occur when that happens. When the embarrassing parts of a teen's identity—imagined or real—are cybercast without permission, humiliation is on the doorstep. Teens, who are just in the midst of forming those identities, are the most vulnerable to these thoughtless disclosures which strike with the full force of barbarians at the gate. When teens are neck-deep in the struggle to figure out who they are, and someone who may not even know them decides to pop something onto Twitter without giving it a second thought, it doesn't help. The kid can't even console himself or herself that it was an innocent mistake made out of love and not a mean spirit.

Fake IDs

Another problem with teen identity that has arisen with the social media is it is easy to fake who you are to others who don't know you well, or who may not know you at all. It doesn't take long for a teen to figure out he or she can present an ideal self (that person who you think you'd like to be) to others in the virtual world. In fact, barring any face-to-face meetings or corrections posted by others who know you are lying, you can actually run with that presumed identity for some time.

This, of course, isn't limited to adolescents. Adults on dating sites engage a lot in this promulgation of ideal selves as opposed to real selves. It would make an interesting study if some researcher decided to study just how much this process occurs. So the Web and its social media can become a kind of escape or netherworld where a teenager can be—for awhile and with some people—who he or she wants to be.

The problem is we can't go for long assuming that both the actual and virtual worlds—and the identities we have created in each—are real.

Cognitive Dissonance

Social scientists and communication scholars study something they call cognitive dissonance,[6] which basically says humans cannot live for long being in dissonance with themselves. We can't go on convincing ourselves that two opposites are both true, or that someone we love and respect is right about a point, yet the point itself is wrong. The only thing that helps us live in dissonance for a time is denial. And denial doesn't do much to help us realize our true identity.

Notes

1. *A River Runs Through It,* directed by Robert Redford (Allied Filmmakers, 1992).

2. Jim Willis, "Fishing for an Identity," A Virtual Unknown blog, October 22, 2011, http://newsok.com/virtualunknwon/2011/10/22/fishing-for-an-identity/.

3. Ibid.

4. Pat Boone, "'Twixt Twelve and Twenty," http://www.youtube.com/watch?v=VoBwauIjUbo.

5. "Your Child in a Digital World," *Cybersentinel*, http://www.cybersentinel.co.uk/your-child/index.aspx.

6. Saul McLeod, "Cognitive Dissonance," *Simply Psychology,* http://www.simplypsychology.org/cognitive-dissonance.html.

CHAPTER NINE

Showing Off Myspace: Examining the Effects of Sociability on Self-Presentation of Myspace Users

Kris D. Boyle and Tom Johnson

Social networking Web sites continue to be one of the more popular destinations on the Internet, particularly among teenagers and young adults.[1] A recent study listed several social networking Web sites in its Top 100 list of most-visited sites, including Facebook (No. 2), Twitter (No. 10), LinkedIn (No. 18), and Myspace (No. 62).[2] With more than two-thirds (67%) of the global online community visiting these sites, they are growing twice as fast as the three more popular major online activities (searches, portals, and PC software).[3] Researchers have offered several reasons why these sites have become popular. In short, individuals use social networking sites to present themselves, to articulate their social networks, and to develop and maintain relationships.[4]

As social networking sites have increased in popularity, so has the attention they have received from researchers, who have chosen to study these sites from a wide range of perspectives, from the role of the sites in society to the nature and characteristics of their users. Of particular interest for researchers has been the way individuals use social networking sites to share information about themselves with others.[5] Other studies have examined the role these sites have played in building and maintaining social relationships.[6]

However, few researchers have examined the relationship between these two elements, which is the focus of this study. This study will employ content analysis to examine the effects sociability has on a user's self-presentation on Myspace, including the amount and type of information users are providing on their Myspace profiles. More specifically, this study examines the extent to which level of sociability, in terms of number of friends and numbers of photos, affects the amount and type of information people are willing to reveal after controlling for motivations for Myspace as well as demographic characteristics. Examining Myspace users' level of sociability will be helpful in better understanding how much information they are willing to reveal about themselves and why.

Because Facebook has emerged as the clear leader among social networking sites, most recent research has focused on that site. However, while the Myspace audience dropped dramatically in 2010, more than 28.6 million still visit it monthly.[7] It continues to maintain a stable membership among younger users, possibly due to its music-based orientation.[8] Also, because it provides more freedom to users in designing the page, it is a more appropriate social networking site to look at than Facebook to examine self-presentation.

Literature Review

Users have several reasons for using personal Web pages. First, it offers an alternative to other communication channels.[9] Individuals will use pages to keep in touch with friends and family, particularly when other forms of communication were not available or were not fulfilling their needs. The Web pages also served as a mode of self-expression for individuals who were comfortable with, and enjoyed, interpersonal communication. At the same time, individuals who were apprehensive with face-to-face communication were less likely to reveal much information about themselves on their Web pages.[10] This would suggest that an individual's ability to socialize with others influences the amount of information they are willing to divulge in an online setting.

Sociability

The Internet has long been viewed as a tool for fostering sociability.[11] In measuring an individual's sociability, researchers have often examined their behavior (i.e., shy vs. outgoing, introverted vs. extroverted).[12] Previous research has shown there are both similarities and differences between users' sociability in online and off-line environments. Specifically, individuals more popular or sociable off-line are more sociable online.[13] At the same time, users who aren't as popular or sociable off-line have used online sites to compensate for a weak off-line social network. They strive to appear more sociable online than they really are, which they feel is important, and they are more willing to reveal things online that they wouldn't tell others off-line.[14]

This may explain why social networking sites are so popular. One of the unique features of these sites is the ability of a user to develop relationships with online friends along with strengthening relationship with those already in their social network.[15] This has led researchers to suggest that social networking sites serve as a bridge between online and off-line connections. Early research argued that the relationship was one-directional, where users established relationships online and then met their new friends face-to-face (off-line). However, more recent work has suggested that the relationship is bidirectional, where the sites are used to create relationships online and to strengthen off-line relationships already established.[16]

Self-Presentation

In his classic work, Goffman defined self-presentation as a process of information management composed of expressions one gives and expressions they give off.[17] The first deals with a more narrow form of communication—words or related symbols—which an individual uses with the express purpose of conveying information in a certain manner. For instance, using certain words to describe oneself in order to plant certain impressions in the minds of others. However, giving off expressions involves a more wide range of action that are more theatrical, contextual, and nonverbal. Others will often use the expressions given off by the individual as the real motivation for providing the information they do.

Goffman suggested it is easier for an individual to control the expressions he or she gives than those he or she gives off. Self-expression then becomes an "information game," where impressions of individuals are formed as a result of the information given or given off.[18]

Web pages are an ideal setting for the information game because individuals can have maximum control over the information they provide on the site.[19] Individuals can use multimedia tools, including audio and video components, in constructing a self-image that can be communicated to a mass audience. Through these pages, users can control the expressions they are giving and giving off, creating an experience that is more satisfying than it would be in an off-line environment. For example, an individual who wants to appear outgoing can include links to pages of friends and photos of gatherings as evidence.[20]

In providing information online, individuals use a wide range of tools including e-mail, hyperlinks, images, animations, color, and font types. For instance, blogging offers individuals an outlet for self-expression.[21] Some researchers have chosen to measure self-presentation through examining how individuals use these tools. Papacharissi measured self-presentation through identifying users' motives for hosting a personal Web page and examining the characteristics of their sites. The latter was measured through dividing the Web pages into different categories, based on the focus of the content (i.e., self-expression, personal interests, family, professional, support, and personal views of host), and counting the number of feedback mechanisms (e-mails, surveys, and guestbooks). Interactivity and vividness of a Web page were also used in measuring self-presentation.[22] The measurements of self-presentation for this study were adopted from the measurements introduced by Papacharissi.

Social Networking Sites

The popularity of social networking sites has grown tremendously in recent years. For instance, in February 2010, 47.1 million active social networking site users visited Myspace, equating for 15 percent of the world's social networking participants.[23] Facebook attracted the largest percentage of global visitors (52%), with 163.2 million users visiting the site in February 2010, more than three times the reach of any other social networking site.[24] Three Web-tracking organizations—Alexa, Complete, and Quantcast—all listed several social networking sites in their lists of top 100 Web sites visited most often by users in the United States.

The backbone of social networking sites are the profiles and lists of users. Profiles are often created when a user signs up for a service and answers questions related to his or her age, location, interest, and background. Like other personal Web pages, the social networking sites allow users to modify their profiles, adding colors, music, photos, and videos.[25]

Myspace Motivations

On Myspace, users can list several reasons for having a page—for friends, for dating, for serious relationships, and for networking. One of the more common reasons was for friendship.[26] Two-thirds of Myspace users said keeping in touch with friends was their motivation for creating their own page.[27] There is evidence that users' motivations were related to the amount of information they posted on their pages. Specifically, those who created a page to keep in touch with friends were more likely to post information about themselves than those who listed a different reason (dating, serious relationships, or networking).[28] This included posting more personal identity items (their interests, their motto, videos and slideshows of themselves, their contact information) and personal interest items (hobbies, favorite books, movies, music, television shows, and heroes). This would make sense because through their page, users can post pictures, blogs, messages, and similar information for the enjoyment of others, while enjoying the same information on their friends' pages.

Sociability and Self-Presentation on Social Networks

As mentioned earlier, researchers have suggested there is a relationship between an individual's off-line and online sociability. Individuals use the Internet—namely social networking sites—to either build upon an already strong social network or to make up for what they may be lacking socially in an off-line environment. Additionally, self-presentation is a large part of these social networking sites. Users of these sites see a certain level of self-presentation and self-disclosure as a requirement of participation. In other words, why have a profile if you aren't willing to say enough about who you are?[29]

The fact that participants use social networking pages for both social and self-presentation purposes would suggest that there could be a relationship between the two. For instance, one of the roles of self-disclosure on social networking sites can be to limit accessibility to the individual by others. Thus, if a user makes it clear in his or her profile that they are in a serious relationship, politically conservative, or that religion is important, this can often weed out those individuals who are not compatible with the user.[30] In other words, the information they provide about themselves can be used in developing their online social network and how sociable they want to be on these sites.

It is worth examining whether this relationship works in the other direction. Specifically, does a user's sociability, including their size of their online network, impact the amount of information they reveal about themselves? Based on previous research, this study aims to more closely examine the effects of sociability on the level of self-presentation by answering the following questions:

RQ1: On average, how sociable are individuals on Myspace in terms of number of friends, number of photos of friends, and number of videos of friends?

RQ2: On average, how much personal information are Myspace users revealing about themselves?

RQ3: What are the most common reasons users provide for having a Myspace page?

Characteristics of Myspace Users

In assessing the impact of social networking sites, researchers have focused a lot of attention on better understanding their user demographics, which can vary from site to site.[31] One study found there were more Asian or Asian Americans on Xanga and Friendster than on Myspace, while Hispanics were more involved with Myspace than other sites.[32] Additionally, females are more likely to use Myspace, but there is little difference between genders on usage of other sites, like Facebook, Friendster, and Xanga.[33] Hargittai warned that researchers need to be careful when generalizing users of one social networking site with users of other sites. However, it is worth noting her findings suggested that the average Myspace user was a white female with some college education.[34]

There are also significant age differences between the user bases of social networking sites. For instance, younger users tend to gravitate toward both Myspace and Facebook, while older users prefer Facebook over Myspace.[35] More than half of the young adult users between the ages of 18 to 30 turn to Myspace, compared to just 36 percent of adult users over 30.[36] There is also evidence that would suggest that is attracting a more mature audience. The percentage of adults using social networking sites has been on the rise, from just 8 percent in 2005 to 27 percent in 2009.[37] Due to evidence in previous research that user demographics and motivations can influence the level of self-presentation on these pages, this study will test the following hypotheses:

H1: The more friends a Myspace user has on their page, the more information they will reveal about themselves after controlling for demographic factors and motivations for going online.

H2: The more pictures Myspace users have of their friends, the more information they will reveal about themselves after controlling for demographic factors and motivations for going online.

H3: The more videos Myspace users have of their friends, the more information they will reveal about themselves after controlling for demographic factors and motivations for going online.

As discussed earlier, social networking sites are most often used to strengthen existing relationship, serving as a link between online and off-line relationships. Within the Myspace context, users can list four reasons for hosting a page: here for friends, here for dating, here for serious relationships, and here for networking. The authors suggest that individuals using their page to keep in contact with friends would be more willing to include information about themselves than those using the page for other reasons.

> H4: Myspace users who list friends as a reason for hosting a page will have more friends and include more personal information on that page than users who list other reasons.

Methods

Data Collection

Researchers coded 502 Myspace personal pages for self-presentation. A random sample of Myspace pages was generated by using the site's browse function, which allows users to conduct both general and specific searches. The more refined searches are conducted by listing specific characteristics one wants to seek out. This study coded individuals by age. The browse function also filters out pages that are not personal homepages such as ones created by bands or organizations.

A comScore study conducted in August 2006 indicated that of the 66,778 unique visitors to pages in that month, 11.9 percent were 11–17, 18.1 percent were 18–24, 16.7 percent were 25–34, 40.6 percent were 35–54, and 11.0 percent were 55 and older.[38] Because the browse function only includes pages of people 18 and older, the researchers collapsed the 11–17 age group with the 18–24 group. The researchers sampled pages in proportion to the different age groups. For instance, for the 18–24 group, 30 percent of the total sample, the researchers coded 150 pages. We then coded an equal number of each age within that group.[39] For each individual age, the browse function provided 3,000 pages to view. We used a random number generator to create a starting point (Myspace page 61) and coded that page. The browse function has an update feature that will provide different 3.000 pages to code and we again coded the page 61. The researchers continued hitting the update button until we had coded the correct number for each age.

Dependent Variables

The self-presentation measures were based on those introduced by Papacharissi in her study of self-presentation on personal homepages.[40] For this study, there were five measures of self-presentation: whether people hid their identity, how many personal identity items they listed, how much personal information about themselves they revealed, as well as number of detail items and personal interests they listed.

First, we measured how many of five personal identity items Myspace users had on their page. Do they have a personal motto? Do they have a details list? Do they list personal interests? Have they created a blog? Do they have a contact box? All of these questions were dichotomous yes or no and were combined into a scale from 0 to 5.

Second, this study measured how much they revealed about themselves. Do they list their interests (i.e., general interests, music, movies, hobbies, television, books, heroes, groups, and other topics)? Do they list their hometown, relationship status, sexual orientation, race, religion, zodiac sign, whether they smoke, whether they drink, whether they want children, as well as their education, their occupation, and income? Scores could range from 0 to 21.

In this study, sociability served as the independent variable. We measured this by accounting for the number of friends listed on the page, the number of friend comments on their page, the number of photos with friends, the number of slideshows with friends, and the number of videos with friends. The number of friends and friend comments were listed on the actual home page, while the number of photos, slideshows, and videos were counted.

Lastly, user demographics and motivations were each treated as control variables. User demographics included gender and age. In terms of motivations, we used the four yes or no motivation questions identified by Myspace: here for friends, dating, serious relationships, and networking.

Data Analysis

Frequencies were first run on all measures. A series of regression analyses were conducted to determine if the level of sociability (number of friends, number of photos, and number of videos) was positively related to the level of self-expression (the number of personal identity items and the number of items they revealed about themselves). User demographics and motivations served as control variables in these analyses.

Results

User Demographics

There were an equal number of male and female Myspace users (52.2% male, 47.8% female). However, they differed in terms of their race and their educational background. Specifically, 61.4 percent were white and 58 percent of those who listed their education had at least some college education. This is different from previous research, which found that only 44 percent of Myspace users were white.[41] Users were almost equally divided in terms of relationship status, with 42.8 percent listing their status as "single" and 47.4 percent listing "married" or "in a relationship" as their status. Of the 83.5 percent who revealed their sexual orientation, 78.7 percent said they were straight and less than 2 percent said they were either bisexual or gay or lesbian. The plurality (45%) did not reveal their occupation or religion. Of those who listed their occupation, 15.9 percent were professionals and 12.2 percent were worker or laborers and 7.8 percent were students. Of those who listed their religion, 26.5 percent said they were Christian and 11.6 percent identified themselves specifically as Catholic.[42] More than 80 percent (80.9%) chose not to reveal their income. Of those who did, respondents were almost equally divided between earning $30,000 or less (4%), 30,000–45,000 (5.2%), and $45,001-$60,000 (3.2%). However, just fewer than 4 percent said they earned $250,000 or more.

These results shared some similarities and some differences with those in previous analyses. Thelwall examined more than 20,000 Myspace member profiles and found that the majority of users were female (54%).[43] There was also a larger gap between the percentage of single users (66%) and those who were married or in a relationship (30%). However, similar to our results, Thelwall found that more users were white, were Christian, and were straight.

Sociability

The first research question explored Myspace users' level of sociability. While there was considerable range in the number of friends people had, most people did not post photos or videos of their friends.

In terms of the number of friends, 39.1 percent had 25 friends or fewer listed on their page, while 29.3 percent had between 26 and 100 friends. Nearly one-third of participants (31.7 percent) had more than 100 friends on their pages. There was a fairly even distribution of friend comments on the users' pages. Just 10.4 percent of users had no comments from their friends on their pages, while 22.1 percent had between 1 and 10 comments. There were 23.5 percent of users who had between 11 and 50 comments left on their page, whereas 12.7 percent had between 51 and 100 comments. Just under one-third of participants (31.3%) had more than 100 friend comments on their wall.

The visual representations of users' friends on their pages were not as frequent as expected. More than half of the users (59%) chose not to have any pictures of their friends on their page, while 27.3 percent had anywhere from one to 10 friend photos on their page. Only 13.8 percent of users posted more than 10 pictures of their friends on their page. Slideshows were used less often, with only 24.5 percent of users posted a slideshow on their pages, and just 16.4 percent had slideshows that featured photos of friends. There were even fewer pages (4.2%) with videos of users and their friends.

Self-Presentation

Research question 2 examined the degree to which people are willing to present information about themselves online. While nearly everyone felt comfortable enough to list certain details about themselves, nearly half of users kept certain information about themselves private.

As mentioned earlier, this study used two measures of self-presentation: the number of personal items on users' pages and how much they are revealing about themselves on their pages. While a solid majority listed a motto (74.7%) had a details list (99.2 %), listed personal interests (79.9%), and had a contact box (99.6%), they were less likely to have created a blog (33.3%).

There were some dramatic differences in the scores measuring how much they would reveal about themselves. Nearly everyone listed their relationship status (99.2%), hometown (97%), and zodiac sign (99.2%). The large majority would also reveal their race (83.3%), sexual orientation (82.5%), whether they plan to have children (79.9%), education (79.9%), and even body type (72.3%). While 79.9 percent listed personal interests, fewer took time to reveal their favorite music (69.1%), movies (60.2%), television shows (59.4%) books (53.0%), or heroes (57.8%). Myspace users were more reticent to list whether they smoke (52.4%) and drink (52.2%), their religion (53%), or their occupation (54.6%). Only a small percentage were willing to list their income (19.1%) or groups they belong to (19%).

The third research question examined what were the most common motivations of Myspace users. In terms of motivations, people said they were motivated to have a Myspace page to stay connected to friends (73.1%), with the second highest score being networking (30.5%). Few people said they used Myspace to seek out dates (14.9%) or serious relationships (10.4%).

Sociability Effects on Self-Presentation

First, a correlation analysis was conducted to better determine how different variables interacted with each other. There was a strong correlation between the number of friends listed on a user's Myspace page and the number of comments left on the page (r = .689, p < 0.01), suggesting that using both measures would result in multicollinearity. Thus, only one of these measures—number of friends—was used as a measure of sociability. There were some additional correlations that, while not strong, are worth mentioning. The number of friends listed on the user's page was significantly correlated with the number of personal identification items on the page (r = .107, p < .05), but negatively correlated with the amount of information the user chose to present about themselves (r = −.164, p < .01). There was also a significant correlation between the number of friend comments and the number of personal identification items (r = .135, p < .01). However, there was not a significant correlation between the number of friend comments and the amount of information an individual revealed about themselves (r = −.081, p > .05). There were no significant correlations between the number of friends and the number of friend photos and videos or between the number of friend comments and friend photos and videos.

A series of regression analyses were conducted using the number of friends, number of friend photos, and number of friend videos as independent variables, while the number of personal identification items and amount of information provided on the page were the dependent variables. Two demographic measures, age and gender, and four motivation measures, here for friends, here for dating, here for serious relationships, here for networking, all served as control variables.

This study hypothesized that the more friends a Myspace user has on his or her page, the more information he or she will reveal about him or her after controlling for demographic factors and motivations for going online. The first model, which included just the number of friends, was a significant predictor of the number of personal items a person would reveal (β = .107, p < .05) and therefore the model was significant (R^2 = .011; R^2adj = .009, $F(7,490)$ = 5.70, p < .05). Number of friends remained a significant predictor after adding in the control variables into the equation (β = .098, p < .05), and the significance of the model was slightly improved (R^2 = .077; R^2adj = .063, $F(7,490)$ = 5.81, p < .01). Gender (β = .096, p < .05), visiting the site for friends (β = .160, p < .01), and here for networking (β = .106, p < .05) were

Table 9.1 Regression analysis (number of friends and sociability)

	Personal Identification Model 1	Personal Identification Model 2	Presentation Model 1	Presentation Model 2
Constant				
Number of friends	.107*	.098*	−.164***	−.156**
Age		−.085		.031
Gender		.096		−.006
Here for friends		.160**		.020
Here for dating		−.036		.082
Here for serious relationships		.043		−.038
Here for networking		.106*		−.078
R^2	.011	.077	.027	.035
ΔR^2	.009	.063	.025	.022
F	5.70*	5.81***	13.77***	2.56*

$* \, p < .05; \quad ** \, p < .01; \quad *** \, p < .001.$

each significant predictors of the number of personal items listed on a page, though the relationship was fairly weak. Specifically, the number of items was higher with female users than male users. Additionally, those listing friends and/or networking as a motivation listed more personal items (see Table 9.1).

Next, regression analyses were conducted using how much users revealed about themselves as a dependent variable. The number of friends was a significant predictor ($R^2 = .027$, R^2adj $= .025$, $F(1,496) = 13.77$, $p < .001$), though the relationship was negative ($\beta = -.167$, $p < .01$). After adding in the control variables into the equation, the second model was also significant ($R^2 = .035$; R^2adj $= .022$, $F(7,490) = 2.56$, $p < .05$). However, the number of friends was the only significant predictor ($\beta = -.156$, $p < .01$). Interestingly, the number of friends was a negative predictor. That is, as the number of friends increased, the amount of information one listed about him or her decreased. Therefore, hypothesis 1 was only partially supported. Number of friends did influence the number of five personal identity items they revealed about themselves (e.g., do they have a details list? Do they list personal interests?), but number of friends were negatively related to how much information they would reveal about themselves (e.g., relationship status, sexual orientation). Also, number of friends only explained a little over 1 percent in the variance in self-presentation (see Table 9.1).

Hypothesis 2 stated the more photos of friends people would post on their Web site, the more they would reveal about themselves. The number of friend photos ($\beta = .097$, $p < .05$) was also a significant predictor of the number of identification items when entered alone ($R^2 = .009$, R^2adj = .007, $F(1,499) = 4.78$, $p < .05$). When including the control variables, the significance of the model increased ($R^2 = .073$; R^2adj = .060, $F(6,493) = 5.58$, $p < .001$), but number of photos dropped out as a predictor of self-presentation . However, two of the motivational items, here for friends ($\beta = .174$, $p < .001$) and here for networking ($\beta = .114$, $p < .05$), were significant predictors of the number of personal items listed on a page.

The number of friend photos was not a significant predictor of the amount of information revealed ($\beta = .027$, $p < $ NS) when it was entered alone in the equation ($R^2 = .001$, R^2adj = $-.001$, $F(1,499) = .373$, $p > .05$). However, none of the control variables were significant predictors either, so the model was still not significant ($R^2 = .013$; R^2adj = $-.001$, $F(7,493) = .953$, $p > .05$).

Hypothesis 2, that number of photos of friends posted would influence how much information people would reveal about themselves was partly supported. Like number of friends in general, number of photos of friends did influence the number of personal identity items people had on their page but not the amount of information they revealed about themselves (see Table 9.2).

Unlike the other two measures, the number of friend videos was not a significant predictor of personal identification items ($R^2 = .001$, R^2adj = $-.001$, $F(1,499) = .305$, $p > .05$) for either the number of personal identity items ($\beta = .025$, $p < $ NS) or the amount of personal information revealed ($\beta = .003$, $p < $ NS) A second model with the control variables was significant ($R^2 = .069$; R^2adj = .055), for the number of personal identity items. Being motivated to use social networking sites for friends ($\beta = .172$, $p < .001$) and for networks ($\beta = .112$, $p < .05$) influenced the number of personal identity items one included. However, no variables significantly predicted how much information a person would reveal so the model was not significant ($R^2 = .013$; R^2adj = $-.001$, $F(6,493) = .910$, $p > .05$).

Table 9.2   Regression analysis (number of friend photos and sociability)

	Personal Identification Model 1	Personal Identification Model 2	Presentation Model 1	Presentation Model 2
Constant				
Number of friend photos	.097*	.080	.027	.029
Age		−.077		.038
Gender		.057		.018
Here for friends		.174***		.006
Here for dating		−.044		.103
Here for serious relationships		.043		−.037
Here for networking		.114*		−.092
R^2	.009	.073	.001	.013
ΔR^2	.007	.060	−.001	−.001
F	4.75*	5.58*	.373	.953

*$p < .05$; ***$p < .001$.

Hypothesis 3, then, was not supported. Number of friends' videos did not predict either measure of personal identification (see Table 9.3).

Hypothesis 4 stated that those motivated to use social networking sites for friendship would have more friends and reveal more about themselves. Using Myspace for friends was a significant predictor of the number of personal identification items ($\beta = .270$, $p < .001$). Using Myspace for networking was a significant predictor of the number of friends ($\beta = .124$, $p < .01$) and the number of personal identification items ($\beta = .100$, $p < .05$). In other words, being motivated to visit social networking sites to make friends and for networking predicted posting personal identity items, but did not influence the amount of information people revealed bout themselves. Therefore, hypothesis 4 was partly supported. Using social networking sites to gratify dating and relationship needs were not related the two personal identity items (see Table 9.4).

Table 9.3 Regression analysis (number of friend videos and sociability)

	Personal Identification Model 1	Personal Identification Model 2	Presentation Model 1	Presentation Model 2
Constant				
Number of friend videos	0.025	0.033	0.003	0.014
Age		−0.084		0.035
Gender		0.079		0.026
Here for friends		0.172***		0.005
Here for dating		−0.046		0.103
Here for serious relationships		0.045		−0.036
Here for networking		0.112*		−0.093
R^2	0.001	0.069	0.000	0.013
ΔR^2	−0.001	0.055	−0.002	−0.001
F	0.360	5.19***	0.005	0.910

*$p < .05$; **$p < .01$; ***$p < .001$.

Table 9.4 Regression analysis (motivations and personal identification)

	Number of Friends Model 1	Personal Identification Model 1
Constant		
Here for friends	.044	.270***
Here for dating	−.078	−.045
Here for serious relationships	.033	.027
Here for networking	.124**	.100*
R^2	.019	.092
ΔR^2	.011	.085
F	2.37	12.59***

* $p < .05$; ** $p < .01$; *** $p < .001$.

Discussion

The explosive growth of social networking sites over the five years has certainly piqued the interest of communication researchers who have examined how individuals use these sites to present themselves online.[44] Other studies have examined how people employ social networks to develop new friendships and to cultivate existing ones.[45] However, few researchers have combined these two areas and examined the degree to which sociability influences how people present themselves online.

Social network replaced e-mail as the preferred way for people to interact with friends they see on a regular basis as well as to keep in touch with geographically distant friends.[46] Users have taken advantage of the interactive elements on Myspace as one study found that users tended to have at least four interactive elements on their set, including photos to click on, videos, blogs, contact box, quizzes, whether they allow others to post messages to the site and whether the individual posts external links to other Myspace sites or to other information.[47]

But just because Myspace provides many venues for allowing interaction with others does not necessarily mean that people will take advantage of them. The current study found a real split in degree of sociability of Myspace users. For instance in terms of number of people users have befriended, the plurality (39.1%) had fewer than 25 friends. On the other hand, about a third (31.7%) boasted more than 100 friends on their page. Perhaps a better measure of how sociable an individual is on Myspace is not the number of friends, but how frequently they maintain contact with these individuals. Again, there was a great divide among Myspace users. While about a third (31.3%) had more than 100 friend comments on their wall, slightly more (32.5%) had 10 comments or fewer. Results from this study lend support to previous studies of sociability. Previous research has shown that individuals who are more sociable off-line are more sociable online.[48] On the other hand, those who are shy in real life may try to compensate by appearing more sociable online than they really are, and revealing information online that they wouldn't tell others off-line.[49] People may present interactive sites where they reveal considerable information about themselves through blogs, photos, and videos and making themselves easily available to others through contact boxes and allowing people to post messages, but have few actual friends to take advantage of these interactive applications.[50]

This study employed three other measures of sociability: the number of photos, videos, and slideshows that feature friends. This study found that more than half of respondents did not have any photos of friends on their pages and more than 8 in 10 had 10 photos or fewer. Creating slideshows and videos and posting them on their page takes more technical expertise than putting up photos, so not surprisingly there were fewer individuals who had created slideshows (16.4%) or videos (4.2%)

Researchers are increasingly exploring how people present themselves through personal Web pages, blogs, and social networking sites because they have nearly complete control over the information they provide on these sites.[51] Myspace, in particular, allows for greater self-expression than its popular cousin Facebook. Myspace allows its users to customize their virtual space with an open format in which design elements, text, video, music, graphics, and photographs can be employed to reflect the users' online personalities and they can therefore construct self-images that can be communicated to a mass audience.[52] Self-disclosure is a critical part of these social networking sites, as why would a person create a profile if he or she isn't willing to say enough about who he or she is?[53]

This study, building on earlier studies by Papacharissi, employed two types of measures of self-presentation: personal identity, which was comprised of five ways individuals could present their self, including whether they had a personal motto, have they created a blog, and do they have a contact box; and personal revelation, which includes 21 measures of how much they reveal about themselves.[54] The results clearly showed that people were trying to control the image they were trying to present.

In terms of personal identity, nearly everyone had a contact box and a details list, and about three-quarters listed a motto and personal interests. However, only a third created a blog, the personal identity item that requires the most self-disclosure.

There were also some dramatic differences in what people would reveal about themselves. Some items were almost universal such as their relationship status, hometown, and zodiac sign. Large majorities would also reveal more personal information, such as sexual orientation, whether they plan to have children, and even body type. Only about half would list behaviors that some might frown upon such as whether they smoke or drink or information such as their religion or education. The only two bits of information that people seemed reticent to discuss was their income or groups they belong to.

The fact that people were willing to reveal so such of themselves on social networking site may be linked to the very nature of these sites that encourages people to open up to others, particularly when most of their contacts are existing friends.[55] However, as previously noted, one reason why people might be so willing to present information about themselves is to discourage some visitors. For instance, users who make clear they are a serious relationship may do so to keep at bay those trolling for dates or those who list their religion or whether they plan to have children may signal what type of people they feel compatible with.[56] Also, Boyle and Johnson speculated one reason why people would be willing to reveal intimate details about themselves is because they hide some basic information such as their actual name, which Qian and Scott characterize as discursive anonymity.[57]

The main focus of this study was to examine the extent to which sociability predicts people's willingness to reveal information about themselves. Results were decidedly mixed. Number of friends and number of friend photos did predict the number of personal identity items, but only number of friends predicted amount of information one was willing to reveal and that relationship was negative. Number of friend videos did not predict self-presentation.

The varying results for the two self-presentation measures may reflect differences in the measures themselves. Personal identity items reflect the number of *structures* people have in place to allow others to interact with the creator (e.g., blog and contact box) and to reveal information about themselves (personal motto, details list, personal interests, and blogs). The second measure examines how much information people wish to reveal about themselves. More sociable individuals were willing to offer mechanisms to interact and present a desired image to others, but they were not necessarily willing to actually reveal more information.

The current results are in line with the findings of Qian and Scott who found that the more a blog was directed toward an audience the user knows off-line, the more the individual is likely to reveal about him or her.[58] However, if the audience includes those who the user doesn't know off-line, the blogger is less likely to share personal information. Someone with a small number of friends has likely limited his or her social network to off-line friends. The more friends that a person has the more likely that list includes people who are mere acquaintances or the person doesn't know off-line and therefore the less likely the person is to reveal about him or her. It should be noted that neither number of friends nor number of friend photos was a particularly strong measure of self-presentation, explaining anywhere from 0.1 percent to 2.7 percent of the variance. Number of friends is a surrogate measure of sociability. Other studies involving surveys have included more direct measures such as shy versus outgoing or introverted versus extroverted.[59]

Past studies do suggest that the reasons people use social networking sites influence how much they are willing to reveal about themselves.

Most people have listed building friendships as their main motivation for going to social sites.[60] There is evidence that creating a page to keep in touch with friends will lead people to reveal more about themselves online more than other motives (such as dating, serious relationships, or networking). The current study partly supports these results. Like results for number of friends, being motivated to create a social networking profile to build and maintain friendships did predict putting structures in place to encourage interaction and to allow people to express personal information if they wish. However, motivations did not actually influence the degree people revealed information about themselves. Results for dating and serious relationships were in line with previous studies that said that people using online data sets are careful to manage their image and will strive to highlight their positive attributes and qualities, although they must also be careful not to present a dishonest image of themselves because they may meet the person off-line.[61]

Limitations and Future Studies

This study examined how sociability influenced how much information people revealed about themselves on Myspace. Myspace was chosen over Facebook, in part, because it allows the creator to better personalize their page to present the image they would like to project. However, because different social networks attract different kinds of users who may visit them for different purposes,[62] results for this study cannot be generalized beyond Myspace. Another limitation is that this study relied on a content analysis of Myspace, not a survey of its users. Therefore, it could not explore more behavioral-based measures of sociability including how shy and introverted a person is. Myspace does ask its users what motivates people to use the site, but actual motivations may be more complex. Finally, this study discovered what people chose to reveal about themselves, but could not address why they chose to reveal certain facts and keep others to themselves.

Future studies should expand the number of sites it examines to determine whether people are more willing to reveal information about themselves on different types of sites. For instance, one would assume that people would be more likely to reveal information about themselves on Facebook, which more than Myspace focuses on connecting people with other people. On the other hand, LinkedIn is a professional site where people network with each other, so people are more likely to craft an image that presents themselves as businesslike and professional.

Future studies also should survey users of Myspace to more clearly discover what motivates them to use that site and why they choose to post certain information about themselves and withhold other information.

Acknowledgment

Portions of this chapter have been adapted from Kris Boyle and Thomas Johnson, "MySpace is Your Space? Examining Self-presentation of MySpace." *Computers in Human Behavior,* 26, (2010): 1392–99.

Notes

1. Joanna Brenner and Aaron Smith, "72% of Online Adults Are Social Networking Site Users," Pew Internet & the American Life Project, http://www.pewinternet.org/Reports/2013/social-networking-sites/Findings.aspx.

2. "Alexia," http://www.alexa.com/topsites.

3. "Global Faces and Network Places: A Nielsen Report on Social Networking's New Global Footprint," Nielsen Online.

4. Kris Boyle and Thomas Johnson, "Getting to Know MySpace: The Effects of Self-Esteem and Self-Presentation on MySpace Profiles of Older Users" (paper presented at the annual AEJMC Midwinter meeting, Norman, Oklahoma, March 2011); Kris Boyle and Thomas Johnson, "MySpace Is Your Space? Examining Self-Presentation of MySpace," *Computers in Human Behavior* 26 (2010): 1392–99; Danah M. Boyd and Nichole B. Ellison, "Social Network Sites: Definition, History, and Scholarship," *Journal of Computer-Mediated Communication* 13, no. 1 (2007): article 11; Nichole B. Ellison, Charles Steinfield, and Cliff Lampe, "The Benefits of Facebook "Friends." Social Capital and College Students' Use of Online Social Networks," *Journal of Computer-Mediated Research* 12, no. 4 (2007): article 1; Eszter Hargittai, "Whose Space? Differences among Users and Non-Users of Social Network Sites," *Journal of Computer-Mediated Communication* 13, no. 1 (2007): article 12; Lisa A. Stern and Kim Taylor, "Social Networking on Facebook," *Journal of the Communication, Speech & Theatre Association of North Dakota* 20 (2007): 9–20.

5. Boyle and Johnson, "MySpace Is Your Space"; Ellison, Steinfield, and Lampe, "The Benefits of Facebook Friends"; Rob Nyland, Raquel Marvez, and Jason Beck, "MySpace: Social Networking or Social Isolation?" (paper presented at the AEJMC Midwinter Conference, Reno, Nevada, February 2007); Stern and Taylor, "Social Networking on Facebook."

6. Boyle and Johnson, "Getting to Know MySpace"; Boyle and Johnson, "MySpace Is Your space"; Jolene Zywica and James Danowski, "The Faces of Facebookers: Investigating Social Enhancement and Social Compensation Hypotheses; Predicting Facebook and Offline Popularity from Sociability and Self-Esteem, and Mapping the Meanings of Popularity with Semantic Networks,"

Journal of Computer-Mediated Communication 14 (2008): 1–34; Catherine Dwyer, Starr R. Hiltz, and Katia Passerini, "Trust and Privacy Concern within Social Networking Sites: A Comparison of Facebook and MySpace" (paper presented at the Thirteenth Americans Conference on Information Systems, Keystone, Colorado, August 9–12, 2007); Boyd and Ellison, "Social Network Sites"; Ellison, Steinfield, and Lampe, "The Benefits of Facebook Friends"; Hargittai, "Whose Space?"

7. Quantcast, "Syndicated Online Traffic Measurement Service," http://www.quantcast.com/myspace.com.

8. David Wilkinson and Mike Thelwall, "Social Network Site Changes over Time: The Case of MySpace," *Journal of the American Society for Information Science and Technology* 61 (2010): 2311–23.

9. Zizi Papacharissi, "The Self-Online: The Utility of Personal Home Pages," *Journal of Broadcasting and Electronic Media* 46, no. 3 (2002): 346–68.

10. Ibid.

11. Zywica and Danowski, "The Faces of Facebookers"; Norman H. Nie, Sunshine Hillygus, and Lutz Erbring, "Internet Use, Interpersonal Relations, and Sociability: A Time Diary Study," in *The Internet in Everyday Life*, ed. Barry Wellman and Caroline Haythornthwaite (New York: Blackwell), 216; John P. Robinson, Meyer Kestnbaum, Alan Neustadtl, and Anthony Alvarez, "Mass Media Use and Social Life among Internet Users," *Social Science Computer Review* 18, no. 4 (2000): 490–501. Paul DiMaggio, Eszter Hargittai, W. Russell Neuman, and John P. Robinson, "Social Implications of the Internet," *Annual Review of Sociology* 27 (2001): 307–36; David Zakin, "Physical Attractiveness, Sociability, Athletic Ability, and Children's Preference for Their Peers," *Journal of Psychology* 115 (1983): 117–22.

12. Zywica and Danowski, "The Faces of Facebookers"; Zakin, "Physical Attractiveness."

13. Zywica and Danowski, "The Faces of Facebookers."

14. Ibid.

15. Boyd and Ellison, "Social Network Sites"; Ellison, Steinfield, and Lampe, "The Benefits of Facebook Friends"; Hargittai, "Whose Space?"

16. Ellison, Steinfield, and Lampe, "The Benefits of Facebook Friends."

17. Erving Goffman, *The Presentation of Self in Everyday Life* (Garden City, NY: Doubleday).

18. Ibid.

19. Zizi Papacharissi, "The Presentation of Self in Virtual Life: Characteristics of Personal Home Pages," *Journalism & Mass Communication Quarterly* 79 (2002): 643–60.

20. Ibid.

21. Boyd and Ellison, "Social Network Sites"; Papacharissi, "The Presentation of Self in Virtual Life."

22. Papacharissi, "The Presentation of Self in Virtual Life"; Papacharissi, "The Self-Online."

23. "Global Audience Spends Two Hours More a Month on Social Networks Than Last Year," Nielsen Wire, http://blog.nielsen.com/nielsenwire/global/global-audience-spends-two-hours-more-a-month-on-social-networks-than-last-year/.

24. Ibid.

25. Boyd and Ellison, "Social Network Sites."

26. Boyle and Johnson, "MySpace Is Your Space"; Stern and Taylor, "Social Networking on Facebook"; Papacharissi, "The Self-Online."

27. Boyle and Johnson, "MySpace Is Your Space."

28. Ibid.

29. Zeynep Tufekci, "Can You See Me Now? Audience and Disclosure Regulation in Online Social Network Sites," *Bulletin of Science Technology Society* 28 (2008): 21–37.

30. Tufekci,"Can You See Me Now?"; Leysia Palen and Paul Dourish. "Unpacking 'Privacy' for a Networked World" (paper presented at the proceedings of the SIGCHI conference on the Human Factors in Computing Systems, Ft. Lauderdale, Florida, April 5–10, 2003).

31. Hargittai, "Whose Space?"

32. Ibid.

33. Ibid.

34. Mike Thelwall, "Social Networks, Gender and Friending: An Analysis of MySpace Member Profiles," *Journal of American Society for Information Science and Technology* 59, no. 1 (2008): 1321–30; Hargittai, "Whose Space?"

35. Amanda Lenhart, Kristen Purcell, Aaron Smith, and Kathryn Zickuhr, "Social Media and Young Adults," Pew Internet & American Life Project, http://www.pewinternet.org/Reports/2010/Social-Media-and-Young-Adults/Part-3/1-Teens-and-online-social-networks.aspx.

36. Ibid.

37. Ibid.

38. comScore. "Social Networking Goes Global," http://www.comscore.com/press/release.asp?press = 1555.

39. If the number of age categories did not divide equally into the number of sampled within that group, we coded an additional page starting with the youngest in that age group.

40. Papacharissi, "The Presentation of Self in Virtual Life"; Papacharissi, "The Self-Online."

41. The authors used the categories created by MySpace. So, for instance, while Catholics and Protestants are Christian, MySpace created three separate categories.

42. Hargittai, "Whose Space?"

43. Thelwall, "Social Networks."

44. "Global Faces and Network Places." Boyle and Johnson, "MySpace Is Your Space"; Boyd and Ellison, "Social Network Sites"; Ellison, Steinfield, and Lampe, "The Benefits of Facebook Friends"; Hargittai, "Whose Space?"; Stern and Taylor, "Social Networking on Facebook."

45. Zywica and Danowski, "The Faces of Facebookers"; Dwyer, Hiltz, and Passerini, "Trust and Privacy"; Boyd and Ellison, "Social Network Sites"; Ellison, Steinfield, and Lampe, "The Benefits of Facebook Friends"; Hargittai, "Whose Space?"

46. "Global Faces and Network Places"; Stern and Taylor, "Social Networking on Facebook."

47. Boyle and Johnson, "MySpace Is Your Space."

48. Zywica and Danowski, "The Faces of Facebookers."

49. Ibid.

50. Boyle and Johnson, "MySpace Is Your Space."

51. Papacharissi, "The Presentation of Self in Virtual Life"; Papacharissi, "The Self-Online." Hua Qian and Craig R. Scott. "Anonymity and Self-Disclosure on Weblogs," *Journal of Computer-Mediated Communication* 12, no. 4 (2007): article 14. Kaye D. Trammell and Ana Keshelashvili, "Examining the New Influencers: A Self-Presentation Study of A-List Blogs," *Journalism & Mass Communication Quarterly* 82 (2005): 968–82; Boyle and Johnson, "MySpace Is Your Space." Tufekci, "Can You See Me Now?"

52. Carolyn M. Kane, "I'll See You on MySpace: Self-Presentation in a Social Network Website" (MA thesis, Cleveland State University, 2008).

53. Tufekci, "Can You See Me Now?"

54. Papacharissi, "The Presentation of Self in Virtual life"; Papacharissi, "The Self-Online."

55. Tufekci, "Can You See Me Now?"

56. Ibid.

57. Boyle and Johnson, "MySpace Is Your Space"; Qian and Scott, "Anonymity."

58. Qian and Scott, "Anonymity."

59. Zywica and Danowski, "The Faces of Facebookers"; Zakin, "Physical Attractiveness."

60. Boyle and Johnson, "MySpace Is Your Space"; Stern and Taylor, "Social Networking on Facebook"; Papacharissi, "The Self-Online."

61. Monica T. Whitty, "Revealing the 'Real' Me, Searching for the 'Actual' You: Presentations of Self on an Internet Dating Site," *Computers in Human Behavior* 24 (2007): 1707–23; Ellison, Steinfield, and Lampe, "The Benefits of Facebook Friends."

62. Hargittai, "Whose Space?"

CHAPTER TEN

Is Jar Jar Racist? Digital Media, Content, and Style Ethics of Spectacle Cinema

Tim Posada

Introduction

A more conservative film critic would perceive *300* (2007)—an over-stylized, comic book adaptation of the classic tale of 300 Spartans battling the Persian army—as somewhat problematic—a film that "feeds vampirically on the past," as John Storey calls products of postmodern culture that sensationalize history for the sake of the present moment.[1] When the story is but a cipher for visual spectacle, what use is there in such skin-deep fair? Special effects erode story, so the clichéd retort goes. Turn-of-the-20th-century filmmaker Georges Méliès believed visuals must be constructed in such a way that the audience can clearly distinguish between trickery and realism; special effects must highlight "the skills of an illusionist or a character's dreams or hallucinations," not replace realism.[2] For Méliès, film was a dangerous tool that could distort reality or create vulgarity through techniques like *intrusive* close ups. James Flint summarizes: "[Méliès] felt film should maintain the 'moral' conventions and framing of the theatre, as these allowed viewers to put what they were seeing in context and thereby dispel any of the real magic that might be lurking behind the heady new spectacle of cinema."[3] More than 70 years after his death, the magician-turned-filmmaker would be disturbed by cinema's current state, for as Lev Manovich points out, the image is no longer authentic as it becomes the primer material for a digital painting:

> [A]lthough we normally think that synthetic photographs produced with computer graphics are inferior to real photographs, in fact, they are *too perfect*. But beyond that we can also say that, paradoxically, they are also *too real*.
>
> The synthetic image is free of the limitations of both human and camera vision. It can have unlimited resolution and an unlimited level of detail.[4]

We have entered a mediatized environment where Photoshop and various visual effects programs displace the realism of the moving and still image. In effects-driven work, the grainiest elements of the film are the live pieces, while the graphics are often completely clear—too clear as Manovich claims. As a form of spectacle, Andrew Darley claims such effects example *impossible photography*—what happens when "'photography' is cut loose, uncoupled from its physical ties to phenomenal reality."[5] What Manovich and Darley note speaks directly to *300*, and a Méliès-esque lens sees this film as irresponsible due to its confused core: heavy metal music in a period piece, overly chiseled men, hyper-sexualized foreign cultures, fight sequences in slow motion, and many other exaggerated elements. Historical accuracy matters far less than (vampiric) exploitation. To borrow the warning from science fiction (SF) film *eXistenZ* (1999), the more dependent we become on virtual reality for entertainment purposes, the more problematic distinguishing between the virtual and real is.

Alas, such simplifications are unsatisfying and far too dismissive, especially considering the lack of empirical evidence to support these end-of-reality claims. Solely on the level of content, support might exist in favor of complaints about spectacle cinema's *stupidity* and *excess*. Yet what most critics ignore are these films' stylistic choices—that bit of excess spectacle cinema is most known for. What if style is content? For Susan Sontag, the moment we enter content, we have already found style.[6] In the case of *300*—one of the top grossing R-rated films which set a new standard for the use of green-screen film[7]—it arguably functions like an epic poem where style matters most. Exaggeration and sensation set the dramatic tone. Excess does not hinder the story but creates it—an idea lost on the Frankfurt School criticism against *the culture industry*. For Theodore Adorno and Max Horkheimer, the culture industry describes the proposed ideological construct to explain mass culture's complete control over the public.[8] It entails the duping power popular culture maintains over the viewing public. But the work of newer theorists, such as Stuart

Hall, Michel de Certeau, Dick Hebdige, John Fiske, and Henry Jenkins, view subcultures, fan communities, audiences, and various communities as far more active. Through various case studies and new theoretical constructs, the public finds various ways to resist, negotiate, and completely reappropriate dominating ideologies. If these ideas, which have been forming over the past 40 years, hold any merit, then completely dismissing *dumb* films seems too in line with Adorno and Horkheimer to hold worth. I am not proposing that duping entertainment does not exist, merely that when the masses flock, groupthink is not insured to follow, hence a blockbuster film should not be discarded so easily.

However, any discussion of special effects must also acknowledge that the spectacle of new technology can also create a blinding spell, through digital means, that allows key elements, like racial irresponsibility to continue. Digital characters like Jar Jar Binks in *Star Wars: Episode I— The Phantom Menace* (1999) and the Twins in *Transformers: Revenge of the Fallen* (2009) recreate classic Hollywood racial stereotypes, but their digital depictions mask their aura. Each film provides important reminders that as new media transform the cinematic landscape, the dangers of Hollywood's greatest sin—the misrepresentation of non-whites—lingers behind each pixel. The use of special effects, far from an inherent evil of film, can easily produce racially disturbing imagery, just as easily as the magnificent spectacles praised in films like *Metropolis* (1927), *2001: A Space Odyssey* (1968), *Star Wars* (1977), and *Titanic* (1997).

This analysis of the spectacle of special effects in cinema is rooted in aesthetic ethics and representation ethics—two often disconnected disciplinary approaches that find a bridge through new media. I contend that as we move into the futurism of filmic graphics, we must not forget the semiotic emphasis on symbolic identity even with the most advanced software, constructing narrative worlds and identities still relies on the process of signification found in its human creators—a process only possible through lived experience. However, current models of film interpretation ignore the pleasure found spectacle cinema, reducing it to content— turning it an easy target—rather than engaging the idea that visual pleasure and emotional appeal is a worthy endeavor.

A Brief History of Spectacle Criticism

Cinematic spectacle has several key climaxes: the trick films of Georges Méliès; epic battle sequences in *The Birth of a Nation* (1915); miniatures in the futuristic cityscape of *Metropolis*; the use of stop-motion in *King*

Kong (1933); paintings as backgrounds in *The Wizard of Oz* (1939); the classic parting of the sea effect in *The Ten Commandments* (1956); the use of front projectors in place of painted backgrounds in *2001*; spaceship models in *Star Wars*; extensive computer animation in *Tron* (1982); the CGI (computer-generated imagery) water tentacle in *The Abyss* (1989) that paved the way for the liquid metal villain in *Terminator 2: Judgment Day* (1991); believable prosthetics in *Jurassic Park* (1993); dubbing news footage in *Forrest Gump* (1994); the first full-scale use of animated CGI in *Toy Story* (1995); use of CGI and scale modeling for a non-SF/fantasy epic that would become one of the most successful films of all time, *Titanic*; stylized uses of slow motion in *The Matrix* (1999); motion capture for Gollum in *The Lord of the Rings: The Two Towers* (2002); and James Cameron's specially developed three-dimensional filming equipment for *Avatar* (2009), the worldwide top grossing film to date.[9] While these films moved film technology forward, many of them received special attention for their content. *The Birth of a Nation* caused various protests due to the negative depiction of a white actor in blackface with an affinity for raping white (implicitly pure) women. Furthermore, the saviors of the film are clansmen. *King Kong* is often perceived as a story about the noble savage, merely replacing tribes people with an enormous ape. Accusations of excessive violence overshadow *Terminator 2*, *Jurassic Park*, and *The Matrix*. Susan Sontag even referred to *2001* as "fascist art" that "scorns realism in the name of 'idealism.'"[10] And as for *Avatar*, many critics share the view of *Los Angeles Times* columnist, David Brookes: "[O]f all the directors who have used versions of the White Messiah formula over the years, no one has done so with as much exuberance as James Cameron in 'Avatar,'" concluding, "[i]t rests on the stereotype that white people are rationalist and technocratic while colonial victims are spiritual and athletic. It rests on the assumption that nonwhites need the White Messiah to lead their crusades."[11] Few discussions of films' technological achievements exist separate from criticism of their creators' limitations, but criticism of spectacle cinema goes far beyond the film industry, as many theorists use the concept of spectacle to declare the complete unhinging of society.

Magic shows, advertising, politics, jazz music, the evening news, and the Sunday matinee all serve as key examples of the spectacle. The spectacle theories of Guy Debord, Neil Postman, Mitchell Stephens, Kalle Lasn, Henry Jenkins, and others move from ideological domination to active participation. Perceptions of special effects draw much from Plato's warning against the arts in general. Much like an Aristotelian analysis of *pathos*—the effectiveness (and deceptiveness) of emotion in persuasion—art exists outside of logic, and this form of pleasure is too divorced from sound reasoning.[12] This clearly sets the stage for modern interpretations of entertainment found in the works of early-to-mid-century Marxists and conservative media theorists. Debord's *Society of the Spectacle* remains the most significant analysis of the spectacle, which he defines as a far-reaching construct that speaks to the way public space (broadly defined) functions. As a Marxist, Debord deems life a commodity—drawing on Marx's "commodity fetishism"[13]—of which the commodity comes to visual fruition in the spectacle, an ideology that "feels at home nowhere because [it] is everywhere."[14] The world is understood through mass-media narratives rather than community stories. While the "spectacle" is visual, Debord makes clear that images are not the spectacle but "mediate" it.[15] As a representation, the spectacle is always what is fake, masquerading as the real, thus we remain fooled by what we think is real.[16] Cinematic spectacle, then, is an affront to the real. Through less hyperbolic language, Neil Postman's classic text, *Amusing Ourselves to Death*, presents a pessimistic vision of contemporary media, claiming we have moved past a text-based society (oral based before that) and into an entertainment one.[17] Postman transforms Marshall McLuhan's "medium is the message" into the "medium is the metaphor," claiming the medium itself limits the type of information that can be transported across its platform.[18] Newer voices such as Mitchell Stephens avoid terms like entertainment society, instead favoring the idea of an image society, which is seen more as a new mode of knowledge gathering rather than a dystopian cry for help. Simply put: "the image is replacing the word as the predominant means of mental transport."[19]

Within popular media, *Adbusters* magazine editor Kalle Lasn, one of the primary advocates behind the recent Occupy protests, provides the most accessible example of spectacle critique in *Culture Jam*. While the book mostly focuses on strategies to use media technology when resisting the dominant discourse presented in mass media, Lasn begins with a list of the "threats" to "the ecology of the mind": noise, jolts, shock, hype, unreality, erosion of empathy, information overload, infotoxins, and a loss of infodiversity. Jolts, in particular, speak directly to many of the changing elements in film editing.[20] For example, a major criticism of *Transformers: Revenge of the Fallen* (*Transformers 2*) can be summed up in Peter Travers's film review: "No one can top [director Michael Bay] for telling a story with such striking, shrieking incoherence."[21] According to Lasn, the goal is to create "the maximum number of jolts per minute."[22] A terrible by-product of contemporary media, then, is the erosion of thought—the fulfillment of Aldous Huxley's prophetic society in *A Brave New World* with spectacle cinema as the soma. Travers agrees, at least in the case of *Transformers 2*, when he calls the film "fast food." Opposing Lasn, Steven Johnson claims younger generations—those who have embraced Lasn's *jolt* culture—are actually smarter than the youth of past generations. Stories have become more complex, forcing audiences to track more information. Television series like *24* and *Lost* are cognitively more beneficial than procedural dramas like *Magnum, P.I.* or *The A-Team* (or recent shows like *Law & Order* and *CSI*), which are too formulaic to provide much critical engagement.[23] Using terminology from John Fiske's *Television Culture*, *24* and *Lost* provide a *multiplicity of access points* while *Law & Order* and *CSI* are *closed narratives*.[24] Lasn's analysis lacks historical examination and, quite frankly, functions more on unproven generalizations. Opera was once popular culture, fiction books were deemed cultural fodder, and now new media are *eroding* our cognitive abilities through mobile technology and spectacles that distract us: new media criticism must do more historical analysis lest it resort to hyperbole.

For Scott Bukatman and Henry Jenkins, audiences are not under the spectacle's spell; they voluntarily suspend logic for the sake of narrative. In an analysis of magic shows, Bukatman discusses how audiences engaged with stage illusions: "The spectacle was a simulacrum of reality, but spectators were not duped by these illusions—by paying admission the customer indicated at least some understanding of the rules of the game. Some pleasure, however, clearly derived from responding to these entertainments as if they were real."[25] Bukatman further addresses the idea of destabilization: "If [SF films] destabilize us, then it should be acknowledged that we welcome the effect. We are moved away from the mundane, away from the ordinary—in some sense, we are moved away from the narrative and into the pleasures of the spectacle."[26] Similarly, Jenkins addresses how exploitation films—low-budget films featuring titillation in the form of special effects, sex, and violence—were not and should not be condemned merely because of their blatant perversions; viewers actually maintain a critical distance due to the absurdity of such offensive content.[27] For Jenkins, the issue is less about content than when it becomes so "formulaic that it no longer provokes an emotional reaction."[28] Rather than emotional responses stunting critical cognition, it is pivotal to insuring an active viewing experience.

Speaking to the emotional impact of the spectacle, fantasy author J.R.R. Tolkien refers to the process of "sub-creation."[29] When he authored *The Hobbit* and *The Lord of the Rings* series, he created an archive of supplemental material to construct his fantasy world: maps, legends, languages, folk songs, and customs of various species. Sub-creation is the world-making process found in religion, mythology, and any detailed narrative that invites the reader into its narrative borders. Tolkien's fictional works stem

from excess—the fantasy genre has often been critiqued for constructing fictional worlds that play into unhealthy fantasies. If psychoanalysis
is correct and we do choose something like the consumption of stories
to substitute for a lack in our lives, then fantasy stories are a prime location for fictional worlds that can make any reader envious and wish to be
spirited away, never to return to reality. Of course, such a generalization
misses out on the process at work. In a cultural history of magic shows,
Simon During places special emphasis on suspension of disbelief, rather
than considering it a process of unhealthy escape, for its ability to guide
audience members through an active engagement with the narrative in a
process called "systematic disavowal." This process acknowledges both
magic and logic, enabling entrance into either sphere without abandoning
predetermined beliefs.[30] Karl Bell finds "systematic disavowal" trite, but
cedes that During's explanation still effectively enables people to maintain
a "sense of enchantment and mystique."[31] What Tolkien and this latter
criticism note is the pleasure found in the spectacle—an aesthetic delight
divorced of context to an extent for the sake of narrative immersion.

Constructing Spectacle Ethics

Considering the history of the spectacle, CGI presents new challenges
for storytelling. For example, the continual one-upping of cinematic special effects often seems to favor forgiveness of a few noticeable imper-
fections rather than complete film cohesion. The Incredible Hulk's three
cinematic appearances—*Hulk* (2003), *The Incredible Hulk* (2008), and
The Avengers (2012)—straddle this peculiar position between believable
and cartoony, and with the advent of even higher definition televisions,
once top-of-the-line graphics are quickly becoming obsolete. So perhaps
filmmakers should just return to a cinema divorced from such technological distractions. In 1995, Dogme 95, led by avant-garde filmmaker
Lars Von Trier, attempted to do just that by creating a 10-point manifesto
of filmmaking techniques, such as on-location shooting, natural sound
with no added scoring, handheld camera work, and color film with no
added lighting. Proving rather difficult, many of the directors, including
von Trier, often broke these rules, and by 2002 it had become more of a
proposal than a movement. *Discretion replaced revolution.*

Dogme 95 created an aesthetic ethics that proved rather unreachable,
yet there is something to be learned from weariness toward using technology at the expense of narrativity. With this warning in mind, I examine
two seemingly disconnected aspects of spectacle cinema and apply ethical approaches: the racialization of digital characters and the excessive

use of visual effects *in place* of story. I argue, first, that no use of CGI exists divorced from cultural signification, and then, that spectacle and excess are not inherent evils. I use close-text analysis of digital content and style—something often absent in most discussions of the spectacle— to determine what spectacle cinema could mean for various moviegoing audiences who often consider films mere escapism.

Racializing the Ghost in the Machine

For Larry Gross, the first step in creating an ethics of representation in film and television begins by allowing various groups to represent them- selves.[32] *But what happens when that representation is completely alien, robot, or digitized?* In 1970, roboticist Masahiro Mori proposed the idea of the uncanny valley to address the growing dilemma present when creating robots. She constructed a graph that examined how robots were per- ceived based on their visual closeness to human attributes.[33] Perhaps the best description of the uncanny valley occurs in television series *30 Rock*, when Frank (played by Judah Friedlander) explains the concept to Tracy (played by Tracy Morgan):

> **Frank:**   As artificial representations of humans become more and more realistic they reach a point where they stop being endearing, and become creepy.
> **Tracy:**   Tell it to me in *Star Wars*.
> **Frank:**   Alright. We like R2D2 and C3PO.
> **Tracy:**   They're nice.
> **Frank:**   And up here (pointing to the top of the uncanny valley graph) we have a real person like Han Solo.
> **Tracy:**   He acts like he doesn't care, but he does.
> **Frank:**   But down here (pointing to the bottom of the valley), we have a CGI Storm Trooper or Tom Hanks in *The Polar Express*.
> **Tracy:**   I'm scared. Get me out of there.[34]

Director Robert Zemeckis's digital animation features—*The Polar Express* (2004), *Beowulf* (2007), and *A Christmas Carol* (2009)—create the oddity at the bottom of the uncanny valley. At certain points these films appear live action, while other moments present Frank's creepy visualizations that look too robotic, and un-relatable as human representations. Transcend- ing the uncanny valley, Pixar Animation took a different path in its first human-starring film, *The Incredibles* (2004). Rather than attempt frame upon frame of realistic characters, Pixar concocted a cast of digital people who had more in common with comic book illustrations than Zemeckis's *off* animation. In place of attempted realism in Zemeckis's films, they chose relatable caricatures, mirroring Jenkins's argument regarding video games: "[w]e have learned to care about creatures of pigment as we care about images of real people. Why should pixels be different?"[35]

Much time goes into projecting human emotion into alien, digital, and robotic creations, often taking personification to new heights. It only makes sense, then, that if digital designers spend so much time making characters look and feel real, then those same characters can and should be held to the same standards of human emotion and attributes. If a digital character is a caricature of humanity it appears fair to use frameworks already in place—categories like race, gender, and class—to decode them. Designers and filmmakers do not create in vacuums; they must find ideas somewhere, consciously or unconsciously. For, HP computers' 2009 Webcam facial recognition feature could not locate the faces of black users.[36] Intentional or not, this *technical error* reflects the social location of its manufacturers who did not think to test the product on a diverse consumer base. Like bandages that read, "Blends to skin tone," when white is the default racial category—even for neutrally constructed computer products—it becomes easy to make assumptions that often go unquestioned—something effects editors and filmmakers faced in films like *Transformers 2, Avatar*, and *Phantom Menace*.

Transformers 2 premiered to mass criticism due to racial stereotypes in the form of CGI robots, two Autobots—the hero team of the film—referred to as the Twins. Rather perplexing though was director Michael Bay's dismissal of these accusations, claiming the film was just "silly fun."[37] Even the screenwriters, Alex Kurtzman and Roberto, expressed reprint for the final product.[38] Fan Web communities approached the debate in various ways. At the forefront of the opposition's defense was the simple claim that *Transformers 2* depicted no racial stereotypes as the two characters under scrutiny were digitally created robots. How can robots be any race? They're robots—digital creations. Apparently, as the defense continued, such claims revealed personal prejudice, rather than calling attention to it, by labeling these robots black stereotypes. Similar defenses surrounded the 2010 hit, *Avatar*, featuring a cast of blue aliens indigenous to the moon, Pandora, which were clearly racialized in the tradition of American Indian. The defense continues that such films transcend race, rather than reinforcing stereotypes, and to use such a *narrow* paradigm stands in the way of the futurism so often stressed in the SF genre. After all, isn't the point of SF to see past such trivial categories as race, ethnicity, gender, sexuality, socioeconomic status, disability, and religion?[39] While the color-blind mentality—known for its ability to ignore diversity and (unintentionally?) provide easy access for the rules and norms of a dominating group to become normalized and universalized—is on its last leg, it is far from gone.

Adilifu Nama provides an extensive examination of classic SF films, finding racial tension in films parading as progressive; instead many often reaffirm "the dominant hegemonic order of the day" though "their meaning can never be fully guaranteed, merely brokered."[40] A simple glance at contemporary popular film examples how old ideas of ethnic representation linger: *Eat Pray Love* (2010) basks in the India-as-mystic-land stereotype Edward Said warned against more than 30 years ago,[41] and *The Blindside* (2009) presents black people as either weak, drug addicts, or gang members, mirroring bell hooks's analysis of black stereotypes— overly aggressive men, drug-addicted women, and passive servants of white people—in popular culture 20 years ago.[42] Returning to *Transformers 2*, now, if a robot with droopy eyes, a golden tooth, professes illiteracy, and speaks in jive cannot be identified by the masses as a stereotype, a digital racial signifier, we have a dilemma. (And this says nothing of the female Autobots, identified by their pink colors, feminine voices, and smaller stature compared to the other characters.)

Even before the Twins or the Na'vi, we come to this chapter's title, *"Is Jar Jar racist?"* In George Lucas's grandiose attempt to set new CGI ground in *The Phantom Menace*, racialized CGI reached new prominence with the introduction of Jar Jar Binks, a clumsy, unintelligent character who speaks in a stereotypically black dialect. Nama refers to Jar Jar as "a SF version of Zip Coon" and even states that other aliens in the film, the villains known as the Neimoidians, function "as caricatures of the Japanese as underhanded plotters."[43] One need only watch classic Hollywood films to note the similarities in dialect between Jar Jar and many house slaves—though other critics interpreted his speech as Jamaican. If this still seems far-fetched, *Phantom Menace* is far from the first film to construct nonhuman racial identity. The jive-talking black crows in *Dumbo* (1941), one of which is actually named Jim Crow, appear as early examples of the many animated racial characters created by Disney. Nama's extensive study argues that various SF characters, digital or in alien costume, construct Otherness in the general narrative framework: white space travelers make first contact with little green men—a completely foreign signifier of Otherness—who are often weak, in need of help, sexualized, or monstrous. For example, when *The Time Machine*'s (1960) protagonist (played by Rod Taylor) travels into the future, he finds a utopian (white) society void of war, poverty, and pollution. However, humanity is completely subservient to the blue-skinned, glowing-eyed Morlocks who have a taste for human cuisine. Nama proposes that the film's absence of ethnic casting coupled with the Morlocks' ape-like demeanor, cannibalism, and tribal air codes them as "symbolically black."[44]

Jar Jar took alien representation to new digital heights in 1999. He was a completely CGI character motion captured and voiced by Ahmed Best, a Jamaican American performer. Following the racial allegations against the character, and a slew of disdain for Jar Jar in general, Lucas responded in familiar fashion, accusing the accusers of racism. Such attacks on Lucas were merely unconscious racial bias projected onto Lucas' *innocent* story.[45] Yet reception theory and the broader project of cultural studies, shows that the real meaning of a story is far from simple, when considering producers, screenwriters, directors, actors, and audiences. In a postmodern narrativescape, no one interpretation overpowers the others, thus Lucas's response in no way marks the end of the debate.

Through a generalized media effects lens, CGI can displace the audience's ability to concretely identify racial coding, allowing dominant ideology—namely, the ongoing racial inequality of film casting and narratives—to go on unnoticed. The problem is the illusive character of ideology which can be defined in Terry Eagleton's terms as a "language which forgets the essentially contingent, accidental relations between itself and the world, and comes instead to mistake itself as having some kind of organic, inevitable bond with what it represents."[46] In short, ideology (intentionally) mistakes itself for a natural formation. But as Eagleton continually reminds us, ideology cannot be all encompassing, and mass media cannot be understood merely as a device of manipulation, completely stripping audiences of agency. Furthermore, CGI and race is but the first part of this analysis, and while it paints a rather pessimistic picture, it by no means concludes what will always remain an ongoing discussion.

The Meaning of Digital Style

Following the Columbine High School massacre, Henry Jenkins spoke in front of the U.S. Senate Commerce Committee regarding media violence. He was shocked by the lack of media literacy among those present who used satiric or exaggerated video game slogans as proof of video games' adverse influence and deficiency.[47] Such ill-researched views are reminiscent of the public response to Ice T's 1992 song, "Cop Killer." Considering only one lens of song interpretation—all songs are the beliefs of the songwriter—"Cop Killer" could only be interpreted literally, rather than as something ironic or positioned from a more narrative point of view, as Ice-T himself said it was: "I'm singing in the first person as a character who is fed up with police brutality. I ain't never killed no cop. I felt like it a lot of times. But I never did it. If you believe that I'm a cop killer, you believe David Bowie is an astronaut."[48] Literality trumps figurative language, and this is the primary problem with criticism that solely analyzes content.

Most examinations of style ethics focus on the need for authenticity and preserving the *truth* of actual events in documentaries and historical fiction. Such an ethical model is insufficient for spectacle cinema and most fiction in general. In fact, ethics have often shown an aversion to visuality, hence the term *iconophobia* which "[foregrounds] the symptoms of hesitancy, suspicion, distrust, denigration, and avoidance that are exhibited by the theoretical practices related to it."[49] Visuals are merely metaphors for what occurs within. Counter to *iconophobia*, Susan Sontag argues that art should not be reduced to content, for style—the telling of content—is impossible to separate from that content.[50] This is not meant as justification for *Transformers 2* and its kin—merely that a stereotype is but one element of a narrative. Any discussion of ethics in CGI is a multidimensional endeavor. So does the story suffer from this emphasis on style over content? Returning to McLuhan's "the medium is the message," the medium through which something is said is more important than its content—its message[51]—thus new media stories must be inseparable from their graphics. Horror films, for example, prove problematic in the battle between content and style. At their most basic, the *Saw* slasher films are morality tales about what people will do to survive.[52] But to stop at the level of content misses the vast appeal of most horror films—particularly the *Saw* series' focus on homemade contraptions specially created for the singular purpose of dismemberment. Screaming or cringing are the emotional responses that cannot be properly equated at the level of the message. Similarly, to solely examine the content of action films misses the ride effect that makes up much of an actioner's appeal.[53]

Furthermore, at the very least, it would appear safe to assume that most television and film viewers care about special effects to some extent. Simply turn on the Syfy Channel at 2 A.M. and watch any number of crocodile, python, and shark monster movies to understand how distracting low-tech special effects can be. The collective moviegoing audience requires a certain level of visual detail to properly enter *suspension of disbelief*. Even in the case of a popular television series like *Doctor Who*, known more for its writing than often campy visual effects, the graphics have greatly improved since the show's origin in the 1960s. Director Sam Raimi had no intention of creating a cult classic with his directorial debut, horror film *The Evil Dead* (1981)—which birthed two sequels (and another on the way) that turned the film property into horror comedies—but he learned the minimum expectation for audiences before they begin to laugh rather than shriek. Contrary to an idealization of content over style, *special effects matter*.

Still, there is a danger at work in excessive style. A recent study found that four-year-olds who viewed *SpongeBob SquarePants* before a class lesson had a lower attention span than children who viewed a PBS cartoon or simply colored. The study concludes that the fast-pace stylization of the animated series cognitively affects children, at least at such a young age.[54] *Requiem for a Dream* (1999) has also been noted for its excessive style, using 2,000 edits throughout the entire film while the average is 600–700. In fact, Barry Taylor and Craig Detweiler argue that *Requiem's* style—not its content—resulted in the film's NC-17 rating.[55] Two films might be equally violent, but the presentation of that violence may cause different critical and audience receptions. Context and style determine how a subject is framed, something that stages the difference between *300* and *Transformers 2*.

While *300* is morally confused at best: Western (white) society is elevated to noble status in the midst of a savage (ethnic) world; people with physical disabilities are sexually deprived and untrustworthy; and women are subordinate to the *stronger* sex; not to mention the film's extremely gory message about the use of violence to bring about resolution. The film was even banned in Iran.[56] All this said, *300* remains a compelling film due to its visual spectacle through film editing to create overly stylized action sequences. Analyzing style instead of content, Slavoj Žižek calls attention to how the film's production, almost entirely in a film studio, brought real actors into an almost entirely artificial space:

> Aesthetically, we are here steps ahead of the *Star Wars* and *Lord of the Rings* series: although, in these series also, many background objects and persons are digitally created, the impression is nonetheless the one of (real and) digital actors and objects (elephants, Yoda, Urkhs, palaces, etc.) placed into a "real" open world; in *300*, on the contrary, all main characters are "real" actors put into an artificial background, the combination which produces a much more uncanny "closed" world of a "cyborg" mixture of real people integrated into an artificial world. It is only with *300* that the combination of "real" actors and objects and digital environment came close to create a truly new autonomous aesthetic space.[57]

Žižek's analysis of 300 helps us understand the post-literal aesthetic of spectacle cinema in the new media age. We cannot find meaning apart from the spectacle rooted in the technology.

Furthermore, *300* constructs a unique internal logic that makes "fascist art," says Orlando Sentinel film critic Roger Moore invoking Sontag's term,[58] part of the point. The entire film is narrated by Dilios (played by David Wenham), one of the 300 who is ordered to return to Sparta when King Leonidas (played by Gerard Butler) realizes the Persian Army will defeat them. The end of the film reveals that Dilios's narration is not in the voice-of-god tradition but is delivered to an army of Spartan and Greek soldiers preparing to attack the Persians. Of course, the sensational depiction of the 300 Spartans' battles and the savagery of the enemy are insensitive to reality since this story is being articulated for an audience preparing for battle. Demonizing the enemy is common practice if a military force wants to defuse sympathizers and empower soldiers to take on a force that outnumbers them. Here, Sontag's resistance to psychoanalytic film theory helps us understand the reasoning behind abandoning interpretation:

> Ingmar Bergman may have meant the tank rumbling down the empty night street in *The Silence* as a phallic symbol. But if he did, it was a foolish thought . . . Taken as a brute object, as an immediate sensory equivalent for the mysterious abrupt armored happenings going on inside the hotel, that sequence with the tank is the most striking moment in the film. Those who reach for a Freudian interpretation of the tank are only expressing their lack of response to what is there on the screen.
>
> It is always the case that interpretation of this type indicates a dissatisfaction (conscious or unconscious) with the work, a wish to replace it by something else.[59]

Sontag resists critics' attempts "to render completely transparent the meaning of the work,"[60] and for better or worse, the internal logic *300* allows us to understand the film from a certain point of view (historical Sparta according to *300*).

Unlike *300*, the connection between CGI and filmed live action is confused in *Transformers 2*. The camera moves so quickly over digital images without allowing enough time to properly examine each computerized frame—most assuredly because the CGI was not properly compressed to match the live-action footage, revealing a lack of coherency in the midst of the spectacle and a greater concern for appealing to exploitative rather than speculative viscerality. While other films take great pains to highlight key objects of the spectacle—such as the Discovery in *2001* or the Enterprise in *Star Trek* (2009)—*Transformers 2* reveals how little faith it has in its own imagery. Yet the primary reason I consider Bay's robotic trilogy too robotic, as opposed to other recent films, like *300*, *The Avengers* (2012), and *Star Trek* (all films that seemingly attempt to out action each other), is simple: the divorce of style from content—the lack of narrative logic. Putting aside the various racial and sexual insensitivities, *Transformers 2* uses the audience's desire for greater spectacle as justification for overlooking plotline, believable dialogue, and the ability to simply dwell on an image for a longer period of time (save Megan Fox's body). Spectacle cannot exist without story. As Darley and Keith Johnston discuss, spectacle is far from a new concept, whether in classic film genres like musicals, SF films, and horror films,[61] or premiering special effects breakthroughs in trailers,[62] thus *Transformers 2* comes from a long history. However, instead of following suit, the film spends too much time on graphics without humanizing digital characters within the confines of a story.

Beyond Content

We must heed the words of Jean Baudrillard, particularly his idea of hyperreality. To describe the function of hyperreality, Baudrillard critiques Disneyland, saying it "is presented as imaginary in order to make us believe that the rest is real, when in fact all of Los Angeles and the America surrounding it are no longer real, but of the order of the hyperreal and of the simulation."[63] In short, if we perceive the world through mass media, like the evening news, then reality is an edited experience that becomes hyperreal. While the all-encompassing power of Baudrillard's thesis remains debatable, his ideas are worth addressing for filmic special effects. It should be noted that *300* specially emphasizes the cinematic spectacle, almost to absurdity, built into its narrative. Films like *300*, *The Matrix* trilogy, and *Sin City* "do not juxtapose their different media in as dramatic a way as what we commonly see in motion graphics. Nor do they strive for the seamless integration of CGI."[64] This is a new media aesthetic that requires more research than the perversion of hyperreality. As Andrew Darley says, "one of the reasons for the lack of alternative approaches [to examining new media genres] may well be that methods designed for understanding literary texts in particular have been imported wholesale into making sense of visual ones."[65] We need theories designed for new media and spectacle, and even more, according to Susan Sontag, "we need an erotics of art."[66]

Since Platonic thought revitalized with 19th-century Christianity, the idea of leisure activity is often on trial, and spectacle cinema becomes an easy target due to its clear focus on the way a story is told over what that story is. How can the pleasure of a horror movie or a fantasy epic stand a chance against a serious film about sex trafficking or racial tensions in Los Angeles? Similarly, *2001*—transcending ethical consideration—is praised for the sublimity of its imagery and narrative abstraction, while other equally spectacular films meet with scorn. Perhaps the film's notably slow pacing insures that audience members are engaging it more like a painting than the fleeting emotionality of a fast-paced action film. Yet *2001* is known more for its momentous special effects than its narrative message (which is still debated). It might be easy to justify the use of special effects in *2001*, while superhero and comic book adaptations are considered too formulaic to ever amount to anything more than trivial entertainment that assaults our senses. Even something like *Rise of the Planet of the Apes* (2011), a prequel to the civil rights allegory, *Planet of the Apes* (1969), provides elements of social commentary, while *Thor* (2011) and *The Avengers* are almost completely adventure driven. For Jean-Pierre Geuens, this form of entertainment conflicts with art since "art opens a space away from the ordinariness of daily life."[67] Aesthetic ethics tends to understand beauty as something that requires deep critical work and ignores the joy of visual pleasures, thus spectacle cinema is a hindrance to beauty not a part of it.

Providing one of the few examples of ethics in film technique, Geuens attacks the Hollywood production process, calling it "the winner-take-all environment [that] has polluted the air, infecting most with the jackpot fever, leaving independents with few options but to look for shock value."[68] Art leads to truth, and truth cannot be found in a capitalist system—which only cares about profit—that suppresses creativity. The ethical model for production appears clear, unless we consider Michel de Certeau's concept, "poaching," which states that even though ideological constructs might prevent individuals from living apart from a dominating system, they can still poach from dominant culture, finding meaning through negotiation and resistance.[69] So if film production limits artistic freedom, filmmakers who desire larger budgets—hence the need for Hollywood support—can at least poach their way to a secondary meaning that subverts the production system. Sadly, this view remains incomplete, especially considering Henry Jenkins's research on vaudeville entertainment, which is defined by an emphasis on spectacle over story to emotionally grab the audience.[70] Applying vaudeville entertainment to contemporary culture, Jenkins says, "Most popular culture is shaped by a logic of emotional intensification. It is less interested in making us think than it is in making us feel. Yet that distinction is too simple: popular culture, at its best, makes us think by making us feel."[71] If we truly are moving past a text-based culture, then we need to engage with visual culture in different ways that both see where reality seeps in (like racialized robots) and where excess requires our attention but not understanding of reality. What special effects and spectacle cinema call attention to is ethics studies' insufficient response to emotion. Like any SF film where an android goes in search of a heart or a soul, we must start considering the greater role emotion plays in ethics for the current generation, lest we turn into in HAL 9000, wondering why no one understands our pure logic.

Notes

1. John Storey, *Inventing Popular Culture: From Folklore to Globalization* (Malden, MA: Blackwell Publishing, 2003), 65.

2. Simon During, *Modern Enchantments: The Secular Power of Magic* (Cambridge, MA: Harvard University Press, 2002), 170.

3. James Flint, "Buzzsaw and Lightyear," review of *Modern Enchantments: The Cultural and Secular Power of Magic*, by Simon During, *The Guardian*, September 27, 2002, http://www.guardian.co.uk/books/2002/sep/28/highereducation.news.

4. Lev Manovich, *The Language of New Media* (Cambridge, MA: The MIT Press, 2001), 202 (italics in original).

5. Andrew Darley, *Visual Digital Culture: Surface Play and Spectacle in New Media Genres* (New York: Routledge, 2000), 108.

6. Angela McRobbie, *Postmodernism and Popular Culture* (London: Routledge, 1994), 84–85.

7. *300* follows the example set by *Sin City* (2005), filmed almost entirely in front of a green/blue screen. Only one scene in *300* was actually filmed outside the studio. While summer blockbusters range in budget from $125 to $250 million, *300* was made for the much lower $60 million due to reliance on special effects over on-sight shooting. See Gerri Miller, "Inside '300,'" *HowStuffWorks*, 2007, http://entertainment.howstuffworks.com/inside-300.htm, for production details.

8. Max Horkheimer and Theodore W. Adorno, *Dialectic of Enlightenment: Philosophical Fragments*, ed. Gunzelin Schmid Noerr, trans. Edmund Jephcott (Stanford, CA: Stanford University Press, 2002), 95.

9. *Time* provides a brief photo slideshow that summarizes special effects history; Allie Townshed, "A Brief History of Movie Special Effects," *Time*, 2009, http://www.time.com/time/photogallery/0,29307,2055255,00.html.

10. Susan Sontag, "Fascinating Fascism," *The New York Review of Books*, February 6, 1975, http://www.nybooks.com/articles/archives/1975/feb/06/fascinating-fascism.

11. David Brooks, "The Messiah Complex," *Los Angeles Times*, January 8, 2010, A27.

12. Susan Sontag, *Against Interpretation, and Other Essays* (New York: Farrar, Straus & Giroux, 1966), 4.

13. Karl Marx, *Capital: A Critique of Political Economy. Book 1: Capitalist Production,* trans. Samuel Moore and Edward Aveling (New York: Appleton & Co., 1889), 43.

14. Guy Debord, *Society of the Spectacle* (Detroit: Black & Red, 2010 [1970]), para. 30.

15. Ibid., para. 4.

16. Ibid., para. 20.

17. Neil Postman, *Amusing Ourselves to Death: Public Discourse in the Age of Discourse* (London: Penguin Books, 1985), 24–26.

18. Ibid., 3–7.

19. Mitchell Stephens, *The Rise of the Image, the Fall of the Word* (Oxford: Oxford University Press, 1998), 11.

20. Kalle Lasn, *Culture Jam: The Uncooling of America* (New York: Quill, 2000), 15.

21. Peter Travers, review of *Transformers: Revenge of the Fallen* (Paramount Pictures movie), by Michael Bay, *Rolling Stone,* June 24, 2009, http://www.rollingstone.com/movies/reviews/transformers-revenge-of-the-fallen-20090624.

22. Lasn, *Culture Jam*, 15.

23. Steven Johnson, *Everything Bad for You Is Good: How Today's Popular Culture Is Actually Making Us Smarter* (New York: Riverhead Book, 2005), 62–72.

24. John Fiske, *Television Culture* (New York: Routledge, 2001 [1987]), 116, 166, 252, 266.

25. Scott Bukatman, *Matters of Gravity: Special Effects and Supermen in the 20th Century* (Durham, NC: Duke University Press, 2003), 81.

26. Ibid., 116.

27. Henry Jenkins, *The Wow Climax: Tracing the Emotional Impact of Popular Culture* (New York: New York University Press, 2007), 112.

28. Ibid., 3.

29. J. R. R. Tolkien, "On Fairy-Stories," in *Essays Presented to Charles Williams* (Oxford: Oxford University Press, 1947), 67.

30. During, *Modern Enchantments*, 286.

31. Karl Bell, "Remaking Magic: The 'Wizard of the North' and the Contested Magical Mentalities in the Mid-Nineteenth Century Magic Show," *Magic, Ritual, and Witchcraft* 4, no. 1 (2009): 34.

32. Larry Gross, "The Ethics of (Mis) Representation," *Image Ethics: The Moral Rights of Subjects in Photographs, Film, and Television*, ed. Larry Gross, John Stuart Katz, and Jay Rudy (Oxford: Oxford University Press, 1988), 191.

33. Masahiro Mori, "The Uncanny Valley," trans. Karl F. MacDorman and Takashi Minato, *Energy* 7, no. 4 (1970): 33–35.

34. *30 Rock*, "Succession, 2.13," first broadcast, April 24, 2008, by NBC, directed by Gail Mancuso, written by Andrew Guest and John Riggi.

35. Jenkins, *The Wow Climax*, 27.

36. "HP Computers Are Racist," December 10, 2009, video clip, http://www.youtube.com/watch?v=t4DT3tQqgRM.

37. John Horn, "'Revenge of the Fallen' Has Turned Off Critics, but It Reaped an Estimated $201.2 Million in Domestic Ticket Sales in Five Days," *Los Angeles Times*, June 29, 2009, http://articles.latimes.com/2009/jun/29/entertainment/et-bay29.

38. Russ Fischer, "No One Wants to Own Up to Racism in Transformers," */Film*, June 25, 2009, http://www.slashfilm.com/no-one-wants-to-own-up-to-racism-in-transformers.

39. Many SF films and television series do address diversity like *Planet of the Apes*. *Star Trek: The Next Generation* even goes so far as creating its own guiding xenoarchaeology principles, such as the "Prime Directive," which states that the United Federation of Planets cannot influence a species' evolutionary course.

40. Adilifu Nama, *Black Space: Imagining Race in Science Fiction Film* (Austin: University of Texas Press, 2008), 126.

41. Edward Said, *Orientalism* (New York: Vintage Books, 1994 [1979]), 306 and 313.

42. See bell hooks, *Black Looks: Race and Representation* (Boston: South End Press, 1992); The defense would claim that *The Blindside* cannot be racially insensitive since it is based on a true story, but any study of film conventions makes clear that nonfiction, still a fictional representation, becomes melodrama when it enters the realm of (Hollywood) cinematic conventions.

43. Nama, *Black Space*, 34.

44. Ibid., 16.

45. Jonathan L. Bowen, *Anticipation: The Real Life Story of Star Wars: Episode I—The Phantom Menace* (Lincoln, NE: iUniverse, 2005), 96.

46. Terry Eagleton, *Ideology: An Introduction* (London: Verso, 2007), 200.

47. Henry Jenkins, *Fans, Bloggers, and Gamers: Exploring Participatory Culture* (New York: New York University Press, 2006), 187–89.

48. Ice-T and Douglas Century, *Ice: A Memoir of Gangster Life and Redemption—From South Central to Hollywood* (New York: One World, 2012), 142.

49. Rey Chow, "Towards an Ethics of Postvisuality: Some Thoughts on the Recent Work of Zhang Yimou," *Poetics Today* 25, no. 4 (Winter 2004): 676.

50. Sontag, *Against Interpretation*, 5–7.

51. Marshall McLuhan, *Understanding Media: The Extensions of Man* (Cambridge, MA: The MIT Press, 1994 [1964]), 8–9.

52. See Jane Graham, "Saw: Brutality Is Only Skin Deep," *The Guardian*, October 15, 2009, http://www.guardian.co.uk/film/2009/oct/15/saw-horror-movie-franchise, for an overview of morality and terror in the film series.

53. Scott Higgins, "Suspenseful Situations: Melodramatic Narrative and the Contemporary Action Film," *Cinema Journal* 47, no. 2 (2008): 75.

54. Angeline S. Lillard and Jennifer Peterson, "The Immediate Impact of Different Types of Television on Young Children's Executive Function," *Pediatrics* 128, no. 4 (October 2011): e4.

55. Craig Detweiler and Barry Taylor, *A Matrix of Meanings: Finding God in Pop Culture* (Grand Rapids, MI: Baker Academic, 2003), 182.

56. Victor Davis Hanson, "'300'—Fact or Fiction?" *Real Clear Politics*, March 22, 2007, http://www.realclearpolitics.com/articles/2007/03/300_fact_or_fiction .html.

57. Slavoj Žižek, "The True Hollywood Left," *Lacan.com*, 2007, http://www .lacan.com/zizhollywood.htm.

58. Roger Moore, "300 as Fascist Art," *Orlando Sentinel*, 7 March 2007, http:// blogs.orlandosentinel.com/entertainment_movies_blog/2007/03/300_as_fas cist_.html.

59. Sontag, *Against Interpretation*, 9–10.

60. McRobbie, *Postmodernism*, 84.

61. Darley, *Visual Digital Culture*, 49.

62. Keith M. Johnston, *Coming Soon: Film Trailers and the Selling of Hollywood* (Jefferson, NC: McFarland & Company, Inc., Publishers, 2009), 122.

63. Jean Baudrillard, *Selected Writings*, 2nd ed., ed. Mark Poster (Stanford, CA: Stanford University Press, 2001), 175.

64. Lev Manovich, "Understanding Hybrid Media," The European Graduate School, 2007, http://www.egs.edu/faculty/lev-manovich/articles/understanding-hybrid-media.

65. Darley, *Visual Digital Culture*, 5.

66. Sontag, *Against Interpretation*, 14.

67. Jean-Pierre Geuens, *Film Production Theory* (Albany: State University of New York Press, 2000), 41.

68. Ibid., 9.

69. Michel de Certeau, *The Practice of Everyday Life* (Berkeley: University of California Press, 1984), xii.

70. Henry Jenkins, *The Wow Climax*, 4–6.

71. Ibid., 3.

CHAPTER ELEVEN

The Twists and Turns of Online Piracy, Privacy, and Surveillance

Jim Willis

In early 2012, when the loud thud heard in Washington was the sound of the PIPA and SOPA proposals hitting the dusty archives shelf, many in the Internet community of netizens breathed a loud sigh of relief. The culture of openness on the Web would remain intact, and people would be allowed to find information, unfettered by any filters or firewalls or disappearing URLs.

To the uninitiated, or just those awash in a deepening sea of the Internet alphabet, PIPA is the Senate bill called Protect IP Act, and SOPA is its House companion, the Stop Online Piracy Act. These proposals were designed to make it more difficult for Web sites to sell or disseminate copyrighted material that they pirated from the Internet. The key targets of the proposed acts were those sites operating outside the United States, although the acts were also meant to catch domestic pirates as well. The kind of pirated material ranges from music to movies to other consumer products, such a counterfeit watches and purses.[1]

In January 2012, *Forbes* magazine wrote of the proposed acts:

> Although its sponsors have said that they would amend the bill, as currently written, SOPA would enable the U.S. Attorney General to seek a court order to require "a service provider [to] take technically feasible and reasonable measures designed to prevent access by its subscribers located within the United States to the foreign infringing site."[2]

The possibility of cutting the domain name server (DNS) records that point to the site led the Obama administration to warn Congress, "Any effort to combat online piracy must guard against the risk of online censorship of lawful activity and must not inhibit innovation by our dynamic businesses large and small." The administration also echoed concerns raised by a number of security experts, including some anti-malware companies that the bill could disrupt the underlying architecture of the Internet.[3]

Even with the DNS provision removed from the bills, search engines like Google would have to delete any links to sites dedicated to the theft of U.S. property.

Forbes noted that it would also prevent companies from placing on the sites and block payment companies like Visa, MasterCard, and PayPal from transmitting funds to the site.

"The problem with this is that the entire site would be affected, not just that portion that is promoting the distribution of illegal material," Forbes wrote. "It would be a bit like requiring the manager of a flea market to shut down the entire market because some of the merchants were selling counterfeit goods. The bill would also cut off funding by prohibiting payment services from cooperating with infringing sites. Opponents say it would create an 'Internet blacklist.'"[4]

The intent of those proposals seemed good (stopping the international piracy of copyrighted material on the Web), and there was bipartisan political support for that goal. The polarizing came with the means of accomplishing that goal, however. To many, the fencing-off of online information made the cure seem worse than the illness. The protests were loud, widespread, and immediate. The argument went: if you can't have an open Internet where information is open to all, what good is the Internet in the first place?

So the two congressional proposals designed to prevent—or at least slow down—Internet piracy were withdrawn early in 2012 "for further review" even more quickly than they had been introduced.

Say What?

What most Americans didn't know, of course, is *just how open* the Internet has become, thanks to some decisions by the secretive Foreign Intelligence Surveillance (FISA) Court. Specifically what the public did not know is how easy it is for the federal government to tap into individual e-mails, chat room discussions, and social media posts, and to develop profiles of individuals based on their Internet usage.

It might be more accurate to say that many Americans knew the *capabilities* for all that existed, but wrongly believed the *permission* did not. That permission, most Americans have since learned, does exist and it came from a court that the majority of the public didn't know exists. The FISA Court oversees requests for warrants, mostly submitted by the National Security Agency (NSA) and the Federal Bureau of investigation (FBI), for surveillance of those suspected of being foreign intelligence agents and living or traveling within the United States. The FISA Court was created on the basis of recommendations coming from the Church Committee in 1978 and operates under the Foreign Intelligence Surveillance Act of that year. It has been amended several times since the attacks of 9/11, but most thought its provisions were not meant to tap into the private exchanges of American citizens. According to leaks by former intelligence analyst Edward Snowden, Americans are fair game for such government surveillance. Some observers believe the powers of the FISA Court to have expanded to the point where it is "almost a parallel Supreme Court."[5]

So the naïveté most Americans operated under, regarding their belief the federal government doesn't monitor individual Internet communications, existed *before* they learned about the NSA program called PRISM, which is part of what American fugitive or refugee Snowden revealed when he leaked classified information to *The Guardian* and *The Washington Post* in early June 2013.

A Key Program

In one of Snowden's leaked documents, PRISM was listed as "the number one source of raw intelligence used for NSA analytic reports." It differs from the surveillance program used to track *cell* phone calls because it stores and tracks information people exchange on the Internet. While government officials dispute some of the reported details of the program, no one is denying that PRISM exists, and has existed for at least six years. Former President George W. Bush affirmed that in a CNN interview in Zambia.[6] He said he put PRISM in place in 2007 to protect the country. It has been operational under President Obama since that time.

The Washington Post has explained the following about PRISM:

> We know that PRISM is a system the NSA uses to gain access to the private communications of users of nine popular Internet services. We know that access is governed by Section 702 of the Foreign Intelligence Surveillance Act, which was enacted in 2008. Director of National Intelligence James Clapper tacitly admitted PRISM's existence in a blog post last Thursday.

A classified PowerPoint presentation leaked by Edward Snowden states that PRISM enables "collection directly from the servers" of Microsoft, Yahoo, Google, Facebook and other online companies.[7]

Google, Yahoo, and Facebook, Microsoft, and Apple CEOs have all denied they give the federal government "direct access" indiscriminate private information to the government about their users, although Microsoft and Google left open the door that the company might honor specific, targeted requests on identified users. *The Washington Post,* however, wonders about some of the language these company officials are using (i.e., "direct access"), even though admitting that the fact so many companies deny the assertions, that they do seem sincere.[8]

A Renewed Blaze

The revelations about the NSA surveillance programs have thrown gasoline on the embers of the fiery debate about individual privacy and the needs of a country to gather intelligence to thwart terrorism. That debate, sparked in 2001 by the Patriot Act, had died down in recent years, but the blaze is now hotter than ever. The reality is that both the needs for individual privacy and the right of the state to collect needed security data do exist in America.

Part of this debate is connected to a parallel debate about whether Americans actually have a Constitutional right to privacy. There is no actual privacy amendment in the U.S. Constitution, and that leads some— including the late judge and legal scholar Robert Bork—to say that there is no Constitutional right to privacy. Others disagree. In a series titled, "Exploring Constitutional Conflicts," Professor Doug Linder wrote:

> The question of whether the Constitution protects privacy in ways not expressly provided in the Bill of Rights is controversial. Many originalists, including most famously Judge Robert Bork in his ill-fated Supreme Court confirmation hearings, have argued that no such general right of privacy exists. The Supreme Court, however, beginning as early as 1923 and continuing through its recent decisions, has broadly read the 'liberty' guarantee of the Fourteenth Amendment to guarantee a fairly broad right of privacy that has come to encompass decisions about child rearing, procreation, marriage, and termination of medical treatment. Polls show most Americans support this broader reading of the Constitution.[9]

So, in a practical sense, the Supreme Court has certainly acted as though Americans are entitled to privacy, and privacy is a value that seems embedded in the American culture. Furthermore, in matters of media law, specific invasion of privacy statutes exist in all states, and many lawsuits are filed seeking redress of grievances over the unwarranted loss of individual privacy.

When it comes to the need for government intelligence gathering, the reasons for allowing that need to be met are obvious. Recent history has shown that America is vulnerable to different forms of terrorist attack, both foreign and domestic. The attacks of 9/11 and the earlier bombing of the Alfred P. Murrah Federal Building in Oklahoma City are two cases in point, as is 2013 bombing at the finish line of the Boston Marathon. The government simply has to be able to collect information to, hopefully, thwart such terrorist plans. To show how vulnerable the United States is to these attacks, *US News & World Report* published a summary of six of the most vulnerable attack sites in the United States.[10] They include military bases, rail and metro systems, chemical plants, liquid natural gas storage facilities, dams, and bio labs. About the first two of these targets alone, writer Alex Kingsbury states:

- *Military bases:* Many are lightly guarded and use only a swing gate. The FBI arrested six radical Islamists in 2007 on charges of scheming to enter the Army base at Fort Dix, N.J., and gun down as many soldiers as possible, using machine guns.
- *Rail and Metro systems*: Even though security has been stepped up in places like New York rail and metro stations, there are still too many vulnerabilities, especially aboard moving trains. The kinds of bombings that have occurred in Madrid, London, and Mumbai transit systems show how vulnerable the rail systems in the U.S. can be.

One of the reasons that many Americans have given about not worrying over government surveillance is, "I don't have anything to hide, so why should I worry about being monitored? Only those with terrorist thoughts or plans should worry." I've actually heard this refrain a lot among some of my college students over the years. One wonders, however, if the recent Snowden disclosures about the PRISM program and other NSA surveillance activities might cause people to reconsider that opinion. One writer, in an article for *The Chronicle of Higher Education*, looked at this "nothing to hide" argument and found it lacking. Daniel J. Solove is a law professor at Georgetown University, and he wrote:

The nothing-to-hide argument pervades discussions about privacy. The data-security expert Bruce Schneier calls it the "most common retort against privacy advocates." The legal scholar Geoffrey Stone refers to it as an "all-too-common refrain." In its most compelling form, it is an argument that the privacy interest is generally minimal, thus making the contest with security concerns a foreordained victory for security.[11]

Solove disagrees the privacy interest is minimal and feels it should be given much more weight in the debate. He decided to ask readers of his blog, *Concurring Opinions,* about it and got some unique and thought-provoking responses, including the following:

- My response is "So do you have curtains?" or "Can I see your credit-card bills for the last year?"
- So my response to the "If you have nothing to hide . . ." argument is simply, "I don't need to justify my position. You need to justify yours. Come back with a warrant."
- I don't have anything to hide. But I don't have anything I feel like showing you, either.
- If you have nothing to hide, then you don't have a life.
- Show me yours and I'll show you mine.
- It's not about having anything to hide, it's about things not being anyone else's business.
- Bottom line, Joe Stalin would [have] loved it. Why should anyone have to say more?[12]

On Candid Camera

An earlier reference to the Boston Marathon bombing needs elaboration in connection with this privacy or security debate, because it brings in another surveillance device: public street cameras. It is no secret that many cities in the United States use these cameras for a variety of law enforcement and investigative purposes. Boston is one of these cities, and the day of April 15, 2013, showed the positive role they can play in helping to identify and locate terrorists.

Twenty-four hours before the first of two bombs exploded on Boston's Boylston Street on April 15, I was walking that very street, impressed with the organized way the city was preparing for the 117th running of the Boston Marathon. As I walked, I was often passed by thinly clad runners doing last-minute preps for the next day's big road race. More than 21,000 runners take part in this mother of all marathons, and it is a sight to behold.

But the excitement of the marathon turned into memories of chaos for what happened at the finish line, and the sorrow that comes from grieving three lives lost at more than 170 wounded; many severely. As that bloody Monday morphed into Tuesday and beyond, the public's attention shifted not only to the hunt to find the bombers, but to the roles that communication technology and the social media played in those man-hunts. It is a story of local government surveillance techniques and of the trade-off the public accepts in the interest of keeping the streets safe.

It began occurring to many, very quickly, that this was probably the most photographed crime in history, and that the chances of the culprits being identified early were much greater than the chances they would not be identified at all. *The Boston Globe* reported on the rise in the use of street cameras back in August 2007. Reporter Charlie Savage wrote:

> The Department of Homeland Security is funneling millions of dollars to local governments nationwide for purchasing high-tech video camera net-works, accelerating the rise of a "surveillance society" . . . Since 2003, the department has handed out some $23 billion in federal grants to local gov-ernments for equipment and training to help combat terrorism.[13]

While many Americans, at times, worry about the threat these surveil-lance cameras pose to our individual privacy, this was not one of those weeks in Boston. Everyone wanted police and FBI to scan as many faces on Boylston Street as possible and, in reviewing those images, to find the guys who did this crime.

Of course, that is exactly what happened.

But it wasn't just the street cameras, or even the camera from Lord & Taylor department store on Boylston Street, that did the job. These cam-eras were joined by the hundreds of cell phone cameras from everyday citizens who had gathered—they thought—to watch the remainder of the marathoners cross the finish line. When those camera images were added to the surveillance camera results, the world saw who the two brothers were who ignited these bombs. Call it citizen journalism at its best.

Interviewed later, New York City Police commissioner Raymond Kelly said, "The use of cameras was invaluable; both surveillance and smart phone cameras." In another interview he asserted he believes the public has accepted the street cameras and that the privacy issue "has been taken off the table."[14] Acknowledging the reality of the street cameras, New York City civil libertarian Donna Lieberman said, "There's no question but sur-veillance is here and it's here to stay." She said, "The question is how we reduce the risk that we turn into a society where the government knows everything there is about you."[15]

Social Media Exposure

But the images from these street cameras and cell phones still needed to be circulated to all of us. Live television was the first to do that, but many young people don't watch television these days. So it was the images uploaded to the social media of Facebook and Twitter that helped complete the job and let everyone see the faces of terror in Boston.

It is no secret that young people get their news from places, such as Twitter, Facebook, YouTube, and the home pages of AOL and Yahoo. So getting the images out on the Web in sites like these helped in many ways to get maximum interaction from people who knew either of the two brothers, or perhaps both.

Not only did people start calling in tips to police, but some *netizens* also became amateur sleuths in circulating, deciphering, and analyzing photos and factoids to piece together theories of the crime and where the suspects might be hiding.

Users Become Sleuths

One site in which Web users became investigators was Reddit.com. One subgroup that was formed almost immediately was classified under "Find the Bomber." On this home page, more than 60,000 users discussed different photos of the crime scene and exchanged ideas about where the suspects might be.

This is a classic example of what has come to be known by journalists as crowdsourcing. Although, in this case, the crowd was not so much used as story sources, but as potential sources of information that might be helpful to police. In the process, one might say that these individuals became soldiers in the fight against terrorism, armed only with information brought to their attention by security cameras and *cell* phone cameras.

No End in Sight

This privacy or surveillance debate will not end anytime soon, and the Snowden affair is guaranteed to make it more of a topic of everyday discussion for some time to come. At the forefront of that debate, of course, stands Snowden who was stranded as a stateless person in the international transit lounge of the Moscow's Sheremetyevo Airport in the summer of 2013 after the United States revoked his passport following his fleeing Hong Kong. It was there he decided to leak information about the NSA surveillance programs to *The Guardian* of London, and *The Washington Post*. As of July 2013, his future remained uncertain, although obviously the United States wants him back since he has been accused of high crimes. Venezuela and Bolivia had both offered him asylum, however, and the drama was playing out on which he might choose and how he might get there, should he decide to accept either country's offer.

Traitor or Hero?

What is certain, and will be for some time to come, is whether Snowden is seen as a traitor or a hero. The response depends on a person's point of view about what Snowden did and what the leaked information says about what the NSA has been doing. There's also that pesky issue of the law itself: the one he apparently broke.

While Snowden was staying in the Russian airport, an opinion piece on CNN.com looked at "Why we're all stuck in the digital transit zone with Snowden." Written by Andrew Keen, it posited the following: "Yes, Sheremetyevo (Airport) is beginning to mirror the Internet, a vast all-seeing digital panopticon, a network in which somebody might be watching everything we do, a place where individual privacy no longer exists. And Snowden's fate—of being watched around the clock, of having zero privacy—could easily become all of our fates."[16]

The Plot Thickens

He gets more specific in his opinions, adding:

By being able to read our emails and Internet usage, by harvesting over a trillion metadata records, the NSA knows absolutely everything about us. They know our tastes, what we think, where we go, what we eat, how we sleep, when we are angry, when we are sad. They have become our eyes and our brains. Hitchcock's 20th century movie about surveillance and voyeurism really has become the truth about 21st century digital life.

Too Much?

Opponents would say this is just a bit much. Both presidents Bush and Obama have gone on record as stating that safeguards are in place to protect individual American privacy, although the specifics on those safeguards is sketchy. They say the programs harvest more metadata than actual data. But it's hard to get details when you're talking about information that is supposed to be classified in the first place.

One week after Andrew Keen delivered his opinion, Quinnipiac University released the results of a national poll that found, "most Americans believe former NSA contractor Edward Snowden is a 'whistle-blower' rather than a 'traitor.'"[17] Some 2,014 Americans were polled in the survey that ran from June 28 to July 8, as Snowden was holed up in the Moscow airport's transit zone, trying to decide his next move.

The poll found that 55 percent of Americans consider Snowden a whistle-blower, while only 34 percent called him a traitor. Respondents between the ages of 19 and 29 were the ones most likely to call him a whistle-blower, with 68 percent of that demographic saying so. Democrats were less likely than Republicans to call him a traitor.[18]

In the U.S. political arena, however, the rhetoric from both Republicans and Democrats appeared to be on the side of calling Snowden a traitor because he broke provisions of the Espionage Act in leaking classified information. Republican Speaker of the House John Boehner called Snowden a "traitor," while Democratic House Minority Leader Nancy Pelosi called him a "criminal," and Democratic Senator Dianne Feinstein said Snowden committed "treason."

The *Other* Reality

Into this debate must, of course, come the reality of how loud the public's clamor becomes when a terrorist incident does occur that costs American lives. Then the question directed at the government is, "Why didn't you know about this threat and stop it from happening?" That chorus has been heard following most every terrorist incident involving American lives both in the United States and abroad, and obviously government and political leaders are sensitive enough to have voted for strengthening intelligence gathering provisions time and again.

No Easy Way Out

There is no easy resolution to this debate. The ultimate question is always what price is a nation willing to pay for a feeling of safety, and does that price become too high if it threatens the value of individual privacy? That, by the way, is a value many social media addicts seem to be giving up willingly by self-disclosing so much revealing information about themselves online in the first place.

Maybe the difference is that, in doing so, leaking that information about themselves is *their own* idea.

Notes

1. Lary Magid, "What Are SOPA and PIPA, and Why All the Fuss?" *Forbes,* January 18, 2012, http://www.forbes.com/sites/larrymagid/2012/01/18/what-are-sopa-and-pipa-and-why-all-the-fuss/.

2. Ibid.

3. Ibid.

4. Ibid.

5. Eric Lichtblau, "In Secret, Court Vastly Broadens Powers of N.S.A," nytimes.com, July 6, 2013. "Unlike the Supreme Court, the FISA court hears from only one side in the case—the government—and its findings are almost never made public."

6. http://www.cnn.com/2013/07/01/politics/bush-interview/.

7. Timothy B. Lee, "Here's Everything We Know about PRISM to Date," *The Washington Post WonkBlog,* June 12, 2013, http://www.washingtonpost.com/blogs/wonkblog/wp/2013/06/12/heres-everything-we-know-about-prism-to-date/.

8. Ibid.

9. Doug Linder, "Exploring Constitutional Conflicts: The Right of Privacy," http://law2.umkc.edu/faculty/projects/ftrials/conlaw/rightofprivacy.html.

10. Alex Kingsbury, "6 Vulnerable Potential Terrorist Targets," *US News & World Report,* July 10, 2013, http://www.usnews.com/news/slideshows/six-vulnerable-potential-terrorist-targets.

11. Daniel J. Solove, "Why Privacy Matters, Even if You Have 'Nothing to Hide,'" *The Chronicle of Higher Education,* May 15, 2011, https://chronicle.com/article/Why-Privacy-Matters-Even-if/127461/.

12. Ibid.

13. Charlie Savage, "U.S. Doles Out Millions for Street Cameras," *The Boston Globe,* August 12, 2007, http://www.boston.com/news/nation/washington/articles/2007/08/12/us_doles_out_millions_for_street_cameras/?page=full.

14. Tracie Hunte, Annmarie Fertoli, and Colby Hamilton, "NYPD Commissioner Calls for More Street Cameras," WNYC, April 22, 2013, http://www.wnyc.org/articles/wnyc-news/2013/apr/22/kelly-cameras/.

15. Ibid.

16. Andrew Keen, "Why We're All Stuck in the Digital Transit Zone with Snowden," CNN.com, July 6, 2013, http://www.cnn.com/2013/06/28/opinion/keen-snowden-digital-monitoring/index.html?iref=allsearch.

17. Steven Nelson, "Poll: Edward Snowden Seen as 'Whistle-blower,' Not 'Traitor,'" *US News & World Report,* July 10, 2013, http://www.usnews.com/news/blogs/washington-whispers/2013/07/10/poll-edward-snowden-seen-as-whistle-blower-not-traitor.

18. Ibid.

CHAPTER TWELVE

Ethical and Legal Perspectives on the Privacy Paradox on Social Networking Sites

Sue L. Aspley

Introduction

The Internet originated as a scientific or military information system, over the past few decades has grown into a technological resource which would not be recognized by its originators.[1] The Internet has grown from a two-dimensional government informational system into a ubiquitous, public system offering commercial, social networking, e-mail, and other informational platforms for users. With the growth and expansion of this medium, we have seen the development of the new phenomena known as social networking sites. The inception and growth of social networking sites have opened new communication channels for individuals while at the same time increasing users' concerns over breaches of privacy by operators of the sites as well as breaches by participating users.

The creation of social networking sites on the Internet approximately 10 years ago has resulted in the growth of these various sites as well as, exponentially the number of users.[2] Examples of such sites include Facebook, Myspace, and LinkedIn. The classic definition of a social networking site, which is generally accepted by most scholars, was developed by Dana Boyd and Nicole Ellison.[3] They define a social networking site as one which permits the users to: "(1) construct a public or semi-public profile within a bounded system, (2) articulate a list of other users with whom they share a connection, and (3) view and traverse their list of connections and those made by others within the system."[4]

Since this technology is relatively new, the scholarship on its operations and issues arising therein is still emerging. Here I will draw most of my discussion on problems and other activities associated with one of the popular sites, Facebook. More specifically, this discussion will focus on the difficulty of protecting privacy on this particular social networking site.

Operations of Facebook and Privacy Concerns

Facebook was started at Harvard University, centered on college students in order to replicate a sense of a college community.[5] On Facebook users register and develop their profile. In developing this profile, users, if they fill out all the information, provide a great deal of personal information. Users are encouraged to provide more detail.[6] Some of the information provided includes name, date of birth, religion, political views, preferences with respect to movies and music, education, employment, and other data.[7] One then chooses contacts that have access to your personal information. The fact that a number of users on these sites have access to other's profiles is one important characteristic of social networking sites.[8] Facebook permits users to post messages on what are known as friends' (contacts) walls. Individuals can leave comments, upload photos, and tag or leave brief comments about photos. These are just some of the features or basic applications on Facebook.

A user who actively participates on Facebook reveals an extensive amount of private information. The amount of personal information users make available presents a paradox with respect to privacy issues. On the one hand, users reveal a great deal of personal information and on the other, users express concerns about privacy protections. Facebook has privacy settings wherein users can select the amount of information available to other users or "friends."[9] Why then do some users ignore privacy concerns?

Scholarly research on the behavior of social networking site users is just emerging. Boyd and Ellison in studies of social networking sites found that the very nature of sites such as Facebook is centered on accessible profiles.[10] The sustainability of the sites is dependent on the users' displays of information which encourages connections to "friends" or other users through availability of information. Both social and technological factors shape users' displays of information. These sites offer a unique social aspect which attracts users.

Social networking sites in a sense offer a venue for socializing which replicates the coffee houses of Europe and café society before the emergence of the Internet. Boyd and Ellison consider social networking sites as public forums with mediated technology.[11] These public forums are similar to parks and malls. The fact that these actually are public spaces is one of the problems vis-à-vis privacy. Grimmelmann sees this social aspect as creating a false security that causes individuals either to misunderstand or underestimate the privacy risks.[12] One aspect of this deceptive comfort zone is related to social grooming and gossip.[13] Tufekci sees individuals' increasing use of social networking sites for social interactions. Gossip is considered an essential human characteristic, and it equates to grooming behavior found in primates. Users on social networking sites develop a public persona and literally type themselves into existence. Part of the lure of social networking sites is developing social contacts, self-affirmation, and the capability of engaging in a self-promotional public performance. Moreover, these social interactions on social networking sites are a means of fulfilling a basic human activity through gossip and chat in order to forge bonds and relationships.

In their study of college students, Kevin Lewis, Jason Kaufman, and Nicholas Christakis, found that students use social networking sites not just to obtain information, but also to present themselves to others and develop social relationships.[14] They concluded that peer pressure can be a primary factor in determining whether or not students adopt private profiles. If their friends have public profiles, there is a strong possibility students will maintain a public profile also. Another factor in deciding between a public and private profile can be the technology. Even aside from effects of peer pressure to publicize private information, there is the fact that this new technology can create uncertainty among users about the current acceptable norms of behavior on social networking sites. Facebook presents new opportunities for social interaction and consequently many individuals do not have points of reference for structuring their behavior or knowing the full consequences of a public profile.

Emily Christofides, Amy Muise, and Serge Desmarais conducted a similar study with similar findings regarding students' disclosure of information on Facebook.[15] A paradox was found: students indicated concerns over privacy and stated they would probably use the privacy settings. However, study of their behavior revealed they were influenced by personal factors on social acceptability by peers and did not always utilize the privacy controls. The researchers found that the strongest influence was an individual's need for popularity. Moreover, the control of who could have access to one's information varied by relationship; those within the chosen circle were given more access, even though not of the closest relationship to the individual. Maintaining popularity among peers and gaining their acceptance were influences in restricting access to personal information.

Alessandro Acquisti and Jens Grossklags, in their extensive studies on sharing personal information found that contradictions existed in individuals' behavior in the digital environment. In evaluating privacy risks, individuals do not have the appropriate knowledge to determine whether to protect or release personal information. Within this singular decision are additional layers of uncertainties. Individuals are not able to predict consequences. It is often unknown whether provided information will be used for an undesirable purpose. This complexity of the issues and inability to predict outcomes could cause some individuals to ignore privacy concerns altogether, even though they may indicate these concerns are important. "Consumers will often be overwhelmed with the task of identifying possible outcomes related to privacy threats and the appropriate means of protection."[16]

Acquisti and Grossklag see a need for future research in five areas:

(a) The *valence effect*, that is, individuals' beliefs that on social networking sites the provision of personal data could create problems for others; however, in contradiction, they are not concerned about their own privacy.

(b) *Overconfidence* is another area for exploration; individuals assumed that they have more knowledge about a situation than the evidence indicated.

(c) *Rational ignorance* is an area for review because individuals may avoid evaluating privacy issues for the same reason they disregard reading the policies or changing the default settings in that they select the "status quo bias."

(d) *Reciprocity and fairness,* which is the desire of people to act fairly in transactions and to retaliate to a perceived affront.

(e) The last area for research would be the *inequity aversion.* Individuals may potentially view the invasion of privacy based on how they look at the use of their personal data. Some might perceive the use of their data as a fair exchange for the use of the Web site.

Social networking sites present privacy concerns that individuals may not understand. While these studies viewed the activities or attitudes of student populations, the potential harms of breaches of privacy are not limited to one particular age group. The problems associated with privacy on Facebook, unfortunately, are more pervasive than just among students. Gelman has characterized this posting of personal information to making it freely available to the world, in spite of options to use privacy controls as "blurry-edged social networks."[17] This theory suggests that individuals will choose the public option because they cannot predetermine all the people to whom they'd like to connect. In this environment one's social network is not yet defined. This undefined territory is the blurry edge.

There are problems and potential harms with choosing this public option. Boyd has chronicled four problems, even though these social networking sites are viewed as public space, however, this is mediated public space. Social networking sites' problem areas are as follows:

(a) "Persistence. What you say sticks around."
(b) "Searchability . . . can be found in their hangouts with the flick of a few keystrokes."
(c) "Replicability. Digital bits are copyable; . . . difficult to determine if the content was doctored."
(d) "Invisible audiences. . . . In mediated publics, not only are lurkers invisible, but persistence, searchability and replicability introduce audiences that were never present at the time when the expression was created."[18]

These problems conceptualized by Boyd are not hypothetical but are evidenced in some of Facebook's actions in the past few years. In September 2006, Facebook, without due notice to users, launched a new feature called "News Feed."[19] This feature just suddenly appeared on users' home pages. There was no opportunity to opt out. This feature made visible every action one had performed on friends' sites. Activities of adding contacts, commenting on status of relationships, and showing who had joined which groups were on the login pages of all Facebook accounts. Within a "friends" group all actions were chronicled for all to view. Boyd has called this the "privacy train wreck."[20] Users were outraged. This information had always been available through searches, but this clearly brought home to users that their actions were indeed visible. Finally, after the outrage of over 700,000 members the CEO of Facebook apologized and eventually offered privacy options.

A new platform called Beacon was launched by Facebook in 2007. This new platform concerned providing behavioral targeting services to advertisers.[21] Information about Facebook users' activities on other Web sites with which Facebook had partnered was obtained. Particularly, their purchases on other sites were tracked. These purchases would then appear on their Facebook pages, along with targeted advertisements. Again Facebook did not advise users of Beacon, nor offer them a choice to opt out. Users' discontent resulted in Facebook changing the terms of use. Beacon now only appears on users' pages if this person has opted in. This aggregation of information and using it in a secondary fashion, never envisioned by users presents ethical and legal concerns.

Tufekci presents a different type of danger. Facebook users can tag individuals' photos that have been uploaded. This means they can link the picture to that person's profile, and thus create a searchable digital trail of a person's social activities. Once this is done, it is almost impossible to have it removed. The photo can be untagged, but still remain online and is searchable. Users also have been known to tag individuals in photos exhibiting inappropriate behavior; they might not want viewed by a future employer. Social networking sites present ethical questions on how the site handles personal information. Users present ethical questions on social norms within contact groups, targeting friends and displaying personal information in a secondary fashion never envisioned.[22]

Privacy Statements

The role of privacy policies on social networking sites is currently under scrutiny. Social networking sites present unique challenges with respect to the protection of privacy. According to Grimmelmann, many privacy scholars, companies, and regulators such as the Federal Trade Commission (FTC) prefer a document that would provide informed consent for online privacy.[23] In this view the U.S. government does not legally establish privacy standards; instead, the corporations operating these online sites should clearly inform consumers on how their personal information will be utilized. This theory encourages self-regulation by the industry.

Jafar and Abdullah did an analysis of the privacy policies of the major social networking sites. They analyzed the readability of the policies of Google, Myspace, Facebook, and Yahoo. Their focus was on individual information which is electronically stored on social networking sites and the potential of publication elsewhere. After extensive research and analysis their conclusion was: "except for Yahoo, the reading level of the privacy policy statement of the major social networks is beyond the reading grade level of the Internet population in the United States."[24]

Joseph Turow of the Annenberg Public Policy Center of the University of Pennsylvania, in his study found that U.S. adults who go online at home misunderstand the very purpose of privacy policies.[25] The study was also one of the first to find that the average U.S. adult using the Internet does not understand the invisible flow of data. Individuals do not comprehend the invisible Internet. Social networking sites mine their personal data and aggregate this data for secondary uses. Some findings from the study provide profound statistics which are alarming regarding the ignorance of the average Internet user.

- Fifty-seven percent of U.S. adults who use the Internet at home believe incorrectly that when a Web site has a privacy policy, it will not share their personal information with other Web sites.
- Forty-seven percent of U.S. adults who use the.Internet at home say Web site privacy policies are easy to understand. However, 66 percent of those who are confident about their understanding of privacy policies also believe (incorrectly) that sites with a privacy policy won't share data.[26]

The FTC has taken action to understand the advertising practices in the online market place and the privacy issues this creates for consumers. In February 2009, it conducted a staff study and issued an *FTC Staff Report: Self-Regulatory Principles for Online Behavioral Advertising*. The FTC concluded that existing self-regulatory efforts were not adequate to protect consumers and the study culminated in the drafting of Four Basic Principles to serve as the basis for industry self-regulation. The development of these principles was intended to provide guidance to the industry and encourage more readable and appropriate self-regulatory actions.

The Four Basic Principles can be summarized as follows:

- *Transparency and control:* Companies should ensure that there is a clear and concise statement on the collection of data of consumers' online activities. It should be clear a statement could be used in advertising. Consumers should have a clear choice on opting in or out of these activities.
- *Security and data retention:* A company that collects data should provide reasonable security for the data consistent with data security laws and FTC policies. Data should be retained only as long as there is a legitimate business need.
- *Affirmative express consent:* For material, retroactive changes to privacy promises. A company must keep any promises it has made in regard to how it will handle the data. A company cannot use previously collected data in a manner materially different than originally indicated.
- *Sensitive data:* Data on finances, health affairs, or concerning children (normally data wherein there may be a special relationship) should only be released with an affirmative, express consent.

In this action the FTC has taken a hands-off approach and is encouraging self-regulation. However, with the recent filing of a complaint against Facebook, the efficacy of this approach may be questionable.

On May 5, 2010, The Electronic Privacy Information Center along with other privacy advocates filed a complaint against Facebook. The allegations centered on actions by Facebook which were perceived to violate consumers' privacy rights. To quote:

> This complaint concerns material changes to privacy settings made by Facebook, the largest social network service in the United States, which adversely impact the users of the service. Facebook now discloses personal information to the public that Facebook users previously restricted. Facebook now discloses personal information to third parties that Facebook users previously did not make available. These changes violate users' expectation, diminish user privacy, and contradict Facebook's own representations. These business practices are Unfair and Deceptive Trade Practices, subject to review by the Federal Trade Commission under section 5 of the Federal Trade Commission Act.[27]

The relief prayed for in the complaint was that the Commission investigate Facebook, enjoin its unfair and deceptive business practices, and require Facebook to protect the privacy of Facebook users. The complaint further wanted the Commission to compel Facebook to restore previous privacy settings and allow users to have choices. In light of this complaint Dan Fletcher of *Time* indicated that, reportedly, in the near future Facebook would unveil enhanced privacy controls. The complaint is still pending and the decision could influence the ongoing debate on whether industry self-regulation is adequate to protect consumers' privacy.[28]

In theory, privacy policies should protect consumers who use social networking sites. However, in the operative world they do not appear to be working. Consumers do not always read them, and even if they do read them, the message is not clear and transparent wherein they understand to what they acquiesced. Many policies require a measure of searching on a Web site to find them and then it takes a savvy computer user to actually set controls.

Susan Gindin found the problem of unreadable privacy polices is more complex. Consumers are in a hurry, and even if the policies are shorter, they will not read them. Most consumers believe these policies are written in legalese that even an astute legal mind would have problems deciphering. Consumers rarely pay attention to disclosures.[29]

The University of California, Berkeley, School of Information, in a 2009 study, concluded that privacy policies are ineffective for the following reasons:

(1) "Privacy policies are too difficult to read."
(2) "Framing: privacy policies lead consumers to believe that their privacy is protected."

(3) "Even if they could understand them, the amount of time required to read privacy policies is too great."
(4) "Even if they could understand and had the time to read policies, there is not enough market differentiation for users to make informed choices."

Privacy: What Is It and How Do We Protect It?

There is no universal consensus on what privacy means. Privacy scholars generally agree that the concept is of immense complexity. The concept can differ depending on the academic discipline of the proponent of a theory: whether philosophers, social scientists, or legal scholars, all may view it differently. Some scholars have suggested that there are four different concepts:

(a) One developed by Westin was the ability of the individual to have control over one's personal information;

(b) Lessing in his "'The Architecture of Privacy" dealt with the concept in terms of a competing dynamic of two different ideas, the monitored and the searchable;

(c) Johnson further had a different take on the concept as 'the immunity from the judgment of others." He is referring to those areas of an individual's life which should be protected from the judgment of others;

(d) The last concept is the legal concept espoused by Warren and Brandeis, sometimes characterized in an abbreviated sense as the "right to be left alone."[30]

These four theories are not exhaustive, just a sampling of the divergence of scholars. This illustrates that privacy is a concept which is vague and elusive. I will focus on the legal concepts. There is a substantial body of law concerning privacy; however, this has not necessarily led to clarification. Privacy issues require continuing analysis in light of the circumstances and most particularly with respect to today's issues presented by new technologies.

"Privacy is an issue of profound importance around the world. In nearly every nation, numerous statutes, constitutions, and judicial decisions seek to protect privacy."[31] The United Nations' Universal Declaration of Human Rights (the instrument widely accepted as encapsulating basic freedoms and fundamental rights of mankind) has stated, "No one shall be subjected to arbitrary interference with his privacy, family, home or correspondence, nor to attacks upon his honor and reputation."[32] The Organization for Economic Co-operation and Development (OECD) in September, 1980 passed recommendations on guidelines concerning the protection of privacy and transborder flows of data. In general the guide-lines apply to personal data whether public or private which if exposed creates a danger to the privacy of the individual. Part Two, under basic principles states, "There should be limits to the collection of personal data and any such data must be obtained by lawful and fair means and, where appropriate, with the knowledge and consent of the data subject."[33]

Robert Sprague and Corey Ciocchetti found that the legal restraints against the invasion of privacy as providing limited protection in the United States.[34] There are three primary legal foundations for privacy in this country.

(a) what is considered a common law right which is derived through the jurisprudence of court opinions or commonly called judge made law;
(b) a constitutional right derived from the Fourth Amendment;
(c) specific federal and state statutes.

In the United States the origins of the protection of the right to privacy is generally acknowledged to be from the 1890 publication of the now iconic law review article, *The Right to Privacy*, by Warren and Brandeis. This law review article is legendary and is credited with adding a new chapter to the law of torts. The Warren–Brandeis conceptualization cre-ated the jurisprudential foundation for the tort of invasion of privacy in the United States.

Dean William Prosser, considered the father of tort law in the United States, in his article *Privacy*, has indicated that the catalyst for the now famous article by Warren–Brandeis was Warren's annoyance over inap-propriate publicity surrounding his daughter's wedding. In the last part of the 19th century it was considered indiscreet for a lady's name to appear in newspapers. Warren was so outraged that he went to Brandeis, his old law partner, and solicited his assistance in crafting an article to demon-strate that the press had crossed a boundary into an individual's life which should remain private and this was subject to protection by the law. This is the legend behind the now famous article.

In as much as this article is considered the foundation for U.S. tort law on privacy protection, it warrants closer scrutiny. In the Warren–Brandeis article itself other commentators have observed other influences behind their article, such as a recent case, from the Supreme Court of New York *Manola v. Stevens* (1890), concerning photographs of an actress appearing in tights on the Broadway stage where the actress was outraged at the publication of the photo without her consent.[35] In their article Warren–Brandeis were also concerned about the new technology of taking photographs and expressed concerns about taking photographs without permission of the subject. Another potential influence on their article may have been an article by E. L. Godkin, *The Rights of the Citizen-To His Own Reputation*.[36]

Despite existing theories of law acknowledging some legal protection for privacy, most of these theories were not so much in tort law but grounded in property rights. In a sense, the enjoyment of one's property and the rights in one's land and injuries to this right could be compensated.[37] Another area where privacy was protected, to which Warren–Brandeis alluded was concerning private letters.[38] There was an existing evolution of the law and concepts of privacy albeit, of a meager nature at the time of Warren–Brandeis's article. Why then did this article have such a lasting impact?

Even though Warren–Brandeis had some discussion about the various theories of protections in property and even the one on the existing protection of private letters they took their discussion into new territory and thus did in essence signal a new path, another approach for protecting privacy. Essentially, they moved the protection of privacy out of the realm associated with property rights and ensconced it as a separate right in and of its self which could stand alone.[39]

In order to establish a new body of tort law one needs to clearly articulate foundations for actions. While Warren–Brandeis skirted the edges of new possibilities of actionable injuries they did not articulate specific elements for those injuries. However fuzzy their discussion may have been on specifics, they had discovered a separate right phrased as an invasion of privacy which would evolve through future courts' opinions to articulate a more coherent framework for the protection of the right.[40]

Part of the legacy of Warren–Brandeis is the inception of the idea of the protection of the right of privacy as more than just a tort action. Brandeis viewed privacy as a basic fundamental right. Brandeis in subsequent writings took this right to another level, by asserting that one must view not what the law prohibits but basically what the law is required to do affirmatively to protect this right. In his dissent in the now famous case *Olmstead v. United States*, Brandeis found that this right was conferred against the government, the right to be let alone and this is one of the most comprehensive rights in civilization. There are echoes of these thoughts in the now legendary law review article of 1890.

Prosser in his article *Privacy* noted their unique contribution:

> Piecing together old decisions in which relief had been afforded on the basis of defamation, or the invasion of some property right, or a breach of confidence or an implied contract, the article concluded that such cases were

in reality based upon a broader principle which was entitled to separate recognition. This principle they called the right to privacy.[41]

In regard to privacy law, Richards and Solove have compared the differing paths taken by the United States and England. English law developed a separate cause of action for privacy which was based on a breach of a confidential relationship. The English law is built around parties expectations of trust in relationships. The United States took the path known as the right to be left alone.[42] These two separate bodies of law have much in common and much that could be learned from each other, even today as these bodies of law relate to privacy.

Solove sees the legacy of the Warren–Brandeis article as the creation of the four common law tort actions that protect privacy.[43] This article has been at the center of any discussion of privacy in the United States for over 100 years. The article was visionary in predicting the necessity for the law to change with the times:

> That the individual shall have full protection in person and in property is a principle as old as the common law; but it has been found necessary from time to time to define anew the exact nature and extent of such protection.[44]

After the publication of the Warren–Brandeis article there was not an immediate change in theories on privacy. Over the next 30 years it was more of a slow evolution which developed through U.S. case law. Eventually, the majority of states came to recognize a separate right to the protection of privacy. Through his analysis of hundreds of decisions by state courts throughout the United States, Prosser in his article *Privacy* identified four separate torts. To this day these are the four torts or causes of actions for readdress of privacy injuries in the United States:

(1) Intrusion upon the plaintiffs seclusion or solitude, or into his private affairs;

(2) Public disclosure of embarrassing private facts about the plaintiff;

(3) Publicity which places the plaintiff in a false light in the public eye:

(4) Appropriation for the defendant's advantage of the plaintiffs name or likeness.[45]

Prosser himself was aware that these four torts were not always the essence of clarity depending on the factual context:

> It should be obvious at once that these four types of invasion may be subject, in some respects at least, to different rules; and that when what is said

as to any one of them is carries over to another, it may not be at all applicable, and confusion may follow.[46]

Prosser made a tremendous contribution to the body of tort law and the causes of actions for the invasion of privacy. However, this synthesis was over 50 years ago and today's technology was not even envisioned then.

Although privacy is now protected by accepted legal theories, numerous laws both in the United States and throughout the world, courts as well as legislators today continue to grapple with privacy issues and the need to provide the appropriate framework to protect these special interests. The challenges presented by today's new technologies and social networking sites add a new dimension to discussions on privacy rights and the best methods to protect these rights.

These recognized rights to privacy protection in U.S. law are dependent on the facts surrounding the alleged injuries. Part of the puzzle has been filled in by existing theories; however, the new technology has created a whole new range of problems that may require the U.S. legal system to review anew these principles to ensure the adequate protection of privacy in the digital age and more specifically on social networking sites.

Problems and Privacy in the Digital Age

Privacy historically and even today is not a concept subject to one definitive explanation. There is no singular essence to privacy. Privacy differs depending on the context in which it arises. Solove in his book *Understanding Privacy* has devised a method of conceptualizing privacy. The starting point is that we have to recognize that privacy is pluralistic and is "a related cluster of problems."[47] Privacy is an umbrella term for a varied group of concepts which are assimilated to each other and interrelated. Privacy is not stagnant or locked in one position in time. What is perceived as private will change over time. As circumstances change so must our analysis of privacy. The problem with a pluralistic and context-dependent concept of privacy is that it must have enough inherent stable characteristics to make it useful as a concept which the law can protect and from which policies can be derived. The failure to understand privacy's role and its value to society can lead to serious consequences. Lack of understanding of the value or economics of privacy results in potential voids of laws and policies that truly address privacy problems faced today, and thus devise solutions. Individuals can suffer significant harm if privacy problems are not adequately analyzed and put in proper context.

Solove responds to the failures of our current approach to protecting privacy by offering a taxonomy of privacy problems.[48] The goal of this framework is to assist law makers and policy makers in effectively resolving current privacy problems. He places privacy invasive activities into four categories, and then each group is carefully examined for privacy problems which arise, and the harms emanating from these problems. Each of these groupings of problems provides valuable insight into privacy issues and his work in this area is a good starting point to synthesize these categories for potential solutions associated with the new technology and social networking sites.

The first group of activities which present problems is *information collection*. One way this occurs is through surveillance. Surveillance involves the unseen listening or in the case of Internet technology the hidden recording of an individual's activities. Also within this grouping is interrogation which concerns the probing for information. Even if this information is never disseminated, the harm can lie in the intimidation factor, open communication can be disrupted and behaviors altered. This clandestine monitoring could deter group associations and here this could apply to Facebook or other social networking sites' users and their groups of associates. In other words, the freedom of association, whether face to face or online, could be infringed or harmed.[49]

The second group of activities which presents privacy problems concerns *information processing*. Here the activities include the aggregation of information; that is, the combining of individual pieces of information which standing alone do not pose a threat or harm to an individual, but once these bits and pieces are combined into a digital or a data profile this aggregated data can lead to abuses. This was evidenced in Facebook's rolling out of Beacon discussed earlier. Facebook aggregated its users' information and provided it to marketers who in turn targeted individuals on their Web sites with advertisements. Another problem under this rubric of information processing is that of identification which concerns the linking of information to particular individuals. We have seen this occur on social networking sites and particularly on Facebook where a member of the friends' group will tag a photo which then can be linked from other online sites. A third problem on information processing is the use of the information or the security. This problem concerns the lack of appropriate protection of stored information, and this comes into play more and more today with respect to identity theft. An additional problem here is the secondary use of information. The information as originally collected ends up being used for an entirely different purpose that was never disclosed to the individual nor was the consent of the individual obtained. As has been seen on Facebook and Google, social networking sites regularly collect information and pass it on to third parties, usually advertisers, without the knowledge of the individual. Facebook in developing its newsfeed created this problem; Google in attempting to provide location information on individuals likewise breached this privacy concern. The last concept in this information processing group is exclusion. This problem concerns the failure to notify the subject of the data collection and this lack of knowledge means one does not have control in the use of this data. These differing problems may overlap and one activity can encompass more than one of these problems.[50]

The third group concerns the release or publication of information that has been collected. Here Solove characterizes this as *dissemination of information* and considers it a breach of confidentiality. As mentioned earlier, this is the path that the English law focused on in dealing with privacy problems. Within dissemination of information the problem of disclosure presents issues of exposure, increased accessibility, blackmail, appropriation, and distortion. All of these categories or problems concern the transfer of personal data or the threat to transfer data. Breach of confidentiality can concern the release of information in what is presumed to be relationships of trust: for example, doctor and patient, attorney and client, and fiduciary and client. Disclosure carries a different harm. Here the information released is true, but its release could threaten someone's security such as revealing an individual's location information which Google was seeking to disseminate on individuals.[51] Even a friend 's release of information on Facebook may be a privacy problem, for example, releasing the whereabouts of a friend who has been the victim of abuse could result in this information falling into the hands of the perpetrator. social networking sites users in this way could harm their peers.

The fourth and final group concerns *invasion problems*. Unlike the previous groups, these may not concern information. This fourth group aligns with the privacy tort of invasion. These invasions interfere in some manner with an individual's personal life. These invasions are disruptive of daily life and can be such activities as: telemarketing, spam, and harassing phone calls. These actions disturb one's solitude or desire to be left alone. Another aspect of this problem is decisional interference, usually this concerns the government interfering with one's personal affairs beyond the mandate of its regulatory authority.[52]

These four groups may not be exhaustive. However, they provide a much-needed guide on how to analyze privacy problems. This taxonomy provides the tools that can help policy makers visualize and, hopefully, create viable policies, norms, regulations, or laws to manage privacy problems. The taxonomy brings to the forefront the wide variety of privacy problems and their potential harms to individuals. Solove's work can assist policy makers in identifying the problems and the privacy risks associated with social networking sites. His practical and detailed approach to privacy problems is a crucial first step in addressing the new social, ethical, and legal norms which must be created to protect individuals' rights on social networking sites.

Conclusion

The manner in which we deal with privacy in this new information age is of paramount importance. Activities of some social networking sites present a complex array of privacy problems. If we expect users to continue to use social networking sites, we need to ensure their education, so they can make informed decisions on privacy risks. Furthermore, we need to ensure privacy protections for users while at the same time protecting the important constitutional interests of free speech. Understanding privacy problems involves analyzing problems within context.

As we deal with the new technology and social networking sites, we need to develop social norms to guide online behavior. Moreover, we must review the legal and regulatory framework to ensure it is relevant to the task of the protection of privacy in this digital environment. social networking sites also need to step up to the plate and take responsibility for self-regulation in the protection of privacy rights. We must continue the research which is relatively new to evaluate and assess privacy challenges in this new digital age.

Notes

1. Walt Howe, "A Brief History of the Internet," 2010. http://www.walthowe.com/navnet/history.html.

2. James Grimmelmann, "Saving Facebook." *Iowa Law Review* 94 (2009): 1137–205.

3. Danah M. Boyd and Nicole B. Ellison, "Social Network Sites: Definition, History and Scholarship," *Journal of Computer-Mediated Communication* 13, no. 1 (2007): article 11, http://jcmc.indiana.edu/vol13/issue1/boyd.ellison.html.

4. Ibid.

5. Grimmelmann, "Saving Facebook."

6. Tatjana Taraszow, Elena Aristodemou, Georgina Shitta, Yiannis Laouris, and Aysu Arsoy, "Disclosure of Personal and Contact Information by Young People in Social Networking Sites: An analysis Using Facebook Profiles as an Example," *International Journal of Media and Cultural Politics* 6, no. 1 (2010): 83.

7. Grimmelmann, "Saving Facebook," 1149.

8. Boyd and Ellison, "Social Network Sites."

9. Lauren Gelman, "Privacy, Free Speech, and 'Blury-edged' Social Networks," *Boston College Law Review* 50 (2009): 1326.

10. Boyd and Ellison, "Social Network Sites."

11. Ibid.

12. Grimmelmann, "Saving Facebook," 1160–61.

13. Zeynep Tufekci, "Grooming, Gossip, Facebook and My Space: What Can We Learn about These Sites from Those Who Won't Assimilate?" *Information, Communication & Society* 11, no. 4 (2008): 547.

14. Kevin Lewis, Jason Kaufman, and Nicholas Christakis, "The Taste for Privacy: An Analysis of College Student Privacy Settings in an Online Social Network," *Journal of Computer Mediated Communication* 14 (2008): 79–100.

15. Emily Christofides, Amy Muise, and Serge Desmarais, "Information and Control on Facebook: Are They Two Sides of the Same Coin or Two Different Processes?" *CyberPsychology & Behavior* 12, no. 3 (2009): 341–45.

16. Alessandro Acquisti and Jens Grossklags, "What Can Behavioral Economics Teach Us about Privacy?" In *Digital Privacy Theory, Technologies, and Practices*, ed. Alessandro Acquisti, Stefanos Gritzalis, Costas Lambrinoudakis, Sabrina De Capitani di Vimercaati (New York: Auberbach Publications, 2008), 363–77.

17. Gelman, "Privacy, Free Speech, and 'Blury-edged,'" 1316.

18. Danah M. Boyd, "Privacy Trainwreck: Exposure, Invasion and Drama," *Apohenia* (blog), September 8, 2006, http://www.danah.org/papers/Facebook AndPrivacy.html.

19. Grimmelmann, "Saving Facebook," 1168.

20. Boyd, "Privacy Trainwreck."

21. Grimmelmann, "Saving Facebook," 1147.

22. Tufekci, "Grooming, Gossip, Facebook and My Space."

23. Grimmelmann, "Saving Facebook."

24. Musa J. Jafar and Amjad Abdullat, "Exploratory Analysis of the Readability of Information Privacy Statement of the Primary Social Networks," *Journal of Business & Economics Research* 7, no. 12 (2009): 141.

25. Joseph Turow, "Americans & Online Privacy the System Is Broken." A Report from the Annenberg Public Policy Center of the University of Pennsylvania. 2003, http://www.annenberpublicpolicy center.org/Downloads/Information_And _Society/20030701_America_and_Online_Privacy/20030701_onlin_privacy_ report.pdf.

26. Ibid.," 3.

27. EPIC Complaint, "In the Matter of Facebook, Inc." May 5, 2010. http:// epic.org/privacy/facebook/EPIC_FTC_FB_Complaint.pdf.

28. D. Fletcher, "Friends without Borders," *Time*, May 31, 2010, 32–38.

29. Susan E. Gindin, "Nobody Reads Your Privacy Policy or Online Contract? Lessons Learned and Questions Raised by the FTC's Action against Sears," *Northwestern Journal of Technology and Intellectual Property* 8 (2009): 1–37.

30. Taraszow, Aristodemou, Shitta, Laouris, and Arsoy, "Disclosure of Personal and Contact Information," 84–85.

31. Daniel J. Solove, *Understanding Privacy* (Cambridge, MA: Harvard University Press, 2009), 2.

32. Universal Declaration of Human Rights, G.A. Res. 217 (III) A, U.N. Doc. A/RES/217 (III) (December 10, 1948), Article 12.

33. Organization for Economic Co-Operation, *OECD Guideline on The Protection of Privacy Transborder Flows of Personal Data*, 1980, http://www.oecd.org/document/18/0,3343,en_2649_34255_1815186_1_1_1_1,00&&en-USS_01 DBC.html.

34. Robert Sprague and Corey Ciocchetti, "Preserving Identities: Protecting Personal Identifying Information through Enhanced Privacy Policies and Laws," *Albany Law Journal of Science & Technology* 19 (2009): 91–141.

35. William L. Prosser, "Privacy," *California Law Review* 48 (1960): 385.

36. David W. Leeborn, "Symposium: The Right to Privacy One Hundred Years Later: Article: The Right to Privacy's Place in the Intellectual History of Tort Law," *Case Western Reserve Law Review* 41 (1991): 775.

37. Ibid., 777.

38. Ibid., 778.

39. Ibid.

40. Samuel D. Warren and Louis D. Brandeis, "The Right to Privacy," *Harvard Law Review* 48, no. 5 (1890): 193.

41. Prosser, "Privacy," 384.

42. Neil M. Richards and Daniel J. Solove, "Privacy's Other Path: Recovering the law of Confidentiality," *Georgetown Law Journal* 96 (2007): 124–81.

43. Daniel J. Solove, *Understanding Privacy* (Cambridge, MA: Harvard University Press, 2009), 15.

44. Warren and Brandeis, "The Right to Privacy," 193.

45. Prosser, "Privacy," 389.

46. Ibid., 389.

47. Solove, *Understanding Privacy,* 40.

48. Ibid.

49. Ibid., 106–17.

50. Ibid., 117–36.

51. Ibid., 136–61.

52. Ibid., 161–70.

CHAPTER THIRTEEN

Online Marketers' Use of Consumer Data Poses Ethical Concerns

Jim Willis

Somewhere in your mall shopping experiences, you've probably seen a store called, As Seen on TV. It's a name that comes from a phrase that has often been a part of some print ads for a long time. It suggests that, because a product has been advertised on television, it must be good.

Even if that suggestion were true, it may well have lost its relevance to today's world. For, if philosophers are fond of hypothesizing that we live in the postmodern era of thought, mass marketers would add that we may be nearing the post-television age of advertising.

Defining postmodernism is not easy, since even philosophers disagree on its exact meaning. At its core, however, the concept suggests that human understanding doesn't actually mirror reality; instead it constructs reality. Postmodernists would deny there is any one reality that is valid for all cultures. Instead, each person constructs his or her own reality.

Relating postmodernism to post-television advertising, marketers would posit that no television network or cable station—no matter how popular it is—now defines reality for consumers.

Instead, each consumer constructs his or her own reality on which products, services, or political candidates are good. Furthermore, this construction of the good is influenced for each consumer by what he or she makes of the particular recommendations and behavior of a unique reference group each consumer has on a Web, mobile, or social media site.

And the most popular of the social media sites is, of course, Facebook.

One statistic that appears a lot these days is an interesting one: while only 14 percent of consumers in America trust advertisements today, some 78 percent trust peer recommendations.[1]

The implication for marketers is obvious, get friends talking about your client and recommendations often turn into changed minds.

As will be discussed later, we are not so concerned ethically about knowing the recommendations of our reference group(s). However, knowing about the personal behavior and interests of those individuals is ethically challenging.

Are individuals aware of how much private information they divulge to others when they interact on a social media site? Do Facebook users know the ramifications of doing something so seemingly harmless as uploading a picture, or video, or clicking a Like button, for example?

Before answering that, let's look at how popular the social media, mobile, and Web sites and search engines have become in relation to consumer searches, shopping, and buying patterns. Google is leading all search engines in user popularity and is therefore leading in search engine advertising, as the world of mass marketing is turning to the sophisticated ability of Google to offer very targeted demographics.

Television is still a major player as an advertising medium; it's just that the Internet is growing in influence at a much faster rate of speed. The reason is twofold:

1. It is an individually targeted medium in a way television can never be.
2. It is a highly interactive medium in which consumers are not only the advertising targets but also the source of information that makes them targets in the first place.

Here's how *Ad Age* magazine describes it: "The theory is that wary financial investors will applaud spending on social media because of its lower cost and growing reach."[2]

This leading magazine on the advertising industry is quick to point out that the single largest share of advertising bucks still goes to television, but that many advertisers are pulling dollars from print and radio to pursue social media marketing.

At present, only the big players in that world are deriving the greatest benefit of the shift to social media.

Ad Age continues, "Online advertising appears vigorous, but look under the hood and you'll find it's running largely on Google and Facebook. 'The rich are getting richer,' said one digital-media executive, referring to the two giants, which continue to put distance between themselves and the pack. 'All our clients call me and ask, 'What is our Facebook strategy?'—despite a wide lack of agreement on the effectiveness of social media advertising, the exec said. 'We are seeing increases in spending motivated less by financial evidence than a belief that 'they have to be there.'"[3]

For its part, Facebook has been on an aggressive campaign of connecting advertisers to targeted consumers. Doing so only enhances its own bottom line. That was especially the case in the weeks and months leading up the company's initial public stock offering. "Brian Weiser, analyst at Pivotal Research, estimates that Facebook grew 46% and Google 22% in online display in the first quarter [of 2012]."[4]

Google outruns all other search engines in popularity. Every second, so many people visit Google that advertisers willingly pay large sums for on-screen advertising space on pages with search results. This is targeted marketing at its best.

Someone who is looking for information on vegetarian diets, for example, is a more likely customer for a store like Trader Joe's than someone who is a meat-and potatoes customer. The algorithms that Google's search engine uses provide an unrivaled linkage of products and potential customers. And that is a dream come true for advertisers. It's not a bad dream come true for Google, either, which sees much of its $23 billion income originate from advertising.[5]

John Vivian, a media scholar says, "In effect, Google slices and dices the mass audience in ways that give advertisers unusual efficiency in reaching the people they seek. In advertising lingo, there is less wastage. Why, for example, should a marinara company buy space in a food magazine whose readers include people with tomato allergies when Google offers a targeted audience of people looking for spaghetti sauce recipes with nary a one among them who's allergic to tomatoes?"[6]

If Google is king or queen of the search engines, then Facebook leads all social media sites in advertising lure, according to Vivian and *Ad Age*.

Facebook is the leading social media site for advertising and the innovation of its Like button is helpful to advertisers but controversial to many.

Facebook focuses more on behavioral targeting, collecting personal information on its users who are, coincidentally, the potential buyers of advertised products. The personal data of Facebook users is organized and catalogued in ways that offer a mother lode of targeted consumer data for mass marketers.

Vivian points out that each month the 200 million-plus users holding Facebook accounts post some 4 billion bits of information, 850 million photos, and 8 million videos, all of which says a great deal about the behavior, likes, and dislikes of these individuals.[7]

One of the marketing companies showing clients how to identify and relate their ads to consumer behavior is Webtrends. In its home-page promotion video, a company spokesperson says: "Relevant messages are exponentially more powerful. To be relevant every time, everywhere, you need deep understanding of your customers across all digital channels. And to have the ability to have those insights drive your marketing in real time."[8]

To do that, digital marketing research firms like Webtrends help clients unite customer intelligence (data about consumer behavior) from a number of different sites, including Facebook, CRM (customer relationship management), mobile, and social media sites, among others.

Those data help to build target groups, often based on personal data that millions of Facebook users willingly post. These data include news updates, pictures, music, videos, and so forth—all of which are collated and analyzed to form individual consumer profiles.

Have you told your Facebook friends what a great time you had visiting a particular vacation spot, staying in a particular hotel, or drinking a brand of wine? These become building blocks of your profile, and your profile becomes a building block of a targeted audience segment.

All of us who use a social media site like Facebook are already self-identified members of a target-audience segment, probably not knowing we've offered up the information that put us into that segment. With that standing comes a flurry of ads on our Facebook page, which may well be a different array of ads than on someone else's page because—in a real sense—you have said to the advertiser, "I'm your most likely customer."

"Facebook has incredible potential to deliver customers to advertisers based on information that members submit themselves . . . when they communicate with friends, identify their 'likes' . . . and share their interests," Vivian notes.[9]

The Like button, which seems to have been around forever but was launched only in 2010, allows advertisers to inundate anyone who clicks it with ads and news updates which feed right into the flow of your news feed.

Within the first year the Like button was on 2 million Web sites, according to Vivian. It has become a vehicle for what's called "referral traffic." Advertisers have already reported that their highways are flooded with the traffic the Like button has created.

Of course, many individuals worry about the further erosion of individual privacy that comes from heavy interactive usage online. That worry is increased by the intentional and successful efforts of marketers to find out more about consumers from their online posts: indeed simply from their online usage patterns alone.

The Like button is only the latest means of finding out how much we like certain things, people, or ideas. The marketer's idea is to use those preferences to influence friends of online friends to buy that product, service, or political candidate.

This button sends an instant message to advertisers that you are a potential target. As a result, many Facebook users are more judicious in deciding when to hit that button. It also loads up your news feeds on Facebook with largely unwanted promotions of whatever product, service, or political candidate you indicated a liking for when you hit the button. For its part, Facebook says it does not pass on information to other parties without the user's permission, although it does use the aggregated data.

The Terms of Use policy can be found in the bowels of the Facebook site and runs 4,579 words long. Much of that is focused on how it can pass your data along to advertisers, and how you might prevent some of these data from going out by controlling the intricate privacy settings available on another part of the Facebook site. The Facebook, Data Use Policy, is located elsewhere in the site and also runs a few thousand words.

Obviously, few users actually take the time to read the entire legal agreements so—more often than not—users do not know they actually do have some control over the uses of their personal data.

Nevertheless, portions of the Facebook policy note the following:

> You own all of the content and information you post on Facebook, and you can control how it is shared through your privacy and application settings. In addition:
>
> - For content that is covered by intellectual property rights, like photos and videos (IP content), you specifically give us the following permission, subject to your privacy and application settings; you grant us a non-exclusive, transferable, sub-licensable, royalty-free, worldwide license to use any IP content that you post on or in connection with Facebook (IP License). This IP License ends when you delete your IP content or your account unless your content has been shared with others, and they have not deleted it.
> - When you use an application, the application may ask for your permission to access your content and information as well as content and information that others have shared with you. We require applications to respect your privacy, and your agreement with that application will control how the application can use, store, and transfer that content and information. (To learn more about Platform, including how you

can control what information other people may share with applications, read our Data Use Policy and Platform Page.
- When you publish content or information using the Public setting, it means that you are allowing everyone, including people off of Facebook, to access and use that information, and to associate it with you (i.e., your name and profile picture).[10]

About advertising specifically, the policy notes elsewhere:

Our goal is to deliver ads and commercial content that are valuable to our users and advertisers. In order to help us do that, you agree to the following:

- You can use your privacy settings to limit how your name and profile picture may be associated with commercial, sponsored, or related content (such as a brand you like) served or enhanced by us. You give us permission to use your name and profile picture in connection with that content, subject to the limits you place.
- We do not give your content or information to advertisers without your consent.
- You understand that we may not always identify paid services and communications as such.[11]

Like so many other aspects of the Internet, the social media seem destined to be here for a long time to come. And anytime a couple hundred million people decide to flock to a media site, you just know the advertisers are going to be there in the midst of them.

The question to be addressed is this: what are the ethical limits of online marketing, especially when it comes to obtaining personal information about consumers?

In some respects, what is occurring with Web marketing companies and research firms is analogous to high-tech wiretapping. One might ask how much daylight is there between tapping into a phone conversation and tapping into a Facebook exchange between friends.

The latter may not be illegal, but the results are the same. Through the Web crawlers that pick up any mention of a client's product, service, or candidate, marketers do seem to be tapping into personal conversations.

The ethics issue has not gone unnoticed by marketing companies themselves. For example, one Web marketer posted this on its home page recently:

Consumers' lack of trust [in online marketing] is illustrated by a recent privacy survey conducted by IBM in which 78% of responding U.S. consumers stated that they did not complete an online purchase because they were concerned about how their personal data might be used by the site.

A survey by Jupiter backs up these results—they found that 58% of respondents worry about companies selling their personal information to others.[12]

Although this is a lack of trust simply related to data emanating from online purchases, users of social media sites and even e-mail users are wary of what they say, click, or respond to on those sites or regarding incoming e-mails.

To avoid losing consumer trust, some Web marketers are advocating policies like this one from Web Advantage blog:

> In order to gain the trust of consumers, online retailers must *clearly* spell out their privacy policies on their sites. Consumers should know *exactly* what the site plans on doing (or not doing) with any personal information or indirect data (cookies, IP addresses, etc.) they divulge as a result of visiting and interacting with a web site. If a site's policy is to sell OR share consumer information with business partners, that fact needs to be disclosed.[13]

In conclusion, the age of interactive, online marketing might promise more tailored commercial messaging—something which many consumers might appreciate—but it comes at a cost. Like most aspects of Internet usage, that cost is more erosion of our personal privacy. The onus has been placed upon us by the online marketers and the social media sites they use, to find out what the terms of use of these sites are, to learn how to set up some level of privacy barriers for ourselves, to implement and monitor those barriers.

Notes

1. David C. Pratt, "Branding and Peer Recommendations: What Can a Mobile App Provide for You?" ezinearticles.com, December 8, 2011, http://idesignmobileapps.com/article/branding-and-peer-recommendations-what-can-a-mobile-app-provide-for-you/.

2. Ad Age staff, "Where Have All the First Quarter Ad Dollars Gone?" *Advertising Age*, March 26, 2012, http://adage.com/article/media/quarter-ad-dollars/233706/.

3. Ibid.

4. Ibid.

5. John Vivian, *The Media of Mass Communication*, 11th ed. (New York: Pearson, 2012).

6. Ibid.

7. Ibid.

8. Hollis Thomases, "Ethics and Online Marketing," Web Ad.vantage blog, May 30, 2002, http://www.webadvantage.net/webadblog/ethics-online-marketing-165.

9. Vivian, *The Media of Mass Communication.*

10. Facebook, "Statement of Rights and Responsibilities," https://www.facebook .com/legal/terms.

11. Ibid.

12. Thomases, "Ethics and Online Marketing."

13. Ibid.

CHAPTER FOURTEEN

The U.S. Government, Social Networks, and Your Privacy

Brooke Van Dam

Standard Twitter maintenance was scheduled for Monday, June 15, 2009, when the U.S. State Department stepped in. The U.S.-based social networking site had become a centerpiece for information on Iranian protests against the election that had taken place days earlier. Twitter agreed to halt its maintenance until it was the middle of the night in Iran in order to aid the people using the network. As journalist Lev Grossman put it, "Twitter didn't start the protests in Iran, nor did it make them possible. But there's no question that it has emboldened the protesters, reinforced their conviction that they are not alone, and engaged populations outside Iran in an emotional, immediate way that was never possible before."[1]

Many praised Twitter and the State Department for backing freedom of speech in a country that ranks as one of the worst regarding press freedom.[2] It is hard to deny the power of social networks after the Arab Spring of 2009, which turned into the Arab Uprising that is still being seen today.[3] However, the intervention of the U.S. government into social networking has the potential to be dangerous precedent, which could threaten our privacy and freedom of speech.

The Rise of Social Networking

It is almost impossible for a young person in 2012 to imagine a life without social networks. When the most visited Web site in the world is

Facebook, it is clear that constant online interaction is a large part of the Internet.[4] However, it was only about 10 years ago that social networks hit the mainstream.[5] Web sites like Friendster, LinkedIn, and Myspace began connecting people all over the world for a variety of reasons.

Facebook, the social networking leader by a large margin, changed the landscape of social media, when it debuted in 2004. Its growth has begun to flatline but its hold and reach are still dominant.[6] There are over 835 million users worldwide.[7]

According to the Pew Internet & American Life Project, two-thirds of American online adults use social media platforms, such as Facebook, Twitter, Myspace, and LinkedIn.[8] Facebook alone boasts almost 117 million U.S. users who log-on at least once per month.[9]

And it's not just adults who are spending time on the Web to connect with others. The Kaiser Family Foundation found that young people in the United States aged 8–18 spend an average of 22 minutes per day on online social networks.[10]

The Unique Case of Twitter

Twitter is a unique social media application because people don't become friends with someone or part of a group. Anyone can follow a person without the relationship having to be reciprocated. And there are only two settings, public or private. According to researcher Dhiraj Murthy, "Twitter allows users to maintain a public web-based asynchronous 'conversation' through the use of various websites, mobile internet devices, and SMS (i.e. text messages). Messages on Twitter are automatically posted and are publicly accessible on the user's profile page on the Twitter website. . . . One does not need even to 'know' the other user or have their permission to direct a tweet at them."[11]

Users have 140 characters to make a statement, tell a joke, link to a picture, or in some cases make up whatever they want. Although a mass audience will not read most of the millions of tweets on Twitter, the potential is still there for one to be reached.

Privacy

One of the concerns for those who choose to interact with online social networks is privacy.[12] The amount of information each individual chooses to share on these networks is up to the user. At minimum, most social networks require a name, e-mail, and password; however, most users are more than happy to share much more than that. On many social networks one can easily find out where a person works, view numerous pictures of one's private lives, and even engage with banal thoughts on pop culture topics.

One of the newer features that most social networks provide, location tagging, is directly related to the increase in the use of cell phones. "These applications are changing the way people experience everyday activities like shopping, eating, traveling, watching a movie, or taking a picture. Location-based service strategies include any application that has the ability to share an individual's physical location, in real-time, with his or her online social networks."[13] There are even social networks, such as Foursquare and Gowalla, whose sole purpose is to share your location with your friends.

According to a recent study by Pew Internet & American Life Project, more women than men are concerned about their privacy. Women are more likely to put their settings on the most private while for men it is below 50 percent. Overall, 58 percent of people who use social networks put their profiles on private with around 20 percent leaving it completely public. The rest of users lie somewhere in between.[14]

After its initial debut in 2004, Facebook quickly increased in popularity and consequently the company was forced to address its privacy-control settings after complaints from users.[15] Facebook and subsequent Web sites such as LinkedIn and Google Plus now allow the user to choose with whom to share information.

However, just because users check a privacy setting box does not mean their information is completely private. According to Joseph Turow and Michael Hennessey, "In the USA, marketers, media and government specialists use people's information in a broad gamut of ways and with varying concerns for how far the data travel. Although many of these emphasize personally identifiable information, not all of them do. Tracking people anonymously still can lead to useful targeting for marketers."[16]

Social networks readily admit they share information, but most claim it is in our interest. On its own easily accessible Web site, Facebook says, "We use the information we receive about you in connection with the services and features we provide to you and other users like your friends, our partners, the advertisers that purchase ads on the site, and the developers that build the games, applications, and websites you use."

The U.S. government's policy guiding the Internet is confusing to say the least. According to researchers François Bar and Christian Sandvig, "The internet's dramatic success is the new crisis point in communication policy. With the advent of digital technologies, the traditional policy mapping we have identified becomes untenable."[17]

Beyond a confusing policy related to the Internet and information communication technology, a changed security environment post-9/11 has seen tighter controls on security.

The loss-of-control theme and sense of impending crisis that pervades this discourse provides a powerful and seductively straightforward justification for an array of regulatory proposals and countermeasures which advocates believe will restore control, thereby safeguarding social and political order. More often than not, these proposals and countermeasures involve the ratcheting-up of electronic surveillance. Invariably, this has precipitated heated debate as to their implications for individual privacy and freedom of expression.[18]

Legal Cases and the Use of Online Social Networks

Much has been made of the relationship between social networks and advertisers in relationship to privacy.[19] Facebook, and other social networking sites, regularly track the online movements of users in order to target ads more specifically. They claim that they are just giving us a more unique experience and since clearly the social Web is growing, people are agreeing.

One of the lesser focuses of the issue of privacy and social networks is the use of governments to gain information in criminal cases. Increasingly, law enforcement agencies on the local, state, and national levels are looking to social networks to locate criminals who may have fled or to use posts as evidence of guilt.

In 2010, a New York man fled from police before facing sentencing for a bar fight. While in hiding, he posted his current address on Myspace and Facebook. He also listed his place of work, the hours he would be in, and placed his "Wanted" poster on both sites.[20] This type of self-disclosure quickly led to his rearrest.

This man was not alone in disclosing his whereabouts while on the lam from the government. *The Week* actually has a Web page devoted to criminals who got caught based on information they posted on Facebook.[21] On it, one young man broke into a journalist's home and stole several items and then hours later posted pictures of himself with those items.

A Dangerous Line?

The aforementioned may be fairly noncontroversial cases of people committing crimes and then self-disclosing them on a public forum. But the use of social networks to gain information on criminal activity might not be so clear-cut when it comes to freedom of speech. A recent example from the social networking site Twitter provides an interesting template for a debate about what role the government should play in social networking and our right to free speech and privacy.

The case of Malcolm Harris, an Occupy Wall Street protestor, may actually be deemed a case of invasion of privacy, as well as illegal search and seizure. Harris and hundreds of other protesters were arrested for marching on the Brooklyn Bridge after police claim they were told to stop. Harris and other protesters claim that they were told to go over the bridge, not stop.

In an effort to prove that Harris knew what he was doing, the district attorney's office subpoenaed Twitter for Harris's account information and deleted Tweets. A judge in April 2012 overruled Harris's initial filing to stop the government from getting his Twitter details.

According to *The Wall Street Journal* the judge wrote that, "the defendant's contention that he has privacy interests in his Tweets to be understandable, but without merit." Furthermore, the judge wrote that Harris accepted Twitter's terms of use, which clearly state that his postings are public and can be used by the company "for any purpose it may have."[22] Harris appealed this decision as did Twitter, in two separate filings.

The company lost its appeal in mid-September. And Twitter, facing the threat of heavy fines and contempt of court, decided to turn over the user information and deleted Tweets.[23] However, the tweets remain sealed until a judge decides Harris's personal appeal.

The issue in this case is less about free speech, although the right to peacefully assemble is guaranteed, and speaks more directly to our concerns about privacy. When a user is signed up to a social network, should the government be able to get the person's information particularly when the crime is related to protests? If the user deletes a post, or picture, should the government be able to subpoena and admit the evidence in court?

The U.S. government is number one in requesting information from Twitter and Google.[24] Twitter decided to release the information on government requests in 2012 after Google began doing so. According the report, "With 679 requests targeting 948 accounts—apparently more than the rest of the world combined—the U.S. government led the charge in terms of volume. U.S. officials also top the list with a 75 percent success rate followed by runner-up the Netherlands at 50 percent while many countries are at zero percent."[25] Other social networks are not disclosing this information but Google's database, which goes back to 2009, is available for anyone to view.

Conclusion

As long as the use of online social networks continues to grow throughout the world, privacy will be an issue. Although it is clear that most users are concerned about their private information available on the Web, unless they stop sharing information completely, assured privacy is impossible.

In spite of this, there is an argument to be made that there is a limit to what the government should be able to use. These two cases show just how easy it is for officials to be able to request information and draw conclusions based on what users say on social networks. In particular, the arrest of a man whose threats exist solely on Twitter is a new frontier in freedom of speech. Also potentially as damaging is the ability of the government to pressure social network companies to deliver personal information and deleted posts.

One good piece of news for users of online social networks is that, in comparison to cell phones, the government is not as concerned with what is happening on Facebook or Twitter. According to a recent study, "All told, wireless providers fielded about 1.3 million requests for user data last year although . . . the number was almost certainly much higher due to lax record-keeping. If you're concerned about privacy, this should be kind of scary. There's some solace in the fact that most providers claim they deny requests they feel are overbroad or unauthorized, but they comply with most and the numbers are rising."[26]

Notes

1. Lev Grossman, "Iran Protests: Twitter the Medium of the Movement," *Time*, June 17, 2009.

2. Reporters without Borders, "Obama Effect in US, while Europe Continues to Recede Israel in Free Fall, Iran at Gates of Infernal Trio," *Press Freedom Index*, October 30, 2009.

3. Simon Cottle, "Media and the Arab Uprisings of 2011: Research Notes," *Journalism* 12 (2011): 647–59.

4. Alexa, "Top Sites: Global," Alexa Internet, Inc., September 15, 2012, http://www.alexa.com/topsites/global

5. Danah Boyd and Nicole Ellison, "Social Network Sites: Definition, History, and Scholarship," *Journal of Computer-Mediated Communication* 13 (2007): article 11.

6. Shayndi Raice, "Days of Wild User Growth Appear over at Facebook," *Wall Street Journal*, June 11. 2012.

7. Internet World Stats, "Facebook Users in the World," *Usage and Population Statistics*, 2012, http://www.internetworldstats.com/facebook.htm.

8. Aaron Smith, "Why American's Use Social Media," *Pew Internet & American Life Project*, November 15, 2011, http://www.pewinternet.org/Reports/2011/Why-Americans-Use-Social-Media.aspx.

9. eMarketer, "Facebook's US User Growth Slows but Twitter Sees Double Digit Gains," *eMarketer Digital Intelligence*, March 5, 2012.

10. Kaiser Family Foundation, "Daily Media Use among Children and Teens up Dramatically from Five Years Ago," Press release, January 20, 2010, http://www.kff.org/entmedia/entmedia012010nr.cfm.

11. Dhiraj Murthy, "Twitter: Microphone for the Masses?" *Media, Culture & Society* 33 (2011): 779–89.

12. Mary Madden, "Privacy Management on Social Media Sites," *Pew Internet & American Life Project*, February 24, 2012.

13. Eric Miltsch, "Location Based Services: The Hottest Segment in Social Media," *Socialmediatoday.com*, October 7, 2010.

14. Madden, "Privacy Management on Social Media Sites."

15. Barbara Ortutay, "Facebook Adjusts Privacy Controls after Complaints," *The Seattle Times*, May 26, 2010.

16. Joseph Turrow and Michael Hennessey, "Internet Privacy and Institutional Trust: Insights from a National Survey," *New Media & Society* 9, no. 2 (2007): 300–18.

17. Francois Bar and Christian Sandvig, "US Communication Policy after Convergence," *Media, Culture & Society* 30 (2008): 531–50.

18. Peter Shields, "When the 'Information Revolution' and the US Security State Collide: Money Laundering and the Proliferation of Surveillance," *New Media & Society* 7, no. 4 (2005): 483–512.

19. Jan Fernback and Zizi Papacharissi, "Online Privacy as Legal Safeguard: The Relationship among Consumer, Online Portal, and Privacy Policies," *New Media & Society* 9, no. 5 (2007): 715–34.

20. Emily Grube, "Assault Fugitive Who Was Found via Facebook Is Back in NY," NewYorkCriminalLawyersBlog.com, March 8, 2010.

21. "7 Suspected Criminals Who Got Themselves Caught via Facebook," *The Week*, April 26, 2012.

22. Tamer El-Ghobashy, "Twitter Evidence Allowed in Occupy Trial," *Wall Street Journal*, April 23, 2012.

23. Joseph Ax, "Twitter Gives Occupy Protestor's Tweets to U.S. Judge," *Reuters,* September 14, 2012.

24. Derrick Harris, "U.S. Number 1 in Demanding Data on Twitter Users," GigaOm.com, July 2, 2012.

25. Ibid.

26. Derrick Harris, "Charts: If You're Concerned about Privacy, Don't Use Your Cell Phone," GigaOm.com, July 9, 2012.

CHAPTER FIFTEEN

Social Media and the Invasion of Privacy by Corporations

Bala A. Musa

When Robert Collins, a Maryland corrections officer, tried to return to his job after four months' leave of absence, he was asked by his interviewer to provide his Facebook password, as one of the conditions for his rehire. Astonished and frustrated by the perceived invasion of privacy, he declined the request. With the interviewer insisting that Collins comply, Collins contacted the American Civil Liberties Union, which then filed a complaint on his behalf.[1] According to Meredith Bennett-Smith, cases like this have been on the rise, requiring state legislatures and courts to weigh in and decide what are legitimate expectations, and what constitutes excesses in employee background investigation.[2] There are no clear guidelines on this subject at the moment. Some argue that such a request from an employer is fair and reasonable. Others disagree. It is obvious that the controversy is bound to linger as social media continue to permeate the culture.

The information landscape is undergoing immense transformation due to rapid innovation in and adoption of new communication technology. The rise of the Internet and the proliferation of social media, such as Facebook, blogs, LinkedIn, Twitter, YouTube, Foursquare, Yelp, Instagram, and so forth, have led to not only a breakdown of physical distance and barriers but also of social and psychological distances and barriers. These technologies are changing the way people live and relate to one another. The reach of modern communication technology is so fast and pervasive that its adoption and application occurs almost without thought and reflection. Concerns about their impact seem to be afterthoughts.

Debate has raged over whether these and other technological inventions are tools to serve us, or whether humans have, instead, become tools of these technologies. This chapter does not seek to engage in that debate in any depth. If the question is, "Do we control our machines or do our machines control us?" the answer would be both "yes" and "no." People and machines control each other, almost equally. Humans invent and use these technologies to accomplish various tasks. At the same time, the technologies and tools we use constrain our choices and determine our actions. It is this author's conviction that technology is neither totally neutral nor completely deterministic. The impact of media and communication technology, and indeed other technologies, as Joseph Klapper has argued, occurs within "a nexus" of intervening factors.[3] Technology influences human behavior, but it is not the sole catalyst for change. Instead, it is one of many overlapping agents of change, alongside cultural, political, and economic forces.

One subject of growing public debate is, to what extent is it okay for communication media to invade a person's privacy? In particular, as more people and organizations use social media, the question becomes, what are the ethical and legal limits of privacy invasion? This chapter joins the debate by looking at the role, rights, and responsibilities of individuals and organizations when it comes to social media use and the invasion of individuals' privacy. As mentioned earlier, this is a subject that is situated at the intersection of technology, culture, and economics.

Changing Dynamic

The right to one's privacy implies the right to be left alone, and to be safe from public scrutiny, if one so chooses. It means a person's sense of self, a person's identity, and integrity should not be violated or exploited or appropriated, whether physically, psychologically, socially, or economically without that person's consent. The courts, and society at large, have long acknowledged that people are entitled to privacy protection. The rise of social media has rekindled the debate because of emerging ways and avenues of invasion of privacy, the scope in which it occurs, the role of the participants, and the consequences for offenders and victims alike.

For a while, corporate media and their agents were regarded as the leading culprits and perpetrators in invasion of privacy incidents. The public was viewed mostly as an innocent, unwilling, and nonparticipatory victim. The press was usually the aggressor who, for many reasons, would cross legal and ethical lines to invade people's privacy in search of salacious and sensational stories. Usually the subjects whose privacy was invaded were celebrities, public figures, and newsmakers. The recent revelations about how News Corporation's British tabloid, *News of the World,* invaded the privacy of many celebrities, and even noncelebrities, in England are indicative of how media violate ethical and legal standards in the pursuit of sensational stories and profit. The taking and dissemination of topless pictures of Catherine Middleton, the Duchess of Cambridge, is another example of egregious invasion of privacy by overzealous and unscrupulous news media.

In today's new (social) media environment, the scope, nature, and threats of invasion of privacy have changed dramatically. The avenues, processes, rewards, and liabilities continue to expand. Social media are interactive by nature. This factor creates a nuanced and delicate relationship between the parties in communication, particularly with regard to invasion of privacy. This is reflected in how organizations apply social media as a means of gathering, storing, and using the personal information of members of the public. One can now say all or most victims of invasion of privacy are passive unsuspecting members of the public. Big corporate media are not the main perpetrators.

Communicating is personally mediated in the new media environment, as opposed to mass-mediated in the traditional (old or legacy) media environment. Communication is shifting from a "one source to many audiences" model to a "many sources to many audiences" format. A distinguishing characteristic of the latter is the anonymity of the audience.[4] Another element is the relative shift in the distance between the source and the audience, as well as between the audience members themselves.

There is greater expectation of privacy when the source is distant from the audience and when audiences are relatively anonymous to the source and to one another. With today's social media, both the distance and the degree of anonymity are significantly diminished. This is even more so in the case of organizations and organizational communication. If there is less personal distance and individual privacy in mediated interpersonal communication as compared to mass-mediated communication, it is even less so in an organizational communication setting. This is partly because organizational communication is defined by boundaries that separate members from nonmembers, and insiders from outsiders. Organizational

communication also assumes a contractual relationship between the organization and its employees or clients. The assumed contract between the
organization and its publics can be manifest or latent. The expectations of
privacy, therefore, vary according the nature of the relationship and how
each party perceives it.

Organizations, Social Media, and Privacy

Thanks to social media, organizations can track current and prospective employees' activities much more easily. There are many reasons
why organizations are interested in the activities and lives of employees
at and away from work. These range from the need to properly vet prospective employees to ensuring professional standards and compliance
with workplace rules and policies. Even before today's social media era,
employers and financial lenders, for instance, did credit history checks
on prospective employers and borrowers. Such background checking
was a way of ensuring the credibility and integrity of the individual
being hired or to whom they are lending money. Other forms of background checks that organizations conducted regularly included asking
for references on behalf of prospective employees. Landlords and land-
ladies routinely checked the backgrounds of rental applicants. Many
organizations did and still do criminal history background checks.
Some require drug tests of prospective employees. These are just some
of the ways organizations have historically tried to get personal information from their members, clients, or associates. One common trait
in these processes of information gathering by organizations is that the
parties being investigated were mostly aware and would often give their
consent.

While these kinds of personal information are still being collected by
organizations, with new media communication, the range of personal
information and means of collecting it have increased exponentially.
Social media make it possible for organizations to snoop on individuals and gather personal information that people may not voluntarily
divulge, often without the subject's knowledge. There have been numerous instances of perceived invasion of privacy by organizations, at least
from the employees' perspective. A restaurant employee lost her job for
posting a negative comment on her Facebook page about her customers.
A lot of people whose jobs require them to travel to and do business on
the road use company phones that have tracking devices. That means
their employers can track their movements and whereabouts around the
clock. A Los Angeles public security employee found out that his personal

calls on a company-issued phone were being accessed by his supervisors, even though the employer authorized the use of the phone for private communication.

Barrett Tyron, a reporter at *The Colorado Springs Gazette*, a subsidiary of Freedom Communication, was ordered to remove a link on his Facebook wall to a story in *The Los Angeles Times* about Freedom Communication's purchase of *The Orange County Register*. When Tyron protested that the posting was on his personal Facebook page, his superior reminded him of the company's policy and expectation that employees would "protect the company's goodwill, brands, and business reputation."[5] The policy reads in part, "Freedom Communications, Inc.'s Associate Handbook/ Confidentiality and Proprietary Rights policy prohibits you from posting disparaging or defamatory statements about the company or its business interests, but you should also avoid social media communications that might be misconstrued in a way that could damage the company's goodwill and business reputation, even indirectly."[6]

Other instances show how organizations jealously guard their reputations and brands in the age of social media. They care about how they are portrayed and perceived online. They are so concerned that they track their employees' social media footprint and online activities. It is obvious that the organizations and the employees have different expectations of which online activities are personal and which ones are business-related. Do these employees have a right to expect privacy, or have they surrendered their privacy by consenting to work for the organization?

Rights and Responsibilities

When companies snoop on people's private communication and activities, are they going too far, or are they within bounds of expected organizational practice? This question has both legal and ethical sides to it. Recent court rulings show that the law recognizes that both organizations and private citizens have rights and responsibilities. In *Citizens United v. FEC* (2010), the U.S. Supreme Court affirmed that as corporate citizens, businesses have the same (free speech) rights as private citizens.[7] This ruling guaranteed them the right to promote and protect their political, economic, and social interests the way a private citizen would. The ramifications of this decision are still unfolding, but continue to be felt in many aspects of society. Yet the courts and policy makers have recognized that individuals and corporations stand on uneven grounds as citizens before the law. That is why government has sought to enact policies that would limit indiscriminate collection, storage, and use of information about private citizens by organizations.

Generally, organizations have more resources and greater capacity to gather information about private citizens than the other way around. Private individuals are not only in a lesser position of power relative to corporations, but they are also more vulnerable when it comes to the amount of harm that can be done to them. Organizations are a collection of persons and interests with shared stakes and liabilities. Therefore, any attacks against their reputations, finances, and resources are absorbed by their size, the depth of their pockets, and the reach of their resources. That is why individuals are often reluctant to take on organizations, knowing that they are not in a fair fight with corporations. Given this reality, one would argue that organizations should not have unlimited power to monitor the activities of their employees, clients, or associates.

When organizations investigate individuals', and particularly prospective employees', social media activities, the organizations expose themselves to legal jeopardy. The Equal Employment Opportunity Act (EEOA) forbids employers from making hiring decisions based on an applicant's race, sex, religion, (dis)ability, marital status, and so forth. This information is often posted on people's social network sites. When an employer requests access to a prospective employee's social network site, that employer risks being charged for rejecting an employee on the basis of such personal information. In this case, one is putting the onus on the organization to exercise caution and responsibility with their power and capacity to invade people's privacy. Digging into people's personal lives and information should be done with utmost respect for individuals' right to privacy. People are legally and morally entitled to privacy. That right should not be violated just because the technology affords us the capacity to do so. It is almost impossible for an employer to argue that the personal information it has at its disposal about employees has no bearing on how employees are treated. Employees and clients should not be put in a situation where they have to overly self-monitor who they relate to online or in their personal lives because their employers or prospective employers may be watching. Should people not disclose that they belong to particular religious groups, support certain causes, or hold certain political views, for fear that their bosses may not share the same values? This is information that employees would, ordinarily, not share with coworkers but would be comfortable sharing with friends in their social network. They should be free to do so without fear of reprisal.

That said, there is a gray area where companies have greater latitude on how far they can go monitoring employee's social media activities:

specifically, company-related activities using company resources. Some companies allow or expect employees to use Facebook, Twitter, Linke-dIn, and other social media for their professional work. In such cases the employee is seen to be representing the organization in his or her online communication. It would be helpful for the company to spell out its policy on the appropriate use of social networks when representing the company. If a person uses Facebook, blogs, Twitter, and so forth, for work, the ideal situation would be to separate personal social Web sites from professional ones.

There is good reason to support Congress's attempt to require businesses to notify individuals of personal information that companies collect and use. The burden should rest on organizations to defend why they need that personal information and to be held accountable for using such information responsibly. The psychological and social harm that is caused by a breach of one's privacy can, at minimum, leave significant wounds, and in extreme cases ruin a person's reputation. That is why a company should shoulder a greater burden when it decides to dig up personal information.

Information posted on the Internet about another person may not always be true. At times, people use the Internet to smear the good names of innocent people with whom they have disagreement. The individual being maligned may not be aware of the negative or false information paraded online about him or her. If an employer finds that information and uses it as a basis for decisions regarding the employee without making the employee aware of the information, that employee may suffer unjustly.

That said, the line becomes murky when the individual is using the company's resources and paid time for online activities. It is fair to assume that the employee is, in such situations, acting on behalf of the company. The company will not be intruding on a person's privacy if it reads employee's e-mails that are sent via the organization's e-mail. This is because if an employee uses company-issued e-mail to sexually harass another employee or create a hostile work environment, the company would be legally liable. Even when there is justification for reading employees' correspondence and other communications, it is appropriate to make employees aware that their e-mail and online activities on company sites will be tracked. Therefore, the public can share the burden of protecting their privacy.

Finally, while individuals have a right to privacy, they also have a responsibility to safeguard their privacy and to protect that right. As the McBride Commission on International Communication rightly observed, people should not be given responsibility without the right to exercise it, and those who act irresponsibility negate their claim to their rights.[8] It is impossible to do business in today's society without leaving the digital footprint of one's financial transactions, leisure activities, and professional life. In some cases, the more online presence one has the better. However, the trail that a person leaves on social networking sites may come back to haunt him or her. If you voluntarily provide more information about your personal life than you want to make public, you cannot turn around and accuse others of violating your privacy. As they say, the Internet is a global notice board. Information posted there can be taken down at will, but is never completely erased. That is why individuals have the responsibility to help draw the line for corporations, the media, and the society by how they conduct themselves online. Just as organizations are committed to managing their online reputations, individuals must do the same. Organizations should not violate the public's privacy in pursuit of corporate goals and interests. Government must take a firm stand by holding companies that overstep their boundaries accountable.

Notes

1. Meredith Bennett-Smith, "Job Interviewer Asks for Facebook Password. Should You Give It?" *The Christian Science Monitor*, June 11, 2012, http://0-www.lexisnexis.com.patris.apu.edu/hottopics/lnacademic/?.

2. Ibid.

3. Joseph Klapper, *The Effects of Mass Communication* (New York: Free Press, 1960).

4. Dennis McQuail, *Mass Communication Theory*, 6th ed. (Los Angeles: Sage, 2010.)

5. Jim Romenesko, "Freedom Paper Tells Reporter to Remove LAT Story from Facebook Wall," Jim Romenesko.com, http://jimromenesko.com/ 2012/06/13 /freedom-paper-tells-reporter-to-remove-lat-story-from-facebook-wall/.

6. Ibid.

7. *Citizens United v. FEC* No. 08–205, Supreme Court of the United States, 130 S.Ct. 876; 175 L. Ed. 2d 753; 2010 U.S. LEXIS 766; 78 U.S.L.W. 4078; 159 Lab. Cas. (CCH) P10,166; 187 L.R.R.M. 2961; 22 Fla. L. Weekly Fed. S 73, March 24, 2009, Argued; September 9, 2009, Reargued, January 21, 2010, Decided. Lexis-Nexis, http://0-www.lexisnexis.com.patris.apu.edu/hottopics/l nacademic/?.

8. International Commission for the Study of Communication Problems, *Many Voices, One World: Toward a New, More Just, and More Efficient World Information and Communication Order* (Lanham, MD: Rowman & Littlefield, 2004).

CHAPTER SIXTEEN

"Racing the Vampire": Exploring Race and Identity in Second Life

Franklin Nii Amankwah Yartey

Introduction

"At the start, Stella Costello was beautiful by most standards of either the real or virtual world, with a slender waist and a neck framed by perfect crests of blonde hair. But something seemed off."[1] As in the off-line world, in the virtual world users desire to look their best: one wants to have perfect hair, great clothes, the best makeup, the most masculine look with bulging muscles, and so forth. Virtual worlds like Second Life (SL) have opened unimagined doors to millions of people. Many have used this virtual platform as a means to make money, create identity, and do many other things that might have been nearly impossible to do off-line.

This study explores what happens to identity when we become three-dimensional, and how communication encounters in the virtual world influence the creation of identity on SL. The study is an ethnographic exploration of the experiences of a black avatar, "Frankie Nubalo," in creating an identity on SL and how the decisions Nubalo makes in SL are influenced by choices he makes off-line. In the virtual world, unlike the off-line world, humanoids (avatars) do not have all the physical constraints that exist off-line in creating identities for themselves. Off-line, individual identities are predetermined: An individual has just one skin color for life. However, in the virtual world, identity is defined by oneself.[2] The characteristics of a virtual world such as SL allow for a unique creation of identity.

Virtual life presents various interests to individuals and offers almost anything one can find in off-line life. Millions of people around the world log on daily to a virtual world. Many stay logged on for hours or days exploring, meeting new people, conducting business, holding training workshops, and engaging in many other activities in virtual worlds like SL. According to Cassidy, "Nearly six million people have joined Linden Lab's Second Life since it went public in 2003 and there are currently 1.75 million 'active' members who have logged on in the last two months."[3] Virtual worlds like SL have opened unimagined doors to millions of people. Many use the virtual platform to make money and do many other things that may be virtually impossible off-line. Bartle asserts that virtual worlds provide settings that consist of people from different backgrounds and countries interacting and making connections. "From their humble beginnings, virtual worlds have evolved to become major hubs of entertainment, education, and community."[4] Lin also confirmed that "virtual worlds offer opportunities, experiences, and pleasures that satisfy many of the basic motivations that drive modern consumption."[5] Gajjala also asserts that with globalization, the world shrinking in time and space, and the dawning of various technologies, the need has arisen for intercultural understanding. Cyberspace offers a platform for intercultural encounters and exchange of ideas.[6]

Identity Defined

Several scholars have given differing definitions of identity. The *Cambridge Advanced Learners Dictionary* defines identity as "the qualities of a person or group which make them different from others."[7] Goffman asserted that society creates ways of classifying people and acknowledging characteristics, both physical and internal, that are felt to be "ordinary and natural" for members of these classifications. According to Goffman, "When a stranger comes into our presence, then, first appearances are likely to enable us to anticipate his [/her] attributes, his [/her] social identity[.]"[8] Appearances matter off-line, and they matter in the virtual world as well. This element of identity cannot be done away with in the virtual world. According to Kroger, "Erickson (1968) described identity as involving a subjective feeling of self-sameness and continuity over time."[9] Therefore, in different environments and in different situations one still has the sense of being the same person.[10] Viken and Pedersen see identity as "[naturally] arising from the way people live and participate in the social life demanded and permitted by nature."[11] Defining identity online can be tricky, because depending on the user, one's online identity changes constantly.[12] Jordan, however, stated that "one of the most touted beliefs about internet communication is that the medium strips away users' identities and leaves them free to reconstruct a [tether-less] online persona."[13] This freedom that individuals have makes the definition of online identities fluid. However, other factors could influence one's identity.

Boellstorff also asserts that once we log on to virtual worlds, we all assume certain "roles." It is this notion of "role" that shapes our conceptions of identity online. For example, in a vampire community on SL, there are different roles that avatars adopt, which help shape identity. Wright also employs the notion of double consciousness in his works on identity and the African Diaspora. He asserts that double consciousness is an awareness of oneself and how others also perceive others. Black people in America historically have had to deal with this notion of double consciousness—the conflating of one's own identity with the identity imposed by others, leading to a constant struggle to establish an identity. This confusion is what leads to double consciousness.

Creation of an Avatar and Race

An avatar's identity starts being molded the moment an individual logs in to a virtual world and begins customizing or creating an avatar. As stated earlier, an avatar's identity changes constantly, depending on how often its controller (human) decides to modify the avatar. Avatars come in all forms: dogs, cats, elephants, humanoid avatars, and so forth. The virtual world provides this flexibility to be whoever one wants to be. You do not have to be constrained to a particular class or race; rather, you define for yourself what you want to be. There are resources in SL to make this possible, though there are limits to the creation of identity in the virtual world. Webb asserted that "avatars are normally, though not exclusively, humanoid in appearance, although some participants use animal representations."[14] Webb adds that human avatars are heavily stereotyped, appear ethnically white most of the time, their features over-emphasized, and look more sexualized and sometimes more masculine when males. According to Gajjala, Rybas, and Altman, "racialization in a technologically mediated global context is nuanced by how class, gender and geography, caste, colonization, and globalization intersect."[15] Racialization and discrimination also exists in the virtual world, depending on the identities that avatars adopt. There is a probability that a particular "humanoid" may face discrimination, depending on the social circles in which the avatar chooses to immerse. Boellstorff affirms that SL does not present options for one to select race, but the availability of different types of skin allows for the unique creation of identity. According to Boellstorff, skins are highly prized items in SL. There have been instances where avatars were discriminated against because of the skin they were wearing.

What is interesting is that in virtual worlds like SL, avatars have rights just as humans do in the off-line world. These "humanoid rights" protect all avatars from humanoid rights abuses. The first two articles in the Declaration of Rights of Avatars, which was instituted on January 26, 2000, are as follows:

> Avatars are created free and equal in rights. Special powers or privileges shall be founded solely on the common good, and not based on whim, favoritism, nepotism, or the caprice of those who hold power. Those who act as ordinary avatars within the space shall have only the rights of normal avatars.[16]

The first article shows that avatars, depending on whether they are ordinary or not, have special rights allocated them. However, the second article on the Declaration states that all avatars, regardless of their classification, have the right to be treated as people and not as "disembodied, meaningless, soulless puppets. Inherent in this right are therefore the natural and inalienable rights of humankind. These are liberty, property, security, and resistance to oppression."[17] There are a total of 19 articles under the Declaration. The articles in this Declaration provide a solid foundation for avatars to create not only an identity for themselves, but multiple identities, and the ability to change identities at will. One can change the appearance of an avatar as many times as they please. Bradford and Crowe explain that "virtual identity (and status) is defined by shifting characteristics."[18] The identity and the characteristics that come with this avatar constantly change at the discretion of the individual controlling the avatar.

Avatar as Identity

The shifting characteristics of the virtual world and virtual identity allow for the unique creation of identity in SL. According to Au, "the most energetic Netizens maintain several avatars in numerous worlds, some for business, with immediate links to their real-life person and their financial/government credentials. Other identities will be for creation and experimentation, and most people will keep these separate from their off-line physical self in order to explore other facets of self and desire."[19]

Identity, as stated earlier, will be a very difficult concept to define in the virtual world due to the versatile nature of this concept. One's avatar becomes one's identity online, and for this reason any alteration to an avatar in a virtual world instantly changes the identity of the avatar. Ivanova affirms that globalization and changing technologies have complicated the definition of identity: "Under the influence of processes of integration and globalization, and the development of information technologies, the sense of identity of today's individual, regardless of his place of residence, is changing its characteristics [. . .]. A factor that creates problems for the selection of appropriate methods to study it."[20] Not only is it hard to define identity, but also the nature of this concept in the light of globalization presents some challenges to its study.

Freedom

Freedom is what individuals who own avatars have online, freedom to mold their avatars into what they want them to be. The freedom to create an identity that will be ideal to the environment in which an avatar finds itself. This autonomy allowed online and in the virtual world allows for shifts in cultural identities.[21] The freedom provided in virtual worlds allows multiuser virtual worlds like Dungeons (MUDs) a virtual environment in which "the construction of identity that is so fluid and multiple that it strains the very limits of the notion. People become masters of self-presentation and self-creation."[22] This newly acquired freedom conferred in some virtual environments enables avatars to move around freely, exploring, trying to be accepted in the new social conditions in which they find themselves, and joining groups that will satisfy their needs and contribute to shaping identity.[23] Nakamura additionally argues that the identity of an avatar is directly linked to the user: "they represent choices made by the user who wishes to build an online identity that is warranted by preexisting offline relationship."[24] For example, if a user does not have the opportunity or the courage to meet new people in social settings off-line, the virtual world, due to the superficial anonymity it provides, offers a milieu that makes it easy for people who are shy or socially challenged to interact.

In the virtual world, unlike the off-line, humanoids (avatars) do not have all the physical constraints that exist off-line in creating identities for themselves. Off-line individual identity is predetermined—one is of a specific skin color. However, in the virtual world, identity is defined by oneself.[25] Adrian goes on to say that the "AlphaWorld bestows upon all avatars the same capabilities at all times. Consequently, a player who defies a social norm in AlphaWorld, if banished, can generate a new avatar immediately, using a different name, which will have all the same capabilities and skills as previously. The community can have no effect on behavior."[26]

As one can construe from the previous extract, identity can be indiscriminately created and replicated in the virtual world with limited constrictions. Consumerism also helps avatars craft their identities.

Consumption and Identity

Consumption in the virtual world contributes to the identity of an avatar. Being able to buy clothes in virtual stores is a way that users and avatars can create identities online. Off-line people also use this idea to create identities: "consumerism has enabled Americans to establish new identities."[27] Lin adds that "consumption occurs not so much because of the intrinsic functional qualities of an item, but rather because of extrinsic values assigned to objects of consumption by society, social subgroups, or individuals."[28] In the virtual world, the consumption of goods and services is also an attempt to buy into what the virtual society has deemed as necessary to consume if an avatar wants to belong and to be accepted in certain groups or organizations. The clothes worn in the virtual world help define the identity of a humanoid—clothing and accessorizing is an important aspect of the virtual world.[29] Identity is a versatile concept in the virtual world, building and sustaining an identity is a nuanced process. Off-line race and consumption also play important roles in the virtual world and contributes to the creation of an avatar's identity. In creating identities online, it is important to have the cultural currency that enables one to fit into certain groups in the virtual world. This could mean dressing a certain way, speaking a particular language, or performing specific acts.

Participatory Observation

A *deep hanging-out* approach was adopted for this cyber-ethnographic study.[30] This involves totally immersing oneself into the virtual environment under study. I have been immersed in SL for five years now. A deep hanging-out approach was adopted because numerous scholars have used variants of this method.[31] I started off by creating an avatar for myself on SL and picking a name for the avatar. An avatar with skin closely representing black skin was chosen. A darker skin was selected because Frankie Nubalo was an extension of my off-line identity. I then proceeded to Orientation Island for the familiarization process in SL. After being oriented, I proceeded to explore, meet other avatars, chat, and tried to find ways to explore and create an identity for Frankie Nubalo. While exploring and meeting new people in SL, I collected data by taking screenshots of different locations with the built-in camera on SL's interface. These images were saved to the hard drive of my computer. The SL interface also allowed me to select, cut, and paste conversations into a Word document. I created separate files for each ethnographic encounter with the date, time, and the location of encounter. I spent an average of 5–7 hours online each time I logged onto SL, chatting with avatars in public places and taking screenshots. According to Boellstorff, Nardi, Pearce, and Taylor, "it is legitimate to see subscription-based virtual worlds as having public areas where it is not necessary to have every person in an interaction sign an informed consent form-just as there is nothing inherently unethical about taking a picture of a tourist in an open, general area at an amusement park, which is a public place."[32] For this study, informant identities were removed and names of avatars were replaced with pseudonyms, so that they cannot be identified or linked to their identities in SL.[33] Details with regards to the time and place of events were also removed while maintaining ethnographic richness.[34]

My methods also included observing myself off-line and making mental notes of my reactions to the different situations presented to me in the virtual world. After each exploration in SL, I documented my various reactions to different situations in SL and tried to deconstruct and unpack these reactions. A descriptive approach will be adopted in analyzing the ethnographic data collected in world. Conquergood, in his study in the Hmong refugee camp, adopted a descriptive method in analyzing data and performances he had witnessed in the camp. Au, Nakamura, Clarke, and Wright have also used descriptive methods in their studies. Pertinent literature was also reviewed for this study.[35]

Analytical Framework

Using theoretical frameworks from scholars like Au; Boellstorff; Gajjala, Rabas, and Altman; Markham and Baym; and Nakamura, this chapter seeks to answer questions about race and identity by chronicling the encounters and experiences of a black avatar, Frankie Nubalo, as he struggles to make sense of SL, be accepted in SL communities and, through consumption, create a distinct identity for himself. Theoretical concepts to be explored for this study are identity and race.[36] According to Nakamura, "visual culture provides a powerful methodology for parsing gender and racial and ethnic identity in these digital signifying practices that became so prominent at the turn of the century."[37] SL is a visual culture that involves immersion and interaction with natives in world. Clarke, in *Mapping*

Yoruba Networks, introduces theoretical concepts of "desire and belonging." The author writes about the desire of African Americans to belong to, or establish ties to a particular African country. Clarke asserts that "Locating *Roots* as a key force in the shift in black Americans' imaginings of their connection to an African heritage is critical for understanding the establishment of a new common-sense notion of racial categories in heritage terms."[38] Parallels can be drawn with avatar Frankie Nubalo, who is also trying to establish an identity online and also has a desire to belong to a community in SL. Through the lens of Clarke's "desire and belonging," the chapter explores how Frankie Nubalo's race, interactions with the "natives" on SL (especially vampires), and consumption influenced by his desire to belong to a community shapes Nubalo's identity online.

Description of Site

SL is a futuristic virtual environment that provides the means for humans to open unimagined doors to creativity, connectivity, and consumption. It provides individuals opportunities to create new and extended identities through exploration, discovery, the initiation of new relationships, and the building of credibility, while also providing an accelerated and eternal approach to living.

I will describe some basic, frequently used functions on the SL interface. Though SL has a user-friendly interface, there is a learning curve and it takes constant use to be well oriented with the interface.

Communication

The SL interface is user-friendly and allows users the ease of navigation once one is well oriented to the program. On the bottom-left corner of the screen is a *chat* icon that one can click on for community conversations. Chatting in this dialogue box means every avatar in the location you are in can see your chat logs, though it fades out after a few seconds. The interface also allows for private conversations and one can either click the *communicate* icon on the bottom-left corner of the screen or right click on an avatar for options to chat with that avatar privately. The only shortcoming to this is with private chat, you will be stuck with a rectangular chat box that occasionally gets in the way of your avatar's vision.

Moving Around

The interface also allows for easy movement either with a mouse or the arrow keys on the keyboard. One also has the ability to fly by clicking on the *fly* icon on the bottom-right-hand corner of the screen. You can also map your avatar's location or search for locations to *teleport* to with the *search* icons on the bottom and top of the screen. Teleporting is the process of transporting an avatar from one virtual location to another. While exploring SL, one also has the option to save landmarks, clothing items, skins, body parts, gestures, and so forth.

Building

SL allows users not only to communicate and explore various locations, but also to build. The interface allows users to construct virtual buildings, shops, offices, bodies of water, and the like. Items and objects can be stored in the avatar's inventory and used for construction.

Appearances

SL offers the option for an avatar's appearance to be modified with body parts, clothing, and so forth, which can be accessed from the inventory. The shape of an avatar's nose or hand can be transformed by manipulating the options available in the *appearance* menu box. One can also choose the sex for an avatar. Switching an avatar's sex during its existence is an unlimited option that users have.

Appearances Matter

On August 22, 2008, Frankie Nubalo comes into existence. Nubalo is about six-feet tall, lanky with barely any muscles on his stick-like figure; a bald shiny head matches his big brown shiny eyes. He passes easily as an African American but that is not how I intended him to look. I attributed an African identity to Nubalo; however, since I was just starting out on SL, I did not have the money to purchase the darker skins. I decided to go with the clothing that was offered because I had not acquired the literacy to shop for my own clothes. On September 8, 2008, I met Alione, a very lovely lady (Avatar) in an undisclosed location. Here is the content of our initial conversation:

> **Frankie Nubalo:** hi
> **ALIONE:** Hello Frankie give me a min
> **Frankie Nubalo:** k
> **ALIONE:** yes Frankie
> **Frankie Nubalo:** well, just making some new friends here
> **Frankie Nubalo:** where u from

Frankie Nubalo: I am from ohio
ALIONE: Oh i see
ALIONE: Utopia
ALIONE: that is the city I am from

Nubalo's clothes were simple. He had on an unbuttoned white shirt (the shirt had no buttons) with black pants. Thirty-six minutes into our conversation, I decided to ask this lady out on a date and she commented on the shirt.

Frankie Nubalo: what works for you?
ALIONE: dancing, shopping and horseback riding
ALIONE: a man with a button shirt
ALIONE: why are your hands white
ALIONE: oh you have on gloves
ALIONE: where do you shop
ALIONE: do you have any cash on you
Frankie Nubalo: cash
ALIONE: yes linden dollars
Frankie Nubalo: I told you I am new
Frankie Nubalo: how do I get cash
ALIONE: you need set an account or get a job

Immediately, Nubalo was being told what to do to fit in, he needed to button his shirt, take off his white gloves, and find a job. Alione took him to a freebee store since he was without money. She proceeded to help him pick out some brand new clothes. I thought Nubalo could get away with the clothes he wore initially, and I did not really pay attention to how he looked in SL. Appearances do matter, if you want to get a date on SL.

Difficulty with using SL's interface was hindering my avatar's consumption and contributing to his appearance. Gajjala, Rybas, and Altman shed more light on how social and cultural problems arise in producing, consuming, and using technology, and this is what we see happening with Nubalo. Not knowing how to make money or get a job on SL influences his encounters with other avatars. I entered SL with the assumption that I was going to fully explore this new world with nothing holding me back on this endeavor. I did not really care what clothes my avatar wore and was not too worried about picking the right or perfect set of clothes to match an appropriate pair of shoes or sneakers. But obviously avatars in SL take dressing up seriously, and this was revealed in my encounter with Alione. I completely transformed Nubalo after my conversation with Alione: No longer did he look scrawny. Instead, he now had some meat on his bones. Frankie Nubalo looked more like a bouncer. My intimidating physique earned more respect from other male avatars. I had transformed into a powerful and more appealing avatar.

I was, however, still struggling to navigate in SL. I was obsessively trying to create an identity for myself in my quest to be accepted into a group on SL. It was difficult and challenging to be accepted into small cliques in SL. Sometimes it could get very frustrating. Is this off-line or SL? I found myself asking this question each time I was faced with a potential interaction with an SL citizen. Are my experiences on SL richer? My adventures continued at an undisclosed club downtown somewhere in a city in SL.

Frankie Nubalo: hi
Frankie Nubalo: wanna dance too
ALIONE: Sure, dance on.
ALIONE: You lookin pretty natty there Frankie.
Frankie Nubalo: thanks
ALIONE: Thank you.

Gone was the unbuttoned shirt. Donned in jeans and a colorful t-shirt, Nubalo and Alione danced the night away in the club. Alione contributed in many ways to my transformation because she had made comments about my appearance and even gave me some tips on how to improve my appearance. It is nice to be noticed in SL. It is especially uplifting when you are told by an avatar that you look nice. As in the off-line world, compliments on SL share the same positive connotation.

"Rezzing" Myself

My appearances were getting me a lot of attention, but what I hoped for was to be accepted into a community on SL. I wanted to belong to a group of people or a community, be able to connect, and have a sense of belonging. Meanwhile, another conversation occurs:

Findor: you need to re rez your self
Frankie Nubalo: rez?
Frankie Nubalo: more cloths [sic]
Findor: no
Frankie Nubalo: ok what
Findor: hold down ctrl alt r
Frankie Nubalo: did that nothing happened
Findor: your here as just smoke
Findor: might need to relog

Frankie Nubalo: ok will do that. be back
Frankie Nubalo: soon
Findor: k

I was gradually gaining some cultural and technological knowledge through my encounters. Findor needed to actually see me to interact; I had no idea I had teleported in the form of pure smoke. This affirmed my continuous struggles with the epistemologies of doing in SL. "Doing" means learning to effectively teleport from one location to the other or learning to navigate the complex landscape in SL.

Encounter with a Vampire

Kitty was her name, and I met her in a shopping mall. I had teleported there to check out some clothes, and noticing a very well-dressed avatar in a beautiful dress, I initiated conversation. However, during our chat, she disclosed who she really was and asked me to be her minion.

Kitty: So would u like to b my minion too? lol
Frankie Nubalo: not sure
Frankie Nubalo: will have to think about it
Frankie Nubalo: after I become one, what next?
Kitty: nothing, you join my clan, great group of people and keep doing whatever u do here
Kitty: just bite people every now and again to stay healthy
Frankie Nubalo: whow
Frankie Nubalo: interesting
Kitty: It all gets explained during the turning dear

She wanted to make me her minion: Frankie Nubalo's very existence would be only to heed her orders and literally be a slave. Did I want to be a minion? I was being presented with the opportunity I had been waiting for to materialize: to become part of a community on SL, belong somewhere, be cared for by others, have a family of friends, confidants, people I could talk to, people with whom I could share secrets. Was I ready to be a vampire? I did not want to be a vampire. The question was why. Why become a vampire when the notion of being or becoming a vampire was repellant to me. At the same time, one must wonder: Who was thinking and making these decisions? Frankie Nubalo or Franklin Yartey? The connection is obvious. There are similarities between Frankie and Franklin. My off-line identity was influencing my SL identity. For me, this was an inevitable part of being part of the virtual world, to constantly keep my avatar in check from antagonizing my off-line identity. In the next encounter, Kitty continues to persuade me to become a vampire:

> **Kitty:** You still wanting to b turned?
> **Frankie Nubalo:** sometime
> **Kitty:** The tool bar u get to bite
> **Kitty:** you know how to open crates in your inventory?
> **Frankie Nubalo:** no
> **Kitty:** Same way u open boxes when u shop
> **Frankie Nubalo:** yes
> **Kitty:** k then thats a start for your turning
> **Frankie Nubalo:** I see
> **Frankie Nubalo:** will I change physically?
> **Kitty:** no silly
> **Frankie Nubalo:** so how will I change
> **Frankie Nubalo:** ?
> **Kitty:** u wont change at all
> **Frankie Nubalo:** so will people know I am a vanpire?
> **Frankie Nubalo:** hmmm
> **Kitty:** not if u dont tell them
> **Kitty:** did u know i was?
> **Frankie Nubalo:** no
> **Frankie Nubalo:** so you just go up to somebody and bite them without warning?
> **Kitty:** Yes if u want to do it that way
> **Frankie Nubalo:** what other ways are there?
> **Kitty:** Whichever ways u can think of..We all hunt different
> **Frankie Nubalo:** how do you hunt?
> **Kitty:** What do you mean?
> **Kitty:** Just hunt while your exploring SL
> **Frankie Nubalo:** I see
> **Kitty:** u dont have to if u dont want to turn Frank
> **Frankie Nubalo:** can I turn back again?
> **Kitty:** No
> **Frankie Nubalo:** what???????
> **Frankie Nubalo:** why?
> **Kitty:** You would betray the one who made u
> **Frankie Nubalo:** so I will be a vampire for ever?
> **Kitty:** Because u work for the family, making it bigger with more vampires

Once a vampire, forever a vampire in the virtual world. I definitely knew I did not want to become a vampire, even at the cost of loosing acceptance into a community for Nubalo. But I really did not want to be a vampire on SL. According to Kitty, it is the goal of the vampire clan to increase the number of clan members. Explaining the benefits she said:

> **Kitty:** Its just a game within the world frank
> **Kitty:** Something to break up the boredom of this place
> **Frankie Nubalo:** okay
> **Kitty:** Something to do besides shop and dance at clubs

Becoming

So why was the process of becoming a vampire such a daunting task? I entered SL with certain preconceived notions—that I could be whatever I wanted to be and that I would fully explore this new world and hopefully, become part of a community. Yet there I was, presented with an opportunity to become part of a community of vampires and yet I kept turning down the offer. My off-line identity conflated my online identity, preventing Nubalo from transforming into a vampire. My off-line values would not allow me to be vampire if vampires truly existed off-line. These are the same values that interfered with Nubalo's transformation. Becoming a vampire is not a normal process that I would participate in off-line and it does not fit the assumption of what I subjectively consider the "normal state." The normal state entails doing things that fit the norms of my day-to-day life, such as teaching, watching television, seeing movies, going out with friends, eating, sleeping, meeting new people, and so forth. Turning into a vampire does not fit these norms and this is why I rejected the notion of becoming a vampire online. My next encounter with Kitty presented another opportunity to become a vampire, which I met with the same mixed emotions as previously. She was at a dance club with one of her minions, and while we danced, this conversation developed:

> **Kitty:** you look great
> **Frankie Nubalo:** thanks
> **Frankie Nubalo:** u too
> **Kitty:** Hey Frank, Can i take you outside and bite u??
> **Frankie Nubalo:** why?
> **Frankie Nubalo:** hmmmm
> **Kitty:** Need the blood
> **Frankie Nubalo:** why me?
> **Kitty:** Cause your [sic] fresh <giggles>
> **Kitty:** Then i'd like to make u my minion if you'll let me

Frankie Nubalo: I will love to be but lets take it slow okay???

Frankie Nubalo: hmmm

Frankie Nubalo: okay?

Kitty: Take what slow?? Just need a little drink lol you wouldnt want to see me die would u? Frankie Nubalo: no

Frankie Nubalo: there are lots of fresh people in here

Frankie Nubalo: lol

Kitty: Lots r in limbo

Frankie Nubalo: true

Frankie Nubalo: so what do l get in return?

Kitty: If you become my minion?

Kitty: or if i bite u? Frankie Nubalo: both

Kitty: Well if you let me bite you you would be strengthening me, i'm under my required intake

Frankie Nubalo: and . . .

Kitty: And if you decide to become my Minion, i would possess your soul for eternity, and you would become a vamp like me, and be part of one of the best Clans in SL, I'm in a great family, Great people, you'de [*sic*] fit right in

Kitty: And of course i'd train u to become a vamp

Kitty: All my sisters would like you too lol

Frankie Nubalo: so what will happen to me if you just bite me

Frankie Nubalo: ?

Kitty: Nuthin

Frankie Nubalo: tempting

Kitty: But if you decide to be my minion, ide [*sic*] have to take your life.. thats a few bites lol

Kitty: Have to drain u

Frankie Nubalo: hmmmm

Kitty: Then you get replenished with vamp blood

Kitty: Then i teach u to hunt, etc

Kitty: You'de [*sic*] be my charge for awhile

Frankie Nubalo: how long?

Kitty: However long it takes for you to catch on to being a vamp

Frankie Nubalo: remember what I said to you the other day???

Kitty: refresh my memory, its been a long week

Frankie Nubalo: oh come on u know where l stand now on this, lets take our time

Kitty: But i need to feed now

Kitty: you can think about the minion thing

Frankie Nubalo: I am not ready for feeding too

Frankie Nubalo: I am sorry dear

Kitty: Np..I had to try

Frankie Nubalo: D

Being a vampire would mean I would be part of a community of vampires, with a whole clan to support me. Yet biting people to maintain health levels was disturbing to me. However, Frankie Nubalo would not physically change, he would not have vampire fangs, and would not have to worry about daylight; there would not be a physical transformation. Reading the process of transformation from Kitty seemed like the induction process to hypnosis, where the hypnotist tries to establish rapport with the subject by explaining what to expect during the process. Nakamura contributes to this off-line and online identity conflation by asserting that "AIM buddy avatars do not stand alone to signify a disembodied self; instead, they represent choices made by the user who wishes to build an online identity that is warranted by a preexisting offline relationship."[39] The preexisting off-line "relationship scripts" were what was interfering with Nubalo's online "relationship scripts": the off-line scripts were meshing with the online scripts, creating a mutual shaping of identity. The online encounters with my vampire friend were triggering specific reactions off-line which caused my off-line identity to dictate to my online identity what to do and what not to do. What does this say about my off-line identity? Is SL an authentic universe for Nubalo? SL seems to be an authentic universe for Frankie Nubalo. He is already in the process of being accepted into a vampire community. He was invited to a vampire wedding, which I believe is a strong indication that he will finally be accepted when his off-line identity finally allows him to go through the transformation process in becoming a vampire.

Conclusion

The study has performatively demonstrated how the experiences of the black avatar Nubalo, through his encounters online, are gradually helping him to create an identity. It also illustrated how Nubalo's off-line identity influences his online identity by interfering with Nubalo's online choices and decision-making processes. The findings of this study affirm that a deep hanging-out approach, as discussed previously, is an appropriate method to use in gathering and analyzing data online and off-line. My findings also affirm that the notion of identity conflation in the virtual world (Nakamura) has some ontological and epistemological implications. This study contributes to previous research on identity (Adrian and Gajjala) and provides another dimension to creating identity in the virtual world. Future study could address Nubalo's transformation into a vampire as he continues to "deeply hang out" in SL, interacting with SL citizens, and continuously shaping his identity.

Notes

1. Wagner James Au, *The Making of Second Life: Notes from the New World* (New York: HarperCollins, 2008), 69.

2. Angel Adrian, "No One Knows You Are a Dog: Identity and Reputation in Virtual Worlds," *Computer Law & Security Report* 24 (2008): 366–34.

3. Margaret Cassidy, "Flying with Disability in Second Life," *Eureka Street* 18, no. 1 (2008): 22.

4. A. Richard Bartle, "Virtual Worldliness: What the Imaginary Asks of the Real," *New York Law School Law Review* 49 (2004): 19.

5. C. Albert Lin, "Virtual Consumption: A Second Life for Earth?" *Law Review* 1 (2008): 47.

6. Radhika Gajjala, "Interrogating Identities: Composing Other Cyberspaces," in *Intercultural Alliances: Critical Transformation,* ed. M. J. Collier (Thousand Oaks, CA: Sage, 2003), 167–88.

7. "Identity," *Cambridge Advanced Learners Dictionary Online,* 2008, http://dictionary.cambridge.org/.

8. Erving Goffman, *Stigma: Notes on the Management of Spoiled Identity* (Englewood Cliff, NJ: Prentice-Hall, 1963), 2.

9. Jane Kroger, *Identity Development: Adolescence through Adulthood* (Thousand Oaks, CA: Sage, 2007), 8.

10. Ibid.

11. Kirsti Pedersen and Arvid Viken, "Nature and Identity—An Introduction," in *Nature and Identity*, ed. Kirsti Pedersen and Arvid Viken (Kristiansand, Norway: Norwegian Academic Press, 2003), 15.

12. See Katherine Bessière, Fleming A. Seay, and Sara Kiesler, "The Ideal Elf: Identity Exploration in the World of Warcraft," *CyberPsychology & Behavior* 10 (2007): 530–35; Adrian, "No One Knows You Are a Dog"; Stephen Webb, "Avatarculture: Narrative, Power and Identity in Virtual World Environments," *Information, Communication & Society* 4, no. 4 (2001): 560–94; Angela Adrian, "I™: Avatars as Trade Marks," *Computer Law & Security Review* 23, no. 5 (2007): 436–48.

13. W. John Jordan, "A Virtual Death and Real Dilemma: Identity, Trust, and Community in Cyberspace," *Southern Communication Journal* 70 (2005): 203.

14. Webb, "Avatarculture," 563.

15. Radhika Gajjala, Natalia Rybas, and Melissa Altman, "Racing and Queering the Interface Producing Global/Local Cyberselves," *Qualitative Inquiry* 14, no. 7 (2008): 1110.

16. Peter Ludlow and Mak Wallace, *The Second Life Herald: The Virtual Tabloid That Witnessed the Dawn of the Metaverse* (Cambridge, MA: The MIT Press, 2000), 270.

17. Ibid.

18. Nic Crowe and Simon Bradford, "'Hanging Out in Runescape': Identity, Work and Leisure in the Virtual Playground," *Children's Geographies* 4, no. 3 (2006): 338.

19. Au, "The Making of Second Life," 83.

20. Natalia L. Ivanova, "Social Identity under Various Sociocultural Conditions," *Russian Education and Society* 47 (2005): 72.

21. See William C. Diehl and Esther Prins, "Unintended Outcomes in Second Life: Intercultural Literacy and Cultural Identity in a Virtual World," *Language and Intercultural Communication* 8, no. 2 (2008): 101–18; Webb, "Avatarculture"; Crowe and Bradford, "'Hanging Out in Runescape'"; Jordan, "A Virtual Death"; Adrian, "No One Knows You Are a Dog"; Lisa Lau, "Virtually Positioned: Investigating Identity and Positionality in a Case Study of South Asian Literature in Cyberspace," *Interdisciplinary Science Reviews* 29, no. 1 (2004): 65–76.

22. Sherry Turkle, "Parallel Lives: Working on Identity in Virtual Space," in *Constructing the Self in a Mediated World*, ed. K. J. Gergen and J. Shotter (North Manchester, IN: Heckman Bindery Inc., 1996), 158.

23. Ivanova, "Social Identity," 71–87.

24. Lisa Nakamura, *Digitizing Race: Visual Cultures of the Internet* (Minneapolis: University of Minnesota Press, 2008), 49.

25. Adrian, "No One Knows You Are a Dog," 366–74.

26. Ibid., 370.

27. Lin, "Virtual Consumption," 60.

28. Ibid., 68.

29. Samara Mamatovna Anarbaeva, "Samarita Ibanez: An Identity Journey from First Life to Second," *Journal For Virtual Worlds Research* 5, no. 1 (2012), 1–14.

30. Soyini D. Madison, *Critical Ethnography: Methods, Ethics, and Performance* (Thousand Oaks, CA: Sage, 2005).

31. See Dwight Conquergood, "Health Theatre in a Hmong Refugee Camp: Performance, Communication, and Culture," *The Drama Review* 3 (1988): 174–208; Gajjala, Rybas, and Altman, "Racing and Queering the Interface."

32. Tom Boellstorff, Bonnie Nardi, Celia Pearce, and Tina Lynn Taylor, *Ethnography and Virtual Worlds: A Handbook of Method* (Princeton, NJ: Princeton University Press, 2012), 134–35.

33. Ibid.

34. Ibid.

35. See Kamari Maxine Clarke, *Mapping Yoruba Networks: Power and Agency in the Making of Transnational Communities* (Durham, NC: Duke University Press, 2004); Michelle M. Wright, *Becoming Black: Creating Identity in the African Diaspora* (London: Duke University Press, 2004); Nakamura, *Digitalizing Race*; J. Adam Banks, *Race, Rhetoric, and Technology: Searching for Higher Ground* (Mahwah, NJ: Lawrence Erlbaum Associates, 2006).

36. Lisa Nakamura and A. Peter Chow-White, *Race after the Internet* (London: Routledge, 2012).

37. Nakamura, *Digitalizing Race*, 5.

38. Clarke, *Mapping Yoruba Networks*, 140.

39. Nakamura, *Digitalizing Race*, 49.

PART III

Information and Values

Uses and Abuses of the Internet by International Students in American Universities

Anne Kindred Willis

Two things have converged recently to affect the education of international students in the American college or university system: the use of the Internet or social media and an increase in the number of these students entering U.S. institutions. What is the process by which internationals gain entrance into the American university system? What role do the Internet and social media play in the lives of students, inside and outside of academia, and before and after they come to the United States? This chapter addresses these and other questions related to the education of international students in the American system of higher education.

The following are acronyms that are common in the field of teaching English, and they are bulleted here to make for clearer understanding of what follows in this chapter:

ESL—stands for English as a second language and is used as an umbrella acronym to cover most instances of instruction to students whose first language is not English. However, in higher education, this term is giving way to TESOL or ESOL. The next acronym explains the reason for the change.

ESOL—English for speakers of other languages is now a more preferred term as it allows for a certain nuance: that we recognize that English is often a third, fourth, or fifth language for students nowadays, and therefore, a more applicable acronym.

TESOL—Teaching English to students of other languages. This is the term usually given to the field of teaching in this area. Most educators who hold a graduate degree in this area usually refer to it as a master's of TESOL or an MATESL.

IEP—Intensive English Program.

TOEFL—Test of English as a Foreign Language.

IELTS—International English Language Testing System.

ETS—Educational Testing Service.

Numbers of Internationals in the United States

Most of us who are regularly on a college campus agree that the face of the American university has changed due to the number of internationals opting to study here. According to Open Doors data from the Institute of International Education (IIE), about 764,495 students came to the United States in 2011 to pursue undergraduate or advanced degrees.[1] IIE data also show that China sent the most students (194,029) followed by India.

As illustrated by the graph in Figure 17.1, the IIE list is completed by South Korea, Canada, and Taiwan. However, according to a May 2013 article on Arabnews.com, Saudi Arabia is now in fourth place, sending just over 34,000 students to the United States for the 2011–2012 academic year.[2] No matter the exact statistics, students come, influenced by America's reputation for excellence in higher education and for the diversity that our system has to offer. Quacquarelli Symonds World University

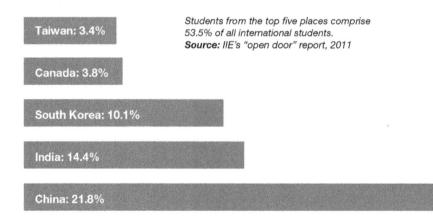

Figure 17.1 Top Five Places of Origin of International Students

ranking reports that 13 of the top 20 universities are located in the United States.[3]

Choosing an American University

What is the process by which students choose the American institution where they will pursue their university degrees? Apparently, this is one area in which the social media do *not* play as important a role as was once thought. According to William Arthur, director of i-Graduate, universities have sorely overestimated the positive outcome of recruitment via Twitter, Facebook, and YouTube. In 2011, the i-Graduate organization conducted a poll of 150,000 students at 1,200 global institutions of higher education with results showing that only 4 percent of students relied on social media to help them choose a foreign university.[4] Students in this poll—and students with whom I have personally conversed in my role as an ESOL instructor—indicate that several things help them make their choices. Forty-five percent of those in the i-Graduate poll said that recommendations from friends had the strongest influence on their choices.[5] In addition, parents' and teachers' opinions play an important role, and many students hire agents to help them find universities that meet their needs. In at least two areas, the Internet is used: to check out universities' rankings and to visit individual university Web sites. This kind of research is being considered when university officials are making decisions about budgeting funds for recruitment of international students.

Admission to a University

Foreign students who want to pursue university degrees in the United States come from a variety of secondary school situations. Some have English as the primary language of instruction, and if this is so, they can often be directly admitted to an institution, assuming that satisfactory completion of an accredited secondary school can be documented. This documentation may include proof of graduation, SAT or ACT scores, high school grades, letters of recommendation—all of this much like domestic students are required to complete. However, in the case of internationals, there must also be proof of a certain level of proficient English skills, via a standardized, globally recognized English test. Individual universities set their own standards for what score on the tests proves proficiency, and this may vary from college to college within a university. In addition, graduate programs typically require a higher score than do undergraduate programs.

When international students are admitted to a university, they matriculate with classes and schedules just as domestic students do. However, if students are not admitted due to weak English skills, and if they still want to seek an American university degree, they must first attend an IEP—an Intensive English Program—to hone their English skills and prepare for the world of academia. This is the kind of program in which I have taught since 2005.

Not all universities have IEPs, but for those who do, it can be a big business and a huge undertaking to get the program staffed and properly housed. Keep in mind: these students and teachers are not a part of the university at large. Classes are on campus, but students are not taking their courses for college credit, and the teachers are usually not part of the tenure-track system. The word *intensive* is certainly apropos here, for the work in an IEP is grueling—as is the teaching and the grading.

On the very first day of class in an IEP, students must take a placement test, and according to the results, they are then placed in an appropriate level. Some students may have to begin at a very low level because they have only minimal command of English, that is, they need to learn how to introduce themselves, speak simple grammatically correct sentences, ask questions, and begin to organize their ideas into short paragraphs. In the highest levels, students are in preparation for graduate school. In these classes, they may be reading advanced texts, working on group projects, and writing research papers. Classes are usually no larger than 15 students, and generally, students attend school every day, not just a typical college schedule of Monday, Wednesday, and Friday, or Tuesday and Thursday. Often, students are in class for 6 hours each day, and then must tend to their homework assignments each evening. It is quite a daunting schedule to maintain.

All with an academic focus, classes are taught in grammar, reading, writing, listening, speaking, and pronunciation. Those are the basics. Some IEPs offer electives, for example, in presentation skills, American culture, American fiction, American films, or American history. Students must matriculate through the program until they meet the required standards. Sometimes this means a certain grade-point average, sometimes a passing TOEFL score, and sometimes both. Admission to a university is based on what the agreement is between the university of choice and a particular IEP; requirements can differ from institution to institution.

Internet Testing

The two most trusted tests of English skills are the TOEFL and the IELTS. Though the instruments and scoring methods of these tests are quite different, both tests seek to measure proficiency in four areas: reading, writing, speaking, and listening.

The IELTS is *only* a paper-based test—no computer is used by the test taker—and it is administered at various "Certified Test Administration Sites" several times a year. Trained professionals are on site to administer and proctor the exam. For the speaking component, the test taker converses face to face with the examiner. On the other hand, the TOEFL *can* be paper-based, but by far, the most acceptable score is from the IBT (Internet Based Test) format. As with the IELTS, testing is in four areas, but for the speaking component, testers speak into a microphone, and trained scorers later evaluate the task. For both tests, the writing component is also individually scored.

Test Integrity and the Web

An issue that begs to be discussed next is the matter of security during and after these types of standardized tests. Because this article is a discussion of Internet issues, let us now focus on the TOEFL-IBT—the test that is taken on the computer. English Testing Services (ETS), the company that generates such standardized tests as the TOEFL and the well-known ACT, SAT, and GRE, is a globally recognized and respected organization that has a plethora of information on its Web site related to its attempts to ensure the integrity of their test instruments, the security of their testing sites and scoring methods, and the validity of test results. First, ETS test designers create new TOEFL questions each year so that test items are up-to-date and to reduce the risk of cheating through memorization of previously administered tests. They also contract with a company that regularly searches the Internet for TOEFL test content to which students have free access.[6]

At each certified testing site, there are rigorous Internet security protocols by which they must abide, such as encrypted software and a delivery system that cannot be accessed prior to the beginning of the test administration. Before the test begins, the test software will close all extraneous windows and applications and will log incidents of someone's attempt to open a non-TOEFL application. ETS claims that their test administrators are highly trained, must pass a certification exam, and must adhere to the policies, practices, and procedures outlined in their manual. According to the Web site, "ETS conducts announced, unannounced and undeclared visits to test sites to observe and ensure that the highest standards are being applied to testing environments around the world."[7]

Two others areas of concern are in the quality and security of test scoring and reporting. ETS tries to limit security issues by assuring that scoring does not take place at a testing site. Administrators are never involved in test preparation or scoring; neither may they administer tests at a site where there may be students whom the administrator has taught. Official test scores are printed on security paper with detailed attention given to color, watermarks, chemical and heat sensitive ink,[8] and much more than will be outlined here.

Test takers themselves must meet a number of security requirements. They are told to expect such things as signature and handwriting comparison, photo ID comparison, voice recognition comparison, videotaping of the testing room, passing through security wanding, and thumb printing. A proctor at the site will take a digital photo of each test taker just prior to the test, and once checked into the testing room, the administrator uses this photo to verify the identification of the test taker. Students must leave all personal belongings in a secure location outside the testing room, and "are prohibited from bringing items into the test center that could be used as a testing aid or to collect, share, or collaborate on the test content."[9] This, of course, includes electronic devices, books, even dictionaries.

It is clear that there are elaborate measures to which ETS goes to guard against compromised test instruments, weakly secured test centers, and fraud during the actual test. Even with all of these safeguards in place, unfortunately, cheating does occur, and according to recent reports it is occurring on a massive scale. Where? You guessed it: China.

Pressures Can Lead to Cheating

Most of us know that China has a one-child policy. What most of us have not considered is what this means to the family. Parents and often both sets of grandparents are heavily invested in the success of their child and will go to almost any length to see that their offspring is successful. This usually means education, and if families have the financial wherewithal, it often means education in an American university. Many of my own students from China have repeatedly told me of the enormous pressure they feel to succeed in an American university. Success means the ability to make a lot of money in the future, principally for two reasons: to make their families proud, and so that they can care for their parents as they age.

What this means for higher education in the United States is this: international students and their families pumped nearly 23 billion dollars into the economy in 2012,[10] and a quarter of this money came from the Chinese.[11] University officials often claim that their goal in recruiting internationals is to bring diversity to their campuses, but at least part of the truth is that the internationals are a pipeline through which big money flows, and many universities see this as a way to ease budget crunches. Therefore, we have the makings of a perfect storm. The Chinese are anxious to pursue university degrees in the United States, and American universities are doing some heavy recruiting on the ground in China. The storm part of this scenario is that, according to a report by *The Epoch Times,* there exists "a thriving underground industry in China—mediated through the Internet—that operates without impunity,"[12] through which students are buying passing scores on their TOEFL exam, the test of English proficiency that most American universities require before admission.

The Epoch Times is a legitimate international newspaper, available both online and in print. It is available in many U.S. cities and was on display at the 2013 Convention of the Association for Education in Journalism and Mass Communication, in Washington, DC. Following is what *The Epoch Times* says about itself:

> Freedom of the press and humanity are the foundation of the *Epoch Times*; our beginnings hailed from a great need to provide uncensored news to a people immersed in propaganda and censorship in China.
>
> Having witnessed events like Tiananmen Square and the persecution of the spiritual group Falun Gong, and at a great risk to themselves and their loved ones, a group of Chinese-Americans started publishing The *Epoch Times* in the Chinese language in the U.S. Some reporters in China were jailed, and some suffered severe torture.
>
> The first English edition launched online in 2003 followed by the first print edition in 2004. The Chinese-language Epoch Times started publishing in response to the growing need for uncensored coverage of events in China. The first newspaper was published in New York in May 2000, with the web launch in August 2000. Local editions published by regional bureaus soon followed, making it the largest of any Chinese-language newspaper outside of Mainland China and Taiwan.
>
> The *Epoch Times* is a privately held news media company. Our network of local reporters throughout the world uncovers stories that are authentically local, yet also globally relevant. Our independence enables us to report widely and present a diversity of opinions. A special strength of The Epoch Times is our coverage of China. We publish in 21 languages in 35 countries across five continents.[13]

I thought it important to verify the authenticity and integrity of this publication because the allegations made by the two reporters, Amelia Pang and Alex Wu, about the rampant cheating on the TOEFL raise serious questions about the qualifications and credentials of Chinese students to whom American universities are granting admission. The reporters of the February 2013 article, "Test of English Easily Bested by Cheats in China," write that, "Methods for beating the test abound: from study guides available online compiled from previous years' examinations, to finding doubles in China to sit the test in person, to, in the most organized and entrepreneurial instance, taking advantage of the time zone difference between China and the United States and feeding answers to co-conspirators across the Pacific."[14]

Apparently, there is a Chinese business known as "Jijing Live Service," which translates roughly to "computer test bible," that can be hired by test takers who want a high TOEFL score.[15] For their clients, Jijing can take advantage of the time difference between the United States and China and will feed the test items to said clients before the start of the TOEFL exam. One *Epoch Times* reporter wanted to see if he could make this happen for himself. He created his fictitious self—a Chinese student who would be sitting for the TOEFL exam in the United States—and set out to see what Jijing was all about.

First, the reporter went to "Taobao," a Chinese Web-based business very similar to eBay. There he found a Web page dedicated to Jijing. After joining and becoming a member, he was then able to register with Jijing for assistance with the TOEFL exam that was to be administered on February 11, 2011. There is a 13-hour time difference between China and the United States. Therefore, the exam began in the United States—on the same date—some 13 hours *earlier* than the start of the same exam in China. The article states, "Just as advertised on the Taobao page, the seller [Jijing] emailed step-by-step notifications, and different parts of the exam streamed in throughout the morning. Hours before he was to take the examination in the United States, the *Epoch Times* reporter had received all of the questions, and answer tips to boot."[16] Clients who use the services of Jijing can also leave comments—again similar to the way customers express their satisfaction on eBay—and one comment brought to light yet another service offered by Jijing. Says one client,

> I would like to share my experience of finding a test replacement. I had a friend who got a good mark with the TOFEL [sic], IELTS Replacement Association, so I went with them too. Their service is really remarkable. They have a very detailed plan for test replacement, with every single step considered properly. I feel I can really count on such a service. Thanks a lot to the help of TOFEL, IELTS Test Replacement Association for my poor English.[17]

What is "test replacement"? It means that a lookalike—and a person with superb English skills—had been paid to sit for the exam instead of the student who will get credit for the score!

The *Epoch Times* reporters contacted ETS and explained their discovery that there is "wide availability of methods by which their [ETS's] tests are gamed." Thomas Ewing, the ETS director of communications responded that while most students are honest, "When a company tests on a global basis there is practically no way to create or administer enough forms of the test to cover the entire world with multiple tests each month, twelve months a year in 180 countries."[18] When cheating is discovered it appears that the consequences are fairly benign. According to a *New York Times/Chronicle of Higher Education* article, the "ETS policy is to cancel a score, but the organization won't say how often that happens and where."[19]

Cheating by the Chinese who want admission to American institutions is apparently becoming more and more flagrant and is going largely unchecked. Thomas Melcher is a Harvard alumnus now living in Beijing who is considered an expert in China about studying in the American university system. In a 2010 white paper, Melcher cites research showing that perhaps 90 percent of applicants have cheated in one form or another: fake recommendation letters, awards or achievements, financial statements, high school transcripts or class rankings, and/or ghostwritten essays. Some of the pressure to cheat comes from parents and some comes from aggressive agents who earn huge sums of money if they can successfully get a student admitted to a university in the United States.[20] Interestingly though, once into their degree program in this country, the Chinese seem to fare as well as their American counterparts, passing and failing at about the same rate.

On a personal note, as an ESOL teacher I have witnessed very little cheating by my students in my classroom. We do have to deal with plagiarism issues, but this is largely because as a socialist society, the Chinese believe in sharing what is in the public domain, and this can mean, simply, copying someone else's ideas. Once our differences are understood, and once the academic honesty policy of a university is explained, there have been few problems for me. In addition, I am in awe of the work ethic demonstrated by my Chinese students. They have phenomenal dedication to their academic success, they are serious and cooperative in the classroom, assignments are done promptly and neatly, and I have frequently seen them study so late into the night that they can barely keep themselves awake in class. I have a great respect for my students from China, and they are a joy to teach.

Other Uses of the Internet

I have often asked my international students about their uses of the Internet. The three devices that most of them own are a cell phone, a computer, and an iPad or other tablet. The uses of the cell phone are obvious save for one exception. In an ESOL classroom, students often make use of an application that is a combination translator and dictionary. Users can translate words and sentences from their first language into English, or vice versa. In addition to reading definitions and translations, users can also *hear* words and sentences spoken in English, a great way to improve listening skills and pronunciation.

One of the biggest obstacles that students are faced with when they come to college in the United States is homesickness. They miss their homes, their traditional foods, their holidays, their friends, and their families —usually parents, but sometimes spouses and children! Nothing has helped to alleviate students' homesickness more than Skype. Most of my students report that they use it every day and plan their meals and outings around times when they converse with their significant others. This is not always easily accomplished due to time-zone differences, but it is important for students to stay connected to their homes.

The Skype anecdotes with which I am familiar are both heart wrenching and humorous. While teaching in a five-week summer program at Ball State University, we got word that a student's father had suddenly passed away. The student was of the Islamic faith whose tradition dictates that burial should occur as soon as possible; thus, if the student had decided to make the long trip home to Indonesia, he would have missed the funeral. Aided by telephone calls and Skype—and of course with support from teachers and classmates—this student was able to connect with his family and weather the tragedy without returning to his country.

On a lighter note is the story about Sharry, from Taiwan, and our dog, Buddy. When I taught at Ashland University in Ohio, Sharry was a homestay student; that is, she paid rent and lived in our home, something that is often preferred by internationals when they want to experience American culture and improve their English. One particular evening, Sharry was eating dinner at our dining room table and chatting on Skype with her mom in Taiwan. Sharry needed to run upstairs to her room to retrieve something that she wanted to show her mother, and while Sharry was gone, her mother watched while Buddy hopped up on the table and quickly gobbled up Sharry's dinner! After that, Buddy was a famous dog among Sharry's circle of family and friends in Taiwan, and it is one of Sharry's favorite memories of living in our home.

Almost every student comes to America with a laptop computer—many also have tablets—and both can enhance learning a new language in countless ways. Very often students need to do research for homework or other assignments. For a project that requires an oral presentation, students will usually support their work with PowerPoint or Prezi. Students who are in the states use the Internet to keep abreast of current events in their home countries. As well, they use YouTube to experience and study the United States. They listen to music, read the English lyrics, watch American movies and television, look at famous cities and landmarks, and listen to examples of conversational English. Of special value are the videos that have English subtitles, for this assists in students' comprehension of the new language they are studying. Google is also used along the same lines as YouTube. And both are being welcomed with open arms into the ESOL classroom.

What better way to enhance learning than to have at the ready color pictures and videos related to the topic at hand? Especially for the lower-level learners, a picture is indeed worth a thousand words. "Teacher, what means goat?" a beginning student recently asked of me. His intent of course, was to ask what the word "goat" means, yet I had no clear way of explaining "goat" to this student. However, I promptly made use of my cell phone, went to Google Images, and found several pictures of goats. "Ahhhhh," exclaimed the student, smiling to express his understanding. "My country," he added, as he pointed to a picture of a group of small brown and white goats. And a teachable moment was met with a bit of enlightenment.

Among the many topics of discussion in the ESOL classroom are how the English language has changed through the years, and how it is growing and changing even now. We make lists of words that we use when we think of our computers, and we come up with fairly recent additions to English vocabulary. As well, we look at how meanings and parts of speech have changed. For example, we now use "friend" and "google" as verbs, as in "Don't forget to friend me on Facebook," and "I don't know . . . but I will google it and find out." We have added to our lists such words as cookies, cyberspace, Internet, CD, spam, LOL, Twitter, tweet, chat, chat room, password, scroll, and so on. I was surprised to learn that the majority of my students even know about Silicon Valley!

Internationals and Friendships

International students come to America, desiring an education that will hopefully enhance their lives when they return to their countries and seek to establish their careers and homes. But an additional hope, expectation, even a fantasy, is to make friends with Americans and experience the culture through them. Sadly, the latter of these goals often does not happen for internationals. According to a couple of surveys cited in a Voice of America blog, somewhere between 10 and 30 percent of international students report that they have no close American friends.[21] We teachers have long known that this is an issue, and in our classes and with international services offices on our campuses, we do what we can to foster cross-cultural friendships.

Why friendships never happen, or why they do not thrive, is a topic for deep discussion at another time. My own students say that they are afraid of instigating a friendship for fear that they will make a cultural mistake or use their English in an embarrassing way. Another concern has to do with being in a group. When several people are in a conversation, even though it is casual and of little importance, the internationals may need a few seconds to process a word or phrase, and by the time they have processed, the conversation has moved on. Thus, they have missed an opportunity to make a contribution. In addition, humor is often very culturally based; many times our students do not understand why people are laughing, and they may feel that they are the brunt of a joke that they cannot grasp. They also know that it is frustrating and time consuming for the native speaker to stop in the midst of a conversation to answer questions, so students often just do not participate.

However, happily, there are many stories of life-long friendships between American students and internationals, and between the international students and their teachers. And long after students finish their English classes, receive their university diplomas, and return to their homes, people are staying in touch via Facebook. With a simple push of the friend button on a computer, two friends from home countries thousands of miles apart can foster their relationships with photos, quick messages, and more lengthy chats. I have been watching a wonderful example of this since the summer of 2011.

During June and July of 2011, Ball State University, in cooperation with *The New York Times*, hosted a group of SUSI students who came to the Muncie, Indiana institution to study the emerging media in America. SUSI is the Study of the U.S. Institute for scholars, and is funded by the State Department. Students are selected through a rigorous series of interviews and essays and are indeed exemplary scholars in their universities. My husband and I were teaching at Ball State at this time, and were privileged to get to know these outstanding young adults from Indonesia, Malaysia, and Singapore. We observed these students with amazement as they learned to communicate in a common language—English—and become a cohesive group of hungry learners who admired and respected each other. Since that summer some two years ago now, we have also watched via Facebook as the students have stayed in close contact with each other, keeping abreast of awards, accomplishments, graduations, and jobs, and they have even had a SUSI reunion for those who could make it. Additionally, I sometimes exchange warm and interesting Facebook chats with several of the students. Recently, Soro, from Indonesia, messaged me about his small village there. He does not have Internet access, so he travels to a café and even there, reception is weak he says, and it may take an hour to watch a short YouTube video. But watch he does, and he makes frequent posts on Facebook for his friends around the world.

What the Future Holds

Just as education in general is changing in response to such things as demographics, family structure, working parents, dying cities, and expanding suburbs, so is the education of international students undergoing some refinements and adjustments, and the Internet and social media will no doubt have a part to play. For example, we ESOL educators expect that online classes for internationals studying English will become more popular in the near future, but first, faultless technology is needed—technology that can provide superior sound and video capabilities so that student and teacher exchanges in speaking, listening, and pronunciation classes can be at an optimal level.

Conversely, it may be the case that the IBT—the Internet-based TOEFL test—will be jettisoned in favor of the old-fashioned way: the paper-based form of the test. If cheating and fraud cannot be controlled more effectively, universities may well decide that the only legitimate score is that from the paper-based test. Though ETS says that it is phasing out the paper-based TOEFL, information from the American Exam Services Web site seems to refute that claim. According to AES, number of American universities now accept *only* the paper-based form of the TOEFL, including such respected institutions as Kent State University, Lehigh University, Texas A & M, and the University of Idaho.[22]

Most data seem to show that in American higher education, foreign students will be a presence for the foreseeable future. It is expected that the Chinese influx will continue, and the Saudi student population is most definitely on the rise. Funded by the King Abdullah Foreign Scholarship Program, it is likely that the number of Saudis studying in the United States will exceed 75,000 by the year 2014.[23] Certainly there will be challenges for administrators, teachers, and students as the faces of our campuses change, but let us hope that in this, the digital age, we can avail ourselves of the best of technology to enhance education for all stakeholders.

Notes

1. "Open Doors Data," Institute of International Education, http://www.ii
e.org/Research-and-Publications/Open-Doors/Data.

2. "Number of Saudi Students in America Up 6 Percent," Arab News, http://
www.arabnews.com/number-saudi-students-america-6-percent.

3. "QS Top Universities," Top Universities, http://www.topuniversities.com
/university-rankings/world-university-ranking.

4. "International Students 'Do Not Use Facebook to Choose Their University,'"
Times Higher Education, http://www.timeshighereducation.co.uk/417479.article.

5. Ibid.

6. "TOEFL," Educational Testing Service, https://www.ets.org/toefl/institu
tions/about/security/.

7. Ibid.

8. Ibid.

9. Ibid.

10. "Special Reports: Economic Impact of International Students," Institute of International Education, http://www.iie.org/Research-and-Publications/
Open-Doors/Data/Special-Reports/Economic-Impact-of-International-Students.

11. A. Pang and A. Wu, "Test of English Easily Bested by Cheats in China,"
The Epoch Times, http://www.theepochtimes.com/n2/china-news/test-of-english-
easily-bested-by-cheats-in-china-353729.html.

12. Ibid.

13. Ibid.

14. Ibid.

15. Ibid.

16. Ibid.

17. Ibid.

18. Ibid.

19. T. Bartlett and K. Fischer, "The China Conundrum," *The New York Times*,
http://www.nytimes.com/2011/11/06/education/edlife/the-china-conundrum.
html?pagewanted=all&_r=0.

20. T. Melcher, "Busted: The Top 5 Ways That Chinese Students Cheat on
Their Undergraduate Applications to American Schools," http://www.washcoun
cil.org/documents/pdf/WIEC2011_Fraud-in-China.pdf.

21. J. Stahl, "Why Aren't Americans and International Students Becoming
Friends?," *Voice of America*, http://blogs.voanews.com/student-union/2012/06/19.

22. "TOEFL Scores—USA Universities," American Exam Services, http://
www.americanexamservices.com/about-the-toefl/toefl-scores-usa-universities.

23. "Number of Saudi Students in America Up 6 Percent."

CHAPTER EIGHTEEN

Ethical Issues in Internet Use: Plagiarism of Internet Sources among University Students in Nigeria

Etim Anim and Stanley Naribo Ngoa

Introduction

The Internet has been described by many authorities in many ways. Mike Ward observed that the world was so awed by the new technology that it conferred the capital "I" on it.[1] Ward's critical introductory text on online journalism came out when the Internet had just surged from the launching pad as the new wonder of the world; but the real wonders of the Internet were yet to unfold.

In later years, Stanley Baran, like many others, was to assert that, "It is not an overstatement to say that the Internet and the World Wide Web have changed the world, not to mention the other mass media. In addition to being powerful communication media themselves, the Net and Web sit at the center of virtually all the media convergence we see around us."[2] Indeed, the Web and the Internet became so interwoven that many who were untutored in the ways of the brave new world often treated them interchangeably. But as Ward reminded us, "They are not the same thing. At the risk of oversimplification, the Internet is the infrastructure that allows computers to talk to each other throughout the world. The Web is the interface that allows people to exchange data, text, pictures, graphics, audio and video on the Internet."[3] For a world that now depends on information as its basic raw material for everything, the interface of the Web and the Net has produced a mine of information that can never be fully harvested. As Ward has summed it up, "there is more information on the Web than you could possibly ever read or want to read."[4]

If we follow the four-phase model of mass media research enunciated by Roger Wimmer and Joseph Dominick, contemporary interest in the Internet would fall into Phases 3 and 4. Phase 3 "includes investigations of the social, psychological and physical effects of the medium."[5] In Phase 4, research is conducted to determine how the medium can be improved, either in its use or in combination with other technological developments. Contemporary communication culture classifies the Internet among new media. New media "is a term which encompasses interactive digital media, computerized, or networked information and communication technologies, such as the Internet, as opposed to traditional media such as print and television."[6] New media thus represent essentially computer-mediated communication technologies and the integration of the traditional media, such as radio, television, film music, images, and text into the interactive capabilities of the computer, often referred to as media convergence in the early days of the Internet.[7]

Closely associated with media convergence is digitization, which enables images, texts, and sounds to be converted into electronic signals "that are then re-assembled as a precise reproduction of, say, a TV picture, a magazine article, a song or a telephone voice."[8]

It is the easy manipulation of digitized media content that has fostered the production and transfer of communication content over the Internet. As James Stovall has argued, the consequence of all these is the actualization of the concept of on-demand access to content anytime, anywhere, on any digital device.[9] However, the unlimited availability of information and the almost unimpeded access to such information on the Internet has created a problem for the world's academic community—both teachers and students. But especially for university students, the temptation to poach material from Internet sources for their work is great and ever present. It has presented a new dimension to an old ethical problem: Internet plagiarism.

Plagiarism

The literature on plagiarism in academia is copious. Shelley Tapp, Barbara Hightower, LaVelle Mills, and R. Nicholas Gerlich give an insight into the scope of available literature on the theme. It is tempting not to copy and paste their summary, but it is instructive of what is confronting the academic world:

> Even a cursory review of academic and business literature reflects widespread theft of ideas by students (Adams 2000; Lathrop and Foss 2000; O'Brien 2000; Fialkoff 1993; and Bugeja 2000). Georgetown, the University of Virginia, Florida State, the University of Maryland, Cornell, and UC-Berkeley, among others, have all reported growing concerns over the use of the Internet to plagiarize course assignments (Diependrock 2002; Fry 2002; Kang 2002; Sessa 2002; Simmons 2001; Townsend and Friedman 2002; and Walzer 2002). Duke's Center for Academic Integrity reports that 70% of college students say that they have cheated (Chard 2002) . . . Young (2001) summarizes a study by the Center for Academic Integrity in 1999 where nearly 70 percent of professors reported one or more instances of plagiarism each year.[10]

Patrick Scanlon and David Neumann surveyed 698 students at nine U.S. universities and found that about 29 percent of those sampled admitted to copying from the Internet without proper citation. About 11 percent of the students also admitted that they submitted an entire paper without citation.[11] Tapp et al. also reported that "Georgetown, the University of Virginia, Florida State, the University of Maryland, Cornell, and UC-Berkeley, among others, have all reported growing concerns over the use of the Internet to plagiarize course assignments."[12]

Not surprisingly, major universities of the world have Web platforms on plagiarism because it is in their interest to prevent their students from being sucked into the rising incidence of Internet plagiarism. Purdue University's OWL Web site defines plagiarism simply as "uncredited use (both intentional and unintentional) of somebody else's words or ideas."[13] The University of Queensland in Australia clearly states the university's definition of plagiarism in its *Handbook of University Policies and Procedures*:

> Plagiarism is the act of misrepresenting as one's own original work the ideas, interpretations, words or creative works of another. These include published and unpublished documents, designs, music, sounds, images, photographs, computer codes and ideas gained through working in a group. These ideas, interpretations, words or works may be found in print and/or electronic media.[14]

Indiana University defines plagiarism as, "Presenting someone else's work, including the work of other students, as one's own. Any ideas or materials taken from another source for either written or oral use must be fully acknowledged, unless the information is common knowledge."[15]. The University of Minnesota subsumes its warning on plagiarism within its concern for Scholastic Dishonesty, which it defines as:

> Submission of false records of academic achievement; cheating on assignments or examinations; plagiarizing; altering, forging, or misusing a University academic record; taking, acquiring, or using test materials without faculty permission; acting alone or in cooperation with another to falsify records or to obtain dishonestly grades, honors, awards, or professional endorsement (*Student Conduct Code*).[16]

Indiana University's Center for Writing Web site invokes some well-known authorities to drive home the issues, among them, two of the world's leading authorities in literary style, the MLA and APA manuals of style. The MLA manual defines plagiarism as "the use of another person's ideas or expressions in your writing without giving proper credit to the source." It cites Alexander Lindey's definition of plagiarism as, "The false assumption of authorship: the wrongful act of taking the product of another person's mind, and presenting it as one's own. . . . In short, to plagiarize is to give the impression that you have written or thought something that you have in fact borrowed from someone else."[17]

Wikipedia's definition is an assembly of the key concepts in definitions offered by dictionaries, namely, "the wrongful appropriation, close imitation, or purloining and publication, of another author's language, thoughts, ideas, or expressions, and the representation of them as one's own original work."

A Nigerian Perspective

Unfortunately, not much has been published on the theme of academic dishonesty in the academic community in Nigeria. A study by B. F. Adeoye, A. M. Olusakin, and Ayodele Ogunleye addressed the issue of "Technologies Students use in Academic Dishonesty." Its aim was "to provide an overview of the literature related to the issue of academic dishonesty in institutions of higher education and suggest some prevention methods."[18] In concentrating on the general theme of academic dishonesty, but specifically what is usually referred to in Nigeria as examination malpractices, the study only obliquely touched on plagiarism. The major concern then was dishonesty in the examination halls. They defined examination malpractices as "any act of wrongdoing that especially contravenes laid down rules of examination practice and which is committed by candidates before, during or after any particular type of examination."[19]

Azuka Alutu and Oyaziwo Aluede also focused on examination malpractices and examination ethics, but this time in the secondary (high) school environment. They concluded "that majority of the students believed that their indulgence in examination malpractice was a common occurrence, which will be difficult to eradicate. Parents, teachers and school principals were found to encourage cheating in examinations."[20]

Another study by two researchers in the University of Wolverhampton, UK, quoted a Nigerian student as saying that, "I never knew much about plagiarism, I heard of the word before, but I never knew what it really meant until I came to Wolverhampton. . . . If one person writes an assignment, every other person copies what the person has written, you don't really get penalised for that as long as you've done the assignment."[21] The aim of the research, conducted among postgraduate students in applied sciences, was to investigate students' needs in academic writing and in understanding and avoiding plagiarism.

J. Bamford and K. Sergiou did a pilot study on plagiarism among international students at the London Metropolitan University and came to the conclusion that "plagiarism was prevalent among that cohort of students."[22] The researchers had proposed to do a follow-up study among home (UK) students in order to have a comparative set of data. But the pilot involved 35 students, a majority of whom "fell into three major regions—West Africa, Asia and China."[23] The authors conceded because the study was a pilot, the findings were only indicative; still they suggested that "all but one of the West African respondents admitted to copying from books at school and the focus group highlighted the fact they had expected to do so at university and could not understand lecturer's 'obsession' with discovering their sources of information."[24]

A report in the Nigerian financial newspaper, *BusinessDay* online, indicated that:

> In recent years, many university students in Nigeria never attempt doing any original research for this research project requirement. Instead, they depend on a market of "professional" project writers who supposedly do the research projects for them, or deliberately plagiarise or recycle research done by others for onward delivery to their "clients," or the students themselves engage directly in plagiarizing research projects executed in other universities.[25]

The tenor of these and other studies is consistent with studies elsewhere in the world: students in their thousands are engaged in intentional acts of academic dishonesty. The efforts of the foreign (non-Nigerian) universities we have cited in this work are representative of the seriousness with which world-class universities consider the issue of academic integrity and the flipside of academic dishonesty. They thus go to great pains to ensure that students are made fully aware of what constitutes plagiarism and the consequences that go with the offence. Our experience is that Nigerian universities seem to be more concerned with plagiarism among university teachers—which is taken very seriously and is judged by the same standards applied elsewhere in the world—than they are with student culprits. While there are instances of unintentional plagiarism in students' works, many students deliberately set out to cheat. One of us, in his capacity as an external examiner for the Graduate School in one of Nigeria's first-generation universities, found that 10 out 15 theses contained evidence of plagiarism—some massive, others hotchpotch. In one of those works, a 63-page study by two professors of an Australian university was cut and pasted as part of the student's review of literature. It was taken from the first page to the last without alteration of even one word. Another cut and pasted a verbatim report of the European Commission on the shift from analogue to digital television. Others pasted a montage of various studies from different authorities, times, and places to constitute their review of literature.

That would mean that the scams went past their theses supervisors and internal committee members without detection. An implication here is that the faculty members are unfamiliar with the Internet. That is to say, their new media competences leave a lot to be questioned and they may have no idea what is going on in cyberspace. This is complicated by the attitude of many academics to their assignments. A good thesis supervisor should be familiar with the quality of his student's work. For example, an average student's research paper which suddenly sounds like a Nobel literature laureate's should send alarm bells ringing in the supervisor's head.

The other possibility is frightening but real: the supervisor simply scans the project and puts it aside; meanwhile he has seen nothing and read nothing. This would mean that the students understand the weakness of their teachers and have no fear of being found out. It can also be inferred here that the students are more wary of copying from books, many of which may be familiar to their lecturers.

A Students' Survey

In response to the dearth of literature on students' involvement in plagiarism in Nigerian academia, we conducted a survey of students in three

Nigerian universities: We sent out a 13-item questionnaire to 835 students in one public and two private universities. These were the American University of Nigeria, Yola, Adamawa State (private); Covenant University, Ota, Ogun State (a private Christian university), and the University of Lagos, Lagos (one of Nigeria's earliest public universities). A total of 805 respondents returned their questionnaires, a 96.4 percent rate of return. The results of the survey were consistent with trends we have seen elsewhere from the literature we surveyed, namely, that the incidence of plagiarism in universities is alarming.

Patrick Scanlon and David Neumann reported that, "In general, self-reports of cheating are high, although estimates vary widely, with 9% to 95% of those asked admitting to some form of academic dishonesty. . . . In a survey of 6,096 undergraduates on 31 campuses, McCabe (1992) reported that 67.4% admitted cheating at least once on a test or major assignment. Davis et al. reported similar numbers in another multicampus survey, also of more than 6,000 students: 76% admitted cheating in either high school or college or both."[26]

Plagiarism of Internet Sources among Students by Frequency and Percentage

The findings from our survey suggested that plagiarism is widespread in Nigerian universities, with slightly more than 75 percent of the students admitting to having used other peoples' works as if they were theirs, a definition of plagiarism which was acceptable to the students: 17 percent said they have plagiarized *often,* 58.2 percent admitted plagiarizing *sometimes* (Table 18.1). A little over 23 percent of the respondents said they had *never* plagiarized; however, from a comprehensive analysis of their responses, this claim is very likely to be more self-serving than true. For example, an analysis of the responses on the motives for plagiarizing shows that only 6.3 percent of the students (51) declined to give any response. As indicated in Table 18.2, clearly 92.1 percent of the students admitted a broad range of motives for plagiarizing. The highest number of students

Table 18.1 Reported frequency of plagiarizing

Acts of Plagiarism	Often	Sometimes	Never	Voided	Total
I have used other people's works as if they were mine	138	469	185	13	805
Percentage	17.1	58.2	23.1	1.6	100

Table 18.2   Motivations for plagiarizing

S. no.	Motive	Frequency	Percentage
1	When I do not understand the assignment	199	24.7
2	When I do not feel like doing the assignment	41	5.1
3	When I am at risk of not meeting deadline	158	19.6
4	When I cannot find materials for the assignment	270	33.5
5	To avoid the rigours of research	74	9.2
6	No response	51	6.3
7	Voided	12	1.6
	Total	805	100

(270) or 33.5 percent claims they plagiarize when they cannot find materials for the assignments given by their teachers. While this response may point to some issues with the teachers who give the assignments, it misses the main issue: the plagiarized resources ought to be part of materials which the students could use to build their own original work.

Respondents' Motives for Plagiarizing

There are clear pointers to an aversion to hard work among the students: 24.7 percent admitted they plagiarize when they do not understand the assignment; 19.2 percent plagiarize when they run the risk of not meeting assignment deadlines; 9.2 percent admitted they plagiarize because they want to avoid the rigors of research, while 5.1 percent plagiarize when they do not feel like doing their assignments. Let us take a student who does not understand the demands of an assignment: that student has two options in a well-run academic department—seek clarification from the teacher who gave the assignment or have a talk with his or her academic adviser. A student who misses the deadline to turn in his paper without a very cogent reason (such as a medical problem) is most likely to be a laggard; still, he has the option of seeking an extension of the deadline. From our survey, the students who admitted they plagiarize *when they do not feel like doing the assignment* or *because they want to avoid the rigors of personal research*[27] appear to be closer to the real motives for cheating. It is reasonable, therefore, to infer that the majority of university students plagiarize intentionally.

Ethical Issues of Internet Use

There may be some instances of unintentional plagiarism which results from poor academic upbringing in the area of research. Many Nigerian students are at a loss when it comes to source documentation in academic writing; they are not conversant with the various manuals of style, even at the doctoral level of research work, where in-text citations and referencing in one paper can be an amalgam of different styles. But the findings of our survey suggest that the majority of students set out deliberately to cheat. All the students (100 percent) in our survey said they knew what plagiarism meant and, indeed, about 65.3 percent also admitted they had been instructed on the risks of plagiarism in the university system.

This brings us to the central issue: Has the Internet made it easier for students to purloin other people's works? Fred Mann cited Diane Lynch as arguing in relation to journalism practice that, "It used to be pretty straightforward: if you copied somebody else's work, you were a bad journalist. Simple. But that's not necessarily how the Internet works; it's designed to allow you to download anything you want, including images and design (in the form of code). Is that sharing or is it plagiarism?"[28] Suzy Hansen observed that, "These days, stressed-out perfectionists and lazy no-goods alike can Google their way to an astounding array of plagiarism Web sites. Many companies sell term papers, essays and book reports by the thousands, for as much as $250 a pop, all just a click and Mom's credit card away, and all in the privacy of an undergraduate's dorm room."[29] Rich added—with reference to journalism practice, another realm where plagiarism thrives—that, "Technology may have contributed to a rampant rise in another form of deception—plagiarism and fabrication of sources. With the click of a mouse, journalists have access to thousands of newspapers on the Web."[30] King, Guyette Jr., and Piotrowski asserted, based on a survey of 121 undergraduate business students, that 73.6 percent of the students in the sample held the perception that it is easier to cheat in an online versus traditional course.[31]

Many authorities in the academic community, therefore, agree that the prevailing technologies, especially the Internet, have exacerbated the propensity of present-day university students to cheat. Scanlon's and Neumann's oft-cited research agreed that the Internet has made it easier for students to cheat in a variety of ways, essentially "cutting and pasting, soliciting papers from others, purchasing papers from online term paper mills."[32] According to Eleanour Snow, the nature of the Internet is partly accountable for this trend. Citing Townley and Parsell as well as Frand, she argued that students do not view the Internet the same way they view a book, which they know is wrong to copy. But the Internet "is somehow anonymous; there is no author, publisher, and copyright date."[33]

Washington State University is among the many universities that take the issue of plagiarism very seriously. On the university's anti-plagiarism Web page, it has argued also that technology has made it easier for students to cheat. "From a purely technical standpoint, sure, it's easier to copy-and-paste chunks of text from one window on a computer to another than it is to re-type entire passages, or even papers. There are even web companies willing to supply would-be plagiarists with canned or customized papers for a fee."[34] There is no doubt that very few students would dare to plagiarize a 63-page paper if they had to sit and hack it out on a typewriter. Our survey certainly supports the contention that it is easier to plagiarize Internet sources than to plagiarize from hard-copy sources.

University students in Nigeria have as much Internet access as they possibly can and the possibility of abuses has increased proportionately. Though Internet access in the country is still considerably limited, it has been growing steadily in the past few years. According to the International Telecommunications Union, as of mid-2010, Nigeria had about 43.9 million Internet users. That figure was up from 23.9 million in 2009, an astounding increase of 83 percent. The Internet penetration of 28.9 percent of the population still leaves a lot of room for improvement but that is mainly because the rural areas are poorly served. But universities in Nigeria are generally urban-based. Some universities have campus-wide Internet coverage; others have information and communications technology (ICT) centers and cybercafes,[35] where students pay N100 (less than 10 U.S. cents) an hour to access the Internet. In addition, town meets gown generally in Nigeria and commercial cybercafes proliferate in the fringes of the universities. In fact, Willie Siyanbola has suggested that, "students' access to the Internet is more through the cybercafés (90.8%) than the universities' networks."[36] Also, most cell-phone companies in the country (MTN, Airtel, Globacom, Etisalat, Visafone, etc.) now enable cell phones (not smartphones) for Internet access. With 116 million active cell-phone subscribers in the country,[37] access to the Internet will certainly continue to rise.

No technology is bad. It is people who make the difference in the use of technology. People use the media for a variety of purposes. The behavioral approach to audience relations with the media emphasizes the needs, motives, and circumstances of the user of the media and media content. This approach is sometimes expressed in terms of the uses and gratifications sought from media use. Denis McQuail has disaggregated the salient strands of this approach into four. Among them are the following:

1. "Media and content choice is rational and directed toward certain specific goals and satisfactions."
2. "Audience members are conscious of the media-related needs that arise in personal (individual) and social (shared) circumstances and can voice these in terms of motivations."
3. Personal utility is a more significant determinant of audience formation than aesthetic or cultural factors
4. Most important factors that shape "audience formation can . . . be measured."[38]

Put differently, the uses and gratifications paradigm essentially asserts that media use is dictated by the satisfactions, needs, wishes, or motives the user desires. This model also draws from Maslow's hierarchy of needs which categorizes human needs into a hierarchy, from the most pressing to the least pressing—psychological needs, safety needs, social needs, and self-actualization needs.[39] Dominick has noted also that "audience members have certain needs and drives that are satisfied by using both non-media and media sources."[40]

Within this purview, university students' uses of the Internet are partly motivated by a generational culture as is evidenced by their heavy presence on the social media. "The phenomenon that perhaps most distinctively characterizes the generation of Americans born since 1990 is its pervasive engagement with social media—media enabled by the proliferation of new digital (and frequently mobile) information and communication technologies," according to the Ohio University Moritz College of Law.[41] The postulate by Rich Maggiani may be used to explain the general attitude of the generation that makes up today's university populations:

> Born plugged in, Generation Y is active and about to turn 30. For them everything is now. For their entire lives everything has been computerized; physical boundaries have never existed, enabling global awareness; mobile phones have keyboards, so communication by voice, text and images is immediate; long distance is irrelevant; Internet access has always been at their finger-tips, replacing archaic cable television and libraries; eroding physical neighbourhoods have been replaced by an online network of friends, many of whom are not physically known, with varying levels of privilege—yet these friends mean everything; essay answers are mailed to teachers; music is downloaded, transported and placed on devices not much bigger than a credit card. . . . Perhaps there has never been a generation of teenagers and 20-year-olds who have had such a profound influence on society than Gen Y.[42]

The media-use habits of contemporary university students appear to be driven by this generational disposition, specifically the culture of immediacy or content on demand, which fits perfectly into the Internet mould. Apparently, then, in following their generational instincts they tend to ignore the culture of the academia, with integrity traditions that date back to the 18th century. All the students who responded in our survey agreed they know what plagiarism is, that it is morally wrong to plagiarize and, in one of the universities we surveyed, 98.4 percent of the respondents agreed that plagiarism is an offence against academic standards. The issue of plagiarism and the general problem of academic dishonesty, therefore, come down to a matter of personal integrity.

The ethical implications of plagiarism go beyond the university systems because today's students are tomorrow's professors, leaders of industry and commerce, leaders of civic society, and political leaders. This means that university students cannot always see themselves as young people who have the freedom to do as they please. As is often said, a university student must be found worthy both in character and learning at the end his or her academic career. Plagiarism as an offence cannot be punished with a jail term; that is to say, it is an ethical issue rather than an issue of law. Therefore, academic dishonesty involves a moral choice.

Ethics are rules of behavior, moral principles that guide the actions of people in any given situation. In our context, as in many others where people are faced with deciding between two or more moral choices, ethics refer to the application of rational thought in making the choice. That is, it usually comes down to a choice between doing what is right or what is wrong. Thus, many authorities (e.g., Scanlon and Neumann[43]) have discussed plagiarism in the context of situational ethics. Robyn McCarthy and Vikkie Hulsart conclude that, "Students hold qualified guidelines for behavior which are situationally determined. As such, the concept of situational ethics might well describe . . . college cheating [as] rules for behavior may not be considered rigid but depend on the circumstances involved."[44]

Students apply the concept of situational ethics, most often unconsciously, to justify plagiarism. Though situational ethics as enunciated by Joseph Fletcher was intended to glorify God's love as the end of all things, it has, in application, affirmed the notion that the end justifies the means. Indeed, Fletcher categorically declared in his work, "For the situationist there are no rules—none at all."[45] Critical expositions on the Fletcher model have opened up a myriad of contradictions that are beyond the scope of this presentation. For our purposes, its flaws include the humanist sub-theme of the inherent goodness of man, which is contradicted

Table 18.3 Rationalizations for plagiarizing

Rationalizations	Frequency	Percentages
It is more difficult to detect	326	40.6
I do not think my lecturer will know the source	107	13.3
My lecturer will not try to verify	118	14.6
No responses	245	30.4
Voided	9	1.1
Total	805	100

copiously by the Bible upon which Fletcher built his work. As every university teacher knows, students are ingenious when it comes to doing wrong. Students may argue that if they cannot meet the deadline for turning in their assignments, it is in order to copy and paste an Internet source so long as they meet the deadline. Or if they cannot "find materials" for their assignments, it is in order to cheat so long as the assignment gets done. In other words, the end is what matters. Yet, asked why they prefer to plagiarize Internet sources, 68 percent of the students in our survey gave reasons which suggest they plagiarize without remorse; they deliberately set out to steal from the Net because they think it is more difficult to catch them if they use its sources: 40 percent said they plagiarize Internet sources because *it is more difficult to detect*; about 28 percent do so because they think their *lecturers would not know the sources* or *would not try to verify the sources*; a large 30 percent declined to give any response—a tacit indication that they do not want to implicate themselves or, in U.S. culture, they pleaded the Fifth Amendment (Table 18.3).

Reasons for Plagiarizing Mostly from Internet Sources

Very few students among the population in our survey will have studied Fletcher, but they live in a world system that has come to accept the basic tenets of situational ethics as excuses for doing wrong, and they have come to function within the same principles (or non-principles). The median age of the 805 respondents in our survey was 20. These people are still growing and are imbibing the culture of their elders who believe in manipulating election results to ensure that incumbent governments stay in power, who alter national constitutions to prolong the rule of corrupt political leaders, and who enact legislations with the advantages accruing to them in mind. McCarthy and Hulsart quote Robbins and Coulter as commenting on societal decadence in the United States:

Many believe we are currently suffering from an ethics crisis. Behaviors that were once thought unacceptable—lying, cheating, misrepresenting, and covering up mistakes—have become in many people's eyes acceptable or necessary practices. Managers profit from illegal use of insider stock information and members of Congress write hundreds of bad checks.[46]

Adeoye et al. made a similar point with reference to Nigeria: "Students who do not participate in any form of cheating are not only at a disadvantage, but can be viewed as being foolish among their peers. Our culture has embraced cheating and the system has grown tolerant of cheating without punishments. The benefits of individual learning and working hard are no longer seen as a goal or focus."[47]

Young people learn more by examples as they see a society without ethics unfold before them. However, having said that, academic institutions have the duty of bringing up their students to believe that they have obligations to their individual communities and the nation and must live within the boundaries of certain expectations. As university students today, they are faced with taking decisions on the simple issues of whether to cheat in an examination or class assignments. Tomorrow as leaders they will be faced with decisions that affect the future and fortunes of the nation and its people. One responsibility of universities, then, is to bring up socially responsible young people who, at the end of their academic careers, should be found worthy both in character and learning.

Plagiarism and Copyright

Sixty-five percent of the students (523) in our survey indicated that they knew what copyright infringement meant. Although plagiarism is not a crime—in other words, you cannot, for example, be sent to jail for plagiarism, it may lead to copyright infringement. Copyright infringement is a criminal offence under the Nigerian Copyright Act 1988 (amended in 1999), a cumbersome 41-article document, followed by Five Schedules. Section 14(1)(c) of the Act states, "Copyright is infringed by any person who without the licence or authorization of the owner of the copyright exhibits in public any article in respect of which copyright is infringed."[48] Copyright violation is actionable under Nigerian law and a convicted violator may be ordered to pay a fine or may be sent to prison for not more than five years under Section 18 of the Act. In fact, both civil and criminal actions may be initiated simultaneously in respect of one act of violation.

Fortunately, copyright protection is limited by the doctrine of fair use. Accordingly, the "Act does not include the right to control . . . the doing of any of the acts mentioned in Section 5 by way of fair dealing for purposes of research, private use, criticism or review or the reporting of current events, subject to the condition that, if the use is public, it shall be accompanied by an acknowledgement of the title of the work and its authorship."[49] Still, it is obvious that the gravity of copying 20 pages of another person's work cannot be obviated by acknowledging authorship. It is usually said that fair use, especially for educational purposes, requires borrowing only what is reasonable.

So a student who plagiarizes may face the sanctions of his institution such as receiving a fail grade in the course, being suspended from the institution for a specified period, or being expelled from college. In addition, the owner of the work may sue the defaulting student, depending on the scope of the violation. It is no comfort that the defaulting student lives in Nigeria and copies the work of an American author: the offence being committed in Nigeria, the copyright owner may seek redress in Nigerian courts. The Nigerian Act is as broad in its purview as to cover Internet sources even though it was enacted before the ascendancy of the Internet.

Curbing Internet Plagiarism

Curbing plagiarism and indeed other acts of academic dishonesty is, therefore, a major task in the Nigerian university system. From the scanty literature available on the subject matter in Nigeria, enough effort has not been put into that task. Since our focus was on plagiarism among students, we did not do any large-scale investigation into the anti-plagiarism policies of universities in the country. But we spoke randomly with some university administrators. The impression that not enough effort is being directed at the problem was supported by their various responses. Indeed, after a discussion on the issue with a senior academic and administrator in Cross River University of Technology, Calabar, in Nigeria's South–South geopolitical zone, he acknowledged the need for a formal policy on academic dishonesty for that university.[50] Idowu Sobowale, a professor of journalism at Covenant University in the country's South–West geopolitical zone (one of the universities covered by our survey), agreed that many universities do not have formal codes on academic dishonesty. He argued that it will be "immoral to harass lecturers without putting in place an express and enforceable policy for students on plagiarism. But he also sounded the warning that lecturers will not be able to influence their students positively if they are themselves not properly grounded in the virtues of intellectual propriety because they can't give what they don't have."[51]

Most universities in the country have well-formulated policies on examination malpractices, incorporating descriptions of various forms of malpractices and appropriate sanctions for each. Examination malpractices have plagued the country since the mid-1960s, which "marked the beginning of governments' onslaught"[52] against the malfeasance. It rose to "epidemic" proportions in 1977, forcing the federal government to set up a commission of inquiry, headed by a former Chief Justice of Nigeria, the late Sir Darnley Alexander. "Ever since, examination malpractices have been the chorus song in the educational system such that today, examination malpractices have become a national disgrace."[53] Universities, polytechnics, and secondary (high) schools have accordingly been waging a vigorous war against examination malpractices.

From the attention given to exams malpractices, it can be deduced that the rather casual attention paid to plagiarism arises from a lack of serious concern for this form of academic dishonesty. To change perspectives and tackle the issue successfully, the following options, based on data from available literature, may be adopted.

Universities Should Formulate and Implement Policies on Academic Dishonesty

A good starting point would be for universities to formulate policies on academic dishonesty. The formats of such policies in major universities in the United States, Europe, Canada, and Australia can be adopted, with appropriate modifications to suit the local environment. Through the appropriate application of rewards and punishments, students may be encouraged to develop ethical standards that would see them through university and beyond.

Education

The purpose of such education could follow the fourfold structure suggested by Snow:

(a) To increase student awareness of plagiarism and the penalties for it.
(b) To teach through examples how to paraphrase material properly.
(c) To teach through examples how to use quotation properly.
(d) To teach when and how to use citation.[54]

It would be helpful to formally take students through the various manuals of style available for documenting sources in academic writing. Few Nigerian universities seem to follow this course of action. Educating them in this direction would help them appreciate the importance of authenticating their works by citing expert sources.

Within this ambit also, university teachers must acknowledge their portion of the blame in encouraging plagiarism. Some of the assignments we as teachers give to students seem designed to push them into cheating. It is a familiar experience in Nigerian universities for students to be asked, for example, to review textbooks in a class that has nothing to do with book reviews, and where they have never been taught the art and techniques of reviewing. But just because a lecturer wants to sell the title to the students, they are compelled to toil through an assignment they were not prepared for. They would naturally resort to the Internet.

Beyond these, the attitude of university teachers toward academic dishonesty needs to change. Ercegovac and Richardson Jr. reported that, "Of the faculty surveyed, 86 percent have suspected, and 65 percent have been certain of, academic dishonesty in their classrooms. Most of the surveyed members did not regularly follow institutional policy but, rather, handled incidents of cheating and plagiarism on an individual basis."[55] That attitude seems to prevail also in Nigerian academia. For example, students caught cheating in exams have been known to receive an automatic F grade by the invigilating or course lecturer and the matter is allowed to end there. It is much worse with plagiarism, which university teachers do not even seem to acknowledge as a serious problem. A change from such a disposition should form part of this education.

Use of Technology to Check or Detect Plagiarism

University teachers need to be more conversant with ICTs and new media and the possibilities that promote plagiarism as well as the possibilities for detecting it. The use of anti-plagiarism software immediately recommends itself; there are many of these online. From students' responses, there seems to be a conception or misconception among students about the Internet competences of their lecturers. Siyanbola has observed that, "In terms of (computer) proficiency, majority of the lecturers are more proficient in MS-Word and a few others in Excel. Not so many are good at web search and Internet surfing activities."[56] Not-so-proficient lecturers may not realize that the same Google that students often use to search for articles to purloin can also be used as an anti-plagiarism program.

Encouraging Academic Integrity through Mentoring of Students by Faculty Members

This may not be a formally structured mentoring program, but an informal one that enables lecturers to adopt some students whose academic progress they can monitor and help to shape. As Kreitner noted, one of the two important functions of mentoring is the psychological support function.[57] The main goal would be to encourage academic excellence, self-esteem, and personal progress of the students involved. That way, they may come to depend on their abilities, rather than dishonest activities, to get ahead in their academic careers.

Conclusion

In this chapter we reviewed many works on plagiarism, especially from online resources, in order to give an idea of the scope of the problem. In the process, we used a number of definitions to help explain the nature and context of plagiarism. A review of literature on the subject in Nigeria revealed a dearth of research and resources. Our survey of students in three high-brow universities (N = 805) appeared to be one of the very few studies in the country on plagiarism. The findings supported what studies elsewhere in the world have suggested, namely, that plagiarism of Internet sources is widespread and likely to continue to increase. Our data showed that at least 75 percent of the students admitted plagiarizing Internet sources *often* or *sometimes*. We situate the chapter in the framework of ethics, drawing attention to the use of the Internet in unethical and antisocial ways as well as the consequences for the nation of turning out university graduates who accept dishonesty as a normal way for getting ahead.

Notes

1. Mike Ward, *Journalism Online* (London: Oxford, 2002).

2. Stanley J. Baran, *Introduction to Mass Communication: Media Literacy and Culture* (New York: McGraw-Hill Company, 2009), 297.

3. Ward, *Journalism Online*, 10.

4. Ibid., 12.

5. Roger Wimmer and Joseph R. Dominick, *Mass Media Research: An Introduction* (Belmont, CA: Thomson-Wadsworth, 2000), 6.

6. Ifeoma Amobi, "New Generation, New Media and Digital Divide: Assessing Digital Divide through Ownership, Literacy, Access and Usage of Social Media by Young People in Nigeria" (paper presented at the 2nd World Journalism Education Congress, Grahamstown, South Africa, July 3–5, 2010).

7. See Joseph Straubhaar and Robert LaRose, *Media Now: Communications Media in the Information Age*, 6th ed. (Belmont, CA: Wadsworth, 2000); Joseph Dominick, *The Dynamics of Mass Communication* (New York: McGraw-Hill, 2004).

8. Robert Campbell, Christopher Martin, and Bettina Fabos, *Media & Culture: An Introduction to Mass Communication* (Boston: Bedford/St. Martin's, 2010).

9. James Stovall, *Writing for the Mass Media*, 6th ed. (Boston: Pearson, 2006).

10. Shelley Tapp, Barbara E. Hightower, LaVelle H. Mills, and R. Nicholas Gerlich, "The Internet and Classroom Plagiarism: Detecting the Problem." *Journal of Internet Banking & Commerce* (2004), http://www.arraydev.com/commerce/JIBC.

11. Patrick M. Scanlon and David R. Neumann, "Internet Plagiarism among College Students," *Journal of College Student Development* 43, no. 3 (2002): 374–73, 385.

12. Tapp, Hightower, Mills, and Gerlich, "Internet and Classroom."

13. Purdue University OWL, http:/owl.english.purdue.edu/owl/resource/589/01/2011.

14. "University of Queensland Policy 3.40.12," http:/www.uq.edu.au.

15. Indiana University's *Code of Student Rights, Responsibilities, and Conduct,* 2005, http://www.umn.edu.

16. Ibid.

17. The definition comes from Alexander Lindey's *Plagiarism and Originality* (New York: Harper, 1952), 2.

18. B. F. Adeoye, A. M. Olusakin, and Ayodele Ogunleye, "Technologies Students Use in Academic Dishonesty," in *Towards Quality in African Higher Education,* ed. Joel B. Babalola, Labode Popoola, Adams Onuka, Soji Oni, Wole Olatokun, and Rosemary Agbonlahor (Ibadan, Nigeria: Herpnet, 2008), 76–85.

19. Adeoye, Olusakin, and Ogunleye, "Academic Dishonesty."

20. Azuka Alutu and Oyaziwo Aluede, "Secondary Schools Students' Perception of Examination Malpractices and Examination Ethics," *Journal of Human Ecology,* 20 (2006): 295–300, http://www.krepublishers.com.

21. Kate Tobin and Joss Granger, "Raising Awareness of Plagiarism in International Postgraduates" (2009), http://www.bioscience.heacademy.ac.uk.

22. J. Bamford and K. Sergiou, "International Students and Plagiarism: An Analysis of the Reasons for Plagiarism among International Foundation Students," *Investigations in University Teaching and Learning* 2 (2005): 2.

23. Ibid.

24. Ibid.

25. An investigative report by Ikenna Obi and Kelechi Ewuzie, published in the February 4, 2010, issue of *Business Day* Online, http://www.businesdayonline.com/ARCHIVE/index.php?options=content.

26. Scanlon and Neumann, "Internet Plagiarism."

27. Italicized portions are taken from questionnaire items.

28. "New Media Bring a New Set of Problems" was written by Fred Mann on Bill Mitchell's blog, August 2, 2002, http://www.poynter.org.

29. Suzy Hansen, "Dear Plagiarists: You Get What You Pay for." *The New York Times on the Web,* August 24, 2004, http://www.nytimes.com.

30. Carol Rich, *Writing and Reporting News: A Coaching Approach,* 4th ed. (Belmont, CA: Thomson-Wadsworth, 2003), 323.

31. Chula King, Roger Guyette Jr., and Chris Piotrowski, "Online Exams and Cheating: An Empirical Analysis of Business Students' Views," *The Journal*

of Educators Online 6 (2009): 1, http://www.thejeo.com/Archives/Volume6Num ber1/Kingetalpaper.pdf.

32. Scanlon and Neumann, "Internet Plagiarism."

33. Eleanour Snow, "Teaching Students about Plagiarism: An Internet Solution to an Internet Problem," http://www.innovateonline.info/index.php?view=article&id=306.

34. See WSU Web site, http://www.wsulibs.wsu.edu/plagiarism/plagtech1.html.

35. Etim Anim, Idorenyin Akpan, Oloruntola Sunday, Bassey Okon, and Terence Eyo, "ICTs and Higher Education in Nigeria," *CRUTECH Journal of Science, Engineering & Technology* 1, no. 1 (2012): 74–82.

36. Willie Siyanbola, "The Information Technology Policy and Higher Education in Nigeria," http://www.nacetem.org.

37. The figure is from the Nigerian Communications Commission (NCC), Nigeria's telecommunications regulator, http://www.ncc.gov.ng.

38. Denis McQuail, *McQuail's Mass Communication Theory,* 6th ed. (London: Sage, 2010), 424.

39. Philip Kotler, *Marketing Management,* 11th ed. (New Delhi: Prentice-Hall of India, 2003), 196.

40. Joseph Dominick, *The Dynamics of Mass Communication,* 11th ed. (Boston: McGraw-Hill, 2011), 39.

41. Adopted from Moritz College of Law, http://www.is-journal.org/socialmedia/index.php.

42. Rich Maggiani, "The Generational Effect on Social Media," 2009, http://www.docstoc.com.

43. Scanlon and Neumann, "Internet Plagiarism."

44. Robyn McCarthy and Vikkie Hulsart, "Faculty's Leadership Role in Creating Climates of Academic Integrity," 2009, http://www.aabri.com.

45. Joseph Fletcher, *Situation Ethics: The New Morality* (Philadelphia: Westminster Press, 1966), 55.

46. McCarthy and Hulsart, "Faculty's Leadership Role."

47. Adeoye, Olusakin, and Ogunleye, "Academic Dishonesty."

48. Federal Government of Nigeria (FGN), *Copyright Act* (Lagos, Nigeria: Government Printing Press, 1988), 8.

49. FGN, "Copyright," Second Schedule.

50. Personal communication with Professor Giddings Arikpo, the Deputy Vice Chancellor (Academic Affairs) of Cross River University of Technology in November 2011.

51. Professor Idowu was at the time the Head of Department of Mass Communication in the university.

52. Adeoye, Olusakin, and Ogunleye, "Academic Dishonesty."

53. Ibid.

54. Snow, "Teaching Students about Plagiarism."

55. Zorana Ercegovac and John V. Richardson Jr., "Academic Dishonesty, Plagiarism Included, in the Digital Age: A Literature Review," *College & Research Libraries* (2004). Downloaded from the Web as a pdf document. This was an extensive study that covered a wide variety of cyber-based works and documents and databases, with some of the works recording very disturbing findings. For example: "Niels cited a massive study of high achievers conducted by *Who's Who among High School Students* in 1993 that found that 'nearly 80% admitted to some form of dishonesty, such as copying someone else's homework or cheating on an exam.'"

56. Siyanbola, "The Information Technology Policy."

57. Robert Kreitner, *Management*, 6th ed. (Boston: Houghton Mifflin Company, 1995), 485.

CHAPTER NINETEEN

The Ethics of Using Social Media in Classroom Interactions: The Tool to Care or to Hurt

Linda H. Chiang

Introduction

Social media have and continue to influence young people worldwide. In August 2011 the London riots involved thousands of people across cities and towns in the United Kingdom. The events were also called "BlackBerry riots." A group of teenagers and young adults engaged in violent behaviors and arson for which the government blamed the social media because these youth used mobile devices and social media to organize the riot.

In Cairo, the social media networks helped Egyptian activists organize massive street protests that resulted in the fall of the former president, Hosni Mubarak. The same media network now serves as a platform for incidents, rumor spreading, utter disinformation, and even violence. In 2013, the social media expert at the Cairo-based Al-Ahram Center for Political Strategic Studies, Adel Abdel-Saddiq, blamed the government for the lack of oversight of the social platform in Egypt that the nation is paying for.

In Malaysia, the ethical issues related to social media are the cyber attacks and the hacking of government Web sites. These incidents caused almost 41 Malaysian government Web sites to be hacked overnight.[1]

The incidents listed earlier have presented the concerns of unethical or inappropriate use of social media. These incidents should serve as an alarm for the educators, due to the worldwide nature of these incidents. The need to safeguard the Internet from being abused by the users as well as to educate the public, especially the young people, on the negative aspects of social media should be paid attention to by countries where social media are used significantly.[2] The world needs to face a new technological society with a new attitude.

Technology has also increased communication and interaction in the classroom as well as widened the generation gap. In the 1960s the term "television generation" was used to explain the social changes. In the 1990s Google became the most popular social medium; after the year 2000 Facebook became the preferred favorite site among young people. The contemporary idea of "Digital Native" has created an era that makes young people live at a fast pace. On the other hand, those who stick with older media become "Digital Immigrants." Three of the more common terms that have been used to describe the young cohort are the "Next Generation,"[3] "Digital Natives," and "Millennial."[4]

Young people today use Internet sites for social interactions. Amanda Lenhart, Kristen Purcell, Aaron Smith, and Kathryn Zickuhr in their report pointed out that by 2009, 73 percent of online teens (ages 12–17) and 72 percent of young adults (ages 18–29) use social networking sites to communicate their lives and update their activities for the their friends.[5] Since these communication media have become the primary media of interaction for today's generation, they have come to be called "social media." Tanya Joosten defines social media as Web 2.0 applications, which include an array of online tools and services that are Web-based and dynamic in nature; in addition to text-based messages (such as Twitter), one can post videos to YouTube.[6] Since we classify these as social media, the primary purpose for using such should be to socialize with anyone, everyone, and everywhere. There are reasons for schools to utilize this method of communication with the popularity of social media among young people. Tanya Joosten considers the reasons for schools to use social media as follows: (1) social media have the potential to enhance learning and meet pedagogical needs and (2) many instructors and students are already users of social media in their personal and professional lives.[7]

Many teachers who are currently teaching in K-12 are considered "Digital Immigrants." For these reasons the teachers have to learn new terms and new devices in order to have the same language that their students are using. In addition, teachers should keep their knowledge of subject matter, pedagogy, and new media technology current through continuing education. In this chapter, the positive aspects of using social media along with teachers' judgments of the extent their students may use devices in the classrooms are discussed. This chapter also looks at the recent trends related to the ethical use of social media, especially involving cyberbullying among teenagers. The following questions are addressed: How are teachers informed about the social media that are commonly used among their students? To what extent will teachers allow students to use their devices and be involved in social networking? How can teachers detect and stop cyberbullying among their students? What is the ethical responsibility teachers need to address in their classrooms? What is the ethical conduct when using social media in a school environment? And, how will teachers model ethical behavior when using social media?

What Is Going on with Social Media in Classrooms?

Most young people in our country use the Internet every day. It is an integral part of a young person's life. The common usages are for them to go online, to get information, play games, write e-mails, talk through instant messaging or in chat rooms, connect with friends through social networking sites, and download music, talk shows, and movies.[8] At the end of 2006, 55 percent of teenagers reported that they use the Internet to socialize and they had a profile on a social networking site, compared with 20 percent of adult users.[9] In more recent years, Facebook has grown to 800 million users,[10] Twitter to 20 million users,[11] and LinkedIn to 100 million users.[12] It has been reported by Lenhart, Purcell, Smith, and Zickuhr[13] that more than 70 percent of adults, young adults, and teens go online to use Facebook. Even though many teachers may not be frequent users of the Internet, they are facing and teaching a group of young Internet users. Schools are facing new challenges as to whether they should allow students to carry their cell phones into the classrooms, whether to provide access for Internet as search engines, and to what extent, students should be involved in online chat rooms while they are in the classrooms.

Teachers have different points of view than students about using social media (cell phone or iPad for Internet) in classrooms. As much as there are benefits for using social media in classrooms, these also bring disruptions and distract students' attention. The following information is a result of a seminar discussion with 30 teachers at a university in Southern California in spring 2013. Most participating teachers did not favor the use of electronic devices by students.

One teacher said, "[Is social media] a solution for effective use of electronics in the classroom? Not really, it just takes constant vigilance"; and "It is more difficult for students to stay on task when you allow students to use their things for the purpose such as a Web Search."

This group of teachers questioned school policies and here are several of the responses: "But first, what is the school's policy? There is a public high school in San Diego that does not allow students to take electronic devices to school"; "My private high school only allows electronics between classes. Or, at the teacher's discretion"; and "I told them to have their backpacks on the floor behind them and all hats off."

As for the teachers' attitudes, they expressed: "I am nostalgic for the days when students were not allowed to have beepers in class. Now I am constantly on 'text patrol'" and "Do you know how to spot a teen using a phone? There is no teen in the country that is looking down at their crotch and is smiling."

Reading from these teachers' reports, technology seems to bother teachers more than help with their teaching. Voices from these teachers and educators may help to transform the need for students to connect into positive social interactions.

Can Chat Rooms and/or Facebook Be Effective Methods for Learning?

Davina Pruitt-Mentle identifies the advantages of using technology for education as improved access to information, improved simulation capabilities, enhanced productivity, and providing technology-based assistance. *Education Week's* Technology Counts 2007 Report indicated that in the United States, 16 states had integrated technology within the standards of other content areas, while 32 states had adopted stand-alone technology standards. These standards predominantly focus on skills other than cyber safety, cyber security, or cyberethics.[14] Without the awareness of these three considerations, no wonder schools and teachers struggle to find a better solution in using technology, especially social media.

Social media offer numerous opportunities for teachers to reach all students. Students used to communicate via e-mails, but more students are either in chat rooms or on Facebook. Many teachers recognize the popularity of social media and have created chat rooms and/or Facebook pages that allow for question and answer activities. Chat rooms and Facebook can also be used for students to collaborate with others and obtain feedback from the teacher as well as from their peers.

One of the concerns expressed by teachers about chat room or Facebook use is the lack of face-to-face interactions. Some teachers remarked: "We are increasingly living in a culture where people don't know how to talk to other people. I feel that a Chatroom isn't the place where people are working on their communication skills." "I am a P. E. teacher; I see the internet as being the main problem for a lot of my students. Kids who cannot catch a basketball being thrown their way, or cannot not run a mile because of all the time spent on computer. The more time people spend on the internet, the less time they are actually being around others, and are getting less vital information on themselves."

But some teachers felt positive about students using the Internet for chat room and Facebook use. One teacher said, "The internet is great when used appropriately. Chatroom forms of discussion are all great ways to communicate when not used furiously." "Students feel far more comfortable sharing and interacting behind the 'safety' of their computer screen. The use of internet Chatroom and Facebook allows the teacher to step aside from the teaching and become a spectator to the students' opinions, ideas, and abilities."

A major downside of students' overreliance on, and addiction to, social media use is that it disengages them from direct physical human interaction. This, in turn, denies students the necessary positive or negative reinforcement.[15]

Teachers also proposed strategies that would help them and students better use the chat room and Facebook. One strategy, mentioned by a few teachers, required Webcam chats at a set time so teachers could see whether students were on task and with the group. Another suggestion was to schedule a video chat with the teacher at least once a week.

Should Students Text or Answer Their Cell Phones in the Classroom?

The popularity of cell phone among youth is due, in part, to psychological needs to belong and to be needed.[16] A recent study found that the majority of cell-phone users started using cell phone at the age of 10–18.[17] The use of a cell phone increases social inclusion and connectedness.[18] Some teens feel secure when they can reach others anytime. However, classrooms are disrupted when cell phones are not used at appropriated times.[19]

Schools have incorporated the digital concept as well by increasing connected classroom and using Web sites and other online tools to reach students and inform parents and the community. However, more and more schools are facing the challenge of students using cell phones to text and read messages, post photos and videos, and make or receive calls. Texting is the instant messaging via cell phones over cellular networks. The emergence of social media requires a new attitude and behavior and thus needs a new ethical consideration.

Teachers reported the following responses from students using devices to text or answer phones in classrooms:

> "It is harder when the teacher allows students to use their cell phones for 'proper' purpose"; "In my school, any phones may be confiscated in class and taken to the VP. The VP assigns a lunch detention, reason: inattention in class and disruptive behavior"; "My wife is a teacher; she has a basket to collect the phones. They trade their phone for a penny candy for the period. It has had limited success"; and "My class knows it is not allowed. Fifty push-ups or get them from the VP. It is their choice, and they still don't get it back until after the class. Boys try to be tough and purposely get caught to prove they can do the push-ups."

Almost all teachers view cell phones as a potential distraction and need to prevent students from using them during class time.

How Does Cyberbullying Influence Students' Lives?

Social media can be seen as a double-edged sword. When used positively, they can build up relationships, communicate, and collaborate positively; however, when these are used to bully and spread negative messages, these can be lethal weapons to hurt or to kill feelings and relationships. Technology has opened a new world for young people to communicate with friends, socialize and interact with peers outside classrooms, and get information they need instantly; however, social media also have the potential to negatively impact young people—from plagiarism and inappropriate sexual messages to excessive disclosure of personal facts and cyberbullying. Cyberbullying and its negative effects are getting more and more attention from the public. Cyberbullying happens when people bully each other online. Such negative behavior can include sending texts messages or e-mails, spreading rumors by e-mails or on social networking sites, and posting embarrassing pictures, videos, and a private communication publicly on Web sites. Bullying can cause physical, emotional, and social consequences for both victims and perpetrators. Bullies often suffer from low school bonding, and poor adjustment, which can be associated with low school competence. They are more likely to be involved in carious self-destructive or antisocial behaviors, such as fighting, and getting in trouble with the law. The cyberbullying behaviors are different from traditional bullying in that they don't need to have physical contact, and it can happen everywhere and anytime. Since content is written, it can have wider and longer lasting negative effects on the victims.

Cyberbullying is on the rise with the widespread use of social media. Technology should instead provide numerous conveniences to young people to interact among their peers; it also causes a dark side effect.[20] It can be used to lift up, cheer up, support, and encourage people; however, it can also be used to belittle, put down, humiliate, or harass others. Such negative behaviors can include sending mean text messages, e-mails, and posting malicious rumors, embarrassing and anti-social pictures and videos online.

Whose Responsibility Is It to Stop Cyberbullying?

In California, a sophomore girl was assaulted by three boys, and one of them took a picture of the alleged attack and posted it online. The picture soon circulated among her classmates. A week later she hanged herself and died. Similar cases happened in Ohio and Canada recently. Parents claimed they were not present when the incident took place in their house. When tragedies such as this happen we may question, "Who is responsible for the death of cyberbullying victims?"

The National Crime Prevention Council reports that 43 percent of teens have been victims of cyberbullying. The report also indicates that ethical and moral decisions are occurring throughout the students' K-12 experiences. Another study was conducted and reported in 2005 through Pew Internet and American Life as Protecting Teens Online. In this report 64 percent of online teens (aged 12–17) reported that they do things online as they don't want their parents to know about it; 79 percent reported that they are not careful enough when giving out their personal information online.[21] It is critical to inform students of the safety and ethics of using technology and social media.

Cyberbullying is found to influence suicidal thoughts among adolescents. In 2007, a survey with a random sample of 1,963 middle-schoolers regarding Internet use and experiences was conducted. Youth who have experienced bullying, either an offender or a victim, had more suicidal thoughts and were more likely to attempt suicide than those who had not experienced bullying aggressive behaviors from peers.[22] Schools and teachers not only need to be familiar with social media, but they also need to be sensitive to the potential harm of cyberbullying. In the 2008 National Cyberethics, Cybersafety, Cybersecurity (C3), Baseline Study showed that local educational agencies place the majority of responsibility of teaching cyberethics, cybersafety, cybersecurity in the hands of educators.[23] However, 75 percent of participating educators felt uncomfortable discussing topics which are getting significant attention from the public such as cyberbullying, even though they felt these 3Cs are important and critical components for teens to use social media and technology appropriately. School districts need to provide training for parents and teachers to communicate cyberethics among students. The collaboration between the school and the community is essential to prevent and stop teen aggressive bullying behaviors.

How Are Technology and Social Media Used in Cyberbullying?

Cyberbullying is considered a common problem faced by children and adolescents throughout the world.[24] In recent years a new form of bullying is using a diverse range of technology in aggressive behaviors and language to harm others. According to the London-based Anti-Bullying Alliance, seven categories of cyberbullying were identified:

(1) *Text message bullying:* Harassing text messages are sent via cell phone and are intended to threaten or cause discomfort and humiliation to recipients.
(2) *Picture/video clip bullying via cell-phone cameras:* Images of the victim are sent to other people and are intended to threaten or embarrass the victim. It involves filming and sharing physical attacks of the victims.
(3) *Phone call bullying via cell phone:* It includes making silent calls or leaving abusive messages without giving the victim time or opportunities to respond or defend for self.
(4) *E-mail bullying:* Abusive and threatening messages are sent via e-mail by perpetrators, often using a pseudonym or someone else's name. It often happens when the perpetrator steals or falsely uses another person's e-mail address.
(5) *Chat-room bullying:* Threatening or sending upsetting responses to someone in an online chat room and spreading negative information.
(6) *Bullying through IM:* Sending negative messages while carrying a real-time conversation with someone online.
(7) *Bullying via Web sites:* Using Web logs (blogs), personal Web sites, online personal sites, and social networking sites to spread unpleasant messages (e.g., Myspace).[25]

Relatedly, these methods of bullying can be used intentionally to hurt or harm others through social media without consideration of their well-being. Studies indicated that middle school and high school years are the peak time for bullying behaviors.[26]

This is also the time that young people are introduced to the Internet and social media and practice using different types of social media. The most common forms of social media among this group of teenagers are e-mails, texting, and chat rooms.

What Is the Ethical Conduct When Using Social Media in a School Environment?

Ethics is a practice to guide and help discern how people should behave.

Citizens in the United States are free to pursue and exercise the freedom of speech. However, being free means each one needs to recognize and accept civic responsibility along with rights and privilege. Society, as a whole, will function more effectively when people help and encourage one another in their social interactions through social media. Social media give citizens a way to connect, communicate, and voice their opinions, but individuals need to be sensitive and considerate of others' rights and privileges. Thus, dialogue and discussion among individuals or groups will be essential strategy to raise the awareness of using social media responsibly. Such ethical interactions, therefore, promote healthy communication, moral actions, and social relationship. There needs to be some code of conduct to regulate or shape cyber users' behaviors.

In the 21st century, students need to be digitally literate. In addition to gaining the skills of technology, they need to be informed of the safety, security, and ethics of using social media. Schools need to provide a framework for young people to make good decisions about their online behavior and attitude in order to use technology and social media responsibly. Schools and students' home environment also need to create a culture of cyber security and safety awareness by offering the knowledge and tools necessary to prevent cybercrime and attacks.

At the dawn of the implementation of California's Common Core Standards in K-12 education, in which collaboration is one of the core standards, exercising ethical social interaction through social media can help to cultivate and develop responsible and respectful collaboration.

Teachers strive to do their best job by trying new ways of teaching, new ways of creating environments in classrooms, and new ways of developing the sense of agency in children, in hopes to reach the sense of expectation for something beyond what is.[27] Social media will help to develop strong links among social experience, learning, and teaching.[28] Teachers can use social media to improve their understanding of students' needs, learning processes, as well as detect and prevent cyberbullying.

How Will Teachers Model Ethical Behaviors in Using Social Media?

Ethical decision is different from legal action even though what is considered illegal is generally considered as unethical. Aristotle discussed ethics "what he does in and by ignorance, he does it involuntarily."[29] Students may not realize the messages that they have posted on social media are hurting others due to their ignorance in using inappropriate language. However, such ignorance may also be due to their lack of knowledge and the result of teachers' negligence. To model ethical behaviors in using social media, this writer proposes the following for attitude changes and pedagogies:

1. Teachers need to be informed of available social media that students are using. Teachers need to learn what their students are interested and involved in using social media. They can be co-learners with their students. Students will take pride when they have something to teach their teachers.
2. Teachers can be cheerleaders. Studies show that the bullied are normally victims. These students need encouragement and understanding. When teachers give them a channel to voice their negative encounters with bullying, it might prevent and reduce cyberbullying incidents.
3. Teachers will be modeling what they preach. The classroom is the place where students will shape their character from their teachers' behaviors. The golden rule "Do to other what you want others to do to you" is a valuable lesson that both teachers and students need to execute. Teachers will not check their e-mails or answer texts while teaching. Teachers need to use humor rather than harsh words when modifying students' defiant behaviors.
4. Teachers may use social media to engage students as teaching pedagogy. Teachers can create a chat room or use Myspace to meet students' needs to interact and use the Internet. Teachers can involve students in content reading discussion or book-sharing projects. Online grading can also give them immediate feedback.

Most importantly, when teachers embrace social media in their class teaching, it narrows the gap of the "Digital Immigrants" and "Digital Natives." Teachers will enjoy getting to know young people's lives, and teaching pedagogy can be more relevant to the young generation.

Conclusion

Social media are an important part of young people's lives. How teachers incorporate social media in their teaching should be an essential issue to be addressed in the teacher training programs. Furthermore, providing staff development to train current Digital Immigrant teachers on how to use social media without feeling intimidated is critical.

The developing and implementing of pedagogy using social media for prospective teachers at the early stage of their training will assist them to work effectively with Digital Native students. K-12 schools are essential to cultivating good citizens, but schools are also the arena in which many citizens in the United States get hurt and humiliated through social media.

In conclusion, social media can help teenagers to build social relationships, search for information, stay in contact, and bring light on people and give them hopes; on the other hand, these can humiliate, embarrass, hurt people, and cast shadow on others' lives. These can build up other humans and are also powerful to tear down self-esteem. The teen years are a time to establish self-images and find self-identity.[30] Without the ethical consideration for others, social media may hurt people and cause lifelong damages emotionally and socially.

Many programs have been developed to prevent cyberbullying. Teachers and parents need to know what Internet or social media their students and children are on, who are engaged in their circle of interaction, as well as pay attention to unusual emotional distress or behavior to detect cyberbullying. Many researchers also recommend developing and publicizing a school-wide anti bullying policy.[31] The youth need to be reminded to conscientiously and responsibly participate in social networking technologies. When every parent, student, and teacher is on the lookout for safe and ethical behaviors of social media, it will greatly avoid the negative effects of social media and reduce the incidents of cyberbullying and enhance the overall positive use of teacher–student cyber time.

Notes

1. Ali Salman, Suhana Saad and Mohd. Nor Shahizan Ali, "Dealing with Ethical Issues among Internet Users: Do We Need Legal Enforcement?" *Asian Social Science* 9, no. 8 (2013): 4.

2. Ibid., 6.

3. Don Tapscott, *Growing Up Digital: The Rise of the Next Generation* (New York: McGraw-Hill, 1998); Don Tapscott, *Growing Up Digital: How the Next Generation Is Changing Your World* (New York: McGraw-Hill, 2009).

4. Marc Prensky, "Digital Natives, Digital Immigrants," *On the Horizon* 9, no. 5 (2001): 1–6; Marc Prensky, "H. sapiens Digital: From Digital Immigrants and Digital Natives to Digital Wisdom," *Innovate* (2009): 6, 3, www.innovateonline .info/index.php?view=article&id=705; Neil Howe and William Straus, *Millennials Rising: The Next Generation* (New York: Vintage, 2000).

5. Amenda Lenhart, Kristen Purcell, Aaron Smith, and Kathryn Zickuhr, *Social Media and Young Adults* (Washington, DC: Pew Internet & American Life

Project, 2010), http://www.pewinternet.org/Reports/2010/Social-Media-and-Young-Adults.aspx.

6. Tanya Joosten, *Social Media for Educators: Strategies and Best Practices* (San Francisco: Jossey-Bass, 2012), 7.

7. Ibid., 3.

8. Julia Wilkins, John Hoover, Plamen Miltenoff, and Traek Downing, "New Communication Technologies & the Emergence of Cyberbullying," *The International Journal of Interdisciplinary Social Studies* 2, no. 3 (2007): 407–12.

9. Pew American Life Project, 2005. *Reports: Teens & Technology: Youth Are Leading the Transition to a Fully Wired and Mobile Nation,* July 2007, http://www.pewinternet.org/~/media/Files/Reports/2005/PIP_Teens_Tech_July2005web.pdf.pdf

10. Facebook, 2011, http://www.facebook.com/press/info.php?statistics.

11. BBC, 2011, http://www.bbc.co.uk/news/business-12889048.

12. LinkedIn, 2011, http://press.linkedin.com/about.

13. Lenhart, Purcell, Smith, and Zickuhr, *Social Media and Young Adults.*

14. Davina Pruitt-Mentle, *2008 National Cyberethics, Cybersafety, Cybersecretary Baseline Study*, www.whitehouse.gov/files/documents/cyber.

15. Robert Sternberg and Wendy Williams, *Educational Psychology* (San Francisco: Pearson, 2010).

16. Abrahan Maslow, *Motivation and Personality* (New York: Harper & Row, 1954).

17. Ishfaq Ahmed and Techmina Fiaz Quzi, "Mobile Phone Adoption & Consumption Patterns of University Students in Pakistan," *International Journal of Business & Social Science* 2, no. 9 (May 2011): 205–13.

18. Ran Wei and Ven-Hwei Lo, "Staying Connected while on the Move: Cell Phone Use and Social Connectedness," *New Media and Society* 8 (2006): 53–72; See also Ahmed and Quzi, "Mobile Phone Adoption."

19. Neil Selwyn, "Schooling the Mobile Generation: The Future for Schools in the Mobile-Networked Society," *British Journal of Sociology of Education* 24 (2003): 131–44.

20. Marilyn Campbell, "Cyber Bullying: An Old Problem in a New Guise?" *Australian Journal of Guidance and Counseling* 15, no. 1 (2005): 68–76.

21. Pruitt-Mentle, *2008 National Cyberethics.*

22. Sameer Hinduja and Justin Patchin, "Bullying, Cyberbulling, & Suicide," *Archives of Suicide Research* 14, no. 3 (2010): 206–21.

23. Pruitt-Mentle, *2008 National Cyberethics.*

24. Debra J. Pepler, Wendy M. Craig, Jennifer A. Connolly, Amy Yuile, Loren McMaster, and Depeng Jiang, "A Developmental Perspective on Bullying," *Aggressive Behavior* 32 (2006): 376–84.

25. Wilkins, Hoover, Miltenoff, and Downing, "New Communication Technologies."

26. Rana Sampson, *Bullying in Schools* (Washington, DC: U.S. Department of Justice, 2002).

27. Maxine Greene, ed., *Variations on a Blue Guitar* (New York: Teachers College Press, 2001), 150.

28. Lev Vygotsky, *Mind in Society: The Development of Higher Psychological Process* (Cambridge, MA: Harvard University Press, 1978).

29. Aristotle, *Eudemian Ethics,* trans. P. Marechaux (Paris: Editions Payot & Rivage, 2008), ch. 9, 3.

30. Erik Erikson, *Identity and the Life Cycle* (New York: Norton, 1980).

31. Edmund Emmer, Murray Worsham, and Carolyn Evertson, eds. *Classroom Management for Middle and High School Teachers* (Upper Saddle, NJ: Pearson, 2009); James Levin and James Nolan, eds. *Principles of Classroom Management: A Professional Decision-Making Model* (Boston: Pearson, 2010).

CHAPTER TWENTY

Rumors on Social and New Media: Ethical Implications for Individuals and Society

Agnes Lucy Lando

Introduction

Mainstream, new, and social media have been all involved in rumors about the identity of witness no. 536. Her family also reported allegedly threatened after the media's coverage rumored about her identity.[1] The rumor resulted in the private sessions of the ICC trials of Kenya's 2007/2008 PEV. The *Standard* newspapers also had a story on that, indicating that social media users forced the International Criminal Court (ICC) to retreat to closed-door sessions.[2] The caption indicated that blogs and social media in Kenya caused the trials of the Kenyan deputy president William Ruto and former radio presenter Joshua arap Sang to go into closed session to protect the first prosecution witness. As this went on, a lady in Kenya presented herself to the police on September 19, 2013, because her picture and profiles were being circulated in social media as the witness no. 536. The ICC scenario is just but one of the many rumors that take place on new and social media with adverse effects. In this regard, Christians, Rotzoll, Fackler, McKee, and Woods hold that ethical journalism includes, among other values, respect for human dignity and truth telling.[3]

The spreading of rumors is not new. Thus, it would not be an exaggeration to state that every adult has encountered a rumor—be it about him or her or someone else. Traditionally, rumors spread via word of mouth. However, the emergence of technologies accelerates the speed and scope of the spread of a rumor. Nonetheless, neither technological advancements nor the emergence of new media alters the reasons why a rumor spreads. Whereas it may not be possible to establish the real reasons why a rumor begins, the primary factors influencing the spread of rumors include, how influential or convincing the rumors is, the credibility of the source of origin, the number of people reached, and the underlying structure of the network used to spread it. When a rumor starts, there are those who hear it and actively get involved in spreading it further; and there are those who choose not to.

Rumors can come from mainstream media through news programs due to sensationalism or news mongering. They can also come from gutter press. Moreover, rumor can also come from people (outside the media) both within and outside the organization. Rumor can happen to anyone. Often, there is no explanation why it happened or who started it, but can cause the longest and most damaging of crises because even outrageous rumors endure or repeat, and they are difficult to battle.[4] The victim of the malicious rumor rarely knows how the rumor started or who has heard it. This makes it difficult to curtail its spreading, which happens quickly and often with disastrous consequences. There are occasions when rumors start from actual truths, but the facts become too intermingled with gossip or misinformation that the rumor becomes louder than the truth. Rumors can ruin the reputation of an individual or product or lead to depression or to death through suicide/homicide. Indeed, as Joe White said, "Rumors are like being stabbed from behind. You are injured before you know what is happening and while the knife might be pulled out later it is going to leave a permanent scar."[5]

Rumors can be negative or positive. For instance, a positive rumor could be, in an organization, that management has increased staff salaries. While this is positive, it could cause untold damage to the organization that has not factored staff salary increment in its budget. Thus, a rumor may be defined as false or misleading information that is purposefully circulated about an individual, organization, or its products in order to harm them.[6] Even though rumor can happen in real life or on social media, this study is concerned with rumors on social and new media. Social media is a phrase that was coined to refer to social networking on new media comprising of e-mail and social networking sites, such as Google +, Twitter, Facebook, and LinkedIn to name a few.[7]

Methodology

This was a content analysis study. The researcher selected some of the most recent rumors that have taken place on new and social media. After the identification of the rumors, the study then briefly describes the nature of the rumors, how the rumors started, and their implication on individuals and society. This study has examined six rumors on social and new media, localized for Kenya, but also others beyond the Kenyan geographical sphere. Then, in some cases, a brief discussion has been done with regard to the impact of rumors in social and new media on individuals and society.

Rumor One

Killer Red Call

On September 1, 2010, Kenyan cell-phone users went into a state of panic due to the red call rumor that was doing rounds in social media sites, specifically on Twitter, Facebook, e-mails, and cell phones. Many phone calls were made and SMSs sent all over the country warning Kenyans not to receive calls from certain numbers:

> Do not pick up calls under given numbers. 9888308001, 9316048121 91+, 9876266211, 9888854137 9876715587. These numbers will come in red color. If the calls come up from these numbers, it's with very high wave length and frequency. If a call is received on mobile from these numbers, it creates a very high frequency and it causes brain hemorrhage. It's not a joke rather, it's TRUE. 27 persons died just on receiving calls from these numbers. Watch AajTak (NEWS), DD News and IBN 7. Forward this message to all your friends and colleagues, and relatives.[8]

The spread of the hoax was rife due to the extreme consequences that were claimed to occur if anyone was to pick a call from a red number. The consequences from the rumor ranged from male impotence to brain hemorrhage to instant death. People began calling their loved ones to warn them. Terming the phenomenon a hoax, the Communications Commission of Kenya (CCK) released a statement a day later, and confirmed that these numbers were nonexistent as mobile, fixed, or international lines. Mobile technology experts also dismissed the rumors as lacking scientific basis because cell phones cannot emit high-frequency radiation as alleged. They argued that if that was the case, then cell phones would not be safe to use. In the midst of the panic, another rumor began to emerge, that the originators and beneficiaries of the red call alert were cell-phone operators and FM stations. Mobile operators benefited from the large volume of calls and text messages driven by panicked and gullible Kenyans, while FM stations generated controversy and tried to get people to tune into their shows and call to contribute to the live debate.

The red-call hoax was one of the first recorded content to go viral in Kenya's Internet space. At this time, the Kenyan telecommunication sector was at a turning point. According to CCK,[9] cell phone use was at its peak with the number of subscribers increasing from 20 million recorded in 2009 to 25 million in 2010. At the same time, the number of Kenyans connected to the Internet grew to 14 million users, a 35 percent Internet penetration rate compared to 21 percent recorded in the previous year. Kenyans were also said to be the largest online community in Africa, after South Africa and Nigeria, both by social media use and by the number of blogs. This setting meant that the country's online space was fertile ground for an Internet hoax.

Additionally, Internet users in the country had never witnessed a local Internet rumor of the scale and rapid spread that characterized the red-call hoax. The ripple effect of the rumor was the heavy losses cell-phone operators and service providers suffered due to the panic. There was a plunge in the profits made from calling rates as people were hesitant to pick random calls.

Rumor Two

The Kenya versus Nigeria "Tweef"

The Kenya versus Nigeria tweet war started early March 2013 after the local media reported that Kenya's national football team, Harambee Stars, had been mistreated on their arrival in Nigeria for a World Cup qualifier match. Kenya turned to the social media site to condemn the poor welcome that was apparently accorded to their national team by the Nigerian Football Federation. Complaints raised by the Kenyan team included poorly arranged transport for the team, lack of security, poor state of training facility, and a two-star hotel accommodation instead of four- or five-star hotel accommodation recommended by *Fédération Internationale de Football Association* (FIFA). To underscore the gravity of the matter, a picture was posted showing an aircraft landing in a bush and Harambee stars players scampering for safety. This elicited negative reactions from Kenyan fans. Photographs of the Kenyan team training on the dusty and unleveled grounds were retweeted.[10] The topic became an instant trend on the social networking site with everyone interested giving an opinion, which were mostly insulting comments between Kenyans and Nigerians.

Al Jazeera identified the following as the earliest trigger tweet that led to the online feud:

Mr YouKnowIGotIt @kmaore
Kenyans should start #SomeonetellNigeria due to the way they are treating our stars!
11:50 PM—20 Mar 2013
7 RETWEETS 6 FAVORITES

The Onslaught

Baba Chausiku ™ @Kisenyajesse
#someonetellnigeria we are disappointed by the way they're treating Harambee. Next time they come here, come with your own airport to land
3:05 PM—21 Mar 2013
124 RETWEETS 22 FAVORITES
Seyyid and Dan @mainadan
#SomeOneTellNigeria to be a president in Kenya one must attain 50% +1vote theirs is just by #Goodluck.
4:44 PM—21 Mar 2013
49 RETWEETS 11 FAVORITES
SaddiqueShaban@SaddiqueShaban
FACT: #SomeoneTellNigeria this weekend alone, we got rugby team in #IRB-HongKong, Cross Country team in #Poland and soccer team in #Nigeria.
222 RETWEETS 15 FAVORITES
@dinobilal: #SomeoneTellNigeria we shall suspend the viewing of their movies if they fail to attend to our players appropriately
@Davynition: #SomeonetellNigeria we thought they were OGAnised. Harambee Stars deserve better; "*#someone tell Nigeria we can throw stones from Kenya and break that African cup of Nation Trophy*"

The Backlash

Amara Nwankpa @bubusn
#SomeOneTellKenya USA—Hollywood, India—Bollywood, Nigeria—Nollywood, Kenya? Firewood.
9:30 PM—21 Mar 2013
37 RETWEETS 3 FAVORITES
RamblersINC.@tee_hidee
#SomeoneTellKenya you know all our Nigerian stars, your TV stations show our movies, but we don't even know where you are on the map.
471 RETWEETS 37 FAVORITES
@Ikharonaj:#SomeoneTellKenya no matter how far Kenyans run, they can't run away from HUNGER." The Kenyans trended in Lagos today. That's as close to civilization as most of them will ever get. #SomeoneTellKenya"
EmekaEnyadike @EmekaEnyadike
6:59 PM—21 Mar 2013
13 RETWEETS[11]

"#there are plans by Dangote to buy Kenya. He needs a new cement depot"
"#Kenyan runners are so fast because they imagine hunger chasing them"
"#You know what the most positive thing in Kenya is? HIV"

As reported by Kenya's Daily Nation news site, the tweet battle with the #SomeoneTellKenya and #SomeoneTellNigeria trended worldwide throughout March 21, 2013. Al Jazeera reported that the use of #SomeoneTellNigeria and #SomeoneTellKenya spanned across many continents, reaching China, United States, Indonesia, United Kingdom, and Saudi Arabia.[12] The mainstream media went ahead and fueled the fight by highlighting the trend. To add to this, they gave conflicting reports from both the Kenya and Nigerian Football Federations. These federations blamed each other with the latter saying there was lack of communication and unwarranted demands such as the use of a chartered plane, a luxury that the Nigerians could not afford.

There were moral implications of this social fight such as resurfacing of strongly held stereotypes. For instance, Nigerians in Kenya are branded as "drug peddling sorcerers who make use of accented Pidgin English." As it is, Nigerians do feel ostracized by Kenyans. It is worth noting that rumors may not necessarily change the exact situation on the ground. For instance, although Kenyans on Twitter (KOT) may have seemingly won the fight on Twitter, this did not change the fact that the Nigerian Super Eagles have proved superior to the Harambee Stars. In any case, they won the match that caused the fight. Thus, Kenyans won on Twitter, but Nigeria won on the football ground.

The Kenya–Nigeria tweef exhibits adverse effects of social and new media communication on African culture in regard to communication and conflict resolution. The supporters of both football teams used negative language. In former times, the African culture did not allow pronouncement, let alone use, of the abusive words exchanged on the social media. Furthermore, it was very rare, literally unheard of, for women and younger generation to openly exchange abuses with men. But on this Kenya–Nigeria tweef, everybody who had something to say did say it in the manner he or she chose. Social and new media are free for all.

Even though freedom of expression is a contemporary basic human right, it is my conviction that while every citizen is equally entitled to the freedom to express himself or herself, it must not be of harm or inconvenience to others. Thus fundamentally, while social and new media are making life bearable and fun, they pose such a great challenge not only on authenticity of what is communicated but also adds to the already myriad challenges of communication and media ethics.

Exposure to social media lowers African cultural values and morals. This does not mean that the new media are entirely to blame. African morals and values disintegrated since the 19th century when African warmed up to the concept of globalization, modernization, and Westernization. What the new media have done is to catalyze the disintegration of morals and values. Words posted on Facebook and Twitter by fans are simply unprintable. People have found a "safe haven" to be explicit in their language, character, and conduct making them audacious. This is the character that is "Not African" and shows the levels Africans have reached in destroying their once treasured values and cultures embroidered in respect and togetherness.

Argument's presented by fans on Twitter and Facebook have made it difficult for one to imagine that such thoughts are good or right. Since most fans were airing their grievances or annoyance, they openly said what was on their minds. Reading all the comments posted on the two social sites, it was clear that the values they believe in were not influenced solely by African culture.

Emergence of social media has weakened legislation making it difficult to draw a line between freedom of speech and civility, individual reputation, privacy, dignity, physical, and emotional security. It could be thus said that the more people use social media, the clashes between these values increase.

Many people use social media as a way of enhancing existing relationships, but when excessively used it usually distracts the users from their surroundings. Due to the freedom that has been accorded to the users, one feels obligated to express him or her in whatever way he or she pleases not considering others who and of what age will access the media. The feud between Kenya and Nigeria's football team and also those who post nude or pornographic images of themselves is an example of misuse of freedom of expression.

Ethical Implications on the Tweefs

Most users engaged in the Kenyan–Nigerian social media battle easily consumed what trended at the time without even questioning whether the cause of the social fight was worth. This was seen from both sides: when a Kenyan user insulted the Nigerians, fellow Kenyans would delve in with full-blown support, adding more insults. Similarly, whenever a Nigerian posted an insulting message, Nigerian users would retweet it to a wider audience.

It seems that new and social communication, with reference to the Kenyan–Nigerian social fight, is giving rise to a new media breed of single-dimensional communicators characterized by fast and easy-undigested consumption of messages. Stanley Baran and Dennis Davis[13] elaborate that cybercitizens have little desire for self-reflection or critical examination of their own biases. This is because in the virtual communities of social media, hidden behind constructed identities, people remain anonymous and irresponsible. The verbal misconduct seen on both sides of the social fight and the spread of it revealed the negative side of social communication and its influence on user behavior. Its ability to facilitate the speedy spread of news simultaneously to a vast audience of different users, transcending geographical borders, further proves its precarious nature and manipulative effect, especially when used for wrong motives.

The case of the Kenyan–Nigerian social fight further demonstrated that the circulation of negative messages via the social networking sites vis-à-vis the spread of positive messages was seen to be higher in negative messaging than positive. Negative or insulting messages got a higher number of *retweets* (recirculation of the message) as opposed to the number of *retweets* from a positive message. This goes further to prove the power of social media to spread negativity across the Internet, while also influencing and promoting negative behavior on users in terms of animosity, anger, abusive language, and utter disrespect for the other.

Social and New Media Communication and Its Effect on Relationships

Everyone, to a great extent, is a product of his or her environment and social media influence people's relationships. It is a culture. The nature of new and social media tends to promote social disintegration. For example, the social communication during the fight promoted political and cultural negativity on both ends with Nigerians scorning the Kenyan politicians and Kenyans ridiculing the Nigerians' president. Each team mocked the other's culture. This goes to show the influence of new and social communication on matters of respect and morality. The fact that users could explicitly disrespect other's political leaders and culture shows the influence new media have, even in its influencing ability to change deep set values of respect for elders and leaders. The social fight saw several media personalities and religious leaders engage in it, with more participating in the exchange of abusive words than the promotion of a cease fire. This social fight also reveals the inflexibility and difficulty of new and social media to adapt to known media ethics. Accuracy, verification, and objectivity to the new media environment is a great challenge, because objectivity was clearly missing from this tweef.

Social and New Media Communication in Relation to African Culture

The social fight violated all known traditional African codes of good behavior toward strangers, setting in its place what Stanley Baran refers to as "a new authority of contemporary culture, setting the pace, norms and values of society."[14] This new authority is social media. Diversity is beautiful, but by emphasizing the cultural differences between Kenyans and Nigerians, social media allowed cracks of disintegration to appear and ugliness to float to the surface. What this reveals is that external circumstances only act as a catalyst for what is already on the inside.

According to W. James Potter, social media have brought about a false sense of connection where people construct faulty meanings to messages. People rely on their friends to give them updates on the world and create new worldviews.[15] These are friends they may have never met or seen except from a social site profile photo. In social media, a friend is anyone who makes a connection online through a common interest. Even if people's social circles grow, the ties of online friendships are never as strong as personal friendships.

New and social communication has also brought about a general sense of disorder. This is because there are no checks and balances in the individual usage of the new and social media. A person has liberty to use and/or abuse these new forms of communication. Whereas within the African setting there were rules and regulations guiding each and every person, we are now in a new dispensation where people feel that they can speak without regard to others. The fact that they do not have direct, face-to-face contact with the recipient of a message seems to give people an excuse to use uncivil language. African culture maintains that relationships and community welfare or oneness is a cherished aspect of a society. Traditionally, disputes between communities were resolved face-to-face; presently however, with the rise of new and social communication, differences go unresolved leading to animosity built up over time and no intervention as seen in the social fight.

Is Social Media Integrating or Disintegrating Our Culture?

Can we term the fact that most Kenyans on social media were speaking with one voice, united in purpose, a form of integration? Ironically, it could have been the same group that only weeks before had spewed vitriol and hate speech at members of other Kenyan tribes in the name of politics. Yet, against a common enemy, they rose as one to post abusive comments at the Nigerians, who, by the way, also gave as good as they got. It is baffling to imagine that right-thinking people generated the context of information and set the tone of the discourse, with scant regard for the consequences. Every choice we make—to do the right or wrong thing, the good or the bad—inevitably affects us and others. Thus, any disintegration will be as a result of what people allow to dominate their thinking, attitudes, and behavior.

The Future of African Culture with the Increased Use of New and Social Media

With the emergence and continuous development of social and new media, I consider the future of African culture bleak. Although new media make communication more effective than has hitherto been possible, its excessive use brings more harm than good in contemporary times. With practically every family member hooked to new media, face-to-face communication is decreasing and the time shared between family members in the same household is minimal. This generally goes against the principle of ethics concerned with what is good and right as contributing to the well-being of a person, and maximize the good in another person. The important role of authority figures or significant figures as custodians of wisdom, knowledge, or guidance is fast fading. "Google it!," "It was on the Net!' are frequent statements.

Rumor Three

Kenyan Deputy President Luxury Private Jet Scandal

Information broke out on social media on May 22, 2013, based on the editorial cartoon in *The Daily Nation* that portrayed women members of parliament massaging different body parts of Kenya's deputy president, Honourable William Ruto, aboard a hired jet.[16] This is an alleged indication that a number of women had accompanied him on the trip.

The cartoon finds its origin in a four-day nation trip that took the deputy president and his entourage to Gabon, Congo, Nigeria, and Algeria. According to the office of the deputy president, the trips reflected a desire by the government to underline its intention to pursue a foreign policy agenda guided by Pan-Africanism. News reports from Nation Media Group, Standard Group, and *The Star* indicated that the hiring cost of the jet was around Kenya shillings 100 million.

This unverified information about women members of parliament massaging the deputy president got further impetus on social media when it was debated in the national assembly with sections of women members of parliament expressing displeasure and demanding disciplinary action against the media house. One female member of parliament, for instance, insisted that "if women MPs massaged Ruto, then I demand that *The Daily Nation* do another cartoon of male MPs massaging me for equality purposes."[17] Since the facts of the caricature and the debate in parliament could not be verified for facts, no main ruling was made on the matter except that members who felt aggrieved were given 14 days to petition the house committee on parliamentary broadcasting.

This coverage of the deputy president degenerated into rumors and name calling on social media. Three main new media platforms were used in discussing the rumor, namely Facebook, blogs, and Twitter. According to Facebook postings on the Nation Media Facebook page, the participating members had no factual information to verify or reject the allegations. The postings took political alignments based on ethnicity and party affiliations. For instance, contributors who seemed to be aligned to the government made disparaging and insulting remarks to those who seemed to question the entire trip and the alleged massaging. Other Facebook posts seemed to be concerned about the quality of journalism and lack of professional writing in the Kenyan media citing the cartoon as an example of low morals of reporting. For instance, Simon Karibuki said, "For the first time since I started reading *Daily Nation* many years ago, today I felt ashamed to see this cartoon on the most respected newspaper. *Daily Nation* is a premier paper and this cartoon lowered its standard to gutter press."

A respectable Kenyan lawyer, Ahmed Ahmednassir, also tweeted "when you move into a new office, you tell the spymaster to swoop it for bugs, listening devices and human moles. Ruto forgot to do so and was set up by Raila Odinga moles." The insults and abuses that followed this tweet were enormous.

Ethically, the cartoon depicted women who had accompanied Ruto in bad taste—submissive and servants. To Hon. William Ruto, the cartoons were a threat to his marriage vows since they showed other women massaging him. He is a married man with kids who are quite impressionable. The cartoon also could have contributed to the public's view that the women who were present in the trip are loose women who seek sexual favors. Being a public figure and senior government official, the rumor depicted the premier as corrupt and a spendthrift. The language used on social media in responding to divergent opinion was both disrespectful and against the good of the public. In some instances, the language used was immoral and unethical and generally aimed at demeaning the integrity of their opponents.

Rumor Four

CNN and Kenya 2013 General Elections and Violence

During March 4, 2013, Kenyan general elections, CNN fell under sharp criticism from the Kenyan masses because of a video clip *"Kenyans armed and ready to vote"* they produced and uploaded on its Web site. The video featured four people whose faces were beclouded carrying what the CNN reporter, Nima Elbagir, described as "guns fashioned from iron piping, home-made swords and bullets bought from the black-market." What sparked more ragging debates was the timing of the online story that only turned out to be a rumor. This rumor sparked immediate reactions from Kenyans on social media, especially Facebook and Twitter.

Benta @taputany

@CNN Who is this woman trying to make a name for herself by using actors with ash on their faces? #SomeOneTellCNN This is NOT right. Shame

6:05 PM—1 Mar 2013

"I don't understand why stories and reports of how Kenyans are preaching peace, is not being told by the International media," tweeted Chris Kirubi.

Unbelievable! Disgusting and Saddening! A fellow human being rejoicing in another's misery? We thank God they didn't find this to report (Sahan Journal, 2013).[18]

So CNN Africa Division does have a PEV department!!!??? To cover war? Seriously? Isn't that just nasty, evil and so annoying? Try fuel conflict then come cover it? And then we have Joe from WSJ who was disappointed because he didn't see machetes in Nakuru? What's this supposed to mean really? Is that what these foreigners want to see in Africa and report it in the west?

Rumor Five

The Death of the Kenyan First Lady

An article was posted on March 10, 2013, on the *Kenyan Daily Express BlogSpot* citing the death of the then first lady, Mrs. Lucy Kibaki. This was after people saw the former president at Agha Khan Hospital and the rumors started spreading that Mrs. Lucy Kibaki was critically ill. *The Star* newspaper took up this rumor and built a story around it, alleging that the first lady had been ill and admitted at one of the hospitals in the city.[19] To date, it is not known whether Mrs. Kibaki had been ill and admitted at all.

The implication that such utterances had the on the first lady, her family, and the society at large is huge. Whereas it takes only a few seconds to click the share button, but how many people ever pause to find out if what they are sharing is true? The trauma, anxiety, and grief that individuals, their families, and relatives feel are indescribable when rumors circulate that one is dead yet he or she is still alive.

The use of social and new media calls on humanity to tread carefully, and conduct ourselves in the social media circles just as we would in any other public circumstances. People encountered online should be treated with fairness, honesty, and respect, just as you would off-line. Verify information before passing it along. Be honest about one's intent when reporting and avoid actions that might discredit one's professional impartiality. Before deciding to pass on information by other news outlets or individuals, be thoughtful.

Rumor Six

The Death of Nelson Mandela

In many African cultures, discussing a person's death is taboo until he or she actually dies. And when he or she dies, wails and mourning dirges would announce the death. This would be a confirmation that the person is dead, as well as announcement to the rest of the community. Mandela was hospitalized on June 8, 2013, with a recurrent lung disease. The scene outside the Pretoria hospital where he spent more than months in intensive care unit (ICU) resembled a mini shrine, with candles and messages of goodwill piling up. In contrast, his rural homestead remained eerily calm apart from the presence of local and foreign media. The peaceful scene is in stark contrast to his suburban home in Johannesburg, where residents and curious tourists had been flocking to leave flowers and goodwill messages—an alien idea in Qunu. On social media, Mandela had been declared dead, but in reality, he was still alive at that time.

Rumors on Mandela's death spread fast on Facebook. Rumors of the politician's alleged demise gained traction after a "R.I.P. Nelson Mandela" Facebook page attracted nearly one million likes. Those who read the "About" page were given a believable account the South African politician's passing:

> At about 11 A.M. ET on Saturday (August 31, 2013), our beloved politician Nelson Mandela passed away. Nelson Mandela was born on July 18, 1918 in Mvezo. He will be missed but not forgotten. Please show your sympathy and condolences by commenting on and liking this page.

Hundreds of fans immediately started writing their messages of condolence on the Facebook page, expressing their sadness that the talented 95-year-old politician was dead. And as usual, Twittersphere was frenzied over the death hoax. The social media rumor on Mandela's death caught many people, including respected persons and celebrities, commenting on his death. For instance: George Bush Snr, 89, also sent condolences which were picked up by an American newswire, BNO, then flashed up by CNN. Jim McGrath, spokesman for Mr. Bush, sent out an email entitled: "Statement by President George H. W. Bush on the death of Nelson." He wrote on behalf of the former president:

> Barbara and I mourn the passing of one of the greatest believers in freedom we have had the privilege to know. "As President, I watched in wonder as Nelson Mandela had the remarkable capacity to forgive his jailers following 26 years of wrongful imprisonment—setting a powerful example of redemption and grace for us all. He was a man of tremendous moral courage, who changed the course of history in his country. Barbara and I had great respect for President Mandela, and send our condolences to his family and countrymen."[20]

But Mr. McGrath tweeted and e-mailed a statement that the earlier comments were based on a flash from *The Washington Post*.

On the rumors about Mr. Mandela's death, Gary Gray, Australian resources minister, had to apologize to South Africa's high commissioner for having told guests attending a Minerals Council of Australia dinner at parliament house that Mandela had died. According to Associate Press, his statement was, "I apologize unreservedly and am deeply sorry to have relayed what I thought was reliable advice." In Amsterdam; people observed a minute of silence marking the death of Mandela; celebrity Rihanna also fell to the rumors tweeting her prayers for Nelson Mandela.

On Sunday (September 1) the politician's representatives officially confirmed that Nelson Mandela is not dead. "He joins the long list of celebrities who have been victimized by this hoax. He's still alive and well, stop believing what you see on the Internet," they said.

Some media houses pitched tent outside the hospital so as to be the first ones to report his "death" live from the hospital.

Rumors can be true or false, but either way, they hurt. Rumors can be prolonged and can be repeated. It is very difficult to battle a rumor because the victim of the rumor never knows who started it. The individual can also start being a rumor monger by checking with friends through social or new media if they have heard it. Therefore, whether the rumor is true or false, it impacts a person's life, leading to depression, breaking the heart, causing death, or even killing people. In view of the fact that most rumors targeting individuals are negative in nature, the persons spreading such rumors choose to be anonymous and therefore use channels that ensure that they are not linked to them.

Rumors can also bring down reputations, alienate friends, and sometimes result in aggression in relationships or ostracizing behavior. In working environments, rumors can start among a small group of individuals and quickly spread to the rest of the organization through channels such as short text messages (SMS) and the Internet/e-mails. With SMS or e-mails, it is easy to spread the rumor because all a person does is click the forward button.

Other social media and users blamed the government for hiding the truth about Mandela's death. Isobel Robertson, on September 1, 2013, at 5:40 A.M. wrote:

> My husband and I lived in SA for 31 years until April 2012. We had the utmost love and respect for Nelson Mandela, but unfortunately could take no more of the crime, corruption and downright lying of this government. We don't believe we will ever be told the whole (and true) story regarding Madiba's death. He was a great man and should be held by all in the highest esteem. The circus being played out at the moment is being led by Zuma the ringleader. They should be thoroughly ashamed of themselves, when the truth outs ... and it will ... it will be very interesting to see how they will explain away all the lies and deceipt that they themselves concocted. Plenty more I can say but will refrain from doing so as I am so angry regarding this cover-up and may say more than I should.

Elsewhere, in the city council of an Amsterdam neighborhood, people observed a minute of silence to mark the death of the South African icon. However, city council members quickly learnt about the misinformation that came about from dozens of messages on Twitter that seemed to confirm the news, including messages like "Breaking News" and "It's official." Perhaps the biggest blow was Rihanna with a following of over 10 million people on Twitter falling into the rumors of Mr. Mandela's death and tweeting her prayers for him.

Eventually South African president, Jacob Zuma cautioned against the rumors. "The presidency is disturbed by the rumors that are being spread about former president Mandela's health. We appeal for respect for the privacy and dignity of the former president." On September 1, 2013, Nelson Mandela was released from the hospital after three months of treatment. This was contrary to a widespread Internet rumor that claimed he was dead.

Mandela's "Death" and Ethical Implications

From the Mandela case study, his whole family was devastated by the news reports that were being circulated that Mandela was dead. One of his daughters, Makaziwe Mandela angrily stated, "It's truly like vultures waiting when the lion has devoured the buffalo, waiting there for the last of the carcass. That's the image we have as a family."

One of the most difficult things in new and social media is chasing down rumors. Social media have increased the speed and breadth of the rumors. But why do rumors thrive on social media? The reasons are pretty much the same as why rumors thrive and spread outside social media. First, if the rumors have elements of believability and are plausible, especially if there are any existing beliefs and prejudices about the subject of the rumor, then the rumor will tend to spread. Second, even if the people who make initial contact with a rumor believe or do not believe it, there is always the desire to tweet it, in the name of sharing or informing others. Additionally, the current reputation of the persons who are the subject matter of the rumor also plays a role. If a person is currently under reputation crisis or image restoration, then audiences will more likely believe and pass on the rumor. But the overwhelming effect of social media is probably due to its nature. For example, Facebook users create subgroups every day where individuals find acceptance among like-minded users.

Because of speed, social and new media put pressure on newsrooms to publish stories before they are adequately checked and verified as to the source of the story and the reliability of the alleged facts. Major news organizations too often pick up rumors online, which is evident from the magazines and reports generated today. Inevitably, when one works at this speed, errors are made, from misspelling words to making factual errors. An ethical question arises, "Should news organizations go back and correct all of these mistakes which populate mountains of material? Or should they correct errors later and not leave a trace of the original mistake?" The ethical challenge is to articulate guidelines for dealing with rumors and corrections in an online world that are consistent with the principles of accuracy, verification, and transparency.

Traditionally, people sat and talked and shared and gossiped. Now the gossip is modernly done on the super high avenue of communication. One of the reasons that make social media attractive to the people is their power to entertain and to keep abreast with the latest information on what is currently trending. Anonymity is one characteristic that users like so that they can get away with whatever they post. This enables the user not to take responsibility for what he or she says sometimes resulting in cyberbullying and harassment. Unfortunately, most users have exploited this privilege and have used it to bring harm to society. For instance, in Latvia, a huge social networking site in Britain with over 70 million users was also caught in a storm after a 14-year-old British teenager committed suicide. She had been repeatedly taunted over her weight, with signed messages telling her to "drink bleach" and "go die."

Negative Revelations

Social and new media communication while boasting many advantages also has some disadvantages. Positively, social media are fast, cheap, accessible, and interactive, and surpass geographical boundaries; thus one can hardly get bored. Social networking offers people with less restrictive opportunities for expression compared to face-to-face interaction. The social sites are known to reduce face-to-face communication because people realize that they can save time and money through its usage. This can affect a person's social skills development because face-to-face communication is different from online communication. It is also important to note that while using social media sites one misses out on forms of communication such as tonal variation and body language.

Social media sites can also lead to irresponsible behavior as was witnessed in the dispute between Kenya and Nigeria. People feel safe to do whatever they want as long as their identities are not associated with the actions, or think they are beyond reach. The social media sites also provide distractions to people and if not careful one can waste a lot of time in these sites. Kenyans and Nigeria insulting each other is a perfect example of how easily people can be lured into activities that waste time on the social sites.

Practical and Applied Issues of Social Media and New Media

Social media come with issues of security risk. This is mainly because in order to use a social media site one has to provide personal information; otherwise none of the friends will be able to find you or in most cases you will not be able to complete your registration. The problem is that providing personal information online offers an opportunity to the wrong people to steal someone's identity (i.e., identity theft).

As clearly put, "it takes 20 years to build a reputation and five minutes to ruin it."[21] But with the rise of social media it appears that it can take just five seconds or less to potentially damage one's reputation. Many social networking sites incorporate an instant messaging feature, which means you can exchange information in real time via chat. The question is whether this platform is adequate for managing customer relations. Many times after a client has raised a concern, social networking sites take a few days to address it. So if someone is being harassed in social media, it will continue until the administrator of those particular social networks comes to his or her rescue.

Ethical Issues in Social and New Media

New media are good yet they bring with them some ethical issues. They have simplified faking or doctoring of photos and make it more difficult to detect. Photojournalists can use computer software like Photoshop to create false impression.

Indeed, social and new media have created tension between traditional journalism and online journalism. The culture of traditional journalism, with its values of accuracy, pre-publication verification, balance, impartiality, and gatekeeping, rubs up against the culture of online journalism, which emphasizes immediacy, transparency, partiality, nonprofessional journalists, and post-publication correction.[22]

According to John S. Mbiti, it is only in relationship with others that one is conscious of one's being, one's duties, one's privileges and responsibilities toward oneself and toward other people: "I am because we are, and since we are, therefore I am."[23] African worldview emphasizes the need for individuals to adhere to social norms in order to preserve human relationships. This was lacking among the Kenyans and Nigerians. Hence failure to promote good injures personal relationship. African cultural norms seem to be shifting from an emphasis on communal and group goals to individual needs, interests, and well-being. Being right maximizes the good and being minimizes the good in a person. In my view, behavior is good when contributing to the well-being of a person and right when maximizing the well-being of a person and that of others—human, objects, and creatures included.

Conclusion

Everyone should endeavor to be social leaders. This means to devote one's life and talents to improving society regardless of social standing, wealth, or privilege.

From this study we can conclude that greater regulation enforcement is required particularly in new and social media to guide official information dissemination from traditional news outlets and social media platforms. Social media is a double-edged sword, powerful communication platform, which can however be used to propagate information that is both unfounded and untruthful. Threats presented by new and social media include national security threats, social disintegration, watering down of the media professional practice and increase in anonymity. Rumors have negative effects on society, but with social and new media, the risks increase with each invention.

Notes

1. "ICC Sits in Secret over Witness Security Fears," *Daily Nation*, September 20, 2013, 1–4.

2. "Social Media Users Force Court to Retreat behind Closed Doors," *Standard Newspapers*, September 20, 2013, 1–3.

3. Clifford G. Christians et al., *Media Ethics: Cases and Moral Reasoning*. 7th ed. (Boston: Pearson Education Inc., 2005).

4. Katherin Fearn-Banks, *Crisis Communications: A Casebook Approach*, 3rd ed. (London: Lawrence Erlbaum Associates, 2007).

5. Joe White, *The Gift of Self Esteem* (Sisters, OR: Questar Publications, 1989).

6. Timothy Coombs W., *Ongoing Crisis Communication: Planning, Managing, and Responding*. 3rd ed. (Thousand Oaks, CA: SAGE Publications, 2012).

7. R. Frazer, *The Nurse's Social Media Advantage: How Making Connections and Sharing Ideas Can Enhance Your Nursing Practice*. 1st ed. (Indianapolis, IN: Sigma Theta Tau International, 2011).

8. http://blog.theonlinekenyan.com.

9. Communications Commission of Kenya 2010/2011 report.

10. www.jambonewspot.com.

11. The previous comments and replies are courtesy of twitter.com.

12. trendsmap.com.

13. Stanley Baran J. and Dennis Davis K., *Mass Communication Theory: Foundations, Ferment, and Future*. 5th ed. (Boston: Wadsworth Cengage Learning, 2009).

14. Stanley J. Baran, *Introduction to Mass Communication: Media Literacy and Culture*. 6th ed. (New York, NY: McGraw-Hill, 2010), 30.

15. W. James Potter, *Media Literacy*. 6th ed. (Thousand Oaks, CA: Sage, 2008).

16. *Daily Nation*, May 22, 2013, 12.

17. Jeff Omondi, Gado's Caricature That Caused Furore in Parliament. *GHAFLA!* May 23, 2013, http://www.ghafla.co.ke/news/tv/item/9179-gado-s-caricature-that-caused-furore-in-parliament.

18. Carolyn Kinya Magiri, Tweet: "Unbelievable! Disgusting and Saddening! A fellow human being rejoicing in another's misery? We thank God they didn't find this to report" *Sahan Journal*, https://twitter.com/SahanJournal, 2013.

19. Franck Mureithi, *The Star*, October 1, 2012, http://www.the-star.co.ke/news/article-166/where-lucy-kibaki.

20. Harriet Alexander—3:34 p.m. BST, September 1, 2013.

21. Warren Buffet, Brainy Quote, http://www.brainyquote.com/quotes/quotes/w/warrenbuff108887.html 2001.

22. Stephen A. Ward, "Ethics for the New Mainstream," in *New Journalist: Roles, Skills, and Critical Thinking*, ed. Paul Benedetti, Tim Currie, and Kim Kierans (Toronto, Canada: Emond Montgomery Publications, 2010), 313–26.

23. John S. Mbiti, *African Religions and Philosophy* (Nairobi, Kenya: East African Educational Publishers Ltd., 1969).

CHAPTER TWENTY-ONE

Scriptures, Social Media, and Social Power

*David Olali, Gbenga Dasylva,
and Saliu Funmi Imaledo*

Introduction

There is justifiable apprehension in the West regarding the future of religion, especially Christianity, ironically more than the fears of the threat posed by Islamic fundamentalism. As we watch Europeans and their American counterparts stampede to re-enter into the continents of Africa, Asia, and Latin America this time, not to take human and natural resources, but join the ship developing and steering into the future economy of spirituality, it is imperative to examine the mediating forces guiding this trend. In this chapter we argue and demonstrate that circumstances and gratification, rather than the doctrine and ethics, dictate preachers' use of social media. The chapter examines the use of social media among selected leading Nigerian Pentecostal churches and ministers. Judgment is postponed and left in the hands of the audience.

The Nigerian church is chosen for this analysis because of its vibrancy and growth trend. The increasingly diversifying religious economies in this most populous black nation on earth, coupled with the rate at which these movements are reinvigorating, provide ample reasons why preachers such as Pastor Enoch O. Adeboye, the present General Overseer of the fast-spreading Redeemed Christian Church of God (RCCG), and Bishop David Oyedepo, of Living Faith Ministries, should not be excluded from the conversation about global spiritual media and politics,[1] except by those with malicious fear of Africa.[2] Founded by Pastor Josiah Akindayomi in 1952,[3] the RCCG of today has, through the innovations the 21st century has brought, and through the spiritual smartness of Adeboye, become a household name in African Christianity. Today, Nigeria's Pentecostal preachers use new social media such as Facebook, Twitter, Google, Yahoo, and so forth to establish their presence and authority on the Web, and in the life of followers.

The subject of ethicality or otherwise is tacitly subordinated to, if not displayed outright by, the primary motif for the presence of these preachers on such social media platforms in the first place, regardless of their self-definitions. By Pentecostalism, the preachers we have in mind are in varying categories from charismatic to holiness preachers, to prosperity gospel preachers, broadly defined, in Nigeria. Good examples of these and their representations are found in Bishop David Oyedepo (Winner' Ministries [aka Winner's Chapel]),[4] Pastor Adeboye, Reverend Chris Okotie (House of God),[5] Pastor Chris Oyakhilome, PhD (Christ Embassy [aka Love World]),[6] and Pastor Williams Folorunsho F. Kumuyi (General Overseer, Deeper Life Bible Church [Deeper Christian Life Ministries]).[7] For the purposes of this chapter, however, focus is narrowed to the generic, rather than an absolute specific, use of social and medial platforms by these "men of God," as the analyzing space to illustrate the *operations of scripture, power via social media*; because on a general scale these represent a fraction—not insignificant—in the number of categories of diviners in Nigeria's thickly prosperous spiritual marketplace.[8] As Vincent Wimbush describes it, "practices, uses—not the truth claims about or within any collection of texts, not the lexical meanings of any text-part—are my interests."[9]

A strong relationship between religion and security is forged in the melting point of social and new media technology. This new movement's approach echoes back to the Protestantism Reformation. It also parallels the Azusa Street Revival which propelled new Christian spiritualisms into the 20th century.[10] The latter was orchestrated through massive personal missionary activities of the devout, particularly those of the charismatic extraction. In this new era, a good number of such charismatic characterizations have dug or plunged deep into the endless possibilities located in the new social and media technology; they forge a totally new creative spiritual-human agency, while at the same time, negotiating space—viral, physical, geographic, and, economic—these order of spiritual paternity also provide radical, innovative significance in the propagation of insights for spiritual symbols, almost to the point of determining the future (if any), but also to a great extent, the very core of several other Pentecostal bodies, as well as other expressions of religiosity in the African spiritual landscapes.[11]

Beyond the underlying assumption of a spiritual responsibility of prop-agating the social-spiritual Goodness of Jesus, and more than merely expanding the Kingdom of God, the fate of these religious leaders conced-edly hinges on how technologically savvy they make themselves *become* in going and making disciples of all nations,[12] which, in Ruth Marshall's view, is a reification of their strong connections with the United States or Britain. She asserts that with "the marked increase of this type of Chris-tianity throughout the continent, many scholars and religious leaders are tempted to view the rise of these churches solely from the point of view of their foreign origins and connections."[13] A regular mistake which some critics of religion, including new science thinkers, often make lies in the natural dichotomy, which is often assumed subsist in the ways we define religion and secularity.[14]

Furthermore, to illustrate the significance of the new social and medial communication technology is the fact that, though an unfortunate exam-ple, even the death-breathing Boko Haram, a fatally notorious Islamist terrorist organization, which bemoans and condemns westernization as sinful, has demonstrated its morbid and patterned aptitude to wreak damage of international proportions antithetically by deploring (West-ern) social and media technology (YouTube and e-mail) to dissipate infor-mation to the global community, in order to send images of its horror, to perpetuate its strongholds in the minds of millions of Nigerians, and others.[15]

To be a Pentecostal preacher, one *must* lay claim to a divine call, then he must go ahead and prove his vocation, first by way of establishing and legitimizing authority within a community of believers; he must have to contend with the already local rivalries or initial competitors; he would have to scale through various huddles including attempts to discredit his forte. By referencing a personalized narrative of the *new born experience,* which is often related, but very connected to the encounter of St. Paul the radical Apostle of Christianity's holy text, a cult of followership begins to build up around the Pentecostal personality; thus acceptance into the orthodox community of preachers is predicated upon redefinition of the self. This imagery of personal transformation has poignant implications and directly points—and inherently—to the social power motif: in regard to the preacher's authenticity, he runs back into the holy book, by making connections through personalized reinterpretations of *what the scriptures says, what is written.* But what is "scripture," and why are their meanings easily accessible particularly to the preacher, and not others? It should be known that the first media that secure a place for expansion is the unwrit-ten socio-cultural platform.

In a similar vein, wife of Archbishop Benson Idahosa, the founder of Church of God Mission International Incorporated, Archbishop Margaret Idahosa—who also is the first female Pentecostal Archbishop in Africa—explains how there was jubilatory "thunderous response from the audience," which removed her innermost apprehension with regard to whether the congregation which her late husband had left behind was prepared to accept a female pastor-leader: "to my greatest surprise there was a great acceptance of the ordination." God also spoke to a lot of people to confirm her calling, to succeed Idahosa. A video showing how Idahosa had authenticated her leadership, a culturally constructed reality,[16] she claimed, was played to confirm how he had, before death, nominated her as the rightful successor, which resulted in "general acceptance"; he is the father of Nigerian Pentecostalism.[17]

This intersectionality between religion and the media sphere had first begun to seriously appear in the mid-20th century, at which time, "presenting problem," as it was called, was the emergence of religious broadcasts not sanctioned by religious and secular authorities. Interest was heightened in the 1970s when another new phenomenon, televangelism, burst onto the scene. Alongside these discussions of religious uses of the media, debates arose about media coverage of religion at a time when religion was playing an ever more important role in domestic and international politics.

Toni Morrison puts it as "authority and absolute power . . . conquering 'heroism,' virility, and the problematics of wielding absolute power over the lives of others,"[18] the dynamics to ascension to ultimate stardom.[19]

Definitely the holy book of Christianity, the Bible and its odyssey and history among Africans is also the history of slavery,[20] unfortunately, a history often set aside as a wholly academic rigmarole in outside of the United States. The impression one gets is that being *born again* (John 3:3ff.), a hallmark in Nigerian Pentecostal doctrines and belief systems, intuitively makes an erasure of memory of this fraught history,[21] giving a new life[22] to those who embrace its tenets (i.e., the saved). The question is: what harm does remembered history do, beyond unsettling the dusts of our present atmosphere of convenience? The intolerant behavior toward recasting a fraught history of a salvific Christianity is understandable, after all the crown jewel of the Christian faith is heaven for the unblemished, not for those asking such questions as to unsettle the privileges of the hierarchs.

The preceding argument also assumes that Pentecostal preachers' emphases on the coming kingdom of God have in earnest made them to commence their own preparation for "the second coming of the son of God." Perhaps one way they do so is by divine encroachment on the Web pages and private online spaces of individuals who are seeking escape from the brutal harsh realities in Nigeria, ensuring automatically that there are no escape routes from their circumstances, as the earth is the Lord's anointed representation. That way, while God speaks through social and new media, listening is not a choice; it's an order. Besides, the invasion of the spiritual into the personal spaces of humans often occurs with or without an invitation to party.[23] The litmus test of the ethics intents of Pentecostal preachers in Nigeria could be best demonstrated if they lead up, and confront, by launching social media campaigns against evil and corrupt government, demand accountability, otherwise, we might as well fear the powerful underlining assumption: the inability and indeed impossibility of Pentecostal preachers to launch moral change in Nigeria because they are also beneficiaries of the oppressive regime and its inviolable structure of power. As recorded history teaches, people become ensconced into their privileged positions in society.[24] But use of social media for the salvation of people's souls, or for the enlightenment of "barbarians" soon become out of place—in Jonathan Z. Smith's phrase, "when the chips are down."[25] Constructions of the *other* as "barbarian" stem directly from an oppressor-episteme, where we are made, locked inside the four walls of our own belief, incapable of fathoming the impossibility of the meaning-making worlds of others, those who are *outsiders*, the so-called barbarians, who had received this notorious label only because of the fact of their not belonging to our own circle of faith community, except of course, such as are conscripted by con-version. With regard to sin and ultimate punishment, this stage in belief-shaping has been greatly facilitated in Dante's artistic-religious creativity. In its ninth chapter the personae Peter reports in frightening imagery how the angel of wrath, Ezrael would "bring men and women, with half of their bodies burning, and cast them into a place of darkness, the hell of men; and a spirit of wrath shall chastise them with all manner of torment, and a worm that never sleeps shall devour their entrails; and these are the persecutors and betrayers of my righteous ones."[26]

Social and new media usage by these Nigerian preachers happens to be an extension of not only their own biography, but actually the continuous creation of a piece of hagiography. Consequently, having positioned themselves as possessors of direct divine encounters with the Jesus, they move along authoritatively demanding compliance with their interpretations of social scriptures, securing coveted position of constant social-economic power within the overall dynamics of national and cultural polity, thus guaranteeing an uninterrupted flow politicalized profits. The use to which these preachers put social media, *read* as the performance of social

canons of [spiritual] strategies of interpretations, can be culturally analyzed as mutually interactive; could not be conceivably stripped of their
locale of cultural particulars. There is no way to ignore the complications,
the unambiguous implications as to how long the status quo could remain
inviolate when society's religious elite control social life through dominant
forms of social and popular media, or participate in the suppression of the
people they are to help Jesus liberate. The answer to the latter might be
derived from the very meaning of religion!

Tendency toward absolute transcendence[27] are meaningless jabbering
unless it collide social control. Buttressing this further is the corresponding
relationship between the so-called Pentecostal personages and the social
methods which they employ in the signifying of power.[28] The different
locales of spiritual leaders in Nigeria do not interfere with the top-down
political leadership in the country; nor they, as we have already noted,
pretend to challenge systemic repressions, except of a different sort. Moreover, in very obvious ways, these preachers perpetuate the same token
of unequal social, political, and economic status quo which the political
and economic elite brandish; since they are assumed to be called by God,
their authorities are not expected to be challenged—they are part of this
world—at least not by the spiritually uninitiated, the uncalled.

Worth mentioning is the fact that Nigerian Pentecostal is not a mono-
lithic religious category. Its variegated nature has been discussed, not necessarily exhaustively though.[29] And instead of profiling these varieties, I
privilege a critical analysis of the assumptions and the behavior of these
preachers, how they represent themselves as masters of spirits, authorities
on behalf of the divine complex.

In his assessment of the gospels' manifest social power Enoch Powell
writes that "what is not foreseeable is that [they] will provide an authori-
tative source of moral and political guidance to those whose form of worship is older than even the church's book itself."[30] Similarly, the argument
by Christopher Lewis that "religion is the same as politics: it is political
activity under cover of God"[31] turns out to be a caustic but true altruism.
On whether it is in fact possible to determine that Nigeria's Pentecostal
preachers use of social and media technology solely for gospel propaga-
tions, for communication with the world beyond them, and importantly,
to remain relevant in the 21st century spiritual, globalized business world
is subject to ethical consideration,[32] it would be greatly helpful if Nigeria's
fraught history, complex in its interplays of colonialism and slavery, literacy mercantilism[33] and missionary actions, are examined as one connected
block of events. The question then is: Are Nigerian Pentecostal preachers
purveyors of British imperial legacies, or ethically and spiritually minded

citizens? Are the success stories of these Nigerian preachers any different from the economic successes of Britain interests in Nigeria, or in India?[34] That is, would it *not* be unethical, for instance, to argue that since Nigeria is a market place for *consumables* (e.g., religion) due to its sheer size, and population complex, thriving spiritualities and pluralistic cultural layers, and fragmented ethnic nationalities,[35] its history of massive social poverty, and oligarchic class structure, accompanied by the hemorrhaging effect of brain drain, to skeptics and nonbelievers there is only slim difference, if any at all, between Pentecostal business of *divide-and-rule* kingdom of pastors' spiritual networks and business empires, and the causal relationship with the British colonial enterprise, in humble acknowledgment of the embarrassing perspectives.[36] The inquest into the use of new social media by these Nigerian Pentecostals singly achieves an unperturbed, *brazen* social feat, which, by a façade of piety, a social phase lacking in reputation for speaking truth to power,[37] as long as their own network of hegemony is not jeopardized. So long as the new social media perpetually further and continually strengthen their flamboyant territorial security; so long as revivals, church events, and services, conferences produce *miracles* that are translatable into larger physical buildings, which make statement of their wealth status, larger campgrounds equipped with modern communication gadgets, then their ethics is normative and scriptural, God-approved, and ethical. Marshall reinforces this manifestation of unholy drama in pastors in fashion show during Archbishop Benson Idahosa's funerals.[38] It cannot be overstated that Idahosa reignited Christianity in Nigeria, if not in Africa, toward the path of reinvention.[39] Not unlike their fellow Christians elsewhere, Nigerian s have been inundated with conflicts over financial returns, outright conflict of authority, over ownership of churches and congregations. One small example was received, hopefully with equanimity, when Bishop Joseph Imariabe Ojo, second-in-command to late Bishop Idahosa, related how he was sent out of the church because he was accused of and embarrassed with being a threat to the authority of succeeding Archbishop Margaret Idahosa.[40] Bishop Ojo "broke out of" the Church of God Mission to found his own congregation, Calvary Kingdom Church, CKC, Lagos. He too was recently ordained Archbishop on April 21, 2013, by Reverend Amos Osadolor.[41]

Perhaps, Archbishop Ojo's predicament is only complimentary when compared to the worsening situation in churches in disputes over personal power and privileges:

Church property disputes often arise when a disagreement—either among members of a congregation or between a congregation and its national denomination—leads to a legal battle for control of the congregation's property. This can include not only the house of worship itself but also financial assets and even the right to use the church's name. A recent example is the ongoing property disputes within the Episcopal Church triggered by conflicts over the issue of homosexuality. Key church property rulings date back to the mid-19th century, when several denominations split over slavery.[42]

We introduce "church disagreement" at this juncture for four reasons: to demonstrate the non-uniqueness of church property ownership conflicts in Nigeria; illustrate the power of the church (through its intelligence) on social issues; to show that running a church is as good as running any other business (except for its label of spirituality); and to locate human interests of politics, economics, canonized by written or holy texts—representing the law and the constitutions. To add another reason, it serves to show that the reformation of the church is in actuality the reintroduction of series of upsetting dynamics into English society and all its mimicry agents, to perpetuate fluxes for which Protestantization became the freighted term.[43]

Running a Pentecostal church is one of the most lucrative private business enterprises in Nigeria; but it comes with heavy price: radical transformation. To start one, the most crucial tools are charisma, and a Bible. As reductionistic as this appears to be, it equally conveys the altruism about the manner by which many of our new-inspired Christian diviners jump on the wagon. Adding an iPad oriPhone for sending and receiving (text) messages, and for instant communication with prospective clients in need of prayer or counseling, and/or other kind of spiritual need; adding a university degree only makes the new "called-preacher" more marketable, more believable, if he is able to apply total aptitude to the trade.[44]

In their use of social medial, Pentecostal preachers are able to reinforce ownership, and occupancy of their enterprise, as well as in *reading* the beats and climate of spiritual and economic benefactors. Equally significant is the fact that as business men in the spiritual marketplace,[45] particularly in a fast globalizing world,[46] *where nothing is certain*; social media creates mobile social security for empire through their ability to monitor their assets while away in foreign lands, doing leisure or extra mission work. This function is facilitated by that fact that the globalized world is a fast space.[47] In such as ours in which most people who are below the stratum of economic empowerment, and are in a dire need of *salvation*, Marx would be right that revolution is around the corner,[48] only he was very wrong as to the modus operandi. This need manifests in diverse shades and colors in Nigeria, amid high economic and social probabilities. Thus, to be poor situates an individual in many of harm's ways. For instance, to be poor there is a likelihood, of all suspicions, to be branded a "sinner," and possibly the result of not having given ones full life to Jesus. In one version of Pentecostal theology, material prosperity is the undeniable proof-fact of living rightly, connected, with the divine. Consequently, "Get rich or die trying"[49] becomes, not a bad idea. After all, Nigerian Pentecostal preachers' preference for political figures is an undeniable fact, contrary to some opinions that these preachers are outright *neutral* when it comes to political issues. As active powerful political participants, and by sheer size of their economic stakes through their numerous fleets of business and mammoth spiritual ventures, it cannot be correct to assume that politics is not for them.

The Middle East was such an unexpected site for the Arab Spring (revolutions). Many, especially in the West, particularly in the United States, had for long never assumed that Muslim countries, generally called the Arab region, could be site where a revolution could take place, being strongholds of Islam and its civilizations.[50] In summer of 1993, Samuel Huntington also wrote very successful article entitled "Clash of Civilizations?" in which he argues that "after War II, the West, in turn, began to retreat; the colonial empires disappeared; first Arab nationalism and then Islamic fundamentalism manifested themselves."[51] Instinctively, evangelicals provide the usual xenophobic answer to the Arab uprisings.[52]

In the case of Nigeria's contemporary preachers the narrative had begun in earnest, determined from distant lands, through the expressive dominance of Western imperialisms. Sir George Goldie, on his colonial conquest to the Niger River area (later christened[53] *Nigeria* by Flora Shaw in 1897)[54] *commenced* the fatalistic determination[55] of the future history of many unborn generations of "pagans." Lord Frederick Lugard perfectly expresses this European supremacist sentiment:

> In character and temperament, the typical African of this race-type is a happy, thriftless, excitable person, lacking in self-control, discipline, and foresight. Naturally courageous, and naturally courteous and polite, full of personal vanity, with little sense of veracity, fond of music and loving weapons as an oriental loves jewelry. His thoughts are concentrated on the events and feelings of the moment, and he suffers little from the apprehension for the future or grief for the past. "His mind," says Sir C. Eliot, "is far nearer to the animal world than that of the European or Asiatic, and exhibits something of the animals' placidity and want of desire to rise beyond the state he has reached."

Through the ages, the African appears to have evolved no organised religious creed, and though some tribes appear to believe in a deity, the religious sense seldom rises above pantheistic animalism and seems more often to take the form of a vague dread of the supernatural.[56]

As mind-bugging as Lugard's perceptions of Nigerians were, and continues to be even into the 21st century, we have no doubts that historical records after Lugard—but certainly also those preceding him and from which he decidedly looked away—would definitely have given him sudden cardiac arrest; that is, if it is indeed correct that he believed that

He lacks the power of organisation, and is conspicuously deficient in the management and control alike of men or business. He loves the display of power, but fails to realize its responsibility—he will work hard with a less incentive than most races. He has the courage of the fighting animal, an instinct rather than a moral virtue. In brief, the virtues and defects of his race—type are those of attractive children, whose confidence when it is won is given ungrudgingly as to an older and wiser superior and without envy. Perhaps, the two traits which have impressed me as those most characteristic of the African native are his lack of apprehension and his lack of ability to visualize the future.[57]

We would hope, however, that reproducing these quotes would serve the purpose of self-reflection and accountability both for all white as well as for black peoples. For as Tope Fashua had countered, "if Nigerian [preacher]sic broaden his mind, he would have since seized the advantage of national and racial integration."[58] Going forward, James Coleman wrote that "it may be permissible to coin a shorter title for the agglomeration of pagan and Mohammedian states which have been brought, by the exertions of the Royal Niger Company, within the confines of the British Protectorates, and thus need for the first time in their history to be as an entity by some general name."[59] Hence, we raise ethical questions about European *textualization* of peoples, witnesses to the massive corrosive erasures of imperial *British civilization*, before we can even jump to analyze the only recent renovation in Nigeria's preachers' use of social media. Yes, figures such as contemporary Pentecostal preachers, à la Flora Shaw, ought to be critically reviewed as we would the historical records (e.g., cultural forms, norms, etc. before texts) which *permit* them to *scripturalize*.[60] To read these figures out of Nigeria's social power structure is to rid ourselves of understanding how extraordinarily spiritual interpretations of life lands safely on quotidian level practical social ordering. On the one hand, this critical reading facilitates accountability atmosphere, and deepens public engagements on the discourse of religion; on the other, most religious followers are hostile to any interrogation of their spiritual head.

For example, "daddy"—a word describing these preachers' place in their spiritual economy—is used by devotees, like those of other major Pentecostal heavyweights, to connote direct relationship like the one between father and daughter. While ordinary members who are in the majority are not direct legal heirs, they unmistakably benefit tremendously from the community.[61] Often, critics of major Pentecostal preachers in regard to their wealth and largesse intentionally ignore or are ignorant about the dynamics of the formed community; but the imposingly western secular versus religious differentiation does not foster basic knowledge of this dynamic.

With a population of over 150 million, Nigeria is a major user of new social media, and despite the challenges which the country is going through, both critics and technology firms recognize an immediate market profitability which this giant of Africa represents. And is it possible to leave out Nigerian Pentecostal preachers out of this socially interactive economy? Ninety percent of Nigerians Muslims live in the north and 80 percent of the Christians live in the south.[62] Interestingly, this religious partitioning of the country played a significant role in 2011 elections, where the north overwhelmingly voted for a Muslim candidate, while the south, a Christian candidate. Armed with these naked data, and running a cursory analysis one might tendentiously assume that this is a unique factor for understanding Nigerians.

Furthermore, the subject of religious fundamentalism in Nigerian is not a newly invented phenomenon. Social life and the daily of existence of humans are made meaningful through the daily productive and valuable interactions that people make with one another. In Nigeria, you will often hear something to the effect, "no man is an island," to reinforce the importance of sentiments of kinship and community. Social lives produce certain profitable effects for members of community. Nigeria is a place where people do not have worries about their present predicaments, endure affliction with tranquilizing insufferableness, which made Diamond once state that "the Nigerian revolution has not yet occurred."[63] This perspective sheds some light on why Nigerian Pentecostals do not dare challenge status quo; with the present attitude there is not going to be any pricy transformation, to change status quo in the polity. Thus, rather than use social media to create platforms where the individuals could engage and challenge oppressive regimes, the spiritual hierarchs recreate social and media technology, first as grounds for proselytism, to save the damning souls, and to enhance their status and establish veritable presence. But the rich-and-mighty in the land receive: *I will lead a protest if the elections don't go well, Nigeria, evil men will not rule you*[64] when everyone knows that "the beatyful ones have not been borne."[65] This does not mean to exonerate the minimalism in *Nigerian imaginary*.[66]

The Nigerian Broadcasting Commission reported that during Nigeria's 2011 elections there were 109 television station channels, 187 radio stations, and 35 cable television outlets in the country, with over 45 million Nigerians actively online[67] falling into categories of private and public stations. Use of these broadcast media, including the new media affiliates of SMS, Twitter, Facebook, YouTube, and so forth by Nigerians to connect to one another, and to the global world was amazingly unprecedented. Again, Barack Obama's second-term election into the White House was an illustration of this marvel![68]

The subject of the ethicality of preachers of social and new media should not come too easy, a reminder of the fluidity of enslavement. Britain only did what other European powers (France, Germany, Portugal, or Spain) did, but on a differentially horrific scale. Soon colonization became trendy, and like any business-of-the-era project, the availability, control, and expendability of new social media capital, such as Facebook, radio and television stations, provides space for virtual progress, peer interactions.

From an idealist perfective, Nigeria ought to have made more progress than it presently has given its human and natural resources; reality, however, forces upon us reflections of social and political dynamics which have been exacerbated after contacts with Euro-American magic. It is the usual forte of preachers to announce glorious days ahead for the country, giving more push to and authorizing political elitism. Unfortunately, we are not allowed to question the pronouncements of "God's spokesmen." Diamond himself was berated by Nigerians what he gave a tasteless picture for Nigerians. Diamond's salvation was history. And I trust history would do us the same kind of favor.

Benedict Carey's research showed interesting intersections in online messaging pattern. He wrote "the emotional tone of people's messages followed a similar pattern not only through the day but also through the week and the changing seasons. The new analysis suggests that our moods are driven in part by a shared underlying biological rhythm that transcends culture and environment."[69] Such use of social media measures the heartbeats of their followers and patrons. The report continued to state that "on Twitter, people routinely savage others with pure relish and gush sarcastically—and the software is not sophisticated enough to pick up these subtleties." Could this report have any direct relations with the self-apportioned roles Nigeria's charismatic pastors legitimately fulfill in a milieu of malaise?

Put differently, why do Pentecostal churches go viral in the first place? At least, I (Olali) do vividly recall as part of my initial reformative religious years, when my denomination founder, Pastor W. F Kumuyi was said to have instructed that we (members) not use the popular media, especially the television, because it was believed to broadcast "evil shows [pornographic material, for instance]." Today, the church uses Web pages, YouTube channel, broadcast messages via satellite. But we now also realize that the Internet of today is less safe if outright otherworldly were to be our sole concern! Jotham Sederstrom affirms this in monetary terms.[70]

Similarly would be sheer naivety to not recognize the role of popular and social medial in the "successful" historical colonialism—for Europe came *to save* to enslave—to take captive free women. In dealing with this entangled history sentimental attachment precludes critical examination Christianity's participation, as though it invalidates the gospel of Jesus! Perhaps, this explains why most Pentecostals are wont on demanding accountability of their religious hierarchs. My former pastor in California, Pastor Blessing Ubani, once said to me: "It makes sense for Christian pastors not to criticize their peers because that is how to protect the fold and make it sacrosanct."[71]

On the whole, the question of *totalizing* absolute truths led the world into World War II because the Germans found the feet of Adolf Hitler to fit into the historic shoes of atomic power. While we continue to listen to the good news from gold-plated podiums, we should also recognize that we live at a precarious time which comes with burdensome leadership responsibility. For the majority, while secular has proven to be inadequate, through repeated failure, to provide needed social political and especially spiritual, leadership, many continue to throng to churches and other religious circles, and into the hands of religious figures in desperation for a grab on life's breath. The right question for persons in this category is, therefore, not about the ethicality or otherwise of the use of social media by their pastors; neither is it one which demands a bland *yes* or *no*, *right* or *wrong*. It has now to do with, not the Manichaean-framed quiz of *black* versus *white* ideology. Rather, it is "preacher, would you do with it if I gave you my trust on the new social media that would not lead up to another Orwellian *Nineteen Eighty-Four*?"[72]

Notes

1. E. A. Adeboye and E. Mfon, "Preparing for Great Works," in *Out of Africa: How the Spiritual Explosion among Nigerians Is Impacting the World*, ed. C. P. Wagner and J. Thompson (California: Regal Books, 2004), 319; Gbenga Osinaike, "How RCCG Started with 13 People to Become One of Nigeria's Fastest Growing Church," October 17, 2012, http://www.churchtimesnigeria.net/

how-rccg-started-with-13-people-to-become-one-of-nigerias-fastest-growing-church/.

2. Ranjana Khanna, *Dark Continents: Psychoanalysis and Colonialism* (Durham, NC: Duke University Press, 2003).

3. O. A. Adeboye, "Josiah Akindayomi: Christian Sect Founder," in *Holy People of the World: A Cross-Cultural Encyclopedia*, ed. Phyllis G. Jestice (Santa Barbara, CA: ABC CLIO, 2004), 29–30.

4. Dominion Ministries. http://domi.org.ng/.

5. Rufus Okikiolaolu Olubiyi Ositelu, *African Instituted Churches: Diversities, Growth, Gifts, Spirituality and Ecumenical Understanding of African Instituted Churches* (Hamburg, Germany: LIT, 2002), 109.

6. http://www.christembassy.org/site/ourministry/AboutPastorChris.

7. Alan Isaacson, *Deeper Life: The Extraordinary Growth of the Deeper Life Bible Church* (London: Hodder and Stoughton, 1990), http://www.dclmhq.org/dclm/features/about-us.

8. Ruth Marshall, *Political Spirituality: The Pentecostal Revolution in Nigeria* (London: University of Chicago, 2009), 51.

9. Vincent L. Wimbush, *White Men's Magic: Scripturalization as Slavery* (Oxford: Oxford University Press, 2012), 13.

10. Vinson Synan, *The Holiness-Pentecostal Tradition: Charismatic Movements in the Twentieth Century* (Grand Rapids, MI: Wm. B. Eerdmans Publishing, 1997), 141.

11. John S. Mbiti, *African Religions and Philosophy* (New York: Double Day and Co. Inc., 1970). Here, argument is toward pushing back to a period before the Eurocentric cataloguing of religion: S. N. Eisenstadt, ed. *The Origins and Diversity of Axial Age Civilizations* (New York: State University of New York Press, 1986).

12. Matthew 11: 29.

13. Ruth Marshall, "Power in the Name of Jesus" in *Fundamentalism in Africa: Religion and Politics. Review of African Political Economy* No. 52 (November 1991): 21–37, http://www.jstor.org/stable/4005954.

14. Lynn Schofield Clark and Stewart M. Hoover, "At the Intersection of Media, Culture, and Religion: A Bibliographic Essay," in Rethinking Media, Religion, and Culture, ed. Stewart M. Hoover and Knut Lundby (California: Sage Publications, Inc., 1997), 14.

15. "Nigeria—Travel Warning," June 3, 2013, http://nigeria.usembassy.gov/sm_06042013.html.

16. Stewart M. Hoover, "Introduction: The Cultural Construction of Religion in the Media Age," in *Practicing Religion in the Age of the Media: Explorations in Media, Religion, and Culture*, ed. Stewart M. Hoover and Lynn Schofield Clark (New York: Columbia University Press, 2002), 1–6.

17. Sam Eyoboka, "How Archbishop Idahosa Died—Wife," April 20, 2010, http://www.vanguardngr.com/2010/04/how-archbishop-idahosa-died-wife/.

18. Toni Morrison, *Playing in the Dark: Whiteness and the Literary Imagination* (New York: Vintage Books, 1992), 44.

19. Walter Rauschenbusch, *Christianity and the Social Crisis in the 21st Century: The Classic That Woke Up the Church* (New York: HarperCollins Publishers, 2007). The affirmation that we make here is to the effect that social dynamics will always present themselves as to lead to the eventual rise or fall of communities, however these may be interpreted, regardless. For instance, the early Christian communities waited in hiding until a Constantine came to the throne to change their destiny, which still remains and continues to be reshaped era after era.

20. Vincent L. Wimbush, *The Bible and African Americans: A Brief History* (Minneapolis, MN: Augsburg, Fortress, 2003).

21. Norman M. Klein, *History of Forgetting: Los Angeles and the Erasure of Memory* (New York: Verso, 1997).

22. Amy K. Levin, ed. *Defining Memory: Local Museums and the Construction of History in America's Changing Communities* (New York: Rowman & Littlefield Publishers, 2007).

23. Sheldon I. Pollock, *The Language of the Gods in the World of Men: Sanskrit, Culture, and Power in Premodern India* (California: The Regents of the University of California, 2006).

24. Allusion here is to the readings from such records as the Bible itself, which shows the church to have once been a persecuted community, before *becoming* a Roman, and now Western mainstream institution.

25. J. Z. Smith, *Relating Religion: Essays in the Study of Religion* (Chicago: The University of Chicago Press, 2004), 1–60.

26. Dante Alighieri, *The Divine Comedy*, 1555; it is not very common knowledge among general Christian readers or users of the Bible that Dante did not originate the symbolism of hell (fire); that was the invention of the Peter figure in "Apocalypse of Peter"; see also Bart Ehrman, *Lost Christianities: The Battles for Scripture and the Faiths We Never Knew* (Oxford: Oxford University Press, 2003), 24–27. See "The Muratorian Canon and the Canon of Eusebius," http://www .ntcanon.org/Eusebius.shtml; J. K. Elliott, trans. *Apocryphal New Testament: A Collection of Apocryphal Christian Literature in an English Translation* (Oxford: Clarendon Press, 1993), 600–609.

27. Max Weber, *On Charisma and Institution Building* (Chicago: The University of Chicago Press, 1968), 11.

28. Elisabeth Schüssler Fiorenza, "Powerful Words: The Social-Intellectual Location of the International Signifying Scriptures Project," in *Theorizing Scriptures: New Orientations to a Cultural Phenomenon*, ed. Vincent L. Wimbush (New York: Rutgers University Press, 2008), 256–67.

29. Allan Anderson, *Introduction to Pentecostalism: Global Charismatic Christianity* (Cambridge: Cambridge University Press, 2004); see also *Spreading Fires: The Missionary Nature of Early Pentecostalism* (New York: Orbis Books, 2007); *Moya: The Holy Spirit in an African Context* (Pretoria: University of South Africa, 1991); *African Reformation: African-Initiated Christianity in the 20th Century* (Lawrenceville, NJ: Africa World Press, 2001); *Zion and Pentecost: The Spirituality and*

Experience of Pentecost and Zionist/Apostolic Churches in South Africa (Pretoria: University of South Africa, 2000).

30. Enoch Powell, "Reading the Gospels Seriously," in *Religion in Public Life,* ed. Daniel Cohn-Sherbok and David McLellan (New York: St. Martin's Press, 1992), 97.

31. Ibid.

32. Shayne Lee and Phillip Luke Sinitiere, *Holy Mavericks: Evangelical Innovators and the Spiritual Marketplace* (New York: New York University Press, 2009), 129–30.

33. Toyin Falola, *A Mouth Sweeter Than Salt: An African Memoir* (Michigan: The University of Michigan Press, 2005), 255.

34. Frederick D. Lugard, *The Dual Mandate in British Tropical Africa* (London: William Blackwood & Sons Ltd., 1929), 69–70.

35. Kenneth Onigu-Otite and Isaac O. Albert, *Community Conflicts in Nigeria: Management, Resolution and Transformation* (Ibadan, Nigeria: Spectrum Books, 1999).

36. Samuel Diamond, *Nigeria: Model of a Colonial Failure* (New York: American Committee on Africa, 1962).

37. Gbenga Osinaike, "Idahosa: How He Turned Down the Gift of a Jet Plus His Historic Meeting with Abacha—Archbishop Ojo (An Interview)," May 7, 2013, http:// www.churchtimesnigeria.net/idahosa-how-he-turned-down-the-gift-of-a-jet-plus-his-historic-meeting-with-abacha-archbishop-ojo/.

38. Marshall, *Political Spirituality,* 179.

39. Ruthanne Garlock, *Fire in His Bones: The Story of Benson Idahosa* (Tulsa, OK: Harrison House, 1986).

40. Ibid. Gbenga Osinaike, "Idahosa."

41. Bose Adelaja, "I'll Volunteer to Lead Jonathan's 2015 Campaign if…—Archbishop Ojo," April 24, 2013, http://www.vanguardngr.com/2013/04/ill-volunteer-to-lead-jonathans-2015-campaign-if-archbishop-ojo/#sthash.HpApXOMC.dpuf.

42. "Churches in Court: The Legal Status of Religious Organizations in Civil Lawsuits," in *The Pew Forum on Religion and Public Life,* http://www.pewforum .org/Church-State-Law/Churches-in-Court%282%29.aspx.

43. Lynn Schofield Clark, "Overview: The 'Protestantization' of Research into Media, Religion, and Culture," in *Practicing Religion in the Age of the Media,* 7–34.

44. Wole Soyinka, *Three Short Plays: The Swamp Dwellers, The Trials of Brother Jero, The Strong Breed* (New York: Oxford University Press, 1969).

45. Ibid. Lee and Sinitiere, *Holy Mavericks.*

46. M. S. Smith, ed. *Globalizing Africa* (Lawrenceville, NJ: African World Press, 2003).

47. Wilfred Cantwell Smith, *Towards a World Theology: Faith and the Comparative History of Religion* (London: Westminster Press, 1981), 18.

48. Stuart Hall, "The Problem of Ideology: Marxism Without Guarantees," in *Stuart Hall: Critical Dialogues in Cultural Studies,* ed. Kuan-Hsing Chen and David Morley (New York: Routledge, 1996), 25–46.

49. *Get Rich or Die Tryin'*. Directed by Jim Sheridan, produced by Sheridan, Jimmy Iovine, Paul Rosenberg, and Chris Lighty. Paramount Pictures, 2005, 134 minutes.

50. P. Samuel Huntington, *Who Are We? The Challenges to America's National Identity* (New York: Simon & Schuster, 2004).

51. Huntington, "Clash of Civilizations?," http://www.foreignaffairs.com/ articles/48950/samuel-p-huntington/the-clash-of-civilizations.

52. Noam Chomsky, *Deterring Democracy* (New York: Hill and Wang, 1991). On ideological analyses, compare Huntington's *Clash of Civilization and the Remaking of World Order* (New York: Simon & Schuster, 1997) with Edward Said's *Orientalism* (New York: Vintage Books Edition, 1979).

53. Falola, *A Mouth Sweeter*, 7.

54. Flora Louisa Shaw, *Tropical Dependency: An Outline of the Ancient History of the Western Soudan with an Account of the Modern Northern Nigeria* (London: James Nisbet & Co., 1905).

55. Onigu Otite, *Themes in African Social and Political Thought* (Nigeria: Fourth Dimension Publishing, 2000).

56. Lugard, *The Dual Mandate*, 69–70.

57. Ibid.

58. Tope Fasua, *Crushed! Navigating Africa's Tortuous Quest for Development: Myths and Realities* (UK: Author House, 2011), 316.

59. James S. Coleman, *Nigeria: Background to Nationalism* (Berkeley: University of California, 1958), 44. Cross reference with Dubem Okafor, *The Dance of Death: Nigerian History and Christopher Okigbo's Poetry* (Trenton, NJ: Africa World Press, 1998).

60. Wimbush, *White Men's Magic*.

61. Peter L. Berger, *The Social Construction of Reality: A Treatise in the Sociology of Knowledge* (New York: Anchor Books, 1967), 1–18.

62. Ogbaa Kalu, *The New Americans: The Nigerian Americans* (Westport, CT: Greenwood Press, 2003), 7.

63. Diamond, *Nigeria*, 55.

64. "Nigeria, Evil Men Will Never Rule You Again … A Prayer for Nigeria," April 10, 2011, http://seriouslydoughnuts.blogspot.com/2011/04/nigeria-evil-men-will-never-rule-you.html.

65. Ayi Kwei Armah, *The Beautiful Ones are not Yet Born* (Oxford : Heinemann, 1988).

66. Diamond, *Nigeria*, 56.

67. Common Wealth Secretariat, *Nigeria National Assembly and Presidential Elections, 9 and 16 April 2011*. Report of the Commonwealth Observer Group, Abuja, Nigeria, April 18, 2011. http://thecommonwealth.org/sites/default/files/news-items/documents/COGNigeriaFinalReport.pdf.

68. Nigeria Profile, http://news.bbc.co.uk/2/hi/africa/country_profiles/1064557.stm#media.

69. Benedict Carey, "Twitter Study Tracks When We Are :)," *New York Times*, September 29, 2011, http://www.nytimes.com/2011/09/30/science/30twitter html?_r=0.

70. Jotham Sederstrom, "The Online Powerhouses Get Comfortable Orbiting Madison Ave," *New York Times*, http://www.nytimes.com/2011/09/28/realestate/commercial/yahoo-and-other-online-giants-are-at-home-orbiting-madison-ave.html?ref=socialnetworking.

71. Blessing Ubani, Upper Room International Christian Fellowship (URICF), www.upperroomglobal.org.

72. George Orwell, *Nineteen Eighty-Four* (London: Secker and Warburg, 1949).

CHAPTER TWENTY-TWO

New Media (II)Literacy and Prosocial Entertainment: Implications for Youth Development

Bala A. Musa and Ibrahim M. Ahmadu

In the past, many have worried about the "digital divide," the separation between those with access to the network and those without access. . . . The harder issue arises when you realize that access to the technologies is not enough. Young people need to learn digital literacy—the skills to navigate this complicated, hybrid world that their peers are growing up in.[1]

Introduction

Infotainment media have become ubiquitous. We find ourselves in a media-saturated "culturescape."[2] When Marshall McLuhan described media as "the extensions of man," or uttered such familiar dictums as "The medium is the message,"[3] even his prophetic insight and vision could not have fully envisage the extent to which this would be realized just a few decades afterward. Mobile media devices have literarily become the extensions of our eyes, ears, mouths, hands, and feet. Media technology enables us to speak to others around and across the globe. Communication technology enables us to see and hear, in real time, events happening thousands of miles away.

The most media-savvy and heavy media consumers, particularly today's youth, are hooked on a sedating drip of entertainment fair. In the past two to three decades, DVD players, MP3s, iPods, smartphones, video game consuls, portable video game devices, Cloud-based content, and others have kept young people connected to their music, information, and games everywhere, all the time. Google Glass and similar new digital media are about to take that connection to a steady stream of media content to yet another level. For this group that, which John Palfrey and Urs Gasser have described as *Born Digital,*[4] new media, in particular, has blurred the divide between the virtual and the real world. This is creating significant paradigm shifts in patterns of relationships, identity, and behavior.

Changing media landscapes change social behaviors and, and vice versa. How this occurs, and its effects on culture, has engaged the attention of media ecologists over. The field of media ecology is concerned with how modes of communication and the communication environment impact culture, and vice versa. This research tradition regards communication media as a substructure, not just a superstructure in the information age.[5] According to Geraldine Forsberg:

> Media ecologists seek to discover how our thinking and behavior changes as we move from oral, to scribal, to print, and electronic cultures. Media ecologists are interested in discovering how various forms of communication influence our moral, physical, social, intellectual, and spiritual development.[6]

Jesuit priest and sociologist, Jacques Ellul, who employed both Marxist critique and sociological theory to analyze the relationship between media technology and society, provided valuable insight into the deterministic role of technology in social change.[7] Neo-Marxist theory categorizes all systems into substructures (that are fundamental and foundational) and superstructures (that are responsive and less foundational). This school believes that institutions in the substructure have causal effects and are determinants of change. If you like, they are the independent variables and driving forces behind social change, while superstructures are dependent on and influenced by substructures. Just as Marxist scholars and other political economists view relations of labor and control over means of production as the most deterministic substructural forces, some media ecologists likewise view communication technologies as having similar relationship to education, politics, family, religions, entertainment, and all other institutions.

Every new medium of communication has deterministic and transformational effects on users. Jacques Ellul saw that society ascribed almost fetish powers to communication technology. He believed people placed so much faith in technology that technology had become a god.[8] Using the Psalmist's analogy, Ellul argues that not only do people worship technology, but that having created this idol, the people are also changed to become like the idols.[9]

George Gerbner and Larry Gross affirm the same view in stating that most people watch television as they would attend a church service, "except that," as they noted, "most people watch television more religiously."[10] Gerbner and Gross hold that media, in this case, television, exert the same force on modern society as religion did in the past. According to them, "Television, the flagship of industrial mass culture, now rivals ancient religions as a purveyor of organic patterns of symbols—news and other entertainment—that animate national and even global communities' senses of reality and value."[11] If the television, which used to be watched from a fixed box set at limited hours of the day, exerted so much influence on the audience, how much more impact does it have in today's society where it is viewed anywhere, anytime, from a variety of mobile devices.

History tends to support the argument that changes in modes of communication naturally occasion changes in other aspects of society. However, the interface and influence are both ways, not just linear. Ellul, for instance, argues that humans invent media technologies, and those technologies in turn (re)make humans. The more we have become technology-dependent, the more we seem to become machine-like in our thinking, actions, relationships, and values. In other words, the transformational relationship is binary and mutual.

Walter Ong, another notable media ecologist, points out how each cultural age has been shaped by the dominant mode of communication. He saw that in oral societies, people had longer memories, were more empathetic, and used more right-brain communication styles. He found literary or print age cultures to be report-oriented, rather than rapport-oriented in their communication patterns. Visual cultures are more aesthetic-driven.[12] Seyyed Hosseini also affirms the position taken by Marshall McLuhan, Neil Postman, and others that, when technology dominates and dictates other realms of culture, it is "capable of imposing its essential form and content on public opinion and, consequently, determines the ideas, ways of thinking, and the sentiments of the people."[13] He and others have noted that when television emerged as the dominant source of information and entertainment, it led to significant change in the nature and process of public discourse. Television, they argue, is essentially an entertainment medium. It uses the language of sensory appeal to arouse emotions. Its aesthetic appeal tends to negate or bypass in-depth logical discourse. Instead of soliciting in-depth reasoned engagement, it invokes passionate and emotional reaction.[14]

Visual media were considered to diminish imagination and creativity, as people didn't have to imagine but went along with the scriptwriter's and director's visualization of scenes and characters. Examples abound of visual media's impact on politics, religion, family, education, commerce, and so forth, that we will not go into much depth in this analysis. Postman described television as a sort of petri dish, that transforms everything deposited into it. Seemingly sacred institutions like marriage and family, faith and religion, the judicial system, and so forth, are served to the public with humor and presented as objects of entertainment. This accounts for the proliferation and survival of television comedies portraying families, friendships, workplaces, court systems, and so forth. In most cases, they are not presented to offer civic lesson. Instead, they exist to amuse the audience. They oftentimes degrade and trivialize these important cultural institutions.

New Media (II)literacy

The term new media generally refers to digital media, which combine text, audio, video, and graphics into a multimedia and multisensory content. It is a convergent media delivery platform that has evolved from just hardware devices into a cultural context.[15] At the dawn of the digital revolution, new media consisted of individual devices, such as cell phones, video games, high-definition television, the World Wide Web, and so forth. In time, the ability to connect these separate devices to the Internet has created a complex and coordinated media environment, which has been referred to as the new "mediascape."[16]

The complexity of this new mediascape calls for new skills to navigate, function, and thrive in it. Just like if you move to a new place, you need to understand the layout and networks of roads, locations, and so forth, to be able to get around and carryout your activities. The new mediascape has its language, the digital language and ethos. As a result, new media literacy requires competence not just in the changing "tecnoscape" of emerging and evolving devices, but how they intersect and interact in a complex relationships of "ethnoscapes," "finascapes," and "ideoscapes" as well.[17]

Arjun Appadurai describes a mediascape as "the distribution of the electronic capabilities to produce and disseminate information . . . which are now available to a growing number of private and public interests throughout the world; and to the images of the world created by these media."[18] A key feature of this environment is its blurring of the boundary between the real and the imagined. According to Appadurai, for the audience:

> The lines between the "realistic" and the fictional landscapes they see are blurred, so that the further away these audiences are from the direct experiences of metropolitan life, the more likely they are to construct "imagined worlds" which are chimerical, aesthetic, even fantastic objects, particularly if assessed by the criteria of some other perspective, some other "imagined world."[19]

To say new media is a context means it is, if one may add, also culturescape, that needs to be navigated. New media literacy is a form of cultural literacy. Just as people need knowledge, skill, and competence to navigate an ethnoscape, similar abilities are needed to navigate the new mediascape.

Media literacy has been of concern to researchers and policy makers at every epoch of technological evolution. In the print media era, emphasis was on reading, writing, and interpretation. The term literacy, itself, is tied to the concept of literature. The person who could read, write, and accurately analyze texts was considered literate. Two elements that characterized literacy in this era consisted of ability to access information and to think critically about the content. James Potter defines media literacy as:

> a perspective from which we expose ourselves to the media and interpret the meanings of the messages we encounter. We build this perspective from knowledge structures. To build our knowledge structures, we need tools and raw materials. The tools are our skills, the raw material is information from the media and from the real world.[20]

In Potter's view, media literacy is not a category of experience that a person has or does not have. Rather it is a continuum, where your level of literacy can be deemed to be high or low, deep or shallow. Like other forms of cultural competence, media literacy is multidimensional. It includes cognitive, emotional, aesthetic, and moral domains.[21] Although the title of this discourse suggests that people can be literate or illiterate, the most accurate way to understand media literacy is to conceptualize it in terms of being more or less literate, not being literate or illiterate.

As media become more sophisticated and pervasive, media literacy becomes more essential for personal well-being and public responsibility. At the same time, the potential for proficient media literacy is becoming both easier and more challenging, as well. To say we live in the information age suggests that we live in an information-rich world. Data and information, in all forms, have become the new social, cultural, financial, intellectual, and political currency. It matters a great deal whether one belongs to the class of information haves or have-nots. That is why media access, as the most basic form of media literacy, still warrants attention. That is why it still makes sense to talk about new media illiteracy, because a person who is not at all familiar with the technology cannot transact business or take online classes from MOOCS. One's ability to function and thrive in this environment is a function of the ability to access, understand, and manage information effectively. This chapter assumes that the world's youth have access to new media, even if it is just cell phones, and that more and more will be able to join the information superhighway in the very near future. That is why there is a need to find ways of enhancing high-level, new media literacy.

The challenge of media literacy or illiteracy in the digital era is that technical competence can easily be equated with literacy. As the opening quote at the beginning of this chapter suggests, access to media technology is only the first step in new media literacy. To maximize the benefits of the new technologies, critical components of media literacy such as the emotional, aesthetic, and moral dimensions can easily be ignored. In doing so, the questions that arise include, to what extent are users aware of the emotional effects of replacing direct personal interactions and relationships with mediated interpersonal interaction? What are the effects of new media on personal and public values? What is the effect of new media enculturation on social development of today's youth?

Social Media Habits of the Youth

The 21st-century youth is in an enviable and, at the same time, very precarious place with respect to information and media literacy. As digital natives, media access and use skills are intuitive to them. They have grown up using cell phones, the Internet, multimedia tablets, and so forth, from early childhood. It is worth repeating that this does not apply to all children because, to some extent, the digital divide still remains. A large number of children and youth in developing countries—being the most of the world's population—do not have ready and reliable access to the Internet. So are also some poor and inner-city kids in advanced countries still cut off from the new media age. However, cell phones are fairly diffused even to the most remote parts of the world. And it has been found that the young in countries like India, Nigeria, Nicaragua, and other developing countries are very savvy in their use of the limited new media devices they have. They are the innovators and early adopters in mobile banking, money transfer, producing mini-movies and disseminating information via phones, skyping, and other cutting-edge technologies of new media.

Beginning with the 2013/14 academic year, the Los Angeles Unified County School District is providing every school child with an iPad tablet. This is one way of attempting to bridge the digital divide, since not all children in the school can afford their own devices. The implication is that this new technology will soon become taken-for-granted component of the learning environment. If Facebook founder, Mark Zuckerberg's initiative to make the Internet available to everyone on the globe succeeds, it will be another giant step toward eliminating the digital divide and extending the information superhighway to the most remote villages or hamlets. Of course, there will be logistic obstacles to overcome, such as lack of electricity and inability to afford the devices.

Assuming these obstacles are surmounted and every kind will trade his or her textbook for a tablet, smartphone, or a computer, what needs to happen for these tools to truly serve as pedagogical tools that will enhance these children's growth? Like it or not, young people are already swimming in an ocean of information. It will only get bigger. The moment people adopt a media device it influences all aspects of their lives. The application of the new technology is not often limited to one intended use. Regarding the use of cell phones for banking, a study conducted by the Futures Foundation and Monitise observed that:

> Users of mobile phone banking are not just heavy users of mobile phones—they are dependent upon them. The phone is *the* key tool for organizing their work and social lives. . . . The phone has become embedded into their everyday lives—enabling access to and control of a variety of a variety of activities through a single device. The phone has become their ultimate remote control.[22]

The research showed that participants in mobile banking also use their phones to access the Internet, to listen to music, to play online games, and to access social networking sites.[23] The implications are that proponents of providing laptops, tablets, smartphones, and other digital devices to young people as tools for learning are in for rude awakening, if they assume such tools are going to be used exclusively for designated teaching and learning. While designers and distributors of these devices may have certain goals and expectations for the applications of the technologies, history has shown that once invented, the technology takes on a life of its own. It is impossible to accurately predict any new technology's reach and impact. Until now advertisers have placed product ads and promotionals in textbooks, lunchrooms, gyms, and jerseys. Now they can be embedded in apps on learning devices.

This gives merit to the arguments put forth by the technological determinists, the cultural determinists, and even the technological neutralists. New media are deterministic in that they impose their mode and structure on users. You can choose to use your television set as a source of light for reading. But, it will not be the best source of lighting. That is because it is not the purpose for which the television set was designed. Instead it functions best as an infotainment medium.[24] Nevertheless, users have often adapted technology to serve functions and needs probably not envisaged by the inventors of those technologies.

Technology continues to serve both intended and unintended functions. It is appropriate to integrate new media technology into the curriculum since they are already a part and parcel of young people's lives. Nevertheless, educators, parents, and policy makers must be aware of potential unintended consequences. A simple starting point for media literacy is being aware that while we control our media, they control us also. Young people may be oblivious of the addictive nature of online interaction. They may not be aware that they are spending more time and money on online transactions than they would have otherwise. Even the fact that while they are viewing media content, they are also been watched, monitored, and tracked is often completely lost on young people.

The trend toward more and more media immersion is irreversible. And it is on the whole a positive development. In a white paper published by MacArthur Foundation funded for the "study of teen online behaviors," titled "Living and Learning with New Media: Summary of Findings from the Digital Youth Project," the authors concluded that "new media have forms have altered how youth socialize and learn."[25] The report stated, "Contrary to adult perceptions, while hanging out online, youth are picking up basic social and technical skills they need to fully participate in contemporary society."[26]

Because new media are part of the social and technological ecology of the youth, the youth understand and speak the language of media very naturally. What they may not realize is, as Postman observed, "(L)anguage is pure ideology."[27] Digital literacy, then, consists in knowing that the medium is imposing a certain value system and ideology on the person who embraces it. For the youth that is the last thing they would think about, particularly the technology is so native to their existence that it is almost invisible to them. New media use is naturally integrated into every aspect of their lives. When they need information, want to connect with someone, purchase something, the first thing they think about is going online. They don't necessarily seek advice from an older adult about schooling, careers, romance, finance, and other important life decisions. Instead they think of going online to get information from anonymous authors, or exchange ideas with their Facebook, Instagram, Twitter, Ask. fm, and others in their social (media) network. For this group, there is little distinction between what is real and what is virtual. If anything, the virtual is more real, because the virtual is more present to them than the physical.

Young people trust their social network friends and acquaintances. They are so trusting of these distant friends or intimate strangers that they would confide in or disclose intimate details to people they have never met or don't really know.

Since young people spend significant portions of their time and lives online, as well as interact frequently with online acquaintances, they essentially are conditioned and socialized by the online environment. This affects their views of relationships and sense of self. As the Common Wealth of Australia stated in its *Early Years of Learning Framework*, technology plays an essential role in young people's sense of belonging, being, and becoming.[28] We will return to the implications of this on young people's development later. Suffice it to say that the complete immersion in the virtual environment created by technology brings George Gerbner's cultivation theory come into the forefront as we seek to understand the potential transformations in culture.[29]

In the era of television as the dominant medium of mass communication, Gerbner and his fellow researchers saw that heavy television watchers were conditioned to see the world portrayed in the media as reflecting the real world. Some, not all, of the claims cultivation theory makes about the effect of media on viewers hold true of the relationship between new media and society today. Among the assertions that hold true is the belief "that 'living' in the world of television cultivates conceptions of its own conventionalized 'reality.'"[30] Cultivation theory holds that television is essentially an enculturation medium. Through the media, young people are socialized into the conventions and values of society.

As indicated earlier, new media have begun to blur the boundary between the virtual and the real. The difference between a person's identity and relationships online and in the real world are becoming more and more intermingled. However, there are limits to the comparison. If television's influence bent toward standardization and uniformity, the DNA of digital media tends toward demassification and retribalization. While new media are fast breaking down social and cultural barriers, they are quickly replacing them with niche group and interest group alliances and identities. New media allow users to express themselves and assert their own voices.

The threat to traditional mass communication was the control and dominance of big business, dominant political parties, dictatorships, and similar powerful institutions that had a strong grip on institutional and legacy media. New media has opened the door of access to as many people and groups who want to use the media to disseminate their messages. Across the globe, traditional media outlets have proliferated. Add on top that the unlimited channels of online communication, from *YouTube* to Weblogs. Digital media have afforded individuals as well as corporations an equal platform to reach a worldwide audience. Philanthropic groups can use social media to raise funds and awareness in support of their causes. Likewise terrorist and hate groups have found social media a fertile recruiting group. That underscores the need for a media literacy approach relevant to the changing times and emerging realities.

Prosocial Entertainment and Youth Development

As stated earlier, media are simultaneously deterministic and neutral. There are certain constraints to how media can be used, that are based on their inherent qualities. However, each medium has, at one time or another, been put to unconventional use. The top primary functions that all media serve are information and entertainment. Even technical information is best received when it is seen to be entertaining. Ethicists view all human activity as value-laden. Therefore, entertainment is not value-neutral. Entertainment can enhance or undermine social good. It is prosocial when it serves good and desirable purpose, and antisocial when it serves negative and undesirable purpose. At its early advent, television was viewed as having the potential to educate and transform society. However, it did not take long for it to be labeled by Newton Minow, then chairman of the Federal Communication Commission (FCC), as a "vast wasteland."[31] This suggests that left to itself, media will breed base, banal, and barren entertainment, rather than what is redemptive, responsible, and edifying.

The digital media revolution is still at its infancy. That is why it is important to pause and observe the mediascape and identify some emergent trends and their potential effect. Back in the mass media era, dominated by television, it was recognized that commercial media would always cater to the lowest denominator, by feeding the audience with popular non-redemptive and, sometimes, antisocial entertainment. Governments and social organizations realizing that commercial media will not invest in public education programming took deliberate steps to create prosocial entertainment programs or embed prosocial messages in entertainment programs. Messages such as those intended to promote tolerance and cooperation, to encourage patriotism and civic responsibility, to discourage drunk driving and gang activity.

In view of the fact that young people, particularly in developed countries, watch less and less television, and also choose their own entertainment sources and content, it is counterproductive to rely on the push model for prosocial entertainment, infotainment, and entertainment education. If the hallmark of the television age was, as Postman said, that we were, *Amusing Ourselves to Death*, one wonders what could be said of today's generation which is hooked on mobile personal entertainment devices like the iPod, digital tables, smartphones, the Internet, and so forth. Young people mostly derive their information and entertainment from preferred Web sites and sources that suit their taste. Not many are choosing media outlets that provide education on health care practices, financial responsibility, or setting career goals. Instead they gravitate to U2, Justin Bieber, and Lady Gaga for lessons on lifestyles, fashions, and moral standards.

In addition to following these stars on Twitter and other social networking sites to learn what is trending, young people look to their peers for their values. The freedom of choice young people have has some positive effects on efficacy, self-determination, autonomy, and decision making. They feel empowered and are proactive in seeking out relevant information needed to address life's daily challenges. At the same time there are many reports of abuse and misuse of new media technology. Examples include the prevalence of cyberbullying, sexting, and posting of inappropriate and embarrassing personal facts online.

Other than religious and advocacy groups, not many organizations are investing in online prosocial entertainment messages. Even if they do, they may not get much traction from the youth, as such messages are not of priority to them. We have cited some of the benefits the youth derived from their digital media. While many have the knowledge and skill to access the information they want, they tend to lack the requisite attitude, aptitude, and critical thinking skills to properly sift through, analyze, interpret, and apply the barrage of information. Even when they immerse themselves in the world of media and consume whatever content is trending online, they need attitudinal competence to comprehend the worldview and lifeview implications of their media consumption and production habits. We use the terms consumption and production together, because the youth are not just passive recipients and consumers of digital media content. Instead, they are both recipients and creators.

They rely on and also use social media to shape sense of self, their values, and their persona. That brings us, again, to the "3 Bs" identified by the Australian government as essential to early learning framework, namely *Belonging, Being,* and *Becoming*.[32] These three are essential to human development. We derive our sense of self from relationships and reach our potential through relationships.

New media both aggregate and isolate. A key component of new media is their capacity to connect people who are physically far apart from one another and bring them into contact with one another. Thus, they are closely associated with social networking. Thanks to social media, one can interact with and learn about others whom they could not have otherwise. Even those confined to one place can relate to others through mediated communication.

Young people growing up in the social media world feel a sense of affinity with lots of people of various backgrounds. They friend all sorts of people. To them, that is real friendship. So it is possible to have hundreds of social network friends, yet have almost no very close friends. And research has demonstrated that people can have lots of social network friends and yet be very lonely.

A University of Michigan study on the effect of social networking sites use on individual's feelings, which was reviewed in *The Los Angeles Times,* pointed in the opposite direction.[33] The study found that the more time a person spends on Facebook, the gloomier the person's mood and outlook on life becomes. Social psychologist and lead researcher, Ethan Kross, noted, "The more you used Facebook, the more your mood dropped." It also showed that "loneliness predicted Facebook use, and loneliness predicted how bad people felt. . . . But the effect of Facebook on how people felt was independent of loneliness."[34] Shimi Cohen reflected on similar findings in his video, where he argues that connecting with people on social networking sites makes us more lonely: http://cargocollective.com/shimicohen/The-Innovation-of-Loneliness.[35]

The previous findings paint only a partial picture of the effect of online relationships on digital natives. Traditional values are replaced by social media values. The values young people pick up from the media are not all bad or wrong. For instance, young people learn to be accepting of people of other backgrounds. They learn to defend their rights and the rights of others. At the same time, social media values are abstractions of values pulled together from multiple sources, not organic or coherent. Just as the move into the atomic age created a paradigm shift, putting the individual at the center, the digital era has also created another paradigm self—one in which the self is discrete but interconnected with other selves.

Young people are familiar with media technology but may not understand attention processes and philosophies behind them. Today's generation navigate identify differently from previous generations. Ancient and traditional societies think about self in terms of their past and their roots. Ancestry and place of origin mean much to them with respect to their sense of identity. The modern and postmodern generations tend to focus on the present and the future. Most people fail to realize the influence of communication technology on one's identity.

Likewise on *Being*, some think that social media sites serve as tools for promoting one's ego. Digital literacy requires understanding the effect of the media on ego. It can be both positive and negative. Some studies have found that, "Looking at your own profile can be self-affirming," and can lead to "increased life satisfaction, social trust, civic engagement and political participation."[36] If new media help young people develop a sense of confidence that is a good thing. Online, people are able to construct and reinforce the kind of self-image they want. Online entertainment or the digital self is not constrained by one's past, present, or perceived future reality. If a person battling with insecurity, addiction, or other struggles is able, through digital narrative and storytelling, to construct a new identity that is healthy and wholesome, then prosocial would have had a positive impact.

Too often we hear of people who have assumed antisocial online identity living out that persona in the real world. Media fantasies of mass murders, hate crimes, cruelty toward spouses, and robberies get carried out in real life.

The value-neutral narrative presented in social media may not have direct harm on young people, but as far as it is helping to promote prosocial values, it is subtracting from the contribution that it is capable of producing. Just as digital characters can be void of soul, likewise young people can be robbed of conscience, compassion, and empathy when virtual characters are viewed only as avatars. If those characters represent neighbors and coworkers and one feels comfortable not treating them negatively, it is only a matter of time that a person will act out the negativity toward the other without remorse.

Healthy personal development requires the nourishment of the total person—physical, social, intellectual, emotional, and spiritual. Technology is incapable of relating to us all these levels. Young people who surf on an excessive diet of media images, symbols, and messages may be dexterous in using keyboards and game consoles, but they will not be necessarily skillful in interpreting, discerning, and applying the messaging. The implication is, as someone has rightly observed, we will become a generation that is "endowed with ton of information, a pound of knowledge, and an ounce of wisdom."

The development of social and emotional skills requires context and proper application of knowledge in given circumstances. New media technology itself is not able to offer that. The science of artificial intelligence is developing at an exponential rate. Yet, there is still a significant gap between the ability of machines to relate a human level. Therefore, concerted effort must to be made to equip young people with the needed skills, knowledge, and attitude that will enable them make media learning and entertainment serve prosocial, rather than antisocial, goals.

The opportunity is there, as more and more schools and organizations are integrating new and social media into the learning and work environment to invest in creating content that not only promotes technical skills for media access, but also provides quality infotainment programming that will help with the total person development of the youth.

Conclusion

If to be human is to be in a relationship, and social media are substituting real relationships with pseudo relationships, and making people more lonely, the question becomes, are the youth who, as the title of Ken Hillis's book rightly states, are *Online A Lot of the Time*,[37] being humanized or dehumanized by new media?

There is no disagreeing with the common saying that "the youth and the leaders of tomorrow." What is of concern is what kind of citizens and leaders will they be? The life stories of many people show that those who were nurtured in an emotionally nourishing and safe environment grew up to have a positive outlook on life to use their influence for the good of society. At the same time, it has been found that some people who turned out to be mass murderers, serial rapists, brutal dictators, and so forth, lacked the necessary emotional nurturing in their formative years.

As society is bringing a generation that is *Born Digital*, it is essential to pay attention to what it means to inhabit a mediascape and culturescape where one's life is dominated by virtual reality, or where individuals can hardly make the distinction between the human and the mechanical. The benefits of new media are enormous. Yet, their potential threats to life as we know it are also enormous. As the common terminology, GIGO, used in computer language suggests, when the entertainment fed to minds in their formative stages consists of garbage, that is what will be reaped from those minds.

Technology is altering the essence of humanness and the value of the person. The idea that humans are created in the image of God and have intrinsic worth is foreign to what Jean Baudrillard calls the culture of simulation, the binary digit, which exists independent of all else.[38] The image is all that matters. Context and moral implications are out of the equation. The image, which has no original, is the idol that has been erected and is worshipped. Postman describes the new religion of the technological society this way:

> The god they serve does not speak of righteousness or goodness or mercy or grace. Their god speaks of efficiency, precision, and objectivity. And that is why such concepts as sin and evil disappear in Technopoly. They come from a moral universe that is irrelevant to the theology of expertise.[39]

The moral imagination of the devotees of digital entertainment is governed by whatever can be mentally conceived, not what is real or beneficial. Personal pleasure and self-distraction take precedence over social responsibility and communal virtue. This is because the entertainment is not grounded in any existing traditions or norms. Its ideology is to be neutral to cultural traditions and boundaries. The nature of community is altered to the point that it questions whether there is any such thing as human nature.[40] And if there is no authentic human nature, it is impossible to expect the attributes of humaneness or to hold the other accountable in improper actions.

Where society has invested in prosocial entertainment, the results have been positive. Where this has been neglected or the weeds of mind-numbing entertainment have been allowed encumber the entertainment and cultural landscape, negative consequences have resulted. As the saying goes, "it is easier to guide a shoot than to bend a tree." If prosocial entertainment is used to inculcate respectfulness, tolerance, compassion, industriousness, integrity, and so forth, to the youth, society will not have to battle the scourge of hate crime, criminal gangs, racism, sexism, human rights abuses, abuse of power, greed, and other negative effects of unhealthy personal development.

In an entertainment-saturated society, the content of media cannot be regarded as morally neutral or socially innocuous. The entertainment contents are educational, whether or not they are intended to be. The question is, what kind of education and values are they imparting? The prosocial entertainment proposition calls for a deliberate commitment to a particular kind of enculturation and cultivation of the responsible and healthy adult. The process begins early in live. It is not a call for brain-washing propaganda effort, but an awareness that enters the ear and eye-gates today, lives, walks, and talks tomorrow.

Notes

1. John Palfrey and Urs Gasser, *Born Digital: Understanding the First Generation of Digital Natives* (New York: Basic Books, 2008), 15.

2. Arjun Appadurai, "Disjuncture and Difference in the Global Cultural Economy," *Theory, Culture & Society* 7 (1990): 295–310.

3. Marshall McLuhan, *Understanding Media* (New York: McGraw-Hill, 1964).

4. Palfrey and Gasser, *Born Digital.*

5. Neil Postman, *Amusing Ourselves to Death: Public Discourse in the Age of Show Business* (New York: Viking, 1985); Neil Postman, *Technopoly: The Surrender of Culture to Technology* (New York: Knopf, 1992).

6. Geraldine E. Forsberg, "Media Ecology and Theology," *Journal of Communication and Religion* 32 (March 2009): 138.

7. Ibid.

8. Jacque Ellul, *The Technological Society* (New York: Knopf, 1964).

9. Psalms 115:4–8, The Holy Bible, NIV (Nashville, TN: Thomas Nelson, 1982).

10. George Gerbner and Larry Gross, "Living with Television: The Violence Profile," *Journal of Communication* 26, no. 2 (1976): 177.

11. Ibid.

12. Walter J. Ong, *Orality and Literacy: The Technologizing of the Word* (New York: Methuen, 1982).

13. Seyyed H. Hosseini, "Religion and Media, Religious Media, or Media Religion: Theoretical Studies," *Journal of Media and Religion* 7 (2008): 61.

14. Postman, *Amusing Ourselves to Death.*

15. Kaveri Subrahmanyam and David Šmahel, *Digital Youth: The Role of Media in Development* (New York: Springer), 2011.

16. Arjun Appadurai, "Disjuncture and Difference in the Global Cultural Economy."

17. Ibid.

18. Ibid., 298–99.

19. Ibid., 299.

20. W. James Potter, *Media Literacy* (Thousand Oaks, CA: Sage), 5.

21. Ibid.

22. Future Foundation, "Emerging Trends in Mobile Banking," http://www.monitise.com/resource_centre_download/28/money-on-the-move-chapter-4-pdf (emphasis in original).

23. Ibid.

24. Bala Musa, "News as Infotainment: Industry and Audience Trends," in *Emerging Issues in Contemporary Journalism*, ed. Bala A. Musa and Cindy J. Price (Lewiston, NY: Edwin Mellen Press, 2006), 131–55.

25. The John D. and Catherine T. MacArthur Foundation, "Living and Learning with New Media: Summary of Findings from the Digital Youth Project," *Report on Digital Media and Learning*, November 2008, 2. Cited in S. Craig Watkins, *The Young and the Digital* (Boston: Beacon Press, 2009), 24.

26. Ibid.

27. Neil Postman, *Technopoly: The Surrender of Culture to Technology* (New York: Alfred Knopf, 1992), 123.

28. Common Wealth of Australia, "Belonging, Being, and Becoming: An Early Years of Learning Framework for Australia," 2009. Cited in Lydia Plowman, Christine Stephen, and Joanna McPake, *Growing Up with Technology: Young Children Learning in a Digital World* (London: Routledge, 2010).

29. Gebner and Gross, "Living with Television."

30. Ibid., 175.

31. Newton Minow, *Equal Time: The Private Broadcaster and the Public Interest* (New York: Atheneum, 1964), 51. Cited in Shirley Biagi, *Media/Impact: An Introduction to Mass Media*, 5th ed. (Belmont, CA: Wadsworth, 2001), 160.

32. Common Wealth of Australia, "Belonging, Being, and Becoming."

33. Geoffrey Mohan, "Facebook Can Leave You Feeling Blue, Study Says," *Los Angeles Times*, Sunday, August 18, 2013, A17, http://eedition2.latimes.com/ Olive/ODE/ LATimes/.

34. Ibid.

35. Shimi Cohen, *The Innovation of Loneliness*, http://cargocollective.com/ shimicohen/The-Innovation-of-Loneliness.

36. Ibid.

37. Ken Hillis, Online *A Lot of the Time: Ritual, Fetish, Sign* (Durham, NC: Duke University, 2009).

38. Jean Baudrillard, *Simulations* (New York: Semiotext, 1983).

39. Postman, *Technopoly*, 90.

40. Andrew Koch, "Cybercitizen or Cyborg Citizen: Baudrillard, Political Agency, and the Commons in Virtual Politics," *Journal of Mass Media Ethics* 20, nos. 2 and 3 (2005): 116.

About the Editors and Contributors

The Editors

Bala A. Musa (PhD, Regent University) is professor and chair of communication studies at Azusa Pacific University. He is recipient of the 2011 Clifford G. Christians Ethics Research Award. He is author of *Framing Genocide: Media, Diplomacy, and Conflict,* and the series editor for the *Communication, Change and Society* series. He is coeditor *Communication, Culture and Human Rights in Africa* (2011), *Communication in an Era of Global Conflicts* (2009), and *Emerging Issues in Contemporary Journalism* (2006). He serves on the editorial board of several publications including *American Communication Journal; Journal of Mass Communication, Delinquency, and Criminology; Journal of African Social Science and Humanities Studies;* and *Global Conversations.* Musa serves on the leadership boards of several nonprofit organizations. An international scholar, trainer, and consultant Musa has taught graduate and undergraduate communication, conflict management, and leadership causes in North America, Africa, Western and Eastern Europe, the Caribbean, and North America. Dr. Musa's research interests include media ethics, media and diplomacy, media and conflict, development communication, intercultural communication, communication and human rights, leadership communication, and media and religion.

Jim Willis (PhD, University of Missouri-Columbia) is professor of journalism at Azusa Pacific University. In addition to his doctorate in journalism, Willis pursued graduate studies at Dallas Theological Seminary. Dr. Willis is a former newspaper reporter and editor in Dallas and Oklahoma City. His reporting assignments have included the Oklahoma City bombing in 1995, and the 10th and 20th anniversaries of the fall of the Berlin Wall.

He is the author of a dozen books, mostly dealing with journalism and the news media. Recent titles include, *100 Media Moments That Changed America* and *The Mind of a Journalist.* Dr. Willis has lectured extensively in Europe, conducting several lecture tours for the U.S. Department of State and serving as guest professor at two German universities.

The Contributors

Ibrahim M. Ahmadu (PhD, University of Jos, Nigeria) is associate professor of religion in the Department of Religious Studies, University of Jos, Nigeria. His research, scholarship, and publications cover New Testament, Christian Ethics, and Comparative Religion. Ahmadu is former national vice president, and current national board member of the Reformed Christian Church of Nigeria. He is also a regional overseer with the denomination. He formerly served as chair, Department of Religious Studies, College of Education, Jalingo; and chair, Department of Religious Studies, University of Jos, Nigeria. Ahmadu has served as editor of several theological journals. He has published numerous academic journal articles and book chapters. He is a leader of thought and a commentator on national and international issues.

Etim Anim (PhD, University of Uyo, Nigeria) is dean of the Faculty of Communication Technology and an associate professor of communication at Cross River University of Technology, Calabar, Nigeria. Anim also holds a master's in communication arts form University of Wisconsin–Madison, and Bachelor of Arts in journalism from the University of Nigeria Nsukka, Nigeria. His research interests include new media, citizen journalism, and print communication in the digital age. He has published several academic journal articles, among them, "Mass Communication Education in the Digital Age in Low-Income Countries: A Nigerian Experience," *The Global Studies Journal*, 1, 1–10; and "Internet Use among Nigerian Journalists," *LWATI: A Journal of Contemporary Research*, 4, 348–61. He has authored two books, which are widely used in Nigerian universities, *Editorial Writing* (1996) and *Creative News Writing* (2006).

Sue L. Aspley (MLLS, George Washington University) is associate professor and head of Copyright Advisory Services, Azusa Pacific University. She is also a practicing member of the library staff for the university libraries. She holds a Juris doctor degree from the University of Louisville' Master of Laws from George Washington University in International Law; Master of Comparative Law from the University of Brussels; MS from the University of Illinois in Library and Information Science; BA *cum laude*, in history, from the University of Miami; and a certification in copyright from the Center for Intellectual Property, University of Maryland, College Park. At present her primary research interests are the ethical and legal issues related to copyright, and information and Internet law. Additionally, she has worked as an attorney for both the U.S. Air Force (JAG) and at the Department of State specializing in international law.

Joseph Bentz (PhD, Purdue University) is a professor of English at Azusa Pacific University. He holds a doctorate in 20th-century American literature. He teaches courses in American literature and writing. He is the author of four novels and three nonfiction books. His most recent books include *God in Pursuit: The Tipping Points, From Doubt to Faith,* and *Silent God: Finding Him When You Can't Hear His Voice.* His novel *A Son Comes Home* won the Silver Angel Award, was selected for Guideposts Book Club, and was chosen as one of the Top Ten Christian Novels of the Year by *Booklist* magazine. He is a former recipient of the Undergraduate Faculty Scholar of the Year Award at APU.

Kris D. Boyle (PhD, Texas Tech University) is assistant professor of journalism at Creighton University. While pursuing his master's degree at Brigham Young University, he worked in several capacities at NewsNet, the university's converged newsroom. This included stints as a campus editor, news editor, and managing editor, where he was responsible for the daily operations of the newsroom. Professionally, Boyle spent more than two years working as a beat reporter for the Idaho Falls Post Register.

Pauline Hope Cheong (PhD, University of Southern California) is associate professor at the Hugh Downs School of Human Communication, Arizona State University. Her research foci are in communication technologies and culture, including how authority and community relations are mediated and changing. She is also known for her publications on religious organizing and media use by various faith groups to build identity and influence. Her award-winning research has appeared in more than 50 journals and books. Journal publications appear in *Journal of Communication, American Behavioral Scientist, The Information Society, Journal of International and Intercultural Communication, New Media and Society, Journal of Computer-Mediated Communication, Information, Communication and Society,* and *Journal of Media and Religion.* She is coeditor of *Digital Religion, Social Media and Culture: Perspectives, Practices and Futures* and *New Media and Intercultural Communication: Identity, Community and Politics,* and is coauthor of *Narrative IEDs: Rumors and the Struggle for Strategic Influence.*

Linda H. Chiang (EdD, Ball State University) is professor of education in the Department of Teacher Education, and the former chair of the Department of Foundations and Trans-Disciplinary Studies at Azusa Pacific University. She is a recipient of Dean's Accomplished Scholar (2008) and Outstanding Researcher (2010) of School of Education. She has held leadership positions at various professional communities. She has served as an assistant executive secretary for Indiana Adult Education Association, secretary/treasurer for Phi Tau Phi Scholastic Society, Associate Council for the Midwestern Educational Research Association, board member of the American Association for Chinese Studies, and Asian Studies Section Chair for the Western Social Science Association. She is an international scholar who is well published in both English and Chinese in the United States, United Kingdom, and Taiwan. Her two books, which were published in Taiwan, are well cited in the fields of multicultural education and positive psychology. Her work is the subject of over 80 articles, books, and abstracts. At present her primary research interests are resiliency, child development, and brain-based learning. Additionally, she has worked as an article editor for SAGE Publishers.

Gbenga Dasylva (MA, University of Ibadan) is a researcher at the University of Ibadan. His areas of interest include conflict communication, history, and the sociology of literature. He published *Communal Communication and the Dynamics of Conflict among Youths in the Niger Delta* in 2012. Dasylva is also a business entrepreneur, who has had tremendous success in the advertising industry in Nigeria. He received the Junior Chambers Ten Outstanding Young Persons Award in 2012. He is also a member of various associations within and outside Nigeria.

Joe Hight is editor of *The Colorado Springs Gazette.* He is the former director of information and development for *The Oklahoman* and Newsok.com. He has spent more than 30 years in journalism as a reporter and editor, and he has served two terms as president of the Dart Center for Journalism & Trauma. He authored and coauthored print and online booklets and columns that are still used by the Dart Center, including *Tragedies & Journalists: A Guide for More Effective Coverage*, that has been translated into three languages. He is a graduate of the University of Central Oklahoma where he was named a Distinguished Former Student.

Saliu Funmi Imaledo (PhD, University of Ibadan, Nigeria) is research fellow at IFRA-Nigeria. His bachelor's was in history and international studies from the University of Ado- Ekiti, Nigeria; and his Mphil/PhD in Peace and Conflict Studies, from the Institute of African Studies, University of Ibadan. He currently resides in Nigeria where he conducts independent researches. His research interests include slave trade, colonialism, ethnicity, race, xenophobia, conflict studies, religion, and society.

Tom Johnson (PhD, University of Washington) is Amon G. Carter Jr. Centennial Professor in the School of Journalism at the University of Texas at Austin. He has authored or coedited three books. His most recent coedited book is *International Media Communication in a Global Age.* He has also published 50 articles in refereed academic journals and has written 19 books.

Agnes Lucy Lando (PhD, Pontifical Gregorian University, Rome) is senior lecturer in the Department of Communication at Daystar University, Kenya. She has published in communication ethics, ongoing higher education in Africa and the idea of a Catholic University in the 21st century. Dr. Lando and her coauthors were 2013 recipients of the George Gerbner Excellence Award, at the Annual George Gerbner Conference in Budapest, Hungary, for their work "Retesting Cultivation Theory on the Origins, Causes, and Predictors of Aggression: The Case of Pre and Post Genocide Rwanda." Dr. Lando's writings have contributed to growing scholarship on media ethics, media studies, and communication theory in the Kenyan and wider East African context. Her research interests include communication ethics, communication and culture, communication theory, and media studies. Dr. Lando is a member of IAMCR, ICA, EACA, and 2013 EACA Conference convener.

Stanley Naribo Ngoa (PhD, Wits University, South Africa) is senior lecturer in the Department of Mass Communication, Covenant University, Nigeria. He is also a senior research associate at the Centre for the Study of Democracy Rhodes University/University of Johannesburg, RSA. His research interests include public opinion and political behavior, mass media and political leadership, media in politics; political communication, issues in African media, political economy of the media. He has published in numerous peer-reviewed journals including *Journal of Media & Communication, International Journal of Humanities and Social Science,* and *Global Media Journal,* among others.

David Olali (PhD student, Claremont Graduate University, Claremont, California; and Research Fellow, International Theological Center's, Atlanta, Georgia) is pioneering research fellow in Global Leadership/Proxy

Director at the T'Ofori-Atta Institute for the Study of the Religious Heritage of the African World at the International Theological Center. Olali's research interests include scriptures (broadly understood as expansive rhetorical device), and their broad—rather than their hermeneutical/exegetical/lexical categorizations, as well as critical comparative scriptures. He combines being a born teacher with acquired research and university teaching experience. As a social critic, he has lectured in Africa and the United States, on religious inscriptions in Africa and the African Diaspora, particularly condemning the burgeoning ethnic and religious fundamentalism, which now finds representations in Nigeria-formed international terror clique, *Boko Haram*. Currently, Olali is researching the intersections between (non-) religious scriptures, and violence, as domains which negotiate or contest *bodies* as sites for the re- and/or de-embodiments of social, political, and religious authorial.

Cindy N. Phu (MA, California State University of Los Angeles) is adjunct professor of communication studies at Chapman University, Santa Ana College, and Pasadena City College. She teaches gender and communication, propaganda and public opinion, intercultural communication, interpersonal communication, argumentation and debate, and public speaking. Her research interests include critical rhetoric, feminist theory, popular culture, pedagogy, and visual analysis, and has presented at her research at local and national conferences. In 2010, she published "Save Africa: The Commodification of Product Red Campaign" in *Kaleidoscope*. She is also an assistant coach for Pasadena City College's speech and debate team.

Tim Posada (PhD candidate, Claremont Graduate University) is a media analyst and critique, specializing in visual culture and media convergence. He teaches journalism, research, and literature at Azusa Pacific University, Biola University, and Vanguard University. He holds a Master of Arts in theology from Fuller Theological Seminary and a master's in cultural studies from CGU. He is currently researching the function of comic book superheroes across various media platforms. He is also the film columnist for the Beverly Press in Los Angeles.

Pavica Sheldon (PhD, Louisiana State University) is assistant professor of communication at the University of Alabama at Huntsville. Dr. Sheldon has published numerous articles in academic journals and has research interests in social media uses and gratifications, media psychology, and interpersonal communication. She is an ad hoc reviewer for several academic journals, including *New Media and Society* and *Journal of Computer-Mediated Communication.*

Brooke Van Dam (PhD, City University, London) is assistant professor of communication studies at Azusa Pacific University. Dr. Van Dam is a 2013 Kopenhaver Fellow of the Lillian Lodge Kopenhaver Center for the Advancement of Women in Communication. Her research interests are in journalism in a changing media and technological environment. Her recently published book chapter can be found in *Making Online News* (Volume 2): *Newsroom Ethnographies in the Second Decade of Internet Journalism.*

Anne Kindred Willis (MA, MED, Azusa Pacific University) is an instructor at Hope International University, in Fullerton, California., where she teaches English to international students. She also holds two bachelor's degrees in music from the University of Kentucky. Willis has also taught at Ball State University, Ashland University, and the University of Laverne. She has presented on issues relating to college student affairs and teaching English to international students at academic conferences.

Franklin Nii Amankwah Yartey (PhD, Bowling Green University) is assistant professor of communication at the University of Dubuque, Dubuque, Iowa. Yartey held graduate teaching and research assistantships at Indiana State University and Bowling Green University. His research focuses on digital media and globalization/social media, with a secondary focus on intercultural communication. His research interests also include online microfinance and its impact on third-world women, health communication, media ethics, and globalization. He has presented papers at many academic conferences. Yartey has professional experience in public relations, and nonprofit promotions in Ghana and the United States. His recent publications include "Jealousy in India and the United States: A Cross-Cultural Analysis of Three Dimensions of Jealousy," in *Human Communication: A Publication of the Pacific and Asian Communication Association*; "More Words, Less Action: A Framing Analysis of FEMA Public Relations Communications during Hurricanes Katrina and Gustav," in *Public Relations Journal*; *Health Communication and HIV/AIDS Patients' Rights* (University Press of America); and *Producing the Global: Microfinance Online* (Lexington Books). He has won several academic awards, including the National Communication Association's Doctoral Honors Seminar and a dissertation fellowship at Bowling Green State University. He has also been elected to who is who in American colleges and universities. Yartey's hobbies include playing table tennis, chess, scrabble, and watching movies.

Index